GENDER, FAMILY, AND POLITICS

Gender, Family, and Politics

The Howard Women, 1485–1558

NICOLA CLARK

OXFORD
UNIVERSITY PRESS

OXFORD
UNIVERSITY PRESS

Great Clarendon Street, Oxford, OX2 6DP,
United Kingdom

Oxford University Press is a department of the University of Oxford.
It furthers the University's objective of excellence in research, scholarship,
and education by publishing worldwide. Oxford is a registered trade mark of
Oxford University Press in the UK and in certain other countries

First Edition published in 2018

Impression: 2

Published in the United States of America by Oxford University Press
198 Madison Avenue, New York, NY 10016, United States of America

British Library Cataloguing in Publication Data
Data available

Library of Congress Control Number: 2018930793

ISBN 978–0–19–878481–4

Printed and bound by
CPI Group (UK) Ltd, Croydon, CR0 4YY

Acknowledgements

WELL. I realise that academic acknowledgements are supposed to be a place for eloquently expressed gratitude, but actually what I most want to say is OMG GUYS, WE DID IT!!! This book began with work undertaken for a PhD thesis and so an enormous number of people have helped along the way—i.e. if I leave you out here, it's because I've not been sensible enough to keep a running list, not because I haven't appreciated your input.

The original thesis was funded by the Department of History at Royal Holloway, University of London, through the Thomas Holloway Scholarship, and both it and subsequent research have been supported by various departmental research funds without which this book could not have come into being. I also want to thank the many archivists who have searched for, found, produced, and copied material for me, particularly Heather Warne and Rebecca Hughes at Arundel Castle Archive, and James Ross and Sean Cunningham at the National Archives, as well as anonymous staff at the British Library, National Library of Wales, London Metropolitan Archives, Cambridge University Library, and record offices of Norfolk, Staffordshire, and Devonshire, and the Royal Collection for permission to use the cover image. I am eternally grateful to those behind the wonder that is State Papers Online for making the obvious stuff so much less painful than for previous generations. Similarly, thanks are due to my editor, Cathryn Steele, for her care of me throughout the publishing process, to the editorial team at Oxford University Press for commissioning the book in the first place, and to the anonymous readers for the most helpful peer review I have yet received.

Colleagues at Royal Holloway and at the University of Chichester have been endlessly supportive cheerleaders (there's an image), and my amazing students at both places have broadened my knowledge, asked pertinent questions, and been incredibly supportive. Attendees of the Late Medieval and Tudor and Stuart seminars at the Institute of Historical Research, plus the Society for Court Studies, have stretched my brain and my capacity for alcohol in helpful and less helpful ways. For academic assistance and friendship in varying combinations, I particularly want to thank Caroline Barron for putting me firmly on the path of studying late medieval and early modern women as an MA student, and for her continued friendship ever since; Anna Whitelock and Peregrine Horden for supervising my thesis, and James Daybell and Michael Questier for examining it and encouraging me to continue. Hannes Kleineke has been consistently on tap for Latin, and managed to find a 'lost' will in the depths of TNA. Justin Colson gave me helpful advice of a network-y, database-y kind, Charlotte Bolland answered several portraiture queries, and Tim Stretton gave me his considered opinion on one of the divorce cases contained herein. Gemma Allen, Sarah Ansari, Jason Brock, Sue Broomhall, Mark Bryant, Clive Burgess, Amanda Capern, Justin Champion, Kirsten Claiden-Yardley, Janet Dickinson, Charlie Farris, Catherine

Fletcher, Olivia Fryman, Steven Gunn, Samantha Harper, Maria Hayward, Simon Healy, Jessica Lutkin, Stella Moss, Hannah Platts, Rob Priest, Glenn Richardson, Mandy Richardson, Kirsty Rolfe, Jonathan Spangler, Edward Town, Sara Wolfson, and Ellie Woodacre, have all been generous with their time, friendship, and expertise. I want to thank Alixe Bovey for inspiring me as an undergraduate at the University of Kent, and for warning me about the perils of academia—I'm not (yet) sorry for ignoring your advice, but I am sorry for apparently making you read a novel by a well-known writer of Tudor fiction?!

Heads up to my writing club girls for advice, food, love, general awesomeness: Rachel Basch, Mariana Brockmann, Sophie Carney, Jo Edge (also for that-which-must-not-be-mentioned), Laura Wood. If you're an early career researcher sick of working in isolation, copy us and meet to work together somewhere—we owe what little sanity we have left to each other. Also to honorary non-academic members Jennifer Gammon and Mick Norman.

To my parents I owe immeasurable gratitude—as I have said elsewhere, to my mother Angela for giving me my love of history, and my father Duncan for the drive to do something with it. My parents-in-law, Jane and Edward Gregory, have been continually supportive, as have Derwin Gregory, Jo Porter, and Michael Chapple. I need to apologise AGAIN to my sister Lyndsey: Lyn, I'm sorry, but there still isn't a camel in this text. There IS still a parrot, on p. 59. However, since you never did get a zebra into your thesis, it's more like #sorrynotsorry. Incidentally, dear readers, if you find the Big Bang Theory quote, give yourselves a gold star.

My feline research assistants, Billy and Lula, deserve no thanks at all, because their arrival as kittens in the summer of 2016 delayed this book by quite some time. Lula, however, has atoned by spending much of the writing time smooshed up by my side.

Finally, the person to whom I and this book owe the greatest debt is my husband Alden Gregory, without whose unfailing interest, support, mastery of clever gene-alogical-table-drawing software, timely production of meals, and occasional grunts in response to my streams of consciousness this book would not exist. I dedicate it to him.

Contents

List of Abbreviations

APC	*Acts of the Privy Council*, ed. John Roche Dasent, new series, 32 vols (London, 1890–1964)
BL	British Library
Bodl.	Bodleian Library
Cal. IPM	*Calendar of Inquisitions Post Mortem*
Cal. Patent Rolls	*Calendar of Patent Rolls*
CCED	Clergy of the Church of England database
CSP	*Calendar of State Papers*
CUL	Cambridge University Library
EEBO	Early English Books Online
EHR	English Historical Review
LP	*Letters and Papers, Foreign and Domestic, of the Reign of Henry VIII,* ed. J. S. Brewer, J. Gairdner, and R. H. Brodie, 22 vols (London: HMSO, 1862–1932)
NLW	National Library of Wales
NRO	Norfolk Record Office
ODNB	*Oxford Dictionary of National Biography*
OED	*Oxford English Dictionary*
PCP	Nicholas Harris Nicolas (ed.), *Proceedings and Ordinances of the Privy Council of England*, 7 vols (London: Record Commission, 1834–7)
Rot. Parl.	*Rotuli Parliamentarium*, ed. J. Strachey et al., 6 vols (London, 1767–77)
SRO	Staffordshire Record Office
TAMO	*The Unabridged Acts and Monuments Online* (HRI Online Publications, Sheffield, 2011)
TNA	The National Archives, Kew
VCH	Victoria County History

Table 1, The Tudor Howards

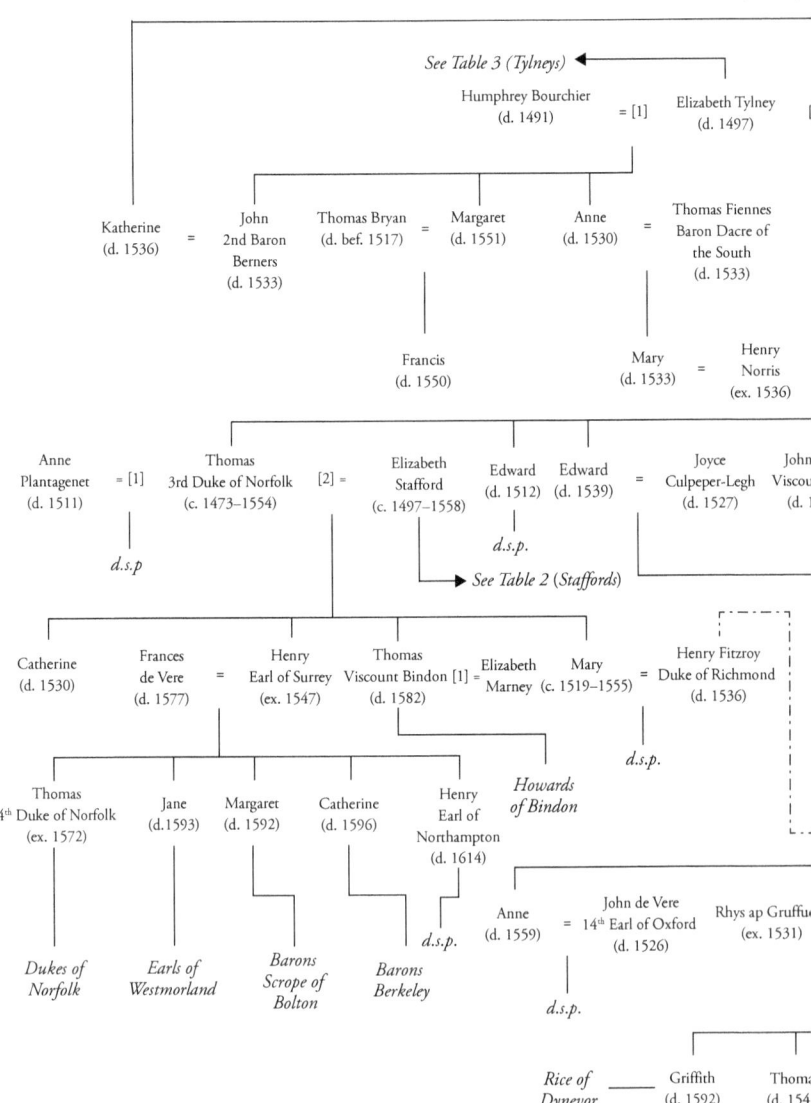

Margaret Chedwode
Norreys / Wyfold
(d. 1494)

See Table 3 (Tylneys)

Humphrey Bourchier (d. 1491) = [1] Elizabeth Tylney (d. 1497)

Katherine (d. 1536) = John 2nd Baron Berners (d. 1533)

Thomas Bryan (d. bef. 1517) = Margaret (d. 1551)

Anne (d. 1530) = Thomas Fiennes Baron Dacre of the South (d. 1533)

Francis (d. 1550)

Mary (d. 1533) = Henry Norris (ex. 1536)

Anne Plantagenet (d. 1511) = [1] Thomas 3rd Duke of Norfolk (c. 1473–1554) [2] = Elizabeth Stafford (c. 1497–1558)

Edward (d. 1512) Edward (d. 1539) = Joyce Culpeper-Legh (d. 1527) John Viscou (d.)

d.s.p

d.s.p.

→ *See Table 2 (Staffords)*

Catherine (d. 1530)

Frances de Vere (d. 1577) = Henry Earl of Surrey (ex. 1547)

Thomas Viscount Bindon [1] = Elizabeth Marney Mary (c. 1519–1555) = Henry Fitzroy Duke of Richmond (d. 1536)

d.s.p.

Thomas 4th Duke of Norfolk (ex. 1572)

Jane (d.1593)

Margaret (d. 1592)

Catherine (d. 1596)

Henry Earl of Northampton (d. 1614)

Howards of Bindon

Dukes of Norfolk

Earls of Westmorland

Barons Scrope of Bolton

Barons Berkeley

d.s.p.

Anne (d. 1559) = John de Vere 14th Earl of Oxford (d. 1526) Rhys ap Gruffu (ex. 1531)

d.s.p.

Rice of Dynevor ____ Griffith (d. 1592) Thoma (d. 154

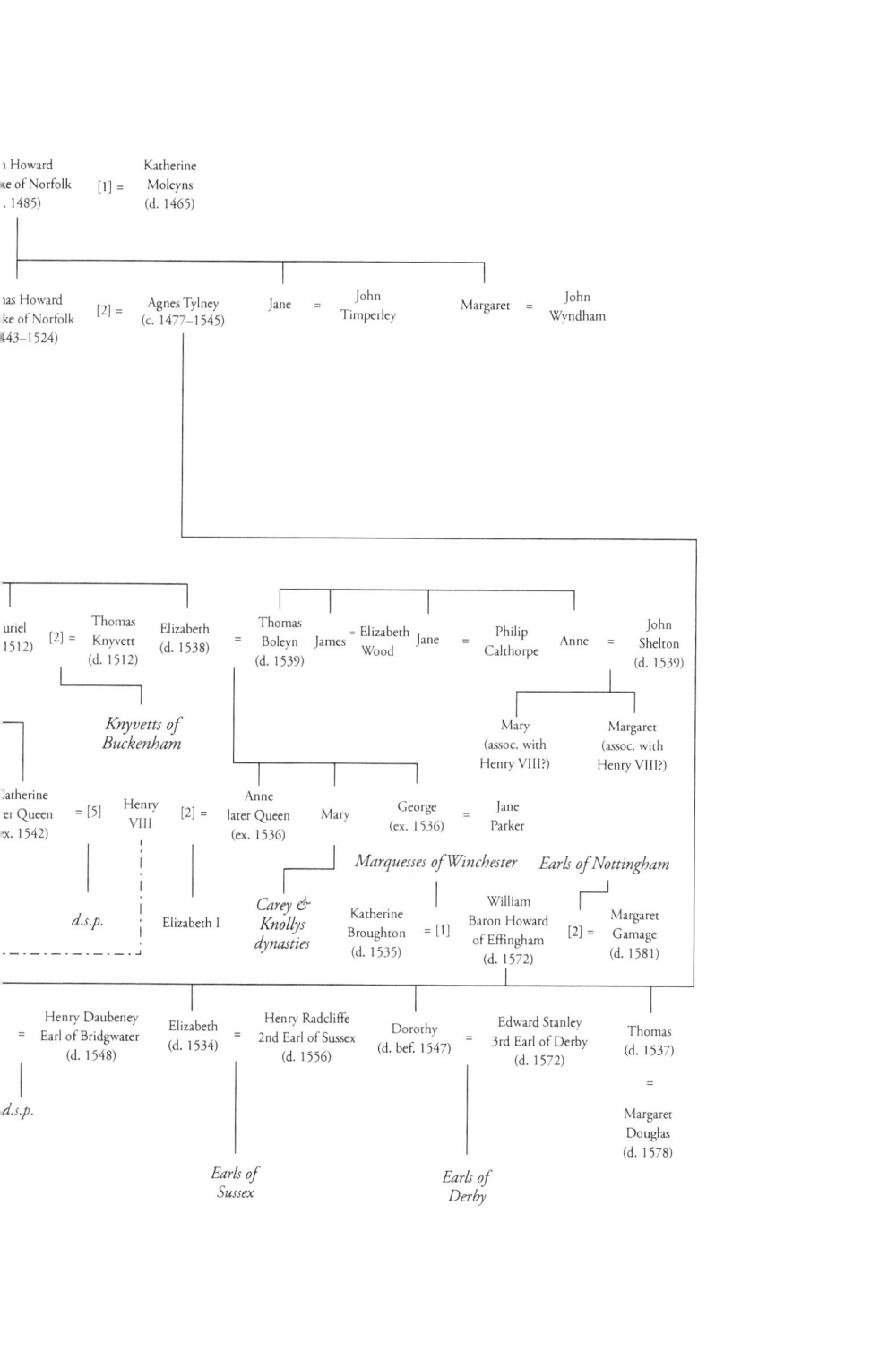

Howard
ke of Norfolk
. 1485) [1] = Katherine
Moleyns
(d. 1465)

has Howard
ke of Norfolk
443–1524) [2] = Agnes Tylney
(c. 1477–1545)   Jane = John
Timperley   Margaret = John
Wyndham

uriel
1512) [2] = Thomas
Knyvett
(d. 1512)   Elizabeth
(d. 1538) = Thomas
Boleyn
(d. 1539) James = Elizabeth
Wood   Jane = Philip
Calthorpe   Anne = John
Shelton
(d. 1539)

*Knyvetts of
Buckenham*

Mary
(assoc. with
Henry VIII?)   Margaret
(assoc. with
Henry VIII?)

atherine
er Queen
x. 1542) = [5] Henry
VIII [2] = Anne
later Queen
(ex. 1536)   Mary   George
(ex. 1536) = Jane
Parker

Marquesses of Winchester   *Earls of Nottingham*

d.s.p.   Elizabeth I   *Carey &
Knollys
dynasties*   Katherine
Broughton
(d. 1535) = [1] William
Baron Howard
of Effingham
(d. 1572) [2] = Margaret
Gamage
(d. 1581)

= Henry Daubeney
Earl of Bridgwater
(d. 1548)   Elizabeth
(d. 1534) = Henry Radcliffe
2nd Earl of Sussex
(d. 1556)   Dorothy
(d. bef. 1547) = Edward Stanley
3rd Earl of Derby
(d. 1572)   Thomas
(d. 1537)

d.s.p.   =

Margaret
Douglas
(d. 1578)

*Earls of
Sussex*   *Earls of
Derby*

Table 2, The Staffords

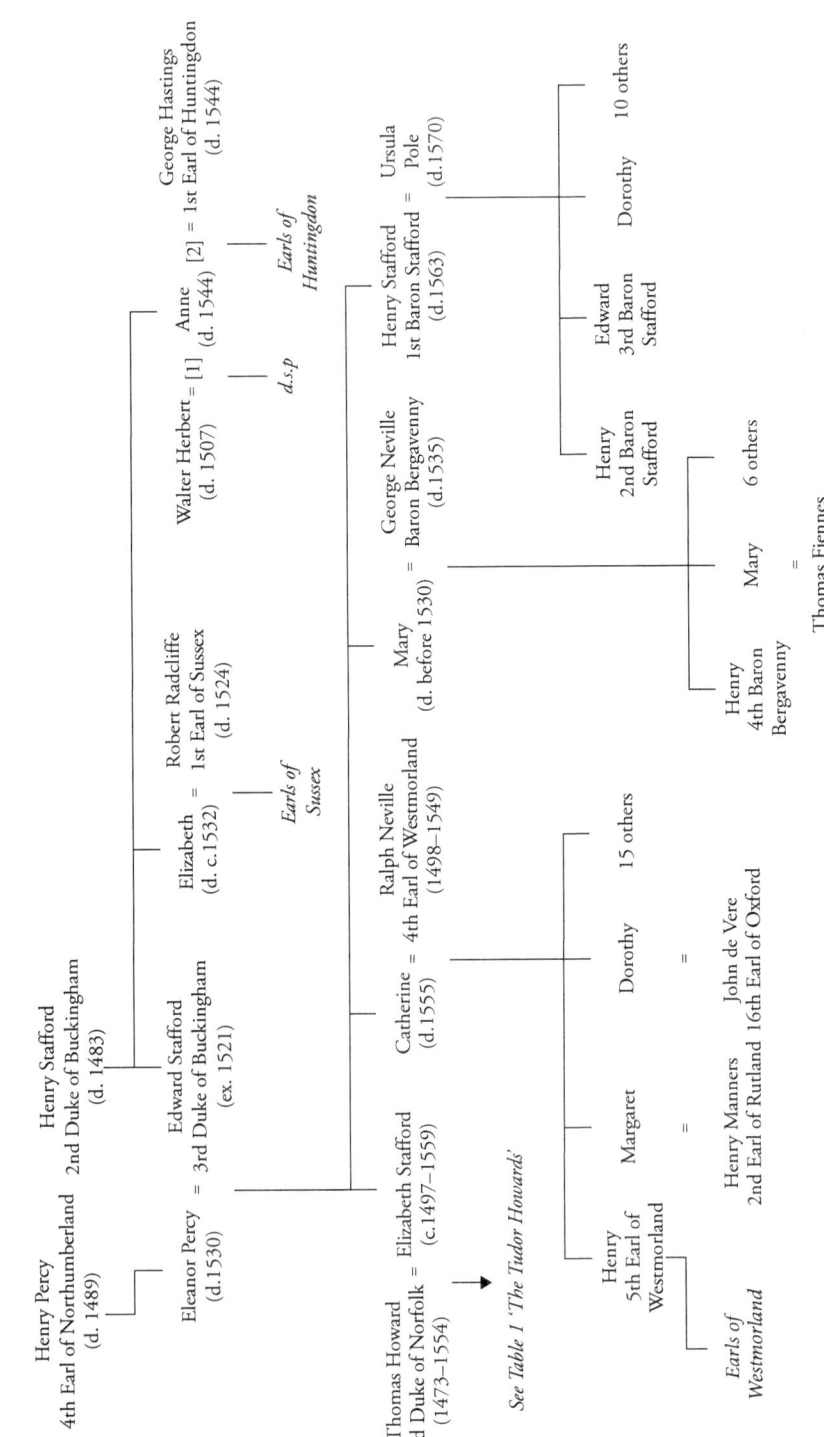

Table 3, The Tylneys

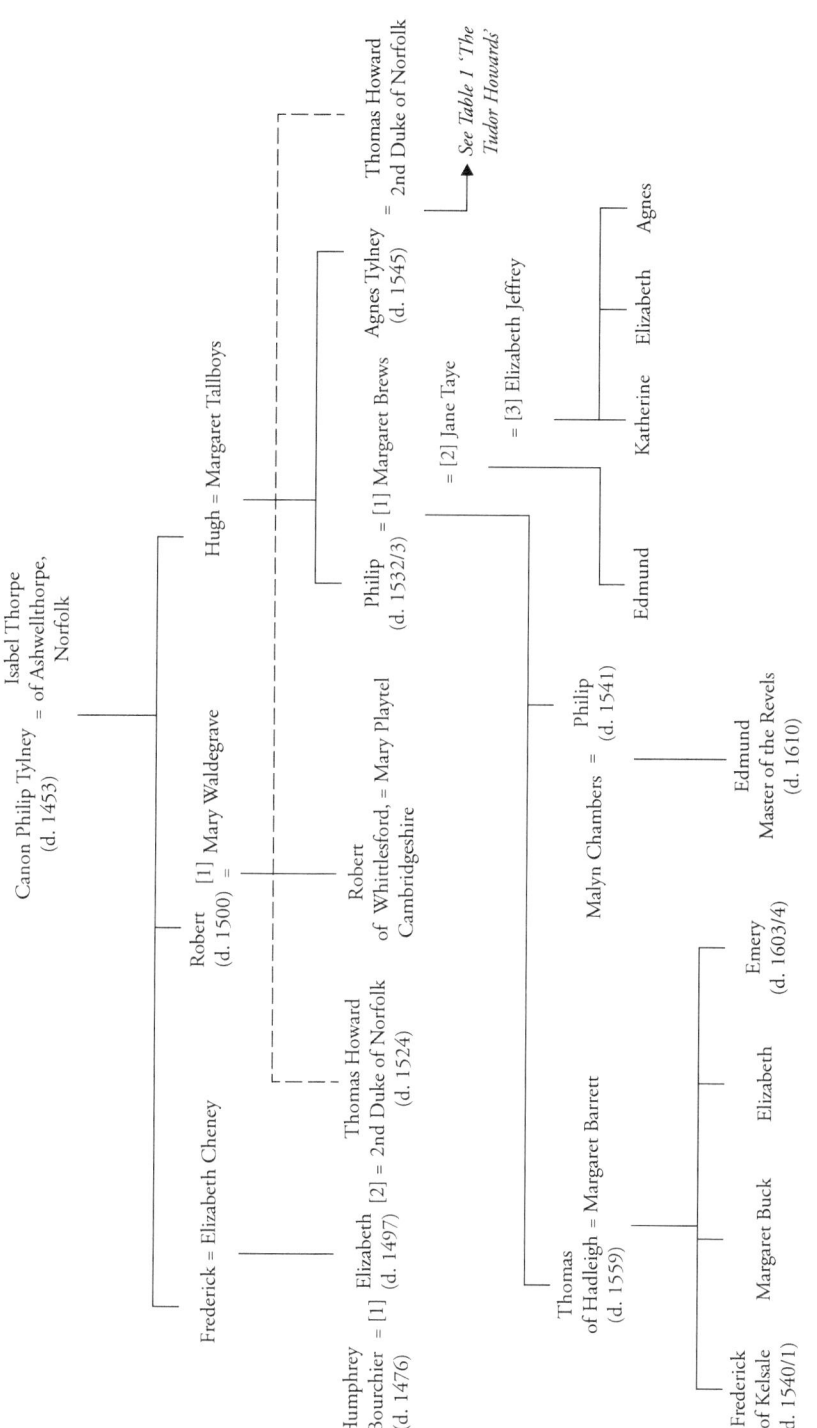

Introduction
'anobull house'

The title quote of this chapter comes from the depositions taken as part of the Queen Catherine Howard treason case in 1541. Mary Lascelles/Hall, the originator of the reports of Catherine's pre-marital sexual liaisons, claimed to have warned Henry Mannox, Catherine's virginals tutor, to steer clear of Catherine, because 'she do cu[m] of anobull hous & yf thow shuld mare here su[m] of here blod wold kell the'.[1] Mannox coarsely replied, 'hold thy pese woman I know here welhenoveghe for I have had here by thow count & know it amongst a C & she loff me & I lof her'.[2] Mary clearly saw the Howard dynasty in this context as a large, cohesive entity primed to enact vengeance against those who wronged its members, and understood that women were among a dynasty's chief assets. Mannox, on the other hand, disregarded this, and seemed to think that Catherine's own individual feelings mattered more than what her family might think. These few sentences lay bare the inherent complexity of the early modern dynasty, and the importance of understanding the position of women within it: for, as this book argues, when women are placed centre stage it becomes evident that both of these interpretations of the function of an early modern dynasty could be valid, and that we need to nuance our understanding of women's agency, dynastic identity, and politics to take account of this.

The study of pre-modern women has gained such momentum in the last few decades that in 2007 Rosemary O'Day was able to state that 'historians...now see women's history as an essential part of any historical writing'.[3] For a long time this was almost exclusively focused on royal women, and pre-modern queenship remains a strong and vibrant field.[4] Scholarship has since expanded, however, to

---

[1] TNA SP1/167, fol. 111.   [2] Ibid.

[3] Rosemary O'Day, *Women's Agency in Early Modern Britain and the American Colonies* (Harlow, 2007), 1. See, for instance, Sara Mendelson and Patricia Crawford, *Women in Early Modern England, 1550–1720* (Oxford, 1999); Bernard Capp, *When Gossips Meet: Women, Family and Neighbourhood in Early Modern England* (Oxford, 2004); Barbara Harris, *English Aristocratic Women, 1450–1550* (Oxford, 2002); Nadine Akkerman and Birgit Houben (eds), *The Politics of Female Households: Ladies in Waiting Across Early Modern Europe* (Leiden, 2013); Gemma Allen, *The Cooke Sisters: Education, Piety and Politics in Early Modern England* (Manchester, 2013); Susan Broomhall and Stephanie Tarbin (eds), *Women, Identities and Communities in Early Modern Europe* (Aldershot, 2008); James Daybell (ed.), *Women and Politics in Early Modern England, 1450–1700* (Aldershot, 2004); James Daybell and Svante Norrhem (eds), *Gender and Political Culture in Early Modern Europe, 1400–1800* (London, 2016).

[4] See, for instance, the many recent and forthcoming titles in the 'Queenship and Power' series edited by Charles Beem and Carole Levin for Palgrave Macmillan.

consider women below royal status, and also to examine the gendered negotiation of power and agency.[5] For late medieval and early modern England, Barbara Harris's work forms the foundation of this and many other studies. Her *English Aristocratic Women, 1450–1550,* published in 2002, not only provided a much-needed survey on aristocratic women across the early Tudor period, but feminized the definition of 'politics' in a way that made it possible to integrate women into existing political narratives.[6] Harris redefined the noble household as a political space, pointing out that many so-called 'domestic' or 'female' activities should be considered as political given that society functioned through patronage and the political was personal. By offering hospitality, arranging marriages, raising children, and so on, women made and maintained the social networks so vital to advancement, and should therefore be considered political actors alongside their menfolk. Other scholars have since capitalized on this work. The role of women in diplomacy is attracting attention, as is their role in the international transfer of culture, both social and material.[7] Thanks largely to the doctoral studies of Dakota Hamilton, Charlotte Merton, Helen Payne, and Sara Wolfson, we now have a detailed picture of the women who served in the households of Queens Catherine Parr, Mary I, Elizabeth I, Anne of Denmark, and Henrietta Maria, and female households continue to provoke new scholarship throughout Europe.[8] Such work has shown that there are many ways in which women engaged with the political sphere: through patronage, literature, religion, and even rebellion, all of which are key themes in the lives of the Howard women explored here.

The position and roles of women within dynasties is a relatively new topic to develop as a result of this increased acceptance of the importance of women and gender relations to political society, and the significance of 'dynasty' likewise. As Helen Berry and Elizabeth Foyster noted in 2007, the history of women and the history of the family do not often intersect.[9] Nor, until recently, did the history of

---

[5] For recent examples of this, see Susan Broomhall (ed.), *Authority, Gender and Emotions in Late Medieval and Early Modern England* (Basingstoke, 2016).

[6] Harris, *English Aristocratic Women.*

[7] Jane Couchman and Anne Crabb (eds), *Women's Letters Across Europe, 1400–1700: Form and Persuasion* (Aldershot, 2005); Allen, *The Cooke Sisters*; Susan Broomhall and Jacqueline Van Gent, *Dynastic Colonialism: Gender, Materiality and the Early Modern House of Orange–Nassau* (London, 2016).

[8] Dakota Hamilton 'The Household of Katherine Parr' (unpublished D.Phil. thesis, University of Oxford, 1992); Charlotte Merton, 'The Women Who Served Queen Mary and Queen Elizabeth: Ladies, Gentlewomen and Maids of the Privy Chamber, 1553–1603' (unpublished doctoral thesis, University of Cambridge, 1990); Helen Payne, 'Aristocratic Women and the Jacobean Court, 1603–1625' (unpublished doctoral thesis, Royal Holloway, University of London, 2001); Sara Wolfson, 'Aristocratic Women of the Household and Court of Queen Henrietta Maria, 1625–1659' (unpublished doctoral thesis, University of Durham, 2010). This work has yet to be done for the households of the rest of Henry VIII's queens. My MA thesis explored the women at the court of Henry VII and Elizabeth of York; see Nicola Clark, '"Richly beseen": Women at the Court of Henry VII' (unpublished MA thesis, Royal Holloway, University of London, 2008). See also Nadine Akkerman and Birgit Houben (eds), *The Politics of Female Households: Ladies in Waiting Across Early Modern Europe* (Leiden, 2013).

[9] Introduction to Helen Berry and Elizabeth Foyster (eds), *The Family in Early Modern England* (Cambridge, 2007), 1–17 (15). For further discussion of this see L. A. Tilly, 'Women's History and Family History: Fruitful Collaboration or Missed Connection?', *Journal of Family History* 12 (1987), 303–15 and M. Doolittle, 'Close Relations? Bringing Together Gender and Family in English History', *Gender and History* 11:3 (1999), 542–54.

the family and what we tend to call 'political history', a broad umbrella of scholarship characterized primarily by its focus on events and individuals of national significance. Instead, they have tended to pass one another rather like ships in the night, or like a Venn diagram without the overlapping middle section. Yet it would be fair to argue that the political concerns of any individual revolved around the concept and reality of family. One had to marry and procreate in order to pass on inheritance and continue one's lineage. Not only were kinship networks formed during this process, but they were also necessary to its success. All of these dynastic and political activities necessarily involved women.

For scholars of continental Europe, 'dynasty' or 'dynastic identity' is an increasingly familiar field of academic study, though so far mostly concerned with royals rather than aristocrats.[10] Work by Jonathan Spangler on the Lorraine–Guise, Liesbeth Geevers on the Hapsburgs, and Susan Broomhall and Jacqueline Van Gent on the Orange–Nassau has explored the definitions, limits, and boundaries of dynasty, as well as its significance to individual identity and, particularly, its trans-national character.[11] The latter focus may be why this concept has yet to be incorporated into work focused on early modern England, since English aristocratic dynasties rarely married across national borders during this period. Though the interest in the English nobility that flourished in the 1990s did occasionally lead to a family-centric outlook, such as George Bernard's work on the earls of Shrewsbury, or his edited volume on the Tudor nobility, this was overshadowed by the louder and more vigorous debate concerning the concept of 'political faction' which was also current coin at that time.[12] Collectively this work barely touched on the women of those families. There remain remarkably few full-length studies of the women of single aristocratic families, and this is particularly the case for early modern England, with the welcome exception of Gemma Allen's recent study of the Cooke sisters.[13]

---

[10] Liesbeth Geevers and Mirella Marini (eds), *Dynastic Identity in Early Modern Europe: Rulers, Aristocrats and the Formation of Identities* (Aldershot, 2015), and Susan Broomhall and Jacqueline Van Gent, *Dynastic Colonialism: Gender, Materiality and the Early Modern House of Orange–Nassau* (London, 2016). See also Jeroen Duindam, *Dynasties: A Global History of Power, 1300–1800* (Cambridge, 2015).

[11] Jonathan Spangler, *The Society of Princes: The Lorraine–Guise and the Conservation of Power and Wealth in Seventeenth-Century France* (Aldershot, 2009); Liesbeth Geevers, 'The Miracles of Spain. Dynastic Attitudes to the Habsburg Succession and the Spanish Succession Crisis (1580–1700)', *Sixteenth Century Journal* 46 (2015), 99–119, and 'Dynasty and State Building in the Spanish Habsburg Monarchy: The Career of Emanuele Filiberto of Savoy (1588–1624)', *Journal of Early Modern History* 20 (2016), 267–92; Broomhall and Van Gent, *Dynastic Colonialism.*

[12] G. W. Bernard, *The Power of the Early Tudor Nobility: A Study of the Fourth and Fifth Earls of Shrewsbury* (Brighton, 1985); G. W. Bernard (ed.), *The Tudor Nobility* (Manchester, 1992). The faction debate became increasingly two-sided, and focused particularly on the fall of Anne Boleyn in 1536, and on the character of the 1590s under Elizabeth I, with one party of historians arguing for the power and pre-eminence of factions in politics, and another insisting on its limitations as a political force, and even doubting its existence. For a recent outline of this, see Janet Dickinson, 'Redefining Faction at the Tudor Court', in Ruben Gonzalez Cuerva and Alexander Koller (eds), *A Europe of Courts, a Europe of Factions: Political Groups at Early Modern Centres of Power (1550–1700)* (Leiden, 2017). The factional potential of aristocratic families, though present in that debate, was never fully addressed. The advent of dynasty as a new focus in European political history may mean that the time is ripe for reconsideration.

[13] Allen, *The Cooke Sisters.*

Natalie Tomas's study of the Medici women of Italy and Helen Nader's edited collection of essays on the Spanish Mendoza women suggest that, again, this concept has been quicker to gain traction on the Continent.[14] There have been a small number of articles focusing on the women of one family, and these are usually to be found within the field of letter-writing due to the nature of family archives and the dynastic information they contain, such as Alison Wall's work on the Thynne women and Alison Truelove's on the Stonors.[15]

Most of this work on dynasty takes as a starting point the assumption that members of a dynasty worked together strategically to achieve shared goals, an idea that seems particularly to carry weight where women are considered. It is clearly true that women did, in general, seek to promote their marital relatives in order that good things might rebound upon the entire family, because what was good for the family was good for them too. But scholars rarely ask what happened if family members had conflicting views of what the dynasty's ambitions should be, or, indeed, how women conceptualized their own dynastic identity. This book reveals that, contrary to much popular belief, there was no identifiably consistent strategy for political survival among the Howards, and this forces us to reconsider our understanding of several key political episodes.

Who were the Howards? As dukes of Norfolk, they were the premier peers of England throughout the early modern period, second only to the royal family. They were, in fact, everywhere: holding office as Lord Treasurers, Earls Marshal, and Lord Admirals, serving the Tudor monarchs at court, even sitting on the throne as royal consorts. Tudor political history cannot be written without them. Unusually, perhaps, their historical infamy is due more to their women than to the men, for two of Henry VIII's six wives, Anne Boleyn and Catherine Howard, belonged to the Howard dynasty. This is one of the reasons why this is a particularly crucial period for which to recover the histories of the remainder of the Howard women, for there were indeed many more of them available to make important marriages, run the estates, serve the queen at court, and, as this book reveals, steer the dynasty as a whole in both helpful and less helpful ways. The existing narrative of the Howards' family fortunes has not prioritized the women. Though there have been some studies of the Tudor Howards, these have either been biographical studies of the men, or have focused on the collective male narrative at the expense of the female.[16]

---

[14] Natalie R. Tomas, *The Medici Women: Gender and Power in Renaissance Florence* (Aldershot, 2003); Helen Nader (ed.), *Power and Gender in Renaissance Spain: Eight Women of the Mendoza Family, 1450–1650* (Urbana, Ill., and Chicago, 2004).

[15] Alison Wall, 'Deference and Defiance in Women's Letters of the Thynne Family: The Rhetoric of Relationships', in James Daybell (ed.), *Early Modern Women's Letter Writing, 1450–1700* (Basingstoke, 2001), 77–93; Alison Truelove, 'Commanding Communications: The Fifteenth-Century Letters of the Stonor Women', in Daybell (ed.), *Early Modern Women's Letter Writing, 1450–1700*, 42–58. See also Sara Jayne Steen, 'The Cavendish–Talbot Women: Playing a High-Stakes Game', in Daybell (ed.), *Women and Politics*, 147–63; Catherine Clarke, 'Patronage and Literature: The Women of the Russell Family, 1520–1617' (unpublished doctoral thesis, University of Reading, 1992).

[16] See, for instance, Gerald Brenan and Edward Phillips Statham, *The House of Howard*, 2 vols (London, 1907), I, chs 1 and 2, pp. 1–59, and John M. Robinson, *The Dukes of Norfolk: A Quincentennial History* (Oxford, 1982). Melvin J. Tucker, *The Life of Thomas Howard, Earl of Surrey and Second Duke of Norfolk, 1443–1524* (London, 1964) and David M. Head, *The Ebbs and Flows of Fortune: The Life*

As this book shows, turning the spotlight onto the female Howards throws much of what we think we know about the family's behaviour into question.

The Howards' own emphasis on the purity of their bloodlines has tended to obscure their real history as political *parvenus*, the lucky inheritors—through the female line—of the extinct dukedom of Norfolk in 1483, only two years before this study begins. Nor did they hold on to it for long. John Howard, the first Howard Duke of Norfolk, was killed fighting for Richard III at Bosworth in 1485, and his eldest son Thomas, then Earl of Surrey, was imprisoned and attainted by the victorious Henry VII. For the Howard women, then, the accession of the Tudor dynasty was something of a baptism of fire.[17] John's widow, Margaret Chedworth/Wyfold/ Norreys/Howard, was left to depend on her inheritance from previous marriages for sustenance, and Surrey's wife Elizabeth Tylney/Bourchier/Howard was forced to scramble to secure the safety of herself, her children, and her inheritance, which she did with aplomb. Immediately she heard the news, she retired with them to sanctuary on the Isle of Sheppey and wrote to the Earl of Oxford, now in charge of the region, to secure the estates that were part of her own inheritance, separate from those of her husband.[18] She and her children remained at her own manor of Ashwellthorpe until Surrey was released and sent to serve as Lieutenant of the North in 1489, when she joined him at Sherriff Hutton Castle in Yorkshire, a household immortalized by the poet John Skelton in his 'Garland of Laurel'. While still in the north, Elizabeth died, and Surrey promptly married her first cousin, Agnes, in 1497. When the family came south in 1499, she too became involved in their political rehabilitation, and in 1503 the couple were chosen to escort the King's eldest daughter, Princess Margaret, to her marriage with the Scottish King James IV, a sign that both were considered responsible courtiers. Though they had not yet regained the dukedom of Norfolk, by the time of the King's death in 1509 the Howards were once again wealthy, high-status, politically powerful aristocracy, and they proceeded to play a central role throughout the rest of the sixteenth century. This narrative is better known; or so it is thought. The Howard men are remembered for their soldiery, playing crucial roles in the Battle of Flodden in 1513—which won them the return of the dukedom of Norfolk—in the suppression of the Pilgrimage of Grace in 1536, and on various military campaigns throughout the first half of the century. Elsewhere, the family as a whole is remembered for its alleged enmity with various royal advisers, for its apparent willingness to groom female relatives into seducing the King, for its support for the royal divorce, and for

---

of Thomas Howard, Third Duke of Norfolk (Athens, Ga, and London, 1995) remain the standard works on the early Tudor Howard patriarchs, and Anne Crawford, *Yorkist Lord: John Howard, Duke of Norfolk, c.1425–1485* (London, 2010) provides a recent prologue for the purpose of this study. Henry Howard, Earl of Surrey, has also formed the subject of several biographies: E. Casady, *Henry Howard, Earl of Surrey* (London, 1938); W. A. Sessions, *Henry Howard, the Poet Earl of Surrey: A Life* (Oxford, 1999); Jessie Childs, *Henry VIII's Last Victim: The Life and Times of Henry Howard, Earl of Surrey* (London, 2006).

[17] See Anne Crawford, 'Victims of Attainder: The Howard and De Vere Women in the Late Fifteenth Century', in Keith Bate (ed.), *Medieval Women in Southern England* (Reading, 1989), 59–74.

[18] James Gairdner (ed.), *Paston Letters*, 6 vols in Microprint edition (Stroud, 1983), VI, 87–8.

its supposed Catholicism, all of which look vastly different when viewed, as they are here, from a female perspective.

The family's position at the heart of the royal court has meant that an active search for political involvement, significance, or impact in the lives of the Howard women has not been necessary: their identity meant that politics was a way of life, a daily lot rather than a special occasion. This is why there is no specific chapter in this book on the Howard women and politics. There is no need to ask *if* the Howard women were involved in politics; we can begin at the point of asking how, why, and what the consequences of political involvement were. Unearthing the records to do so, however, is a particular skill of historians of pre-modern women and one that often goes unrecognized. The vast majority of calendars and catalogues were compiled by men during the twentieth century, before the study of women was considered important. Indexes are not always entirely accurate or thorough, and women were sometimes ignored in the brief descriptions of the original sources. Digitization, however, has meant that we can now access many of these original sources and are no longer reliant on the short calendared versions, and this has been particularly fruitful for the study of aristocratic women. Where a calendar might provide a mere three-line summary of a woman's letter, resources like the State Papers Online might reveal an original which is actually three pages in length. It remains the case that several archive catalogues are not geared towards finding women, but in many cases this is a side effect of coverture. Married women could neither file lawsuits, make wills, nor administer property under their own names, which means that historians need to research in a backwards fashion, searching instead for a woman's male relatives. It hardly needs saying that the higher a woman's status, the easier she is to find, but even where aristocratic women are obvious in original sources, a woman's identity is not always clear. There could be several women with the same title, and contemporaries did not always differentiate between them. This means that it is sometimes difficult to know whether, for instance, one has found Agnes, the dowager Duchess of Norfolk, or Elizabeth, the junior Duchess.

Studying a family through its women is theoretically as well as practically tricky. Who was a Howard woman, and how long did she remain one? In a patrilineal society, women could accumulate a number of different family memberships across the course of their lives. They began with the family into which they were born—'natal' family—but would then add a new 'marital' family with each successive marriage. Was a woman still a Howard woman after she had married into a new family? Women's wills make it clear that they did not cut ties with each family group every time they moved on, but maintained those relationships, collecting families over time, and so many of the means by which historians, anthropologists, and sociologists define men's family identity simply do not work for early modern elite women.[19] This is why this book refers to women throughout by all of their accumulated family names, separated by slashes and followed by title, for example, Agnes Tylney/Howard, Duchess of Norfolk. This not only creates a swift visual understanding of the way in which women accumulated family identities, and

---

[19] On women's wills, see Harris, *English Aristocratic Women*, 127–8.

what those were for each woman under discussion, but also implicitly allows for the idea that a woman's 'current' surname was not necessarily more important than those she had previously borne.

This does, however, create boundary issues for a study like this one, where decisions need to be made on who to include and who to leave out. One of the ways in which this has been done in recent years is by examining the language that early modern people used to and for family members.[20] While anthropologists generally divide pre-modern kinship into three categories—blood (known as consanguineal or biological) kin, marital (affinal) kin such as in-laws and step-relations, and fictive or spiritual kinship, like godparents—historians cannot study early modern families or individuals in such a structured way, because early modern people did not distinguish linguistically between these different forms of kinship.[21] Relations who were not mother, father, brother, sister, aunt, uncle, nephew, niece, or grandparent, whether full, half, step, or in-law, were almost uniformly referred to as 'cousin' or 'kinsman'.[22] This meant that virtually any relation, however distant, might be considered kin. In most cases both male and female Howards used kinship terminology in this way. Thomas, Third Duke of Norfolk, described his daughter-in-law Frances de Vere/Howard/Staynings, Countess of Surrey, as 'my doughter of Surrey', the same formula he used for his biological daughter Mary Howard/Fitzroy, Duchess of Richmond.[23] Anne Howard/de Vere, Countess of Oxford, signed letters to her half-brother Norfolk 'youre loveyng sister', and he referred to her in kind; Elizabeth Stafford/Howard, Duchess of Norfolk, referred to her 'suster Stafford', meaning her sister-in-law, in her will.[24] Anne, Countess of Oxford, mentioned several times her 'cosyn Tylney', and Mary, Duchess of Richmond, called Sir William Fermor 'my cossen'.[25] While the former was a clear connection—the Tylneys were the natal family of Anne's mother Agnes—the latter between Mary and Sir William Fermor is far more distant by modern standards, showing that family boundaries could be stretched and contracted at need.[26]

The language of kinship could be flexibly applied for all sorts of reasons. At the beginning of the letter that Thomas, Third Duke of Norfolk, wrote to the King after the arrest of his niece and other relatives in 1541, he referred to his attainted half-siblings Lord William Howard and Katherine Howard/ap Rhys/Daubeney, Countess of Bridgwater, as 'myn unhappy brother' and 'my lewde suster'; further on he simply referred to them as his stepmother's 'ungracious childern', clearly

---

[20] Emphasized originally by Naomi Tadmor in 'The Concept of the Household-Family in Eighteenth-Century England', *Past and Present* 151:1 (1996), 111–40, and *Family and Friends in Eighteenth Century England: Household, Kinship, and Patronage* (Cambridge, 2001). See also David Cressy, 'Kinship and Kin Interaction in Early Modern England', *Past and Present* 113:1 (1986), 38–69.

[21] Will Coster, *Family and Kinship in England, 1450–1800* (London, 2015), 40.

[22] Ibid.   [23] TNA SP1/130, fol. 43; TNA SP1/131, fol. 24.

[24] TNA SP1/30, fol. 134; TNA PROB 11/42A/285.

[25] TNA SP1/27, fol. 152; TNA SP10/7, no. 1.

[26] This was most probably the William Fermor who was Sheriff of Norfolk and Suffolk in 1540, son of Sir Henry Fermor of East Barsham. William Fermor married Catherine Knyvett, who was the daughter of Sir Thomas Knyvett of Buckenham (d. 1512) and Muriel Howard/de Lisle/Knyvett, Viscountess Lisle (d. 1513), daughter of Thomas Howard, Second Duke of Norfolk.

hoping to imply that he really had nothing to do with them or their behaviour and illustrating the way that language could change within a single piece of correspondence in order to create the effect of familial distance.[27] The Howards did not necessarily use kinship terms to describe even close relations. Sometimes this was simply common sense. The term 'my son' would have been no good as an identifier for those who had more than one son or many sons-in-law, and this certainly applied to the prolific Howards. Thus the use, or lack thereof, of kinship terminology does not always bring us significantly closer to understanding the boundaries of the Howard dynasty, for to do so we need to understand not only who is identified as 'kin', but who is specifically identified as a Howard.

To do so we need to step back even further. Although scholars use the word 'dynasty' frequently, it was rarely used in early modern England.[28] 'House' was sometimes used instead, as in the title quote of this Introduction.[29] Often, though, early modern individuals used the word 'kin' to mean both individuals to whom they personally were related, *and* the noble dynasty to which they belonged. In 1541, Thomas Howard, Third Duke of Norfolk, wrote to the King in sorrow at the behaviour of his family members concerning the fall of his niece Catherine Howard, anxious that the King would 'conseyue a displesure in yoᵣ hert agaynst me and all other of that kyn'.[30] In this context, 'kin' is used in the way that we would use 'dynasty', 'house', or 'family': anybody alive who was directly related to Catherine Howard. This is known as a 'horizontal' understanding of kinship, the dynasty in its present, 'live' state. There was also, however, a 'vertical' definition of kinship, meaning the family line or lineage passed down the generations. This was the kind of kinship commemorated on the vast genealogies beloved by the early modern aristocracy. Since the emphasis was on the passage of a family name and/or title through the male line, it was not only a strongly patriarchal understanding of kinship, but tended to be narrower than its horizontal counterpart.

These various contemporaneous definitions of kinship suggest that surnames might be of some help in uncovering contemporary understandings of a dynasty's membership, since a family name united different branches of the same dynasty, but did not encompass all those who were 'kin' to each individual bearing that name.[31] However, as explained above, this reveals only an initial circle of patrilineal dynastic membership which is highly problematic for the study of women, who might have several surnames across the course of their lives. Names were also open to manipulation, both by their owners and by others. When Katherine Howard/ap Rhys, Lady Rhys, daughter of the Second Duke of Norfolk and wife of Rhys ap Gruffudd, became involved in a situation of rebellion in south Wales in the late 1520s, the King's justiciar wrote to Thomas Wolsey to demand his intervention

---

[27] TNA SP1/168, fol. 143.

[28] The *OED* has the first usage of 'dynasty' to mean 'a succession of rulers of the same line or family' as 1464. A search of State Papers Online for the word 'dynasty', limited by date between 1400 and 1559, finds no results; Early English Books Online (EEBO) finds only one, dated to 1559.

[29] See, for instance, *LP* XVI, 1090.   [30] TNA SP1/168, fol. 143.

[31] Many of the separate branches of the Howard dynasty had yet to form, but in later periods we can see this happening and see the name acting as a unifier.

and consistently styled Katherine incorrectly as 'my Lady Howard' in his letter, probably in order to have his complaints taken seriously by invoking the name of England's premier peerage family.[32] Though Katherine's own letter to Wolsey followed correct naming procedure, calling herself 'Katherine Ryx', she did specifically mention her Howard relations in order to try to get herself out of trouble, thus clearly continuing to identify as part of the Howard family as well as the Rhys.[33]

Where did this leave those who were related to the Howards, but did not possess the Howard name; were they members of the dynasty or not? Status and gender are key here. If a woman married a Howard, she too became a Howard while maintaining connections to her natal family, but her natal family did not change their own dynastic identity. If a man married a Howard woman, he became kin to the Howards, but whether his dynastic identity changed appears to depend on whether he was of equal or lower status. If he belonged to another very aristocratic family, such as the Radcliffes, earls of Sussex, or the Stanleys, earls of Derby, he did not count himself, or become counted, as a member of the Howard dynasty. If, on the other hand, his original status was lower, and he was a member of a family like, for instance, the Knyvetts, or the Sheltons, his new dynastic identity was now much more nebulous, though not necessarily consistent. Dynastic identity was therefore affected by, and could affect, the conflation of kinship and patronage. Lower-status families loosely related to larger, higher-status dynasties are often called 'client families', because though kin, they were essentially drawing on their relations for patronage purposes, and would not have identified themselves or been identified by the name of the larger dynasty.[34] This, though, could change rapidly in reaction to circumstances, as the example of the Boleyns shows. Had it not been for Sir Thomas Boleyn's position at court and his daughters' apparent charms, the Boleyns would most likely have remained in this kind of subordinate position relative to their Howard relations. After Anne's fall in 1536, they were relegated back to that position. This elasticity in linguistics and in dynastic boundaries is the reason it is so difficult to define who did and did not belong, and it is the reason that this very elasticity of kinship and of dynastic membership is a key argument and exploration of this study. In an effort to stay true to contemporary ideas of kinship and dynasty, then, this book considers a Howard woman to be any woman who held the Howard name in some guise at some stage of her life, whether she had been born into or married into the family.

The thematic structure of this book begins by unravelling the strength and expression of the women's kinship ties, not only at times of crisis, but on a daily basis, to create a holistic impression of the dynasty's cohesion from a female perspective. Chapter 2 considers dynastic identity through the women's use and management of material resources, and Chapter 3 takes a case study approach to the high instance of marital issues within the dynasty during this period. Chapters 4 and 5 address the role of the women, and of dynastic identity, in some of the best-known episodes

---

[32] TNA SP1/54 fol. 93.   [33] TNA SP1/54, fol. 87.
[34] On patronage and clientage, see Sharon Kettering, *Patrons, Brokers, and Clients in Seventeenth-Century France* (Oxford, 1986).

of the early Tudor period, and through their roles as courtiers, and Chapter 6 queries the validity of the assumption that whole families responded in the same way to religious change. This study not only brings the Howard women's own narratives to the fore, thereby altering the traditional narrative of the Howard dynasty, but questions the very nature of women's familial identities. It examines the strength of political bonds and loyalties, the strain put upon them by crises, and whether and when family connections could be mobilized. It investigates the networks that existed, the ways in which they were built and sustained, and the uses to which they could be put, and it explores the construction of family or dynastic identity. It argues that we need to appreciate the importance of the Howard women, but that we can only fully understand this by placing them in their many contexts: at court as well as at home, as sisters and cousins as well as wives and mothers; and by appreciating the interaction and intersection of their full kaleidoscope of identities, as Howards, as evangelical, conservative, or otherwise in religion, as subjects of the crown, as both patronesses and petitioners. None of these categories is sufficient explanation of their role taken in isolation, and all need to be seen side by side. This highlights the ongoing need to integrate women into sixteenth-century political historiography, and also a need to nuance our understanding of the triangular relationship between elite women, the aristocratic dynasty, and the early modern state.

1

'Many kyne and few that dothe for me'
Kinship Relations

Family relationships are known to have been the cornerstone of society and politics during this period, especially for women, whose time was often spent advancing their kin in any way possible.[1] At the same time, it is evident that not every relationship between kin could be positive all, or even some, of the time—as scholarship on early modern litigation has shown—and this is as true for women as for men.[2] Where the aristocracy is concerned, scholars sometimes have difficulty persuading these two interpretations to coexist comfortably. Noble dynasties are often presented either as a series of coherent family groups united in pursuit of shared goals, or, conversely, as disparate individuals as likely to fight as unite, and women are not always given space in these interpretations.[3] The Howards themselves have fallen victim to both of these; they are often presented as a united force at court, notably during the rise of Anne Boleyn and again for Catherine Howard, but described as 'wholly disunited' at other points.[4] Yet this need not be an either/or choice. While both these interpretations might approach the truth at specific times of crisis or under extraordinary circumstances, even the Howards did not live every moment under such intense pressures. To fully appreciate the strengths and weaknesses of these family networks, we need a broader consideration of the everyday expression of relationships between kin. This chapter examines the relationships between the

---

[1] Harris, *English Aristocratic Women*; the essays in James Daybell (ed.), *Women and Politics in Early Modern England, 1450–1700* (Aldershot, 2004); James Daybell and Svante Norrhem (eds), *Gender and Political Culture in Early Modern Europe, 1400–1800* (London, 2016), 3.

[2] Amanda Capern, 'Emotions, Gender Expectations, and the Social Role of Chancery, 1550–1650', in Susan Broomhall (ed.), *Authority, Gender and Emotions in Late Medieval and Early Modern England* (Basingstoke, 2016).

[3] Much recent scholarship on dynastic identity tends to take as a starting point the notion that families worked as united groups. See, for instance, L. Geevers and M. Marini (eds), *Dynastic Identity in Early Modern Europe* (Leiden, 2015). As early as the 1990s, however, scholars were questioning this assumption. See the introduction to George Bernard (ed.), *The Tudor Nobility* (Manchester, 1992), 1–48 (29–30) and his essay therein on 'The Downfall of Sir Thomas Seymour', 212–40, and Michael A. Hicks, 'Cement or Solvent?: Kinship and Politics in Late Medieval England: The Case of the Nevilles', *History* 83 (1998), 31–46.

[4] E. W. Ives, *The Life and Death of Anne Boleyn: 'The Most Happy'* (Oxford, 2004), Lacey Baldwin Smith, *Catherine Howard* (London, 1969), and Retha Warnicke, 'Family and Kinship Relations at the Henrician Court: The Boleyns and Howards', in Dale Hoak, (ed.), *Tudor Political Culture* (Cambridge, 1995), 31–53, all paint a picture of the Howards as a family faction. Diarmaid MacCulloch, conversely, has described them as 'wholly disunited' in the later 1540s. MacCulloch, '"Vain, Proud, Foolish Boy": The Earl of Surrey and the Fall of the Howards', in David Starkey (ed.), *Rivals in Power* (London, 1999), 86–113 (87).

Howard women and their kin on just such a basis, arguing that the family were not automatically united and did not consistently function as a coherent unit, but neither were they ever wholly disunited. What might seem a close relationship in one context could look utterly different in another context, and this has implications for the way that we should understand their behaviour on the political stage.

A considerable amount has been written about kinship with reference to the aristocracy. We know that for the early modern nobility, kinship was both vertical (in the form of lineage, or dynasty) and horizontal (living family); both nuclear or 'close', and extended; and that all relations could be called upon for assistance in times of need.[5] We know that family for women was complex, because over the course of their lives almost all women would marry, and thus accumulate at least one new family group. Women did not, and were not expected to, abandon their natal families on marriage, but maintained connections and loyalties with each of their families as they moved through successive life stages.[6] Nevertheless, our under-standing of the dynastic roles women played usually comes from source material which prioritizes women's interactions with men, which meant that for a long time 'family' for women was conceptualized as male–female or mother–child relation-ships. This chapter therefore takes three less commonly considered forms of kinship as its focus: women's familial relationships with each other; their interaction with the male head of the dynasty, the paterfamilias; and their engagement with extended kin. It has been made clear that female networks were perceived to be as, if not more, influential than those of exclusively male kin.[7] Among the Howards, not only were female kinship networks of particular strength, but they could sometimes operate outside of dynastic approval, to the detriment of the family's political position. Relatedly, this 'dynastic approval' is usually presumed to have been patriarchal, and usually took the form of the nominal male head of the dynasty—the firstborn, or paterfamilias—who is generally thought to have functioned as the daily embodiment of authority for noblewomen.[8] Authority was, of course, a negoti-ation, a two-way street, and some dynastic patriarchs were notably more successful

---

[5] For several decades the study of the early modern family was based around a theory of 'grand narrative' change over time, allegedly from 'extended' families in the late medieval age to 'nuclear' families by the middle of the eighteenth century, a theory which has by now been heavily disputed, particularly where the aristocracy are concerned. Naomi Tadmor summed this up in 'Early Modern Kinship in the Long Run', *Continuity and Change* 25:1 (2010), 15–48. More recently attention has turned to the concept of 'dynasty' as linked to, yet separate from, mere 'kinship', as explained in the Introduction to this book. See Geevers and Marini (eds), *Dynastic Identity in Early Modern Europe*, and Broomhall and Van Gent, *Dynastic Colonialism*.

[6] Harris, *English Aristocratic Women*.

[7] Karen Robertson, 'Negotiating Favour: The Letters of Lady Ralegh', in Daybell (ed.), *Women and Politics*, 99–113; Barbara J. Harris, 'Sisterhood, Friendship and the Power of English Aristocratic Women, 1450–1550', in Daybell (ed.), *Women and Politics*, 21–50; Amanda E. Herbert, *Female Alliances: Gender, Identity and Friendship in Early Modern Britain* (New Haven, 2014).

[8] Susan Broomhall and Jacqueline Van Gent, 'In the Name of the Father: Conceptualizing Pater Familias in the Letters of William the Silent's Children', *Renaissance Quarterly* 62:4 (2009), 1130–66. See also Susan Broomhall and Jacqueline Van Gent (eds), *Governing Masculinities in the Early Modern Period: Regulating Selves and Others* (London, 2011), and Alexandra Shepard, 'From Anxious Patriarchs to Refined Gentlemen? Manhood in Britain c.1500–1700', *Journal of British Studies* 44:2 (2004), 281–95, esp. 291–2.

than others at marshalling their relations into some semblance of collective order.[9] This chapter argues that this assumed patriarchal control did not always, or even mostly, extend into daily reality among the Howards during this period, and that this becomes clear when viewed from a female perspective. This allows us to question the perceived coherence of aristocratic dynasties as described in existing political histories.

SISTERHOOD: FEMALE KINSHIP RELATIONS

In December 1529, imperial ambassador Eustace Chapuys reported to his master Charles V, Holy Roman Emperor:

> I likewise deem it advisable to try, in my own name of course, what can be done with the duke of Norfolk, and see whether we could not gain him over to our cause by means of some promise of help and assistance in the marriage of his son to Princess Mary...I have no doubt that such motives would strongly work upon the Duke and yet there is ground for fearing that such a plan, if proposed will be rejected; for should the Queen regain her influence and position before his son's marriage takes place she is sure to have it broken off...*for he knows well that the Queen has never forgiven him some angry words which he and his wife, the Duchess, said on the occasion of her not allowing the latter to take precedence of her mother-in-law, by which both were much offended, especially the Duchess, who belongs to the house of Lancaster.*[10]

The dispute between the two Duchesses of Norfolk was only noteworthy to Chapuys in light of its potential impact on the Duke of Norfolk's sympathies in the royal divorce, and the episode has generally gone unnoticed by historians. However, it is extremely significant in the context of kinship relations within the Howard dynasty. Several scholars have explored female networks, and these studies reveal general warmth between female kin, noting particularly the close relationships between mothers and daughters, and between sisters.[11] Women relied on their female kin for practical support and friendly advice, and were supposed to act as network brokers between their natal and marital families to the advantage of both.[12] This is manifestly not what was happening here. The report makes it clear that on some unspecified occasion, Elizabeth Stafford/Howard, the junior or 'current' Duchess of Norfolk, had tried to take precedence ahead of Agnes Tylney/Howard, the widowed dowager Duchess. The Queen (Catherine of Aragon) had refused to allow this, and Elizabeth and her husband, the Duke of Norfolk, had not taken her refusal well.

---

[9] On conceptions of authority and gender, see Susan Broomhall, introduction to Broomhall (ed.), *Authority, Gender and Emotions.*
[10] *CSP Spain*, IV, 232. My italics.
[11] Karen Robertson, 'Negotiating Favour: The Letters of Lady Ralegh', in Daybell (ed.), *Women and Politics*, 99–113. See also Charlotte Merton, 'Women, Friendship, and Memory', in Hunt and Whitelock (eds), *Tudor Queenship* (Basingstoke, 2012), 239–50; James Daybell, 'Social Negotiations in Correspondence between Mothers and Daughters in Tudor and Early Stuart England', *Women's History Review* 24:4 (2015), 502–27; Amanda Herbert, *Female Alliances: Gender, Identity and Friendship in Early Modern Britain* (New Haven, 2014).
[12] Harris, 'Sisterhood', 22.

This can be read on several different levels. Most obviously, this was a spat between two holders of the same title, and this was specifically a female issue. There could only ever be one male holder of an aristocratic title at a time, but it was possible for several women to have a right to the same title simultaneously. If a noblewoman was widowed, she retained her courtesy title, but the wife of her husband's successor also gained it. This could, in theory, happen several times over if male heirs died in quick succession, and thus at one point in the early sixteenth century there were three contemporaneous Countesses of Oxford.[13] Although a relatively common occurrence, it is easy to see that this might cause friction between the women concerned if it led to queries over authority or entitlement. Elizabeth, the wife of the 'current' Duke of Norfolk, apparently felt that she ought to take precedence over the previous Duke's widow.

Whether she had any right on her side was largely a matter of opinion. Though precedence was important to the early modern nobility, evidence suggests that rules were in reality adapted to circumstances, and were in any case more nebulous for women than for men.[14] In every English list containing noblewomen that I have found from this period, however, including those in which these very individuals are mentioned, the dowager is listed before the current titleholder.[15] Thus while it is not entirely outrageous that Elizabeth might think that her higher natal status and position as the current Duchess entitled her to precedence, this does not seem to have been usual practice at the English court at this time. As the junior, or 'young', Duchess of Norfolk, Elizabeth should normally have given way to Agnes, the dowager, and the Queen upheld this model.

It is inconceivable that Elizabeth and her husband would not have known what was normal practice, and this makes it appropriate to read beyond the surface and think about the other points of contention present in this dispute. It could, for instance, also have been an expression of conflict between different family lines or branches within the dynasty. While Elizabeth's immediate Howard relations formed the inheriting line, Agnes, as the previous Duke's second wife, headed the 'junior', and thus the subordinate, line, and there is evidence that widows in Agnes's position were sometimes sidelined.[16] There is no evidence that this was routinely the case among the Howards, though, and an aside in Chapuys's report suggests that there was more to it. Both Norfolk and Elizabeth were offended by the Queen's decision to place Agnes first, but Elizabeth especially so, because she 'belongs to the house of Lancaster'. This was a reference to Elizabeth's natal status as a daughter of Edward Stafford, Third Duke of Buckingham, who had strong links to the royal line through his Woodville ancestry. Though women nominally gave up their natal

[13] In 1526 there were two dowagers (Elizabeth Scrope, widow of the Thirteenth Earl, and Anne Howard, widow of the Fourteenth Earl) and one 'current' (Elizabeth Trussell, wife of the Fifteenth Earl).

[14] Susan Broomhall, 'Gendering the Culture of Honour at the Fifteenth-Century Burgundian Court', in Broomhall and Stephanie Tarbin (eds), *Women, Identities and Communities in Early Modern Europe* (Aldershot, 2008), 181–94.

[15] For example, New Year gift lists from 1528: E101/420/4, 1532: E101/420/15, and 1534: TNA E101/421/13.

[16] See the essays in Sandra Cavallo and Lyndan Warner (eds), *Widowhood in Medieval and Early Modern Europe* (London, 1999).

family name and status when they married, Chapuys's statement demonstrates the relevance of natal status even after marriage, since even he, a foreigner, knew Elizabeth's lineage. Agnes, the dowager Duchess, did not come from such exalted stock. Her natal family, the Tylneys, were Lincolnshire gentry. If not for their marital titles, Elizabeth would have been far above Agnes in every respect. It appears that Elizabeth felt that this ought to carry weight even after marriage had brought them into the same family and nominally levelled the playing field, and this shows just how complex the issue of dynastic identity could be for women.

On yet another level, Agnes and Elizabeth's marriages to successive dukes of Norfolk meant that not only did they share a title, but that they were also step-mother-in-law and stepdaughter-in-law. Then, as now, this relationship could be particularly fraught.[17] That it was reported in this way by Chapuys, an outsider to the network, is significant. He, not Elizabeth, insinuated that natal status and familial relationship played a role in Elizabeth's reaction, and although we cannot therefore be sure it accurately reflects Elizabeth's own feelings, it does tell us that outsiders thought that it did, and that they accepted the continued importance of women's natal status after marriage. It was Chapuys, too, who highlighted the personal relationship between the two women as mother and daughter-in-law, again showing that all of these layers were perceived by outsiders as well as those involved. Clearly, the Howard dynasty did not behave in a united fashion all of the time, and what is more, outsiders did not expect it to; Chapuys does not appear to be surprised that the two senior Howard women quarrelled so publicly.

The consequences of this episode lie more in what did not happen than in what did. The immediate dispute, Chapuys tells us, was resolved by the Queen in favour of the dowager Duchess. The offence taken by Elizabeth, the junior Duchess, and her husband the Duke, had annoyed the Queen, as well it might, and Chapuys feared that she would not now be keen to see Norfolk's son marry her daughter, Princess Mary. A seemingly minor fracas may therefore have cost the Howards a royal marriage. Female kinship relations could clearly have serious impact on a family's fortunes. It was not enough that two Howard women were of sufficient status to be present at court; certain family members felt the need to quibble for individual status beyond that, and publicly enough for Chapuys to hear of it.

That he did not seem surprised may suggest that the two women simply did not get along particularly well together. This is implied in a letter written by Agnes, the elder Duchess, to Thomas Wolsey in early September 1528. Much of her letter was taken up with the sweating sickness, which had broken out in London and across the south-east that summer. In it she said that she had heard that the Duke of Norfolk had contracted the disease and that several in his house had died, 'as I thinke through defaulte of keping'.[18] It has been plausibly suggested that this was a dig at Elizabeth, who, as the Duke's wife, would have been nominally responsible for

---

[17] See Alison D. Wall, 'Deference and Defiance in Women's Letters of the Thynne Family: The Rhetoric of Relationships', in Daybell (ed.), *Women's Letters and Letter-Writing*, 77–93.

[18] TNA SP1/50, fol. 83.

housekeeping, including preventative medicine.[19] Certainly it can be read as carrying a snide overtone. Moreover, we know that the Duke was indeed sick and absent from court for almost the whole of July, and the last mention of him before this places him at his Suffolk home, Kenninghall.[20] As there are no mentions of Elizabeth during this summer, it seems likely that she was there with him and would indeed have been in charge of his 'keping'. This criticism carries the same connotations and the same insult that it would today, but in a sixteenth-century context it had further-reaching implications. To criticize a woman's household management was to query her fitness for the role of nobleman's wife, which in aristocratic families was a public, political role. Agnes was implicitly suggesting that Elizabeth was not fit to be Duchess of Norfolk or to undertake the public responsibilities of the title. This was not a private comment, but sent in a letter to the King's chief adviser, Cardinal Wolsey. As an experienced courtier it is likely that Agnes's word on such matters would carry weight, and might seriously damage Elizabeth's career at court, which might then harm the whole family.

It is interesting that these disputes only arose once both Agnes and Elizabeth shared the same title, and were thus more equal in terms of rank. This highlights the need to consider the linear narrative of relationships rather than assuming that the character of a single snapshot incident can be applied across time. Prior to 1524, when Agnes held the title of Duchess of Norfolk and Elizabeth was the more junior Countess of Surrey, their relationship appears to have been unproblematic. This is understandable. Whilst Elizabeth was so clearly junior in rank there was no argument to be had on this point. The evidence suggests neutrality, rather than friendship, and while this may be due to the lack of more personal material, it may also relate to their physical locations during this period. It was common for daughters-in-law to live with their husband's parents during the early years of marriage, which often allowed them to form close, supportive relationships with their mothers-in-law.[21] This was not the case here, because Agnes was a second and much younger wife. Elizabeth's husband, Agnes's stepson, was the same age as his stepmother and had lived in his own household for a number of years, which meant there was no need for Elizabeth to live under Agnes's roof. Instead, Elizabeth lived mainly at Framlingham, Kenninghall, and Tendring Hall in Stoke-by-Nayland when she was at home, while Agnes spent most of her time either at Chesworth House in Sussex, or at Norfolk House in Lambeth. They would mostly likely have met at court and at family occasions, but lack of geographical closeness may explain why they never appear to have developed a friendship.

Elizabeth had stormier relationships with her female Howard kin in any case. Her position within the Howard family became increasingly marginal as time wore on, largely due to her marital breakdown during the mid-1530s but perhaps also because of her apparent prioritization of relationships of friendship and service over kinship before this. In May 1531, in the midst of the King's 'great matter',

---

[19] Catharine Davies, 'Agnes Howard [née Tilney], Duchess of Norfolk, Noblewoman', *ODNB* [accessed 22 July 2016].
[20] TNA SP60/1, fol. 130.   [21] Harris, *English Aristocratic Women*, 192–3.

Chapuys reported that Elizabeth had been sent home from court, 'because she spoke too freely, and declared herself more than they liked for the Queen'.[22] She had, in fact, allegedly told the Queen that the latter's opponents were trying to draw her, Elizabeth, over to their 'party', but that 'if all the world were to try it she would remain faithful to her'.[23] Elizabeth's husband, the Duke of Norfolk, was supporting the King's fancy for his niece Anne Boleyn at that point. Self-evidently it was less than ideal for his wife to take the opposite 'side', and though there is nothing to tell us how he reacted to her behaviour it seems fair to suppose he was not particularly pleased. This apparent rift between the family was noticed by outsiders, one of whom noted that Elizabeth had refused to attend Anne Boleyn's coronation in 1536.[24]

Her refusal to accept her husband's mistress also rendered her persona non grata, even an embarrassment, to her natal kin.[25] Her brother wrote despairingly of her 'acustomed wild langaig' and worried that her behaviour might rebound onto his own and his family's reputation, stating that 'the redresse of this standythe not in the adu[er]tysement of her kynne'.[26] The Stafford women joined their menfolk in remonstrating with her. In a letter of 1536 she mentions her 'Aunt Hastinges'— Anne Stafford/Herbert/Hastings, Countess of Huntingdon, her father's sister—but only to relate how this aunt had written to her demanding that she return to her husband, hardly an act of female solidarity.[27] Nor were Elizabeth's Howard female kin a source of support at any stage. As we have seen, her relationship with the Howard matriarch Agnes, dowager Duchess of Norfolk, was far from positive, and there is likewise no evidence for any friendship between Elizabeth and any of her sisters-in-law. Her refusal to knuckle under affected her relationship with her children, and she never seems to have been particularly close with her surviving daughter, Mary Howard/Fitzroy, Duchess of Richmond. During the 1530s she wrote to Cromwell lamenting how she had been 'bourne in an unhappy hower to be matched with...so ungracious a sonne and a doughter'.[28] To be fair to Mary, this was most likely because she knew on which side her bread was buttered. When this letter was written in 1536 she had recently been widowed and was reliant on her father's support to obtain her jointure from her father-in-law the King.

For Elizabeth, then, kinship relations—female or otherwise—were not always her priority, and her loyalties did not automatically align with either her natal or marital kin. Though it is no surprise that women could be at odds with their relatives, it was unusual for a woman to stand out from the combined pressure of natal and marital kin as Elizabeth did.[29] There is a danger here in assuming from these episodes that her relations with kin were uniformly negative throughout her lifetime; as is often the case for women, even high-status women, the surviving evidence for Elizabeth prioritizes those times when she transgressed what was considered the norm. In fact, Elizabeth's relationships with her kin do seem to have recovered later

---

[22] *LP* V, 283.   [23] *LP* V, 70.   [24] *LP* VI, 585.
[25] Barbara Harris, 'Marriage Sixteenth-Century Style: Elizabeth Stafford and the Third Duke of Norfolk', *Journal of Social History* 15 (1982), 371–82. See also Chapter 3.
[26] TNA SP1/76, fol. 39.   [27] BL Cotton MS Titus B I, fol. 384.
[28] Ibid.   [29] Harris, 'Marriage Sixteenth-Century Style'.

on in the 1540s. Her letters show that she was in contact with her sister Katherine Stafford/Neville, Countess of Westmorland, had forgiven her aunt the Countess of Huntingdon for taking her husband's part, and took in one of her Stafford nieces as a ward, knowing them well enough to specify which one she wanted.[30]

Her will shows that by the end of her life she and her brother were close once more, as she made him her executor and left considerable bequests to her sister-in-law Ursula Pole/Stafford.[31] She also revealed a particular care for her female natal kin, as was often the case in elite women's wills of this period.[32] Her will includes several bequests to 'lady dacres and her ij daughters', and though she did not use a kinship term here as she did for her sister-in-law ('my suster stafforde') Lady Dacre was in fact her niece, the daughter of her sister Mary Stafford/Neville, Lady Abergavenny.[33] By the end of her life, she had also reconciled with the Howards, though it is unclear when specifically this occurred as she spent her last four years, from 1554 to 1558, as a widow and may thus have waited until her husband had died before resuming these relationships. This renewal may have owed something to her position within the dynasty as the matriarch of its direct inheriting line, for by 1554 she was the grandmother of the Fourth Duke of Norfolk. Her will reflects this, leaving bequests to him and his wife, her son Thomas, Viscount Howard of Bindon, and Lady Margaret Howard, wife of Lord William.[34] Thus, although Elizabeth was at odds with both natal and marital relations at certain points during her life, this was not a persistent or default position. Relationships could and did alter, and therefore the level of unity within an aristocratic dynasty as perceived from within and from outside might also be subject to change.

Among the rest of the Howard women, the more usual pattern of strong and close relationships as observed by scholars of early modern women reasserted itself.[35] This was particularly so between the mothers and daughters of this dynasty. In her 1494 will, Margaret Chedworth/Wyfold/Norreys/Howard, Duchess of Norfolk, widow of John, First Duke of Norfolk, left bequests to three of her daughters, making no linguistic distinction between daughters from different marriages.[36] Her successor Agnes, second wife of Thomas, Second Duke of Norfolk, continued the tradition. She and her eldest daughter Anne, Countess of Oxford, were close enough to engage in friendly competition over whose patron was the most effective. In a letter to Cromwell in 1534, Anne said that she was sorry the illegal hunters in her park had disappeared, 'specly be cause I [told] my mother that ye wold a caussyd them be payne to a [confessed] the matter as my lord chanseler dosse ffor

---

[30] BL Cotton MS Titus B I, fol. 162.   [31] TNA PROB 11/42A/285.
[32] Harris, 'Sisterhood', 22.   [33] TNA PROB 11/42A/285.   [34] Ibid.
[35] Harris, *English Aristocratic Women*, 117, 138, 185–8; Lisa M. Klein, 'Lady Anne Clifford as Mother and Matriarch: Domestic and Dynastic Issues in her Life and Writings', *Journal of Family History* 26 (2001), 18–38. Work on female friendship has also touched upon this: see Laura Gowing, 'The Politics of Women's Friendship in Early Modern England', in Gowing et al., *Love, Friendship and Faith in Europe, 1300–1800* (Basingstoke, 2005), 131–49; Sara Mendelson, 'Neighbourhood as Female Community in the Life of Anne Dormer', in Broomhall and Tarbin (eds), *Women, Identities and Communities in Early Modern Europe*, 153–64; Merton, 'Women, Friendship, and Memory'; Herbert, *Female Alliances*.
[36] TNA PROB 11/10/195. The Duchess referred to her daughters by their marital surnames.

her'.[37] This letter was written following a visit that Anne had made to London, where she had probably stayed with her mother at Norfolk House. Agnes had bolstered this friendship with more practical support during Anne's marital difficulties in the 1520s. In 1525, the ill health of Anne's husband John, Fourteenth Earl of Oxford, caused the Howards to inveigle him into signing an indenture granting Anne more of his estate in jointure, for her to use for her upkeep after his death.[38] While it is usually assumed that Anne's brother Thomas, Third Duke of Norfolk, was the moving force behind this, in fact Agnes is the first signatory, suggesting that she was the chief representative on the Howard side here and had taken the initiative in securing the best settlement that she could for her daughter.[39] This is a good example of the ways in which close female relationships might affect a woman's dynastic behaviour.

This was exactly what early modern mothers were supposed to do. Older women gave younger relatives legal advice, or even handled such matters for them; Melissa Franklin-Harkrider has noted that Katherine Willoughby's mother Maria de Salinas used her court connections to secure her daughter's inheritance in the 1530s in a similar fashion.[40] Agnes came to the fore again in arranging the marriage of her youngest daughter Dorothy in 1530. Earlier that year the Third Duke of Norfolk had managed to secure the wardship of young Edward Stanley, Earl of Derby, and had married him to his own eldest daughter Catherine.[41] However, he was brought up short by Catherine's death on 15 March 1530 from plague.[42] By October 1530 he had solved the dilemma by asking for a dispensation for 'one of his sisters' to marry the Earl.[43] This was Dorothy, Agnes's youngest daughter, Norfolk's youngest half-sister, and the couple were married by January 1531.[44] Again, this story is invariably told with Norfolk as chief player, but Chapuys thought that if he (Norfolk) had not been reminded of Dorothy's existence, he would have broken his second daughter Mary's engagement and married her to Derby.[45] Who reminded Norfolk about Dorothy? The Derby match was evidently on Agnes's mind during that year, as in her deposition for the royal divorce case given in July 1529 she described the late Prince Arthur rather endearingly as 'a bowt the stature that the yong [earl] of derby ys nowe att'.[46] The financial arrangements for him and Dorothy

---

[37] TNA SP1/88, fol. 83.   [38] TNA C54/394, m. 17.

[39] Steven Gunn, *Charles Brandon, Duke of Suffolk, c.1484–1545* (Oxford, 1988), 84–5; TNA C54/394, m. 17.

[40] Melissa Franklin Harkrider, *Women, Reform and Community in Early Modern England: Katherine Willoughby, Duchess of Suffolk, and Lincolnshire's Godly Aristocracy, 1519–1580* (Woodbridge, 2008), 1–2.

[41] Though it is often assumed that Derby's wives Catherine and Dorothy Howard were one and the same, it is clear from the surviving evidence that they were two separate Howard women; in December 1529 Chapuys reported that Derby had been married to a daughter of the Duke of Norfolk at the King's command, and in February 1530 Norfolk was pardoned for the 'abduction' of Derby, probably a smokescreen to prevent accusations of marital interference on the part of the King: see E. Zevin, 'A New Wife for Edward, 3rd Earl of Derby', *Transactions of the Historic Society of Lancashire and Cheshire* 134 (1985 for 1984), 1–16; TNA WARD 9/149/28; *CSP Spain*, IV (i), 228 (p. 360); TNA C66/655, m. 23.

[42] *CSP Spain*, IV, 270 (p. 477).   [43] *CSP Spain*, IV (i), 460 (p. 762).

[44] *Statutes of the Realm*, III, 357–61.   [45] *CSP Spain*, IV (i), 460 (p. 762).

[46] TNA E30/1456.

were in fact made by Agnes, not by Norfolk, so it is likely that she was the mover behind this match.[47] On this occasion, a mother looking out for her daughter's interests had secured a considerable financial and social coup for the dynasty.

Agnes had a particularly close relationship with her second daughter Katherine, Countess of Bridgwater, especially during the late 1530s and 1540s. Although Katherine had her own house in Southwark during the late 1530s, the depositions dating from the fall of Queen Catherine Howard show that she spent a great deal of time with her mother in Lambeth, and her three children were being fostered there.[48] Katherine's only daughter was named Agnes, presumably for her mother, which implies that Agnes was also her godmother. Their relationship was documented clearly in Agnes's will of 1542, where she bequeathed 'the fourthe parte of all my gooddes both householde stuffe Juells and plate and of all other stuffe whatsoever it be | And also the fourthe parte of all my raiment' to 'my lady Brigewater my doughter'.[49] Katherine was the only one of her surviving daughters to receive a bequest. Later, in her own will of 1554, Katherine asked 'to be buryed in my Ladie my mother tombe in the chapell w[ith]in the p[a]ryshe churche in Lambeth', which was an unusual request for this time and argues for an especially close relationship.[50] Their closeness was also recognized by contemporaries, though not in a positive way. During interrogations regarding Catherine Howard in 1542, Wriothesley wrote grimly that 'as for bridgewater she sheweth herselff her motheres dowghter, that is oon that will by no menys confesse any thing that may towche her'.[51] Perhaps Agnes had given Katherine tips on how to handle questioning of this kind.

This closeness between mothers and daughters was present among the next generation as well. Katherine, in her turn, was close with her daughter, Agnes ap Rhys. During the late 1540s and early 1550s they both lived in Lambeth, and Katherine's will of 1554 made Agnes her sole executrix as well as bequeathing her many movable goods.[52] She also remembered her granddaughter, Agnes's illegitimate daughter Mary, bequeathing her several small, but very personal items: '...gilt spoyne of silu[er] | angell of noble of gold | a stone called Jacent & nother stone called Amediste set in golde | silu[er] salt gilt w[i]t[h] cou[er] & all other small thinges beinge in my coffers in Lambeth.' Further, she evidently left Mary a portion for her dowry that she was to receive when she reached the age of 16.[53] Given Mary's illegitimacy—her mother Agnes was the mistress, not the wife, of her father William, Lord Stourton—this was a wise financial precaution, as Mary would not receive any dowry from her father's

---

[47] *Statutes of the Realm*, III, 357–61.
[48] Nicolas, *PCP* VII, 280; TNA SP1/168 fols 76–7 and 159v.
[49] TNA PROB 11/30/596.
[50] I have found no directly comparable examples. Examples of other 'all female' commemorations, such as the monument to four women of the Neville and Manners families at St Leonard's Shoreditch, were set up after all four women had died in 1591, and not all were buried within it.
[51] TNA SP1/168, fol. 112.
[52] John Tanswell, *The History and Antiquities of Lambeth* (London, 1858), Appendix V, Subsidy of 1548 (229–30); Thomas Allen, *The History and Antiquities of the Parish of Lambeth, and the Archiepiscopal Palace, in the County of Surrey* (London, 1827), 439; TNA PROB 10/27.
[53] TNA PROB 10/27.

kin.[54] Katherine's testamentary remembrance of her illegitimate granddaughter suggests that what mattered to her was not patrilineal descent, but their relationship through the female line. This perpetuation of close mother–daughter relationships was not unusual. Women who had been close to their own mothers were then likely to create a similar relationship with their daughters, and thus female kinship ties remained strong throughout generations of women of the same matrilineal descent.[55] This was as advantageous for the entire family as it was for the women themselves; as we have seen, mothers who were close to their daughters worked hard to secure them the best marriages, inheritances, and court positions.

Though Agnes, Duchess of Norfolk, had four surviving daughters with her husband the Second Duke, it is worth remembering that she was his second wife, and that he had already had five children with his first. When she joined the family, therefore, Agnes gained five stepchildren. Although early modern people tended not to distinguish linguistically between step- and 'full' offspring when describing horizontal relationships, it could often make a difference to understandings of vertical, dynastic, relationships, because parentage had important implications for inheritance. Agnes's five stepchildren were first in line for her husband's inheritance. The earldom of Surrey and the bulk of his estates would descend to his eldest son, her stepson, and not to any children she might bear him. Although the trope of the wicked stepmother was alive and well during this period, there is no evidence that relations between Agnes and her stepchildren were poor in either direction. In fact they appear to have been cordial. In 1503 when Agnes and her husband, then Earl of Surrey, escorted Henry VII's daughter Princess Margaret to Scotland to marry King James IV, Agnes's youngest stepdaughter Muriel accompanied them.[56] At some point during the visit, Agnes and 'hir dochtir' Muriel shaved the King's beard apparently as a prank, because Princess Margaret had said she did not like it; the King paid them in cloth of gold.[57] That they did this together suggests friendship, and it also suggests that Agnes fulfilled a key role in introducing her younger female kin to court life. However, Agnes cannot have been much more than ten years older than Muriel, which potentially adds another layer to our understanding of their relationship. Though stepmother and stepdaughter, their nearness in age may have meant that the relationship between them was not one of maternal authority or daughterly submission. This may also be why Agnes does not appear to have been involved in typical maternal activities, such as arranging marriages, for either Muriel or her sister Elizabeth.

Howard sisters and sisters-in-law also appear to have maintained friendly relationships, and again this is representative of early modern noblewomen.[58] Anne

---

[54] Stourton was married to Elizabeth Dudley, sister of John, later Duke of Northumberland, *c.*1516.

[55] Lisa M. Klein, 'Lady Anne Clifford as Mother and Matriarch: Domestic and Dynastic Issues in her Life and Writings', *Journal of Family History* 26 (2001), 18–38 (21).

[56] J. Leland, *De Rebus Britannicis Collectanea*, ed. T. Hearne, 6 vols (London, 1774), IV, 265–300.

[57] Sir James Balfour Paul, II (ed.), *Accounts of the Lord High Treasurer of Scotland A.D. 1500–1504* (Edinburgh, 1900), 314.

[58] Sibling relationships is a field that has not traditionally received sustained scholarly attention, though this is slowly beginning to change. See Patricia Crawford, *Blood, Bodies and Families* (London, 2004), 211–25; Naomi J. Miller and Naomi Yavneh (eds), *Sibling Relations and Gender in the Early*

Howard/de Vere, Countess of Oxford, and Katherine Howard/ap Rhys/Daubeney, Countess of Bridgwater, supported one another in a time of serious crisis in 1542. At the time of Katherine's arrest in the wake of the discovery of Queen Catherine Howard's pre-marital adulteries, letters were sent to Anne from the Privy Council to order her to take temporary custody of Katherine's daughter Agnes.[59] That Katherine's two sons were sent not to kin, but to the Archbishop of Canterbury and the Bishop of Durham, suggests that it was not necessarily the policy of the Council to farm children out to their kin, and this might mean either that Katherine had nominated her sister, or that Anne had herself come forward.[60] Similarly there appear to have been relationships of some kind between Howard half-sisters and sisters-in-law. Katherine was chief mourner at the funeral of her half-sister Elizabeth Howard/Boleyn, Countess of Wiltshire, in 1538, and Anne's chief mourner in 1559 was her sister-in-law Margaret Gamage/Howard, Lady Howard of Effingham.[61]

A particularly useful way for women to foster relationships among their female kin was through service, and the Howard women took full advantage of their ability to offer patronage in this way. In fact, the Howards are a good example of the way in which female networks could shape a noble dynasty, for the two wives of Thomas, Earl of Surrey and later Second Duke of Norfolk, were first cousins. His first marriage in 1472 was to Elizabeth Tylney/Bourchier, daughter and sole heiress of Frederick Tylney of Boston, Lincolnshire, and wealthy widow of Sir Humphrey Bourchier, and his second was to her first cousin on her father's side, Agnes Tylney, daughter of Sir Hugh Tylney. Both these women took care to use their marriages to promote their Tylney relatives. Elizabeth Tylney was married to Thomas Howard for twenty-five years, but the list of her ladies-in-waiting to whom John Skelton wrote verses in 1494-5 shows that natal relations remained important to her throughout.[62] Her women were mostly kin and included three of Elizabeth's daughters from her first and second marriages respectively (Anne, Lady Dacre of the South; Elizabeth, later Elizabeth Boleyn, Countess of Wiltshire; and Muriel, later Viscountess Lisle); her half-niece Margery Wentworth;[63] Margaret Tylney;[64] and Jane Blennerhasset, described as Elizabeth's 'cousin-german'.[65] This underlines the natal obligations of noblewomen marrying above their status—by bringing female kin into the Howard household, she furthered their connections and future prospects.

Modern World: Sisters, Brothers and Others (London, 2006); Christopher H. Johnson and David Warren Sabean (eds), *Sibling Relations and the Transformations of European Kinship, 1300–1900* (New York, 2011).

  [59] Nicolas, *PCP* VII, 283.   [60] Ibid.
  [61] TNA SP3/12, fol. 42; *The Diary of Henry Machyn*, 189–90.
  [62] Greg Walker, *Skelton and the Politics of the 1520s* (Cambridge, 2002), and M. J. Tucker 'The Ladies in Skelton's "Garland of Laurel" ', *Renaissance Quarterly* 22:4 (1969), 333–45.
  [63] Probably the daughter of Henry Wentworth, Sheriff of Yorkshire, and Anne Saye, who was Elizabeth Tylney's half-sister. She later married Sir John Seymour, and was the mother of Henry VIII's third queen.
  [64] Probably the first wife of Elizabeth's first cousin Philip Tylney, Margaret Brewse (d. 1533).
  [65] Probably née Le Strange (of Hunstanton?) the wife of Sir Thomas Blennerhasset, steward to Thomas, Second Duke of Norfolk.

Indeed, it is likely that this is how Agnes Tylney, Elizabeth's successor as the Earl's wife, entered the Howard household, although she does not appear to have been there in 1494. Agnes's brother Philip was in service to the Earl at this time, and the 'Margaret Tylney' among Elizabeth's ladies-in-waiting was probably his wife. It would have made sense for Agnes to have joined the household as well, and she was probably *in situ* when Elizabeth died, suddenly and apparently unexpectedly, in May 1497. It certainly seems that Agnes and Thomas were already acquainted, because by August that same year, a mere three months later, Thomas had applied for a dispensation to marry her, and by November they were married.[66] The fact that Agnes married upwards is important in understanding her kinship obligations. The previous Tylney–Howard match between her husband and her cousin Elizabeth meant that the Tylneys' star was already attached to that of the Howards, and the Tylneys undoubtedly intended Agnes to help to continue the upward trend in their fortunes.

Female kinship relations among the Howards, then, were variable. Like Longfellow's little girl with a curl, when they were good they were very very good, but when they were bad they were horrid—and carried serious repercussions for the family's fortunes. That both these extremes could be simultaneously true of different relationships demonstrates the need to rethink the usual readings of the Howards as *either* united *or* disunited, and accept that at times they might be both, or neither.

PATERFAMILIAS: MALE–FEMALE RELATIONSHIPS

The household, many contemporary advice manuals proclaimed, was a 'little commonwealth', ruled hierarchically by a male patriarch in precisely the same way that the king ruled his kingdom.[67] The same analogy applied to the early modern family. The father, or equivalent male patriarch, was expected to keep decent control over his wife and children.[68] This extended to noble dynasties too, where the primary male figure was responsible for policing the behaviour of his relatives, and for protecting the interests of the dynasty as a whole. Broomhall and Gent have used the term paterfamilias to describe this male figure, and they and others have been at pains to point out that his role was not a one-way exercise of control.[69] Authority of this nature was a negotiation, and depended, to some degree, on the cooperation of those subject to it. While men were nominally in control of women, it is by now well established not only that this control was rarely absolute, but that it was not straightforwardly oppositional either.[70] The paterfamilias was permitted a degree

---

[66] *Calendar of Papal Letters*, vol. XVII Part 2, appendix 1, pp. c–ci, no. 34.

[67] Introduction to Broomhall and Van Gent (eds), *Governing Masculinities*, 10.

[68] Ibid. See also Elizabeth Foyster, *Manhood in Early Modern England: Honour, Sex and Marriage* (London, 1999) and Alexandra Shepard, *Meanings of Manhood in Early Modern England* (Oxford, 2003).

[69] Broomhall and Van Gent, 'In the Name of the Father'. See also the essays in Broomhall and Van Gent (eds), *Governing Masculinities*.

[70] Broomhall and Van Gent (eds), *Governing Masculinities*; Michael J. Braddick and John Walter (eds), *Negotiating Power in Early Modern Society: Order, Hierarchy and Subordination in Britain and Ireland* (Cambridge, 2001); Julie Hardwick, *The Practice of Patriarchy: Gender and the Politics of*

of government over his family members only because he was also supposed to support, aid, and protect them and their interests: no support, no authority. The relationship with the paterfamilias might therefore be among the most important male–female relationships for noblewomen like the Howards, and it is also one that has yet to be fully explored in the context of the English nobility.[71]

When we think of paterfamilias, we should not think of it as the apex of a defined hierarchical structure among dynasties that were as large, and containing as many smaller nuclear families, as the Howards. While an institution like the royal court had a structure of hierarchical authority that was routinely written down and reinforced by court ritual and ceremony, dynasties did not operate a formal system in this way. As Broomhall and Gent have argued, paterfamilias was as much an 'imagined', ideological concept as a lived reality, since much of what we think we know about it comes from prescriptive literature rather than lived experience, and the paterfamilias was not always either obvious or automatic.[72] Nor was he necessarily the father of everybody in the dynasty, and so this relationship was negotiated alongside other familial ties. In the realm of film, television, and fiction, and even some non-fiction, scenes of secret 'family councils', usually around a long table and headed by a family patriarch, are commonplace, but while it is tempting to imagine dynastic authority taking such a concrete form, this picture is indeed a fiction and not an archival reality. The paterfamilias did not have the power to move every individual family member around like a pawn on a chessboard for the greater good of the dynasty, and any 'family strategy' that there might have been was often politically reactive, rather than proactive.

Though it is true that it was not always obvious within a dynasty who held, or ought to hold, the role of paterfamilias, in the case of the Howards it was in fact relatively straightforward during this period. Between 1485 and 1558 the Howards saw two major family patriarchs, both called Thomas Howard, successively the Second and Third Dukes of Norfolk. Their individual reputations for family management are quite strikingly different; while the Second Duke is best known for building the dynasty back to full political strength following the accession of Henry VII in 1485, the Third Duke is better known for his conflict with various family members, which makes him a useful case study for female relatives' lived experience of patriarchal authority. If we follow the model of paterfamilias as a role of negotiated authority, it may seem surprising that the Third Duke fulfilled that

Household Authority in Early Modern France (University Park, Pa, 1998); Alexandra Shepard, 'Manhood, Patriarchy and Gender in Early Modern History', in Amy E. Leanard and Karen L. Nelson (eds), *Masculinities, Childhood, Violence: Attending to Early Modern Women and Men* (Newark, Del., 2011), 77–95; Judith M. Bennett: *History Matters: Patriarchy and the Challenge of Feminism* (Manchester, 2006).

[71] Broomhall and Van Gent's recent work on this deals with the Orange–Nassau dynasty, based primarily in the Low Countries but spread across much of the rest of continental Europe. Likewise, the essays in their collected *Governing Masculinities* volume (London, 2011) that deal with the nobility and gentry are, by and large, continental, with the exception of the essays by Jared van Duinen and Peter Sherlock. I have already noted that most work on dynasties and dynastic identity, which implicitly handles the concept of paterfamilias, is focused on (a) royalty and (b) continental Europe.

[72] Broomhall and Van Gent, 'In the Name of the Father', 1131.

status at all. Yet it is clear that he was unequivocally viewed as his father's successor here, and this was probably because there were no other likely candidates at the point of changeover in 1524. The other Howard males were all younger full or half-siblings of the Third Duke, since the family did not yet have as many disparate branches as it would go on to develop later in the sixteenth century. The most likely rival would have been his brother Edward, who was of a similar age, beloved by the King, and had he not suffered an untimely death in 1513, would no doubt have gone on to a glittering political career and founded a dynastic branch of his own. As it was, Norfolk's remaining full brother, Edmund, was something of a wastrel, and his half-brothers William and Thomas were still children. What we are watching here, then, is a dynasty at an early stage of development, before it had birthed endless side shoots and rival branches, but one that was already large and politically powerful for its age.

Where, then, was the authority of the paterfamilias felt by women like the Howards, and where could they count on his support? One of the few situations in which a paterfamilias might indeed assist in moving family members like pawns on a chessboard was in the creation of marriage alliances, which has been understood as the most obvious form of 'dynastic strategy' to exist at this time, and one which directly impacted female family members.[73] We should note that it was not necessarily the case that each family member intending marriage had to secure the 'permission' of the paterfamilias before they could go ahead. While this was the case for the royal family, and while it was true that daughters were generally supposed to follow their parents' wishes where marriage was concerned, there is no evidence that, for instance, the brother of the paterfamilias required his say so. Nevertheless, the brides that that brother would be able to attract were based largely on the status of the dynasty as a whole, as caretaken by the paterfamilias, and thus the latter remained notionally influential even if not personally involved in the arrangements. Looking at Howard marriage alliances reveals clear patterns related to the position of the dynasty at different points, and this does suggest that at least one individual was giving an eye to the strength of the dynasty as a whole.

Early on under the Second Duke of Norfolk, then the Earl of Surrey, marriage strategy initially revolved around trying to regain money and status following the loss of the dukedom after fighting on the wrong side at Bosworth in 1485, an action which cost the dynasty its first paterfamilias, John Howard, First Duke of Norfolk. Despite this, the marriages that they were able to negotiate across the rest of Henry VII's reign, shown in Table 1.1, show a swift recovery, and indicate that they had not lost all of their former glamour.

The Earl of Surrey's son and heir, another Thomas, later Third Duke of Norfolk, was able to marry the Queen's sister, Anne Plantagenet, in 1495, a coup indeed. Surrey's much younger half-sister, Catherine, daughter of John Howard and his second wife Margaret, was married to a cousin, John Bourchier, Lord Berners, by

---

[73] See, for instance, chapter 3 of Jonathan Spangler, *The Society of Princes: The Lorraine–Guise and the Conservation of Power and Wealth in Seventeenth-Century France* (Aldershot, 2009), the title of which refers to dynastic marriage as a 'corporate merger'.

Table 1.1 Howard marriages 1485–1509

Name	Bride/groom	Date arranged	Date occurred
Thomas, Lord Howard (d. 1554)	Anne Plantagenet, dau. Edward IV	?1484	Feb. 1595[a]
Catherine (d. *c.*1536)	John Bourchier, Lord Berners	Unknown	Nov. 1497[b]
Thomas, Earl of Surrey (d. 1524)	Agnes Tylney	Aug. 1497	Nov. 1497[c]
Edward (d. 1513)	Elizabeth Stapleton	Unknown	*c.*1500
Elizabeth (d. 1538)	Sir Thomas Boleyn	Unknown	*c.*1500[d]
Muriel (d. 1513)	John Grey, Second Viscount Lisle	Unknown	*c.*1504[e]
Edward (d. 1513)	Alice Lovell/Parker, Lady Morley	Unknown	Aft. Dec. 1505[f]
Muriel (d. 1513)	Sir Thomas Knyvett	Aft. 1504	Bef. July 1506[g]

[a] Sir George Buck, *History of Richard III* (1619), ed. Arthur Noel Kincaid (Gloucester, 1979), 212; *Statutes of the Realm*, III, 610.

[b] Crawford, *Yorkist Lord*, 67–8.

[c] *Calendar of Papal Letters*, vol. XVII Part 2, Appendix 1, pp. c–ci, no. 34 (dispensation for marriage); *Test. Ebor.*, III, 360 (licence to marry).

[d] *Statutes of the Realm*, III, 411.

[e] *Cal. IPM*, 2nd ser. Vol. III, nos 72, 134 (John Grey, Viscount Lisle, IPMs 1504).

[f] *Cal. IPM*, 2nd ser. Vol. III, 938; *LP* I, 257 (53).

[g] *Cal. Patent Rolls* 1494–1509, 465 (pardon for marrying without licence); *LP* I, 257 (40).

1497, in a match calculated not only to cement relations between these branches of the family—Berners was the son of Surrey's wife Elizabeth Tylney/Bourchier/Howard by her first marriage—but to bolster the family pedigree.[74] Surrey also had his eye on the newer nobility like his own family, and married his younger daughter Muriel to Sir John Grey, Second Viscount Lisle, whose title had been granted to his father in 1483, the same year in which the Howards had gained the dukedom of Norfolk. In this way matches were made both with old, established aristocratic dynasties and newer, up-and-coming families in order to boost the Howards' dubious lineage. Surrey also took care to bring rich heiresses and widows into the dynasty, like Alice Lovell/Parker, Lady Morley, heiress of William Lovell, Lord Morley, and widow of Sir William Parker, who married his second son Edward Howard *c.*1505/6. Interestingly, Surrey did not appear to obey his own common-sense dictates regarding his own second marriage to Agnes Tylney in 1497. First cousin to his first wife, Agnes may well have been serving in the household and caught his eye in this way. Though respectable gentry stock, she was not of an ancient aristocratic pedigree; not an heiress; not a rich widow; and indeed, it is commonly said that she brought no dowry, though there is no evidence to prove this. The paterfamilias, it seems, was permitted to make a love match even if none of his family appeared to be able to do so.[75]

The general strategy continued in a similar vein during the early years of Henry VIII's reign, with marriages made for Surrey's children from his second wife, Agnes, to old nobility like the de Veres, earls of Oxford; useful alliances with existing

[74] *Rot. Parl.*, 6, 479; Crawford, *Yorkist Lord*, 67–8.

[75] None of the other marriages shown in Table 1.1 are known to have been love matches, though this does not necessarily mean that they were not, or did not become strong relationships.

Table 1.2 Howard marriages 1509–24

Name	Bride/groom	Date arranged	Date occurred
Thomas, Lord Howard (d. 1554)	Elizabeth Stafford	Nov./Dec. 1511	*c.* Feb. 1512[a]
Anne (d. 1559)	John de Vere, later Fourteenth Earl of Oxford	Nov. 1511	Bef. Sept. 1512[b]
Edmund (d. *c.*1539)	Joyce Culpeper/Leigh	Unknown	Bef. *c.*1520[c]
Katherine (d. 1554)	Rhys ap Gruffudd	Mar. 1514	Bef. Aug. 1522[d]
Elizabeth (d. 1534)	Henry Radcliffe, later Second Earl of Sussex	Aft. 1520	Bef. May 1524[e]

[a] BL Cotton MS Titus B I, fol. 390r–v (Eliz to Cromwell, Oct. 1537); *Statutes of the Realm*, III, 317.

[b] TNA PROB 11/17, fols 88v–89r; *LP* I, 2964 (80).

[c] Three sons born to the couple were mentioned in their grandfather's will of 1523, which means they must have been married by 1520 at the latest. TNA PROB 11/21/241.

[d] NLW MS A 59.

[e] The biographical description of Elizabeth's father, the Second Duke of Norfolk, on his tomb, describes her as married by the time of his death in 1524. John Weever, *Antient Funerall Monuments* (1630), printed by Thomas Harper (London, 1631), 834–40.

East Anglian allies like the Radcliffes, earls of Sussex; and a strategic match with an old Welsh family, the Rhyses of south-west Wales, probably in an effort to counteract the influence of Charles Brandon, Duke of Suffolk, elsewhere in the country (see Table 1.2).

By Thomas, now Duke of Norfolk's, death in 1524, the family had regained what they had lost, and then some. Marriage strategy under his son and successor, the Third Duke, became both more exalted and more erratic, proof of the Howards' increased status and desirability as marriage partners.

This Duke had two daughters and two sons for whom to arrange marriages, as well as several half-siblings. He arranged matches opportunistically and seems to have been more likely to break betrothals in favour of a better option (see Table 1.3). The very first match arranged after his succession in 1524 was for his eldest daughter, Catherine, who was betrothed to Maurice Berkeley, second son of Thomas, Fifth Lord Berkeley, in 1525. This betrothal must have been broken, since Catherine was instead wed briefly in 1530 to Edward Stanley, the minor Earl of Derby, before her unexpected death later that same year. Norfolk's second daughter Mary was betrothed to John de Vere, Lord Bulbeck, heir to the Earl of Oxford, until 1529, when this betrothal was likewise abruptly broken in order to wed her to the King's illegitimate son Henry Fitzroy, Duke of Richmond.[76] This match allegedly became available thanks to the influence of his niece Queen Anne Boleyn, whose maid of honour Mary was, and this demonstrates the way in which marriage alliances were indeed a family affair.[77] Indeed, the paterfamilias rarely contracted a

[76] *CSP Spain*, IV (i), 228 (p. 360); TNA SP1/111, fol. 204.

[77] According to Mary's mother Elizabeth, Duchess of Norfolk: BL Cotton MS Titus B I, fol. 390r–v. See Diane O'Hara, *Courtship and Constraint: Rethinking the Making of Marriage in Tudor England* (Manchester, 2000).

Table 1.3 Howard marriages 1524–47

Name	Bride/groom	Date arranged	Date occurred
Catherine (d. 1530)	Maurice Berkeley	1525	N/A—betrothal broken[a]
Thomas, later Viscount Howard of Bindon (d. 1583)	Elizabeth Marney (joint heiress)	Unknown	Aft. May 1526[b]
Mary (d. *c*.1555)	John de Vere, Lord Bulbeck	Bef. 1529	N/A—betrothal broken[c]
Catherine (d. 1530)	Edward Stanley, Third Earl of Derby	*c.* Dec. 1529	Bef. Jan. 1530[d]
Dorothy (d. *c*.1534)	Edward Stanley, Third Earl of Derby	*c.* Oct. 1530	Bef. Jan. 1531[e]
William, later Lord Howard of Effingham (d. 1572)	Catherine Broughton (joint heiress)	Aft. Nov. 1529	Bef. June 1531[f]
Katherine Howard/ap Rhys (d. 1554)	Henry Daubeney, later First Earl of Bridgwater	Aft. Dec. 1531	Bef. 1535[g]
Henry, Earl of Surrey (ex. 1547)	Frances de Vere	Feb. 1532	1533[h]
Mary (d. *c*.1555)	Henry Fitzroy, Duke of Richmond	*c.*1529	1533[i]
Thomas (d. 1537)	Margaret Douglas	Mar./Apr. 1535 (clandestine)	Bef. June 1536[j]
William, later Lord Howard of Effingham (d. 1572)	Margaret Gamage	Aft. 1535	Bef. June 1536[k]

[a] John Smyth, *Lives of the Berkeleys*, 3 vols, ed. John Maclean (Gloucester, 1883), II, 225.

[b] *LP* IV, 2203.

[c] *CSP Spain*, IV (i), 228 (360); TNA SP1/111, fol. 204.

[d] *CSP Spain*, IV (i), 360, 477.

[e] *CSP Spain*, IV, I, 762; *Statutes of the Realm* III, 357–61.

[f] *LP* IV, 6072 (21); *LP* V, g.318 (21).

[g] TNA SP1/97, fols 118–120v.

[h] TNA E211/83.

[i] *LP* VI, 351; BL Harl. MS 6148, fols 38–9.

[j] TNA E36/120/65.

[k] TNA E36/120/65.

marriage alliance all by himself; as we have already seen, other family members, including women, were usually involved alongside him, suggesting candidates and even guaranteeing financial arrangements.

First marriages were one thing, but second marriages for women of the Howard dynasty were quite another. Few Howard widows remarried at all, a point to which we will return, but this sometimes ran counter to the wishes of the paterfamilias. Mary Howard/Fitzroy, Duchess of Richmond, daughter of the Third Duke of Norfolk, was unexpectedly widowed at the age of 17 in 1536, and, due no doubt to her tender years, returned to live under her father's roof. Thus began a struggle to obtain her sizeable jointure from her father-in-law the King, who insisted that because the marriage had not been consummated (both parties were considered too young) he did not owe her anything.[78] Letters written by Norfolk make it clear that he intended to arrange another marriage for Mary. She was still very young, and she had not yet fulfilled her dynastic duty. However, there was difficulty in finding one suitable, because 'at this tyme ther is neyther lord nor lords son nor other gode inherito[r] in this realme that I can remeber of convenient age to marry her so that in maner I rekon her halff undone'.[79] Moreover, he was anxious to arrange something soon, before his own imminent departure to the north to deal with the Pilgrimage of Grace, because 'I am somwhat jalous of her that being out of my company she myght bestowe her selff otherwise then I wold she shuld.'[80] This was a tacit admission that he could not control his own daughter, which is relatively unusual for this time, as illicit matches were few and far between. This underscores the aspect of negotiation underlying the governance of the paterfamilias.

Apparently Norfolk managed to rescue this situation, since Mary did not after all marry whoever Norfolk thought she had in her mind. Neither, however, did she ever marry anybody else. After some time attempting to secure her jointure from the King, a convenient work-around was proposed and agreed between Norfolk, the King, and Thomas Cromwell. According to a report written by Ralph Sadler, Norfolk suggested two candidates for Mary's remarriage, but the one 'to whom his herte is most inclyned' was Sir Thomas Seymour, brother of the late Queen and uncle to Prince Edward.[81] Mary should remarry, to Seymour, which would legally place her under his name, meaning that her former marital identity could be quietly forgotten and, presuming Seymour could be persuaded to accept this, the jointure issue need never be resolved. The match seems to have been arranged—Sadler recommended that they move quickly so that it could 'take effecte' while Mary was still at court—but there the matter falls silent. Since Sadler is clear that all parties other than Mary had agreed, it seems that she herself must have refused. A letter from Norfolk less than a week after her scheduled departure from court shows that he was on his way back to his estates, and it has been plausibly suggested by David Head that this was surely connected with his daughter's recalcitrance.[82] Her behaviour here is remarkable. Though widows were permitted to refuse matches agreed for them by the King it was rarely done, and those that did were usually older widows with greater experience and thus authority.[83] For Mary to refuse to obey not only the King but also her father, the paterfamilias, shows clearly that his authority was not absolute in either role.

For Mary, this was probably linked to what she perceived as his neglect of the other key element of his role: support for family members at times of crisis. When the King delayed over paying her jointure, Mary, quite reasonably, expected her

---

[78] TNA SP1/128, fol. 69.   [79] TNA SP1/111, fol. 204r–v.
[80] Ibid.   [81] TNA SP1/134, fol. 160.
[82] BL Cotton MS Vespasian F XIII, fol. 86v; Head, *The Ebbs and Flows of Fortune*, 154–5.
[83] Harris, *English Aristocratic Women*, 160–2. Harris advances the example of Anne Savage/ Berkeley, Lady Berkeley, who was widowed at the age of c.38 in 1534; Cecily Lady Dudley, Dorothy Lady Mountjoy, and Thomas Wriothesley all petitioned for her marriage to their relation Edward Sutton, which she refused without repercussions.

father to back her up, since it was in the dynasty's interest that her status as a royal widow should be recognized. Yet six months later matters were no further forward, and Mary blamed her father for this. In a letter to him written in January 1537, she wrote that all she had received thus far from her father's suit was 'no effect but wordes'.[84] She asked, as she had 'oftymes' asked before, that her father would 'grante me lewe to com up and sue myne owne caus... [I] do not dowt bewt wrapon the rygthe ther of hes hyeghns shuld be mowed to hawe compasyon on me'.[85] In short, she did not believe her father had done his best for her, and she thought she would be more successful on her own, though she was careful to couch her letter in traditionally dutiful terms. To be fair to Norfolk, he was worried about angering the King, and many of his letters to Thomas Cromwell did include some variation of 'please help my daughter's cause'.[86] But it should also be noted that of these many letters, only one was written before Mary's accusation in January 1537.[87] Norfolk, indeed, was indignant, and wrote to Cromwell that 'in all my lif I never comoned w[ith] her in any seriouse cause or nowe, and wold not haue thought she had be suche as I fynde her, wich as I think is but to wise for a woman'.[88]

For another year he held his ground. But in January 1538 Mary took up the cudgels on her own behalf once more, writing directly to Cromwell to ask him to deliver her supplication to the King, because Norfolk continued to refuse her permission to go to London.[89] She had consulted her own legal counsel and was convinced of her right. Later that month, Thomas Cranmer, Archbishop of Canterbury, delivered his own verdict, stating that the marriage was valid and that the jointure ought therefore to be paid.[90] Presumably hearing this, Mary pulled out all the stops. An exhausted Norfolk wrote to Cromwell in 1538 that 'My doughter of Richemond doth contynewally wth wepyng and wayling crye owte on me to have me yeve her licence to ride to London... I am so afrayed that the kings highnes shold not be content with me to bring her uppe, that unto this tyme for all her pitefull lamenting I wolde not grawnt to her desire'.[91] This clearly demonstrates that Mary had upset the entire household, because Norfolk was now so near the end of his tether that he had actually written to Cromwell to ask him to 'feale his gracs mynde, whither I shold displease his maiestie in bringing her uppe or not'.[92] Eventually her manipulation was successful and he did take her to court, only to try to arrange the marriage that she then successfully refused. Finally, in March 1539, Mary's title was recognized and she received the first of a series of grants of jointure.[93] She remained under her father's roof until the end of Henry VIII's reign, and she never did remarry, despite him once again attempting the alliance

---

[84] Cotton MS Vespasian F XIII, fol. 144.   [85] Ibid.

[86] As Beverley Murphy, Jessie Childs, and others have pointed out. See Murphy, *Bastard Prince: Henry VIII's Lost Son* (Gloucester, 2001), 220, and Childs, *Henry VIII's Last Victim: The Life and Times of Henry Howard, Earl of Surrey* (London, 2006), 129.

[87] This is the explanatory letter in which he first asked for Cromwell's aid in November 1536: TNA SP1/111, fol. 204r–v.

[88] TNA SP1/114, fol. 48.   [89] TNA SP1/128, fol. 11.

[90] TNA SP1/128, fol. 69.   [91] TNA SP1/131, fol. 24.

[92] Childs, *Henry VIII's Last Victim*, 129; TNA SP1/131, fol. 24.

[93] *LP* XIV (i), 595.

with Thomas Seymour in 1546.[94] Norfolk's position of paterfamilias was ignored and even jeopardized by his own daughter, whom he could not control, and who exhibited a strong tendency to act independently, counter to what he perceived as the dynasty's interests and counter to his own authority. While this appears to indicate a lack of unity within the dynasty, even this apparently stormy relationship looks different in a different context. When Norfolk was arrested for high treason in 1546, Mary spoke up for him, at the expense of her brother, the Earl of Surrey, and visited him in the Tower during his lengthy imprisonment, petitioning several times for his release.[95] Conflict was not a permanent state of affairs between the two of them.

Mary was not the only Howard widow to remain single. Few Howard widows remarried at all, whether they were born into or had married into the family. Jonathan Spangler has noted the same phenomenon among widows in the Lorraine–Guise family of seventeenth-century France, and explains it as a status issue; having married into a princely family, they could go no higher unless they remarried into the royal family itself, which was not an opportunity that arose very often. If they were to remarry to a man of lower status, they would lose their own princely status. Consequently, they remained widowed matriarchs and formed what he has termed a 'matriclan' within the dynasty whose influence could be strongly felt, particularly in their guardianship of property and connections.[96] Though in England a widow retained the highest marital title that she had gained, even if she had since remarried to a man of lower status, the same could be applied to the Howards. Certainly by the 1520s, their status was the highest that it had ever been, as one of only two ducal families in the kingdom, and, like the Lorraine–Guise, it is clear that this caused Howard wives and daughters to retain a strong sense of Howard identity throughout their lives.

In some cases Norfolk himself seems to have supported both their strong natal identification, and their singledom. His half-sister Anne, who had married John de Vere, Fourteenth Earl of Oxford, in 1512, for instance, enjoyed her brother's full support when she ran into difficulties with her marriage in the early 1520s.[97] This was an interesting time for the Howards, because it was clear that the existing paterfamilias, the Second Duke of Norfolk, was reaching the end of his life, and that his son and heir, another Thomas, would succeed him. The transfer of power between successive patriarchs was often a strenuous time for dynasties, but the Howards seem to have had it well planned, with the Second Duke gradually resigning his major offices in favour of his son, and retreating to Framlingham.[98] Interestingly, he also seems to have drawn back from dealing with family crises at the same time. When Anne, who was his eldest daughter from his second marriage, began to suffer problems in her marriage with her young and wayward husband early in 1523, it was her brother, not her father, who mediated with Thomas Wolsey on

---

[94] BL Cotton MS Titus B I, fols 99–101v.
[95] In 1546 Mary told the King's commissioners that her father was a 'trew and faithfull subiect'; TNA SP1/227, fol. 82. See also Epilogue.
[96] Chapter 3 of Spangler, *The Society of Princes*.   [97] See Chapter 3.
[98] *LP* I, Addenda, 365. See also Head, *The Ebbs and Flows of Fortune*, 68–9.

her behalf, going to some lengths to ensure that the matter was brought before the King, and even giving Anne shelter in his own house.[99] Her father's name only appeared on the final legal ordinance drawn up to regulate the Earl's behaviour in February 1524, sternly exhorting him to 'lovinglie, familiarlie, and kindlie intreate and demeane himself towards the said Countesse his wife', and stating that the couple would now return to live under her father's roof.[100]

The Second Duke died, however, before this could be effected, and from this point it was Anne's brother, now the Third Duke, who continued to support her. Oxford's health was poor, and the family appear to have seen his death on the horizon. On 5 June 1525, the year before his death, he signed an indenture assigning an additional seven manors of his estate to Anne for the term of her life, augmenting her jointure from fourteen manors to twenty-one.[101] Though the indenture states that Anne's husband had offered to do this of his own free will, due to the 'great zeal' he had found in her, as well as the 'manyfold kindness eyed and help' from her family, specifically her mother Agnes, dowager Duchess of Norfolk, and her half-brother Thomas, Third Duke of Norfolk, it is entirely plausible to suppose that he had been encouraged, even strong-armed, into this by the Howards.[102] Here, clearly, is an instance of the paterfamilias offering up the kind of dynastic support that his role implied. Norfolk continued to do this during Anne's widowhood, writing to the King and to Cromwell on her behalf when her husband's successor broke into her property.[103] She never seems to have been placed under any pressure to remarry—perhaps because the de Vere estates were useful to the Howards, and they did not want them in the hands of a new husband—and she remained single for the rest of her life.

Things seem to have been somewhat different with another of Norfolk's half-sisters, and this sheds light on the level of negotiation present in these relationships. Katherine Howard/ap Rhys/Daubeney, Countess of Bridgwater, the second daughter of the Second Duke of Norfolk and Agnes Tylney, was—like her half-niece Mary Howard/Fitzroy, Duchess of Richmond—an independent spirit, and even something of a rebel.[104] Her behaviour has direct relevance to the role of paterfamilias. After her first husband's execution for alleged high treason in 1531, Katherine had remarried, to Henry Daubeney, later First Earl of Bridgwater. There is no evidence as to how, why, or when this match came about; it is possible that it was the product of west country links between Daubeney and her mother-in-law Katherine St John/ap Gruffudd/Edgecombe, whose third husband Sir Piers Edgecombe was based in Cornwall, but it may also have been negotiated by her Howard relatives, including her half-brother Norfolk.[105] Within a short space of time, however, Katherine wanted out. In October 1535 letters between herself and Thomas Cromwell, and from her husband too, make it clear that there was a divorce

---

[99] TNA SP1/27, fols 154v–155; SP1/30, fol. 134. UCB, MS UCB 49.

[100] Henry Ellis, 'Copy of an Order made by Cardinal Wolsey, as Lord Chancellor, respecting the Management of the Affairs of the young Earl of Oxford', *Archaeologia* 19 (1821), 62–5.

[101] TNA C54/394, m. 17.   [102] Ibid. See also Gunn, *Charles Brandon*, 84.

[103] TNA SP1/30, fol. 134; TNA SP1/39, fol. 78.   [104] See Chapter 5.

[105] See discussion in Chapter 3.

settlement under negotiation, and that it was an acrimonious separation, with Katherine afraid of her husband's spies, and he furious at having to pay her anything at all, since he had had 'no man[ner] of commodyty bey her', i.e. no land, money, or children.[106] A woman in such straits would usually lean on her natal relatives for support. Katherine's letter, however, explained that though she had many kin, she had 'few that dothe for me', and that the only person who had given her any assistance at all was the Queen, then Anne Boleyn, Katherine's half-niece.[107] Apparently her brother Norfolk, paterfamilias, did not give her the support that she felt he owed her in such a situation. Divorce settlement procured nonetheless, Katherine allegedly went on to involve herself in activities which could have brought the dynasty into serious disrepute. A spy report from the Pilgrimage of Grace in late 1536 stated that 'Lady Rhys' had sent troops and plate for coinage to the rebels, and, as Chapter 5 explains, this—if true—can only have been Katherine.[108] Of course she cannot have done this purely to annoy her brother, but it does suggest that if a paterfamilias was perceived to have failed in his duty to his female relatives, they might conceivably decide to disregard his authority in their turn.

This was all the more likely if the female relative in question was an older widow. Agnes Tylney/Howard, Duchess of Norfolk, wife of the Second Duke, was another who remained single after her husband's death in 1524, and lived another twenty-one years as a widow. The next Duke of Norfolk, the new paterfamilias, was her stepson, but the same age as herself, and she now headed the junior branch of the family. I have written elsewhere about the negotiations of power and influence between Agnes, as a dynastic matriarch, and the Third Duke of Norfolk in the context of the movement of family tombs after the Dissolution of the Monasteries.[109] The dissolution of Thetford Priory, the Howards' mausoleum, created something of a dilemma; though there was another Howard burial space in the parish church of St Mary, Lambeth, it was strongly associated with Agnes, its founder, and her particular dynastic branch, and thus the Third Duke began a new commemorative scheme in St Michael's, Framlingham, the major family seat. Naturally there was overlap between the two, particularly concerning the body of the Second Duke of Norfolk, Agnes's husband and Norfolk's father. While there is nothing to suggest that this caused open conflict, it undoubtedly involved a level of negotiation. The fact that Agnes was able to move her husband's body to a new resting place in her own chapel, rather than Norfolk automatically including his father in St Michael's Framlingham, demonstrates that widows were a force that the paterfamilias needed to take into account in his governance of the dynasty, since on occasion their rights

---

[106] TNA SP1/97, fols 118–120v.   [107] TNA SP1/97, fol. 120.

[108] TNA SP1/112, fol. 34.

[109] Nicola Clark, 'The Gendering of Dynastic Memory: Burial Choices of the Howards, 1485–1559', *Journal of Ecclesiastical History* 68:4 (2017), 747–65. See also Rowena E. Archer, 'Rich Old Ladies: The Problem of Late Medieval Dowagers', in Tony Pollard (ed.), *Property and Politics: Essays in Later Medieval English History* (Gloucester, 1984), 15–35; Robert J. Kalas, 'The Noble Widow's Place in the Patriarchal Household: The Life and Career of Jeanne de Gontault', *Sixteenth Century Journal* 24 (1993), 519–39, and the essays in Sandra Cavallo and Lyndan Warner (eds), *Widowhood in Medieval and Early Modern Europe* (London, 1999).

and authority might trump his own. There were plenty of occasions when Agnes and her stepson appear to have worked together harmoniously. We have already seen that the arrangements for the marriage of Agnes's youngest daughter, Norfolk's half-sister Dorothy, for instance, were made between them. Norfolk made no bones about his stepmother caretaking Howard estates as her jointure for term of her life, even though she was not the mother of the inheriting line, and this is significant: Barbara Harris has analysed widows' legal petitions for the period 1450–1550 and discovered that of 59 disputes between widows and their relatives, women were the mothers of the heir in only 9, showing that often a widow whose connection to the inheriting line was weak might struggle to maintain her position within the dynasty.[110]

Yet there were also times when they very definitely were not working together, and when Agnes's authority and behaviour were in direct contradiction to Norfolk's. The spat between Agnes and her junior counterpart, Norfolk's wife Elizabeth Stafford/Howard, over precedence in the late 1520s, related at the beginning of this chapter, can be viewed in this way; while certainly it was primarily an argument between the two women, Chapuys was clear that Norfolk had weighed in on his wife's side and was therefore upholding her status over Agnes's in a way that cannot have helped their relationship.[111] This conflict became particularly obvious during the fallout of the discovery of Queen Catherine Howard's affairs in 1541. The evidence given at the time made it clear that Agnes, along with other female kin in and around her household, had known about Catherine's pre-marital affairs, but had not declared them either to the King and his Council, or, significantly, to the Duke of Norfolk as paterfamilias, before Catherine's marriage to the King. It was female kin—Katherine, Countess of Bridgwater, and Lady Margaret Howard—who sued to the new Queen to accept her old lover Francis Dereham as her secretary.[112] Catherine's affairs whilst at court were also arranged and kept secret by female kin; her cousin Katherine Tylney who had been with her in Agnes's household, and Jane Parker/Boleyn, Lady Rochford.[113] That Norfolk was apparently oblivious to this demonstrates the way in which female kinship networks could operate outside of patriarchal control and bring the dynasty into danger and disrepute.

When this was discovered, Norfolk promptly distanced himself from his relations, joining the investigation temporarily before leaving London for Kenninghall and his family to their fate.[114] Duchess Agnes seems to have understood that this would be the case, as she burnt incriminating papers before Norfolk visited to examine them on behalf of the Council.[115] Later, Norfolk would state that he had informed the authorities of her treasonous speech at this time.[116] Was this the behaviour of a good paterfamilias? It is easy to react emotively and condemn Norfolk for his actions, fleeing when his family needed him, but in fact he was doing what he was supposed to do: protecting the core of the dynasty. Those involved

---

[110] Harris, *English Aristocratic Women*, 135.   [111] *CSP Spain*, IV, 232.
[112] TNA SP1/168, fol. 87.   [113] TNA SP1/167, fol. 136.
[114] *LP* XVI, 1426.   [115] TNA SP1/168, fol. 96.
[116] BL Cotton MS Titus B I, fols 99–101v: 'Who shewed his maieste of the words of my mother in law for wich she was attaynted of mysprision but only I.'

in the Queen's fall were half-siblings, in-laws, step-relations; close family ordinarily, but not so necessary to the continuance of the lineage as his more immediate relations. Neither his wife nor his children—future inheritors—were involved in this episode. By removing his support from the guilty parties he was publicly demonstrating his loyalty to the crown, which was a far safer strategy for the protection of the family patrimony. It is likely that he did not even perceive this as a choice between two competing courses of action: if he were found complicit, the dynasty itself was doomed.

The role of paterfamilias, then, was not always straightforward, and the Third Duke of Norfolk arguably had a difficult time negotiating authority with the female members of his dynasty. While he could act the part of dynastic protector after family members had transgressed and threatened the dynasty's reputation, his authority with them was not sufficient to stop them doing these things in the first place. It is too simplistic to say that this was his 'fault', or even that it was anybody's fault, though it may not have been helped by the personalities of those involved. His position depended on his support for these women at appropriate times; but who was to define when it was appropriate for him to support them, and when it was best to turn his back? This is why the idea of the Howards as disunited has become accepted, and it is true that there were a number of episodes where one could read gender relations here as oppositional. Sometimes Howard women simply behaved in a way that was not beneficial to the dynasty as a whole, and this could be because they had different goals that did not chime with the supposedly collective goals of the family; because they did not respect the authority of the paterfamilias; because they felt he had forfeited this for some reason; or a combination of these factors.

EXTENDED FAMILY AND FICTIVE KINSHIP

The Howard women's kinship networks were not solely comprised of immediate family, and scholars have long recognized the importance of extended kin to the early modern aristocracy.[117] As Cressy explains, distant kin generally remained in the background unless called upon to exercise obligations of kinship in the form of patronage or other assistance, but nevertheless these connections remained important for those occasions.[118] For this reason, extended kinship relations might appear even more elastic and circumstantial than other, closer, connections, since they would move in and out of the dynastic foreground according to need, so that the dynasty could appear to swell and contract continuously. The Howards were related to a large number of East Anglian gentry or lower nobility families. Among their closest 'extended' kin were the Boleyns, Timperleys, Wyndhams, Knyvetts, and Bryans, with looser connections to the Sheltons and Calthorpes. They also spent much of the early period of their own elevation to the peerage making marital

---

[117] Cressy, 'Kinship and Kin Interaction'; Broomhall and Van Gent, *Dynastic Colonialism*.
[118] Cressy, 'Kinship and Kin Interaction'.

connections to local nobility, such as the Barons Dacre of the South, Morley, and Marney. Though all nobility were well connected in this way, the Howards were particularly so from the 1520s onwards. Often, the way we learn about kinship relations within these large families is through negative events, not least, litigation between family members.[119] Interestingly, that is not the case for the Howard women or even the Howard men. While all participated in litigation, this was rarely, if ever, against kin. While we have already seen instances of less than positive relationships or difficult episodes for the Howard women with family members, much of the evidence surviving for the relationship between them and their more distant kin is of positive cooperation and patronage.

Surviving household accounts for the Howards show regular visits by kin outside of immediate family. In 1523–4, Margaret, Lady Wyndham, paid lengthy visits to her first cousin-by-marriage Thomas, Earl of Surrey.[120] Accounts from 1526 show Knyvetts, Sheltons, Mr Timperley, Lady Marney (Bridget, widowed mother of Elizabeth Marney, then a ward of Thomas, Third Duke of Norfolk), Sir Philip and Lady Tylney making regular visits.[121] Accounts for the deer park at Framlingham between 1509 and 1515 list numerous kin as recipients of gifts of venison, including Sir Thomas and Lady Boleyn, Lord Dacre of the South, members of the Calthorpe family, Tylneys, Wyndhams, Bryans, and Timperleys.[122] Accounts of Sir Thomas Boleyn, Lord Rochford, as treasurer of the King's household in 1526, show that he reciprocated these attentions, sending a hogshead of wine to Agnes Tylney/Howard, dowager Duchess of Norfolk.[123] He also later offered assistance to Agnes's daughter Katherine during a time of financial need, showing that patronage was not one-way, but flowed in both directions between the Howards and their kin.

The difficulty in differentiating between close kin and extended kin is exemplified by the Tylney family and their relationship to the Howard women. For Agnes Tylney/Howard, dowager Duchess of Norfolk, the Tylneys, as her natal family, were close kin and it is clear that she remained very involved with them throughout her life and took her obligations to them seriously. She named her 'nephew Tylney' as an executor of her will in 1542.[124] Her niece Katherine Tylney was among the maids within her household in the 1530s and went with her cousin Catherine Howard to court in 1540.[125] A niece-by-marriage, Malyn Chambers/Tylney, also came to Agnes for assistance at this time following the death of her husband Philip, Agnes's nephew.[126] Though Agnes was chiefly concerned to wring information from Malyn regarding the Catherine Howard case, she did promise to 'do for her as she myght', underlining the continued loyalty she felt towards natal kin forty

---

[119] See, for instance, Antonio Terrasa-Lozano, 'Legal Enemies, Beloved Brothers: High Nobility, Family Conflict and the Aristocrats: Two Bodies in Early-Modern Castile', *European Review of History* 17:5 (2010), 719–34, and Lloyd Bonfield, 'Seeking Connections between Kinship and the Law in Early Modern England', *Continuity and Change* 25:1 (2010), 49–82.

[120] UCB, MS UCB 49.   [121] CUL, Pembroke College MS 300.

[122] BL Add. MS 27421, and Add. Ch. 17745. It is not always possible to identify the specific individual from each family.

[123] TNA SP1/59, fol. 100.   [124] TNA PROB 11/30/596.

[125] TNA SP1/167, fol. 119v.   [126] TNA SP1/168, fol. 145.

years after her marriage.[127] It also highlights her value to them; she continued to fulfil her obligations even in the midst of accusations of treason.

These networks of kin were not only important for Agnes, but for the rest of the Howard women as well. Agnes's eldest daughter Anne, like her mother, employed Tylney relations within her household.[128] When her husband's successor the Fifteenth Earl of Oxford broke into her house at Castle Camps in 1526, Anne wrote a complaint to Wolsey dated from 'Wyttysforth': this was almost certainly Whittlesford in Cambridgeshire, a house owned by a branch of the Tylney family.[129] The fact that she had gone to her mother's kin for safety reveals the continued importance of these ties. Katherine, Countess of Bridgwater, also valued her Tylney kin, leaving jewellery in her will to 'Emorye tylney my kinesmane', who also witnessed her testament.[130] The endurance of these ties down the line of female descent within the Howard family underlines the strong sense of kinship possessed by these women.

A common expression of extended kinship ties was through the practice of fostering. Aristocratic children were often sent away to be brought up within a noble household of equal or greater status in order to promulgate links between the two families, provide the fosteree with useful networks for advancement, and potentially cement the alliance through intermarriage.[131] Some households served as a springboard to a place at court, which held even greater advantages for noble families. Women played major roles in fostering other children, and while these were not necessarily kin, where the Howards were concerned they often seem to have been, and fostering functioned for them as a way to promote lower-status natal kin. Agnes Tylney/Howard, Duchess of Norfolk, in particular, has a reputation for fostering, based largely on her guardianship of her granddaughter Catherine Howard. Catharine Davies and Lacey Baldwin Smith have stated that Catherine was simply one among many young female relatives brought up concurrently within Agnes's household. Indeed, Smith states that 'the children of innumerable Howard relations and dependents' were brought up by Agnes, and David Starkey has described her household as 'a slackly run mixed boarding school'.[132] Though Agnes probably was the Howards' most prolific fosterer, this was not as pronounced as has been thought. Of the women mentioned in the Catherine Howard evidence, only a few can be clearly pinpointed as relations Agnes was fostering. We know that she fostered her granddaughter Agnes ap Rhys, and Agnes's two brothers Gruffudd and Thomas.[133] She probably fostered her son William's first

---

[127] Ibid., fol. 145.   [128] TNA SP1/27, fol. 152.

[129] In the 1520s it was held by Robert Tylney, a first cousin of Agnes's. See Cyril Bristow, *Tilney Families* (Tonbridge, 1988), 29–30.

[130] TNA PROB 10/27. Emery Tylney was a second cousin of Katherine's, a grandson of Agnes's brother Sir Philip Tylney.

[131] Adams, 'Fostering Girls in Early Modern France', in Broomhall (ed.), *Emotions in the Household*, 103–18.

[132] Davies, 'Agnes Howard [née Tilney], Duchess of Norfolk', *ODNB* [accessed 25 January 2013]; Smith, *Catherine Howard*, 42; David Starkey, *Six Wives: The Queens of Henry VIII* (London, 2004), 646.

[133] Nicolas, *PCP* VII, 283.

wife, Katherine Broughton, who became her ward in 1529.[134] Her niece, Katherine Tylney, and of course the famous granddaughter Catherine Howard, were there. Others such as Mary Hall, Joan Bulmer, Alice Wilkes, and Dorothy Dawby were servants who shared a sleeping chamber with the noble fosterees. Nevertheless, her activities in this regard proved immensely useful to her natal and marital kin, for both Katherine Tylney and Catherine Howard gained places at court, and Agnes was later able to advise Catherine on how best to treat the King.

Other Howard women also undertook to foster natal kin. During the 1530s and 1540s, Elizabeth, Duchess of Norfolk, fostered her brother's daughters Susan and Dorothy Stafford.[135] This was no doubt seen as a good opportunity by their father, Elizabeth's brother Henry, Lord Stafford, because Elizabeth's status was now above his own and the chances were that she could secure them better marriages than he himself could, particularly since there were many young Staffords and his was a limited income. Elizabeth's household, however, may not have been the most pleasant place for young female relatives. Her letter to her brother in 1537 stated that if he wanted to send her another daughter, he should send Dorothy, 'for I am well a quyntyd w[i]th hir condycons all redy & so I am nott w[i]th the other & se ys yongyst to & yf she be Inynged therfore she ys better to breke as consarnyng hir yowth'.[136] The idea that girls were sent to be 'broken' is not one espoused by any other noblewoman during this period, indeed Tracy Adams underlines the positive nature of most fostering relationships.[137] Nevertheless, Dorothy stayed with Elizabeth into the 1550s, and later became one of Elizabeth I's favourite ladies-in-waiting, which suggests that Elizabeth's household was indeed a springboard into court society.

The tradition of godparenting could also function as an expression of kinship networks, though not exclusively so.[138] In England, children were given three godparents; two godmothers and one godfather for a girl, the opposite for a boy.[139] Without specific records of christenings it is often difficult to track godparents, though the principal godparent was usually the 'naming' godparent and often gave the child their own name, hence the term 'given name'. This in itself can often function as a means of tracing godparenthood where a name is particularly unusual, because names were understood as an important way to document family connections.[140] Two of Agnes, Duchess of Norfolk's, granddaughters were also named Agnes (Agnes ap Rhys and Agnes Howard, daughter of Lord William), which suggests that she was their main godmother, and a Tylney niece was also

[134] *LP* IV, 6072 (21).　　　[135] BL Cotton MS Titus B I, fol. 162.
[136] Ibid., fol. 152.　　　[137] Adams, 'Fostering Girls in Early Modern France', 110–14.
[138] There is a considerable body of work on early modern godparenting, most notably Coster, *Baptism and Spiritual Kinship*; J. Bossy, 'Blood and Baptism: Kinship, Community and Christianity in Western Europe from the Fourteenth to the Seventeenth Centuries', in D. Baker (ed.), *Sanctity and Society: The Church and the World* (Oxford, 1973), 129–44; Philip Niles, 'Baptism and the Naming of Children in Late Medieval England', in Dave Postles and Joel T. Rosenthal (eds), *Studies on the Personal Name in Later Medieval England and Wales* (Kalamazoo, Mich., 2006), 147–58. For the significance of godmothering as a sign of female kinship ties, see Harris, 'Sisterhood', 23–4.
[139] Coster, *Baptism and Spiritual Kinship*, 175.
[140] Merton, 'Women, Friendship and Memory'.

named Agnes.[141] Elizabeth Stafford/Howard, Duchess of Norfolk, also undertook the role of godparent. She was chosen as godmother to her great-grandson Philip, Earl of Arundel, in 1557.[142] This reveals that she was only invited to take this role once she was reconciled with the Howard family after the death of her husband in 1554. Clearly, godparenthood, like kinship itself, was a two-way street; if godparents were supposed to help children advance through life, clearly it was only worth choosing those who were already valued within their families and within wider aristocratic society. That the Howard women were considered in this way shows that they often functioned as linchpins between extended kin and the core of the dynasty, particularly in the case of their own natal kin, to whom their sense of obligation was especially strong.

CONCLUSION

Unsurprisingly, kinship connections of all kinds were of vital importance to the Howard women. Like most other aristocratic women of this period, the evidence shows that they valued both natal and marital connections throughout their lives, and often passed on those relationships to the next generation, creating matrilineal kinship bonds that were distinct from the usual patriarchal line of inheritance. Female kinship connections, then, were significant too, and this exposes an aspect of the Howard dynasty hitherto overlooked. These networks performed vital functions for the women's natal and marital families, including fostering, godmothering, the arrangement of marriages and placement of women at court, and securing inheritances. All of these served to strengthen the connections between the women's natal and marital families, and augment the Howards' status.

Female networks were also of importance to the lives of these women themselves. We see them giving advice, providing useful patronage connections, accommodation, and doing so even for female kin who had temporarily dropped from favour among patriarchal kin. This demonstrates that the Howard women's networks could function outside of, and sometimes in opposition to, those of the men, and while this could be positive for the women themselves, episodes like the precedence dispute between the duchesses of Norfolk show that the Howards' female kinship networks could also be very damaging to the political fortunes of the entire family. While a strictly oppositional model of gender relations is in many ways outdated and unrealistic, this evidence suggests that we should not go too far in the opposite direction and assume that noblemen and women consistently worked harmoniously towards shared goals. The negotiation of power and authority was a delicate one, particularly for those at the apex of power like the Howards, and this is demonstrated by the way in which Thomas Howard, Third Duke of Norfolk, the paterfamilias

[141] Coster, *Baptism and Spiritual Kinship*, 175; Bristow, *Tilney Families*, 31.
[142] J. G. Elzinga, 'Philip Howard [St Philip Howard], Thirteenth Earl of Arundel', *ODNB* [accessed 20 April 2012].

for much of this period, struggled not only to keep tabs on his family's behaviour, but to implement effective damage control in the aftermath of their activities.

And yet we have seen that this was never set in stone. As this book goes on to reveal, kinship relations at times of crisis did not necessarily reflect more ordinary, daily, lived experience as a member of this family. Relationships among the Howards were just as likely to be positive as negative in different contexts, and it is unfair to assume either that they were consistently a strong, united 'faction', or that they were continually at odds with one another. As a result of this, there were myriad ways in which it was possible to define dynastic identity, and these were apt to morph to suit the circumstances under question. There were times when the actions of one or more of these women do not appear to have taken broader dynastic goals into consideration, which means that their identity as a member of the Howard dynasty cannot always have been uppermost in their minds. The dominant patrilineal mode of lineage meant that women's dynastic identities were open to interpretation by themselves and by those around them. To us, this seems vague and unclear. The examples discussed here, however, make it clear that early modern people themselves did not feel a need for 'clearer' dynastic boundaries, and the elasticity of kinship relations suited, and were crucial to, the society in which they lived.

2

'Trashe baguaige and many od endes'
Material Culture and Patronage

For elites, probably more than other social groups, objects and belongings held great dynastic significance. Their objects, and the means by which and spaces in which these were produced, displayed, and exchanged, told their dynastic story and were also used to construct, or re-construct, it.[1] Materiality was also the way to show off wealth and status, and, in the patronage-based political system of this period, acquire and exhibit agency through control over local material economies, the offer of hospitality, and through gift-giving. The influence of material culture on individual lives and early modern society as a whole has gained such recognition in recent years that we are now in the midst of what has been termed the 'material turn' in humanities scholarship, but women's place in this remains complex.[2] They were much more likely to own and have direct control over objects like jewels, clothes, and furniture than they were land or property. We know, too, that they were involved in the production, design, and purchase of these objects, and that there are definably female patterns of exchange at certain levels of society.[3] What is largely missing from this narrative is an analysis of gendered materiality in a familial

[1] As demonstrated most recently by Susan Broomhall and Jacqueline Van Gent, *Dynastic Colonialism: Gender, Materiality, and the Early Modern House of Orange–Nassau* (London, 2016). See also Richard Cust, 'The Material Culture of Lineage in Late Tudor and Early Stuart England', in C. Richardson, T. J. Hamling, and David Gaimster (eds), *The Handbook of Material Culture in Early Modern Europe* (London, 2016), 247–74; M. Evans (ed.), *Art, Collecting and Lineage in the Elizabethan Age: The Lumley Inventory and Pedigree* (London, 2010); T. J. Hamling and C. Richardson (eds), *Everyday Objects: Medieval and Early Modern Material Culture and its Meanings* (Aldershot, 2010); T. J. Hamling, '"An Arelome To This House For Ever"; Monumental Fixtures and Furnishings in the English Domestic Interior, *c.*1560–1660', in A. Gordon and T. Rist (eds), *The Arts of Remembrance in Early Modern England* (Aldershot, 2013), 59–83; Peter Sherlock, *Monuments and Memory in Early Modern England* (Aldershot, 2008).

[2] Introduction to Richardson, Hamling, and Gaimster (eds), *The Handbook of Material Culture in Early Modern Europe*.

[3] See relevant sections in Maria Hayward, *Dress at the Court of Henry VIII* (Leeds, 2007), and *Rich Apparel: Clothing and the Law in Henry VIII's England* (Aldershot, 2009); Elizabeth V. Chew, 'The Countess of Arundel and Tart Hall', in Edward Chaney (ed.), *The Evolution of English Collecting: Receptions of Italian Art in the Tudor and Stuart Periods* (New Haven and London, 2003), 285–314; Susan Broomhall and Jacqueline Van Gent, 'Gendered Strategies of Porcelain as Power in the Early Modern House of Orange–Nassau', in James Daybell and Svante Norrhem (eds), *Gender and Political Culture in Early Modern Europe* (London, 2016); Jane Donawerth, 'Women's Poetry and the Tudor–Stuart System of Gift Exchange', in Mary E. Burke, Jane Donawerth, Linda L. Dove, and Karen Nelson (eds), *Women, Writing, and the Reproduction of Culture* (Syracuse, NY, 2000), 3–18; Lisa M. Klein, 'Your Humble Handmaid: Elizabethan Gifts of Needlework', *Renaissance Quarterly* 50 (1997), 459–93.

and dynastic context.[4] If men could use materiality to develop and display agency, then clearly so could women. However, the use of material culture is often considered as a collective enterprise within families like the Howards. Though many scholars maintain that a woman's primary role was to support their husband's family, material evidence for the Howards shows that they were able to use objects to transmit their complex accumulation of familial identities. In doing so, they also used material culture to enhance their social standing, to secure the ties of kinship and political alliance, and to cement ties of familial affection and friendship, thereby revealing an intense level of direct agency.

IMMOVABLE GOODS: WEALTH AND STATUS

A brief outline of the Howards' material situations, in terms of the estates they owned, houses they lived in, and general wealth, serves to highlight the material disparities within the dynasty, something not often acknowledged. Though noble households were peripatetic, most families nevertheless owned a main family seat in which the patriarch and his immediate family spent the majority of their time. For the Howards, these main residences changed several times, but were all clustered around the Norfolk–Suffolk border. Under John Howard, First Duke of Norfolk, the family lived mainly at Tendring Hall at Stoke-by-Nayland in Suffolk until he gained the dukedom of Norfolk and with it Framlingham Castle in 1483.[5] The move to Framlingham must have marked a major change in their living situation, for Framlingham was a fully-fledged castle, where Tendring, though a respectable house meant for a knight or baron, cannot have been anything like as large.[6] Having previously introduced such luxuries as glass windows, elaborate chimney pieces, and expensive wall hangings to Tendring, John Howard's accounts show that he spent the years between 1483 and 1485 bringing Framlingham similarly up to date, both by repairing existing buildings and by adding new ones. He is usually credited with building the Great Chamber across the Inner Court, linking up the two sides of the castle, introducing fashionable brick chimneys, and possibly also adding pleasure gardens.[7] The importance of Framlingham, though, was not solely scale and splendour but also its dynastic symbolism, since houses, as well as objects, could function as dynastic heirlooms. As the seat of the dukes of Norfolk, ownership of and residence at Framlingham helped to confer legitimacy

---

[4] With the recent exception of Broomhall and Van Gent, *Dynastic Colonialism*, and some work on gender and early modern commemoration and memory; see Peter Sherlock, 'Patriarchal Memory: Monuments in Early-Modern England', in Megan Cassidy-Welch and Peter Sherlock (eds), *Practices of Gender in Late Medieval and Early Modern Europe* (Turnhout, 2008), 279–99; Catherine Howey Stearn, 'Grave Histories: Women's Bodies Writing Elizabethan History', in Donald Stump, Linda Shenk, and Carole Levin (eds), *Elizabeth I and the 'Sovereign Arts': Essays in Literature, History, and Culture* (Tempe, Ariz., 2011), 69–84; and Nicola Clark, 'The Gendering of Dynastic Memory: Burial Choices of the Howards, 1485–1559', *Journal of Ecclesiastical History* 68:4 (2017), 747–65.

[5] Crawford, *Yorkist Lord*, 142–3 and 150–2.　　　[6] Ibid.

[7] Ibid. 150–2, 159; John Ridgard, *Medieval Framlingham: Select Documents, 1270–1524* (Woodbridge, 1985), Suffolk Record Society 27, p. 6.

upon its occupants, and stress continuity between the previous titleholders, the Mowbrays, and the Howards.

Alas for the Howards, Framlingham was lost along with the rest of the family estates after Bosworth in 1485, though as Tendring Hall formed part of John Howard's second wife Margaret's jointure she was allowed to keep it and lived there until her death in 1494.[8] At this point, it passed to Norfolk's son and heir Thomas, Earl of Surrey, later Second Duke of Norfolk. His family had been living primarily on his wife Elizabeth Tylney/Bourchier/Howard's much smaller manor of Ashwellthorpe in Norfolk, while Surrey himself was imprisoned in the Tower.[9] After his release in 1489, they decamped to Sheriff Hutton Castle in Yorkshire during his ten-year stint as Lieutenant of the North. It was at Sheriff Hutton that Elizabeth died, and it was here that her first cousin Agnes Tylney became Surrey's second wife.[10] Once the family returned south in 1499, they resumed living at Tendring Hall and kept it as the major residence until Framlingham Castle was returned to them in 1514 along with the dukedom of Norfolk.[11] They remained there until Thomas Howard's death in 1524. After this, the Third Duke and his immediate family continued to live at Tendring Hall for the summer and Hunsdon for the winter, as surviving household accounts suggest, but they also began to include Framlingham in their peregrinations, keeping an extravagant Christmas there in 1526.[12] Between 1526 and 1528 Norfolk spent a considerable sum building a new, lavish, house on the site of an old Mowbray hunting lodge at Kenninghall in Suffolk, and this then became the main family residence during the 1530s and 1540s.[13] Elizabeth Stafford/Howard, Duchess of Norfolk, her children, including Mary Howard/Fitzroy, Duchess of Richmond, all spent time living here, as did her daughters-in-law Frances de Vere/Howard, Countess of Surrey, and Elizabeth Marney/Howard, later Viscountess Howard of Bindon, along with their various children. Kenninghall seems to have been a triumph of fashionable architecture. Built on a similar scale to many royal palaces, in an 'H' shape for 'Howard', it had four storeys, multiple courtyards and ranges, many outer buildings, tennis courts, and fishponds.[14] Kenninghall was used as the main family house until the arrest of the Duke in 1546, after which it was granted to Princess Mary.[15] It was returned to them on her accession in 1553 and continued as the major family residence under the Fourth Duke until he purchased the Charterhouse in London in 1565.

While many of the Howard women spent time in the family's major houses as wives of successive patriarchs or as daughters growing up, the majority married out

---

[8] Anne Crawford, 'Victims of Attainder: The Howard and De Vere Women in the Late Fifteenth Century', in Keith Bate (ed.), *Medieval Women in Southern England* (Reading, 1989), 59–74.

[9] Head, *The Ebbs and Flows of Fortune*, 18.

[10] *Calendar of Papal Letters*, vol. XVII Part 2, appendix 1, pp. c–ci, no. 34.

[11] Head, *The Ebbs and Flows of Fortune*, 21; Ridgard, *Medieval Framlingham*, 6.

[12] CUL, Pembroke MS 300.   [13] Head, *The Ebbs and Flows of Fortune*, 84.

[14] TNA LR2/117, inventory of Kenninghall, 1547, unfoliated.

[15] See J. L. McIntosh, *From Heads of Household to Heads of State: The Preaccesion Households of Mary and Elizabeth Tudor, 1516–1558* (Gutenberg <e>, 2009), chapter 3, 'Property and Politics: Land Acquisition and Political Status', <http://www.gutenberg-e.org/mcintosh/chapter3.html> [accessed 6 September 2017].

and then lived elsewhere. The wealth of their new husband, not that of their birth family, determined the location and quality of their new residences, and this was naturally somewhat uneven across the family. Some settled fairly locally. Elizabeth Howard/Boleyn, Countess of Wiltshire, would have spent time at Blickling Hall in Norfolk as well as Hever Castle in Kent, but neither of these could rival Framlingham. Her much younger half-sister, Anne Howard/de Vere, Countess of Oxford, was also within easy reach of Howard territory, spending much of her married life at the impressive de Vere seat of Hedingham Castle in Essex. The remainder of her sisters were far-flung. Katherine Howard/ap Rhys/Daubeney, Countess of Bridgwater, spent her first marriage living in south-west Wales, principally at the large and newly refurbished Carew Castle, but her second marriage saw her live primarily at what was then a much smaller house in South Petherton, Somerset.[16] By contrast, her sister Dorothy married Edward Stanley, Third Earl of Derby, in 1531 and would have lived at the much more luxurious Knowsley Hall in Derbyshire.

Once widowed, most of these women moved to alternative properties included within their jointure and would then have run their own households. Agnes Tylney/Howard, Duchess of Norfolk, spent her widowhood at Chesworth House near Horsham in Sussex, and at Norfolk House in Lambeth, which was bequeathed to her in her husband's will of 1520.[17] This meant that she became the hub of the family's London activities. Norfolk House was across the road from Lambeth Palace, the home of the archbishops of Canterbury, and across the river from Westminster, very close to the royal palace and therefore the royal court when it was in residence there. When family members came to London, it was Agnes who put them up at Norfolk House, meaning that she remained intrinsically connected to the core of the dynasty even after widowhood.[18] Other Howard widows also gravitated to London. Agnes's daughter Katherine, Countess of Bridgwater, had a house in Southwark after her separation from her second husband in the 1530s, and records show that she lived at Lambeth, though on the estate of the archbishopric of Canterbury and not at Norfolk House, during the 1550s.[19] Mary Howard/Fitzroy, Duchess of Richmond, wrote letters from Stepney in the late 1540s.[20] Anne Howard/de Vere, Countess of Oxford, moved to the manor house at Castle Camps in Essex after she was widowed in 1526, and though initially she struggled to keep it safe from her husband's successor, she spent the rest of her life living there.[21] Elizabeth Stafford/Howard, Duchess of Norfolk, spent a considerable portion of her married life living at a house in Redbourn, Hertfordshire, from the 1530s possibly until her death in 1558.[22]

The houses that they lived in were often broadly representative of these women's general financial status both as wives and as widows. Attempting to calculate the

---

[16] Her second husband Henry Daubeney, Earl of Bridgwater, began extensive rebuilding of another house at Barrington Court, but did not finish it. See <https://historicengland.org.uk/listing/the-list/list-entry/1000505> [accessed 6 September 2017].

[17] TNA PROB 11/21/249.   [18] TNA SP1/168, fol. 48.

[19] Nicolas, *PCP*, VII, 280; Thomas Allen, *The History and Antiquities of the Parish of Lambeth* (London, 1926), 439.

[20] TNA SP10/7, no. 1 and no. 3.   [21] See Chapter 3.   [22] See Chapter 3.

Howard women's worth in terms of monetary wealth is a difficult thing to do during this period. Any 'official' written record of a woman's wealth may not have matched the reality, because though coverture meant that a married woman could not legally own or manage material assets, she may have done so in practice under her husband's name.[23] For most noblewomen financial worth was keyed into the dowry and jointure payments agreed at the time of her marriage, and these represented differences in status carefully translated into financial sums.[24] Dowry and jointure sums grew across the early modern period due to inflation, competition from increasingly wealthy under-classes, and increasing land prices swelling incomes.[25] Women marrying into the Howard dynasty therefore brought larger and larger dowries as the period progressed, partly as a result of this inflation and partly because of the dynasty's own increasingly inflated status. While Elizabeth Stafford allegedly brought 2,000 marks to her marriage with Thomas, then Lord Howard, in 1512, Frances de Vere would bring double that amount to hers with their son Henry, Earl of Surrey, twenty years later in 1532.[26]

The portions given to Howard daughters marrying out increased in a similar fashion. In 1520, when he wrote his will, Thomas Howard, Second Duke of Norfolk, left his widow £300 (500 marks) for the marriage of each of his remaining daughters.[27] Among these was Dorothy, whose dowry when she later married the Earl of Derby in 1531 was inflated to 4,000 marks.[28] For women marrying into the Howard dynasty, however, jointure amounts remained relatively stable despite the increase in dowries, which suggests that others were paying through the nose for the privilege of marrying into the family. Both Agnes Tylney in 1497 and Frances de Vere in 1532 were granted jointures of 500 marks, as was Elizabeth Stafford/Howard, Duchess of Norfolk, in 1512, and all three women enjoyed this sum during widowhood.[29] For Howard daughters marrying out, jointure could vary considerably depending on the status and wealth of the family into which they married. Katherine Howard/ap Rhys/Daubeney, Countess of Bridgwater, held a jointure of £200 from her first marriage to Rhys ap Gruffudd in the 1520s, whereas Mary Howard/Fitzroy, Duchess of Richmond, had the highest jointure of 1,000 marks from her marriage to the King's son Henry in 1536.[30] It goes without saying that all of these women were vastly wealthy by comparison with the population

---

[23] Susan Broomhall, 'Materializing Women: Dynamic Interactions of Gender and Materiality in Early Modern Europe', in Amanda L. Capern (ed.), *The Routledge History of Women in Early Modern Europe* (epub. London, 2017).

[24] Broadly speaking, a woman of high status marrying downwards would offer less dowry, but expect more jointure, whereas the opposite was true if a woman of lower status married upwards.

[25] R. B. Outhwaite, 'Marriage as Business: Opinions on the Rise in Aristocratic Bridal Portions in Early Modern England', in Neil McKendrick and R. B. Outhwaite (eds), *Business Life and Public Policy* (Cambridge, 1986), 21–37.

[26] BL Cotton MS Titus B I, fol. 390r–v (Eliz. to Cromwell, Oct. 1537); *Statutes of the Realm*, III, 410.

[27] TNA PROB 11/21/249.   [28] *Statutes of the Realm*, III, 357.

[29] Arundel Castle MS G1/4, copy of the livery of Thomas, Second Duke of Norfolk, 1524; TNA E211/82; NRO MS NRS 27260 361x3.

[30] For Katherine's jointure, see NLW A 59; for Mary's, BL Cotton MS Titus B I, fol. 383c, *LP* XV, 1032 (p. 540), and TNA SC12/23/40. While Mary's mother Elizabeth stated that Mary was owed £1,000, 1,000 marks (a third less) was the amount finally agreed upon.

at large, yet direct comparison between them shows that the Howard name did not necessarily equal comparable wealth or status for women.

MOVABLE GOODS: CLOTHES, JEWELS, AND DYNASTIC BRANDING

Naturally, this disparity also applied to the objects that they owned. Nobles would generally seek to obtain the best quality that they could afford commensurate with their status. Thus, while all of the Howard women dressed richly in velvet and damask, cloth of gold, cloth of silver, and cloth of tissue appear only to have featured occasionally in the clothing of Elizabeth Stafford/Howard, Duchess of Norfolk, though it is likely that Agnes Tylney/Howard, the senior Duchess, also wore these fabrics.[31] It is worth remembering that although the sumptuary laws of this period did not mention women, in theory giving them licence to wear whatever fabrics or colours they chose or could afford, in practice coverture meant that married women did not legally own the clothes and jewels that they wore, or, indeed, the money to purchase them.[32] This meant not only that their clothing generally reflected their husband's status, but that men were within their rights to withhold access to material goods as a form of control over their wives. Elizabeth Stafford/ Howard, as the wife of the dynasty's patriarch, was of the highest noble status and this was reflected in the quality of her clothing. In 1534, however, in punishment for her objections to his mistress, her husband seized her jewels and apparel.[33] An inventory of Kenninghall taken in 1546 includes a long list of apparel belonging to her in coffers in the inner nursery, even though she had not lived at Kenninghall for over ten years. Unfortunately for Elizabeth, she never seems to have recovered these items; all were then sent to Protector Somerset in 1552 after her husband's arrest.[34] The list shows that in the 1530s, her favoured colour aside from the ubiquitous black was purple. Jewellery, too, was status-bound. Evidence from inventories and wills shows that in general, the Howard duchesses followed the trends of their time, and like other aristocrats favoured primarily diamonds, rubies, emeralds, and pearls. They also owned jewels made with white sapphire, a cheaper substitute for diamond, and there are a number of references to amethyst, 'jacent' (a red coloured stone), and carnelian.[35] These were apparently of a higher quality than those belonging to Katherine Howard/ap Rhys/Daubeney, Countess of Bridgwater, in the 1540s, which included 'foure ringes of golde sett with course stones and Angell of golde with certen course peerles'.[36]

---

[31] TNA LR2/117, unfoliated.

[32] Maria Hayward, *Rich Apparel: Clothing and the Law in Henry VIII's England* (Aldershot, 2009), chapter 11, 'Women: Wives and Spinsters, Vowesses and Widows', 225–50.

[33] BL Cotton MS Titus B I, fol. 383a, Elizabeth to Cromwell, 26 June 1537.

[34] TNA LR2/116, fols 19–20v.   [35] TNA LR2/116, fols 3v–7v; TNA PROB 10/27.

[36] David Starkey (ed.), *The Inventory of King Henry VIII*, 3 vols (London, 1998), I, 93.

Status was strongly linked to dynastic identity, and this too was showcased for women through materiality.[37] Inventories show that the Howard homes were drenched in dynastic 'branding', with textiles, plate, and suchlike emblazoned with coats of arms and badges. More particularly, they make it clear that objects could be used to document a dynasty's marital history, which meant, for women, a way to signal continued connections to natal families. At Framlingham in 1524 there remained a pair of cruets engraved with the letters C and M, which might have belonged to Catherine Moleyns, the first wife of John Howard, First Duke of Norfolk, and items including waterflowers (water lilies) may well have related to his second wife Margaret Chedworth/Norreys/Wyfold, since in her will she left a chain of waterflowers to one of her daughters.[38] By 1546, at Kenninghall, 'branding' was even more in evidence, in part because the Third Duke appears to have owned many more items than his father had done. The white lion badge of the Howards themselves was the stand-out embellishment, but it was often combined with Stafford knots, marking Norfolk's marriage with Elizabeth Stafford. For the same reason, there were many textiles embroidered with the letters T and E, with a few T and A left over from the previous Duke and his second wife Agnes. Other instances of combined dynastic branding included a salt—an important piece of plate designed for display—engraved with a falcon, which was the Boleyn badge, and plate combining Howard lions and Marney half-wings, belonging to Elizabeth Marney/Howard, wife of the Duke's youngest son Thomas.[39] The plethora of dynastic symbols clearly show that women brought their own branding into their new situations when they married, rather than either being forced, or choosing, to use only the badge of their new family. Materially, as well as figuratively, it made sense for families to document the alliances between them to mutual benefit, and for women to signal their continued connections to their natal families as well as their new marital connections.

Dynastic branding could also be used to attempt to bolster familial identity, and, by association, relationships. The inventory of Kenninghall taken in 1546 shows that among Elizabeth Stafford/Howard, Duchess of Norfolk's, coffers was an unfinished counterpoint for a bed, suggesting that she had been engaged in this work at the time of her sudden departure from the house at Easter 1534.[40] Rather poignantly, given the breakdown of the relationship between herself and her husband at that point, it seems that this was intended for her own and her husband's bed: the components included 140 of the letters T and E, for Thomas and Elizabeth. Susan Broomhall has pointed out that women of this social class had no practical or economic need to produce such items themselves, and suggests that they continued to do so as an engrained, traditional means to display feminine traits of 'modesty and propriety'.[41] While this is undoubtedly true, there could clearly be other, more immediate motivations as well. Elizabeth, making a bed for herself and

[37] Susan James, *Women's Voices in Tudor Wills: Authority, Influence, and Material Culture* (London, 2015), 260.
[38] CUL, MS 173 Dd. III. 86 no. 3 (unfoliated); TNA PROB 11/10/195.
[39] TNA LR 2/117, unfoliated.   [40] Ibid.   [41] Broomhall, 'Materializing Women'.

her husband, seems to be doing so as a deliberate performance, performing her marriage and her identity publicly in the face of her husband's continued relationship with his mistress, Bess Holland, who also lived in the house. Domestic production might be seen as one of the few acceptable forms of resistance that she was able to offer as a woman, and it was perhaps made more powerful by the very fact that the items she made were not strictly necessary.

Such activity could have political implications. We know from the surviving embroideries of Mary, Queen of Scots, for instance, that women were well aware of the political import of needlework and other materiality.[42] Not only was Elizabeth, Duchess of Norfolk busy with a bed cover designed to showcase her disintegrating marriage in the 1530s, but she was also embroidering 'a greate pomegranet of gold and two of yellow satten not ffynesshed'.[43] Pomegranates were the badge of Catherine of Aragon. Elizabeth was therefore stitching her support for the Queen. Moreover, this was in the 1530s, after Catherine had been sent from court, but before her death in 1536, which was a particularly dangerous time to signal such support, especially given the family's relationship to the new Queen, Anne Boleyn. Clearly, women were able to use material culture to signal political allegiance, even in the face of familial disapproval, and embroidery, indeed, was a peculiarly female form of material resistance.

Colour and material could also be used for performative, political purposes. In 1546, the commissioners responsible for taking the inventory of Kenninghall listed an embroidery frame set up in the chamber of Mary Howard/Fitzroy, Duchess of Richmond, the Duke's daughter, containing unfinished embroidery of purple satin with cloth of gold.[44] Mary had had difficulty claiming her jointure, and therefore her royal status, as the widow of the King's illegitimate son, Henry Fitzroy, Duke of Richmond. In 1538 her father attempted to marry her to Thomas Seymour, which would have side-stepped the jointure question entirely, and though she was able to avoid this fate, the match reappeared as a possibility in the mid-1540s.[45] Mary's choice of embroidery colours could be taken as a determined show of royal status. In her coffers there were also textiles for a bed, again purple satin embroidered with cloth of gold bawdekin and cloth of tissue and pearls. While this was in one sense a personal issue relating to Mary's own identity, the fact that it involved the royal family meant that her use of materiality had political ramifications.

Style, too, played a role here. Elizabeth's complaint that her husband had taken all of her clothes, made in a letter to Cromwell in 1537, is borne out by the Kenninghall inventory of 1546, which includes a fairly lengthy list of apparel belonging to her despite the fact that she had not lived there in over ten years.[46] Three of her six gowns were described specifically as 'English' style, which pre-dated Anne Boleyn's preference for French style and, as Maria Hayward has noted, suggests

---

[42] Susan Frye, *Pens and Needles: Women and Textualities in Early Modern England* (Philadelphia, 2010), chapter 1, 'Political Designs: Elizabeth Tudor, Mary Stuart, and Bess of Hardwick'.

[43] TNA LR 2/117, unfoliated.   [44] TNA LR 2/117, unfoliated.

[45] TNA SP1/134, fols 160r–v, Ralph Sadler to Thomas Cromwell, 14 July 1538; BL Cotton MS Titus BI, fols 99–101v, Duke of Norfolk to Thomas Cromwell, December 1546.

[46] BL Cotton MS Titus B I, fol. 383a, Elizabeth to Cromwell, 26 June 1537.

that though costly, by the mid-1530s Elizabeth's wardrobe would not have been considered particularly fashionable.[47] Could this mean that Elizabeth deliberately showcased her allegiance to Catherine of Aragon through her clothes as well as her embroidery? It may be worth noting that Elizabeth's favoured colours were black followed by purple, and so were Catherine's.[48] The wardrobe of Norfolk's mistress Bess Holland, conversely, contained mainly French-style gowns, which would make sense for a woman serving in the household of Anne Boleyn.[49]

As well as dynastic branding in terms of patriarchal lineage, the Howard women used material goods as a means of perpetuating matriarchal memory and descent, and this is particularly obvious in their wills. Several Howard women left items of jewellery or clothing to their daughters, granddaughters, or other matrilineal kin in a way that suggests that these items carried something of the spirit of the wearer and were intended as means of remembrance as well as useful and valuable gifts. Margaret Chedworth/Wyfold/Norreys/Howard, Duchess of Norfolk, bequeathed her daughter 'a cheyne of waterflowres'—waterlilies—which may have been a heraldic symbol relating to either her natal family or a previous marriage.[50] In 1545, Agnes Tylney/Howard, Duchess of Norfolk, left 'the fourthe parte of all my gooddes both householde stuffe Juells and plate and of all other stuffe whatsoever it be | And also the fourthe parte of all my raiment' to her daughter Katherine, Countess of Bridgwater, and also remembered her natal kin in the form of her 'nephewe Tynlay' who received 'a goblet of siluer and gilte w[i]t[h]out a cover'.[51] Her daughter Katherine then continued this practice in 1554, leaving an angel noble of gold, a jacent, and an amethyst set in gold, and 'all other small things being in my coffers at Lambeth', to her granddaughter Mary Baynton, as well as clothing and silver to her daughter Agnes.[52] She continued to remember her mother's kin through her bequest of a gold bracelet to her 'kinsman'—a cousin—Emery Tylney.[53] Elizabeth, Duchess of Norfolk, left apparel and 'ewry stuffe' to her niece and great-nieces in 1558, as well as various items of clothing and plate to her sister-in-law Ursula Pole/ Stafford, Lady Stafford, her granddaughter the Duchess of Norfolk, and Lady Margaret Howard.[54]

While wills provide us with a useful snapshot of an individual's state at the time of their death, analysis of material status enables us to track changes in circumstances throughout their lives. For women this was, as ever, irrevocably entwined with marital status. We know that Mary Howard/Fitzroy, Duchess of Richmond, struggled to claim her jointure, and therefore her royal status, from her father-in-law the King after the untimely death of her husband Henry Fitzroy, Duke of Richmond, in 1536. Because the couple had yet to consummate the marriage due to their youth, the King insisted that it was therefore invalid, largely because this meant that he could avoid having to pay Mary her jointure

[47] Hayward, *Rich Apparel*, 234.   [48] Hayward, *Dress at the Court of King Henry VIII*, 179.
[49] TNA LR 2/117, unfoliated.   [50] TNA PROB 11/10/195.
[51] TNA PROB 11/30/596.   [52] TNA PROB 10/27.   [53] Ibid.
[54] TNA PROB 11/42A/285.

of 1,000 marks a year, a not-inconsiderable sum even for the royal treasury.[55] In the meantime, she had returned to live under her father's roof at Kenninghall, and after much petitioning she received grants of land to the correct yearly value for her jointure in 1538–9.[56] By 1546, however, the commissioners who took the inventory of Kenninghall described her closet and coffers as 'soo bare as your maiestie wolle hardlie think' and stated that her jewels had been sold to pay her debts.[57] Without this evidence we might have assumed that Mary lived materially happily ever after, since 1,000 marks a year was more money than any of her contemporary female Howard relatives received in jointure. It remains unclear why she continued to struggle for money during this time, unless she had been forced to enter into debt between 1536 and 1538 before she received her jointure and was unable to repay in entirety afterwards, or unless her income was syphoned off by relatives. This must have created a strange juxtaposition between the status of the house and of the Howards, versus the comparatively poor state of Mary's personal living conditions.

Many Howard women lost material goods through attainder and never regained them, and in this way their material well-being was directly related to their individual behaviour. Often this was explicitly stated. During her arrest, Queen Catherine Howard's officers were ordered by the King to allow her only 'vj frenche hoods w[i]t[h] thapp[er]tinnces w[i]t[h] edges of goldesmythes worke so there be no stone nor perle in the same and likewise asmany paire of sleves vj gownes and vj kyrtells of saten damask an velvet w[i]t[h] suche things as belong to the same Except always stone and perle'.[58] As a result of the same episode, the Queen's aunt, Katherine Howard/ap Rhys/Daubeney, Countess of Bridgwater, also lost material goods. Plate, jewels, and boxes, rolls, and books of documents and accounts belonging to her were discovered 'in a wicker hamper sent to the Towre founde in the litell studie nexte the kinges olde bedchambre' in the Tower of London in the royal inventory of 1547.[59] The jewels—a few rings, an 'Angell of gold', a girdle, cramp rings, and a chain—were described as 'coarse', which might suggest that these were the things that she had been allowed to bring with her for everyday use during her imprisonment. The fact that the biggest piece of plate bore the badge of her first husband, Rhys ap Gruffudd's, family, suggests that at least some of the items that she used in the Tower dated from her first marriage. Was this because they were older and worth less than other of her possessions, or was she choosing, through material culture, to associate herself with this time rather than with her more recent, unsuccessful, marriage to Henry Daubeney, Earl of Bridgwater? That these items remained in the Tower after Katherine's release in 1543 may suggest that they had been initially forgotten and that it was then thought imprudent to

---

[55] TNA SP1/128, fol. 11 (Mary to Cromwell, January 1538), SP1/128, fol. 69 (Cranmer to Cromwell, January 1538).

[56] *LP* XIV, i, 595, g. 651 (29), ii, 236 (74).   [57] TNA SP1/227, fol. 84.

[58] TNA SP1/167, fol. 127v.

[59] David Starkey (ed.), *The Inventory of King Henry VIII*, 3 vols (London, 1998), I, 93.

attempt to reclaim them, which shows how attainder and imprisonment continued to affect women's material status even after rehabilitation.

While both the Queen and her aunt were effectively single women during their imprisonment in 1541, married women were equally materially affected by attainder, whether or not they were themselves attainted. There was no law regarding a wife's position if her husband was attainted. The crown was free either to bestow or with-hold her personal goods and jointure estates, and thus much depended on the wife's petitionary zeal and the contacts she was able to mobilize to speak for her.[60] Elizabeth Tylney/Bourchier/Howard, Countess of Surrey, was forced to flee to sanctuary with her children after her husband's capture at Bosworth in 1485, and then had to fight for the return of her jointure property and manage without her marital wealth during the term of her husband's imprisonment. Her mother-in-law, Margaret Chedworth/Norreys/Wyfold/Howard, Duchess of Norfolk, was compara-tively lucky; though widowed, she was able to live off the jointures of her previous two marriages without having to fight for them.[61] Agnes Tylney/Howard, dowager Duchess of Norfolk, was attainted for misprision of treason in 1541, and also suf-fered confiscation of goods and property. She was, however, re-granted a portion of these once pardoned in 1542, though she did not regain the same level of material wealth as previously before her death in 1545.[62]

There is no doubt that this did reflect poorly on the dynasty as a whole, but other family members could hardly intervene to prevent the damage to their col-lective material status. Confiscation was explicitly designed as a visual reminder of that very thing. In response, there seems to have been a feeling that it was not the problem of the rest of the family, even the family patriarch, to mitigate the material status of other family members. Instead, they fought tooth and nail for their individ-ual goods. The commissioners responsible for searching Agnes, dowager Duchess of Norfolk's property during the same episode wrote that inventorying her goods would take several days more, because although she had 'moche good apparel and stuff', she also had 'moche trashe baguaige and many od endes', suggesting she may have been something of a hoarder.[63] She had also apparently hidden money and plate, her most valuable items, since the same letter stated that she admitted she had a thousand pounds more than she had told them previously, and that more plate had also been found. Wealth was clearly important to Agnes as a marker of status, but evidently she was also very aware of its potential transience. She agreed to go to the Tower only after they promised her she would have 'monay in her purse | to provide her of thinges necessarie and for her dietes w[i]t[h] women to waite upon her | and stuff necessarie'.[64] Here was a woman who understood that without these trappings, her own status might be forgotten and this might be reflected in the treatment she received.

---

[60] John Bellamy, *The Tudor Law of Treason: An Introduction* (London, 1979), 216–17.
[61] See Crawford, 'Victims of Attainder'.   [62] *LP* XVII, 296 (58).
[63] TNA SP1/168, fol. 129.   [64] Ibid.

PATRONAGE

Many of the Howard women's activities with objects and material resources fall under the vast umbrella of 'patronage', an area where women's activities have received considerable scholarly attention.[65] They used the resources of their great households to offer hospitality to local clients, and other peers. They commissioned artwork and literature, giving employment to craftspeople which again afforded them a measure of agency within those economies, as well as a way to publicly document and display status and wealth. They gave these objects, and objects that they had made themselves, as gifts. All of these material activities were effective ways of building and maintaining economic and social networks that were politically and personally beneficial. In this way, the Howard women's various engagements with material culture were a means of gaining direct agency, be it political, religious, economic, dynastic, or a combination thereof.

A key way in which early modern women used the material resources at their disposal was in the exercise of hospitality. Hospitality used the space and resources of the great household as a stage for the magnificent, munificent display expected of the nobility during this period.[66] Hospitality was not gendered—it was an obligation for both women and men, and both women and men would partake in others' hospitality. The way that space was used in terms of hospitality was fairly standard across all noble establishments at this time, in that visitors of gentle birth would usually dine with the lord and/or lady in the comparative privacy of the dining chamber or privy chamber at the 'board's end', and their servants plus visitors, workmen, or household officials of common ancestry would eat in the hall with the rest of the household.[67] Lodging as well as food was offered. This meant that aristocratic women had to be canny managers of their household resources.

We have already seen that the Howard houses were, generally speaking, on the large side, and this meant that their household staff were also numerous, as the

---

[65] See Sharon Kettering, 'The Patronage Power of Early Modern French Noblewomen', *The Historical Journal* 32 (1989), 817–41. See also Karen Robertson, 'Tracing Women's Connections from a Letter by Elizabeth Ralegh', in Susan Frye and Karen Robertson (eds), *Maids and Mistresses, Cousins and Queens: Women's Alliances in Early Modern England* (Oxford, 1999), 149–64; Sara Chapman, 'Patronage as Family Economy: The Role of Women in the Patron–Client Network of the Phelypeaux de Pontchartrain', *French Historical Studies* 24 (2001), 11–35; Pauline Croft, 'Mildred, Lady Burghley: The Matriarch', in Croft (ed.), *Patronage, Culture and Power: The Early Cecils* (New Haven and London, 2002), 283–300; Sara Jayne Steen, 'The Cavendish–Talbot Women: Playing a High-Stakes Game', in Daybell (ed.), *Women and Politics in Early Modern England, 1450–1700*, 147–63; D. Eichberger, 'The Culture of Gifts: A Courtly Phenomenon from a Female Perspective', in Eichberger (ed.), *Women of Distinction: Margaret of York and Margaret of Austria* (Turnhout, 2005), 286–95; Susan James, *The Feminine Dynamic in English Art, 1485–1603: Women as Consumers, Patrons and Painters* (Aldershot, 2009); Giulia Calvi and Isabelle Chabot (eds), *Moving Elites: Women and Cultural Transfers in the European Court System* (EUI Working Papers HEC, 2, 2010); Amanda E. Herbert, *Female Alliances: Gender, Identity, and Friendship in Early Modern Britain* (London, 2014). Recently there has been a particular flurry of interest in women's role in literary production (Helen Smith, *'Grossly Material Things': Women and Book Production in Early Modern England* (Oxford, 2012), and Julie Crawford, *Mediatrix: Women, Politics and Literary Production in Early Modern England* (Oxford, 2014)).

[66] Felicity Heal, *Hospitality in Early Modern England* (Oxford, 1990).

[67] Christopher Woolgar, *The Great Household in Medieval England* (London, 1999), 25.

surviving household books for Thomas, Earl of Surrey and later Third Duke of Norfolk, and his second wife Elizabeth Stafford/Howard, from 1523–4 and 1526–7, begin to reveal.[68] These books are essentially kitchen accounts, which not only include daily lists of visitors, but numbers of staff and menus, allowing us to build up a picture of the family's networks, and of the way that household resources were used to maintain these networks. The contrast between the two books is especially valuable because the earlier book (1523–4) covers a period where Elizabeth was managing the household alone during her husband's absence. We do have to bear in mind that the primary purpose of these books was to record the food distributed, and so they leave out any servants who did not receive this as part of their employment.[69] The 1523–4 book is most likely recording a reduced household, since the Earl was away for much of that year.[70] Thus on ordinary days there were usually five messes of gentlemen, yeomen, and grooms dining in the hall, and four other messes of servants dining in the kitchen, which—if the usual distribution of four people to a mess was observed here—adds up to only thirty-six people, with the addition of the twenty or so who dined with the Countess in her chamber.

In 1526–7, the household was much larger. By this point, Thomas Howard had been made Duke of Norfolk, and his finances and household had increased exponentially. This book too was designed to record the food consumed, so once again it is only a rough estimate of the true number of people residing in the household. At dinner on a typical day, there were twenty people dining with the Duke and Duchess in their chamber, twenty-two people making up the nursery staff, and, again presuming the usual system of four people to a mess was observed, around seventy servants dining in the hall, which adds up to a household of 112 people. This, though, is a conservative estimate; it does not, for instance, include the clerks and yeomen cooks of the kitchen, who are listed but not counted.[71] This was a large household, comparable to that of the Duke of Buckingham at Thornbury in 1507–8, which had on average 157 servants.[72]

The books do show that the number of personal servants who dined with the Duke and Duchess in their chamber could fluctuate considerably.[73] When both were at home at the beginning of the 1526–7 book, they dined together with anywhere between twenty-two and twenty-six people.[74] When Elizabeth dined alone

---

[68] UCB, MS UCB 49, unfoliated (1523–4) and CUL, Pembroke MS 300, unfoliated (1526–7). These are the two most complete records of visitors. There is also a 'household book' for Surrey and his family for the year 1519–20, but as is often the way with such records, the information it records is not comparable with the two later books because it does not include kitchen accounts, recording instead more general expenses (NRO NRS 2378 11 D4). Likewise, though there are also some short, less detailed kitchen accounts from Kenninghall in 1525 (NRO Rye 74, fols 1–14), analysed by Richard Howlett as 'The Household Accounts of Kenninghall Palace in the year 1525', *Norfolk Archaeology* 15 (1904), 51–60, these cover only 26 days.

[69] For more on using household accounts in this way, see Woolgar, *The Great Household*, 8–29.

[70] UCB, MS UCB 49.   [71] CUL, Pembroke MS 300.

[72] Woolgar, *The Great Household*, 12.

[73] By this time, nobles no longer dined publicly in the great hall or even the great chamber except on special occasions; meals were taken in the lord's chamber, or in the lady's chamber when the lord was absent. See Woolgar, *The Great Household*, 145–6.

[74] CUL, Pembroke MS 300.

during this year, that number reduced to somewhere between twelve and sixteen. In 1523–4 while her husband was away for an extended period during his service as Lieutenant of the North, she dined with around twenty people at dinner in her own chamber, which could suggest that when she had been officially left 'in charge' of the household, she augmented the level of service she received accordingly to provide a visual sign of her temporary authority.[75]

The kinds of visitors welcomed into the Norfolks' home in both these years are what we would expect. They included kin, other nobles, local gentry, household officials, workmen, clergy, travellers, and their servants. Unsurprisingly, overall visitor numbers were far higher when Elizabeth's husband was present in 1526–7 than in 1523–4 when she entertained alone, but this was probably not only to do with her gender and position. In 1523, her husband had yet to become Duke of Norfolk, which meant that his father was the major patron for most of the local gentry, whereas by 1526 this had changed, so the number of visitors probably reflected this. The difference—broadly speaking—lay in the visits of local gentry men. While the 1526–7 book records a steady stream of Knyvetts, Wingfields, Sheltons, Waldegraves, Jerninghams, and other East Anglian gentry, the 1523–4 book is far more limited. This strongly suggests that these men's patron was Elizabeth's husband, and not Elizabeth herself, which makes sense since she could not promote them to office or offer the same kinds of financial perks. It may also suggest that Elizabeth was not perceived to be able to influence her husband, since the gentry do not seem to have approached her as a conduit for his patronage.

Nevertheless, Elizabeth did offer considerable hospitality on specific occasions during her husband's absence. In August 1523, she welcomed her in-laws for what appears to have been a family celebration. Her parents-in-law Thomas and Agnes, the Duke and Duchess of Norfolk, and their children Anne, Countess of Oxford, Elizabeth, Dorothy, and Thomas, along with her aunt-in-law Lady Wyndham, all ate dinner and supper in her chamber, and stayed until the next day.[76] The reason for this gathering is not given, but clearly there were good relations between the branches of the family at this stage. Elizabeth also extended continual hospitality to her husband's aunts, Ladies Wyndham and Timperley, and to her half-sister-in-law Anne, Countess of Oxford, who stayed at Stoke and Kenninghall for short periods to escape marital problems.[77] Clearly a noblewoman's household could offer a refuge to kin. Elizabeth also hosted a wedding celebration for a member of the local gentry, Thomas Redding, in 1523. The bridal party dined in 'the bryde chamber', a room designated for the event.[78] As was usual, very few members of the aristocracy came to dine with the Howards, as most peers were too busy holding court in their own localities to venture any great distance to visit one another. However, in September 1523 when Elizabeth was 'in charge' but absent in London, one of the more local peers, the Earl of Essex, visited, and was served in the great chamber even though the lord and lady of the house were absent, as a reflection of his status. Likewise, though Elizabeth and her husband

---

[75] UCB, MS UCB 49. [76] Ibid. [77] Ibid. [78] Ibid.

spent Christmas at court this year and were away until mid-January, 'my lord marques' (Thomas Grey, Marquess of Dorset) visited on 3 January 1524 and was also feasted in the great chamber.[79]

Elizabeth also used hospitality to maintain her own friendships made during her time at court. Across the year 1523–4, several of Catherine of Aragon's ladies-in-waiting visited her. While several were also distant Howard kin, and might therefore have visited in that capacity rather than as court friends, Ladies Parr and Gray, and Mistress Parker, with 'another of the Queen's maids', all visited during this year, some of them more than once.[80] The fact that East Anglia was not remotely close to home for most of them demonstrates the importance of hospitality in maintaining these kinds of networks, as well as the emphasis that Elizabeth attached to them. Elizabeth continued to visit court at regular intervals, suggesting that she continued to serve as a lady-in-waiting for set periods of time. The 'default' image that we have of Elizabeth is usually that of her in isolation following her objection to her husband's mistress in the 1530s, but this household book shows that this was by no means the case earlier in her life.

The household books not only show who visited the Howards but also the food placed before the family and their guests. This, too, was a form of material display; the lord and lady were expected to eat a broad range of expensive and elite foods, and they were expected to offer the same to their high-status guests. Meat, bread, and beer were staples for everybody. What singled out the elites was the variety of different kinds of meat that they consumed, and the fact that it included venison. Venison was the food of the rich, since only they could afford to possess and maintain deer parks, and consumption of it was a deliberate and overt marker of status. As well as venison from the parks, the Howards' estates also provided some fish from the ponds, and mutton and chicken from the fields. Nevertheless, the weekly lists of purchases for Tendring Hall in the 1526/7 book show that pork, chicken, beef, rabbit, and so forth were regularly bought elsewhere.[81] This was the same for most of the items consumed by the household. The 1546 inventory of Kenninghall shows that there was a bakehouse, brewhouse, fishhouse, millhouse, and slaughterhouse all on site, which meant much of what was eaten was prepared then and there even if produce had come from further afield; once again, the existence of all of these specialist household departments was a marker of the nobility of the house owner.[82] As was usual, the household observed a fish day on Fridays. Those dining in the hall could expect the less exciting foods like flounders and whiting, while the lord, lady, and higher-status guests would be offered an enormous variety of freshwater and seawater fish from pike to herring, as well as stockfish and saltfish. They also consumed shellfish in the form of oysters.

The variety of food on special feast-days vastly exceeded that on ordinary days, because these were days on which extra guests might be expected and culinary magnificence was therefore required. While in 1523 the lord and lady spent Christmas at court, in 1526 they spent it at home at Tendring Hall.[83] The book shows that

[79] Ibid.   [80] Ibid.   [81] CUL, Pembroke MS 300.
[82] TNA LR 2/117.   [83] CUL, Pembroke MS 300.

Christmas Day itself was not the time for feeding the masses. Boxing Day, and the Saturday following Christmas Day, were the big visiting days in Christmas week and on that Saturday 362 people were fed in the hall at dinner. Across the week there were so many extra people dining with the lord and lady that some were accommodated on tables in the parlour. New Year's Day, too, was a big day for visiting, and probably also for gift-giving, and 60 messes of people were served in the hall. Interestingly, of the food purchased in advance of Christmas, much of it was birds, including plovers, curlews, woodcocks, redshanks, ducks, and goose, which was an expensive luxury already becoming associated with Christmas. Other high-status birds, notably swans and a peacock, were received as gifts. On Christmas Day itself, there was the traditional stuffed boar's head served to the lord, the lady, and their highest-status guests at dinner, among the birds mentioned above, with venison and 'ginger brede'. The household did not have boar, but they did enjoy custards, brawn (a kind of terrine), and 'bakemetes' which appear to have been pies. The expenditure on food for the week of Christmas came to £26 6s. 3½d., and the week after, which included New Year's Day, it came to £31 9s. 6½d.[84] While between Christmas and New Year the food was mostly 'ordinary' fare, on New Year's Day itself boar's head, venison, small birds, and roast veal made another appearance, highlighting this as another feast-day.

The exercise of hospitality demonstrates, perhaps more clearly than any other form of materiality, the inescapable significance of 'stuff' as an indicator of status. The Duke and Duchess had no option but to entertain on this scale; magnificence and munificence were a duty even more than they were a pleasure. This had more to do with individual than collective status and was based on social hierarchy. A duke and duchess were at the top of the aristocratic pile and, correspondingly, more was expected of them materially than those with lesser titles, though consequently they also had more to lose from failing to be bountiful in this way.

Noble generosity was evidenced further through the practice of gift-giving. Gift-giving, or gift exchange, was at the core of the early modern political system during this period, for both men and women.[85] Gifts were given to create or maintain social connections, and to reinforce requests for favours, or build up 'credit' for future requests. Gifting was a non-optional social convention across society, but the many different kinds of gifts all held their own subtle implications. One of the most ubiquitous among elites as well as other social echelons was the gift of food. Food gifts carried particular connotations of social dialogue because they were consumable. Once the item was eaten, the giver was within her rights to send another, thereby initiating a continuing dialogue between herself and her recipient.[86] Gifts of food were especially personal when the item had been handmade by the giver, and this was more likely to be the case with food gifted by women. Interestingly, all the extant examples of this nature from the Howard women show them gifting food products to other women, suggesting that food

[84] Ibid.   [85] On gifting, see Felicity Heal, *The Power of Gifts* (Oxford, 2013).
[86] Felicity Heal, 'Food Gifts, the Household and the Politics of Exchange in Early Modern England', *Past and Present* 199 (2008), 41–70.

was used by them as a means of maintaining female networks. Dorothy Howard/ Stanley, Countess of Derby, sent 'oringe pyes' to Princess Mary in 1538. It is likely that this gift was homemade, and as it contained both oranges, which had to be imported, and copious quantities of sugar, it was expensive and therefore a mark of the esteem in which the giver held the recipient.[87] Agnes Tylney/Howard, dowager Duchess of Norfolk, sent cakes to Mary in 1544, which were probably also homemade, and brawn to Anne of Cleves in 1539.[88] Elizabeth Stafford/Howard, Duchess of Norfolk, recorded that she had sent almond butter and wafer cakes to her sister's family in the late 1530s.[89]

Elizabeth also used a gift of food in 1531 as a 'cover up' for a greater gift. She sent Catherine of Aragon poultry and an orange, 'enclosing' a letter from Gregory Casali, the King's papal envoy dealing with the matter of the divorce in Rome.[90] This was immensely risky for both Elizabeth and Catherine. Though Chapuys, whose report this was, thought that Elizabeth might have done this with the knowledge of her husband, it became clear that this was not the case, which meant that she was not only defying the King by passing on this information, but also her family. Whether she had merely rifled her husband's papers and removed or copied those of interest to her mistress, or whether she was an established conduit between Casali and Catherine, is unknown. The material aspect to this is equally fascinating. Chapuys does not say whether the letter was merely given to Catherine alongside the gifts, or whether it was somehow concealed within them, nor who had been employed to deliver it. Luckily for both women, Elizabeth's espionage does not seem to have been detected, which demonstrates that the practice of gift-giving was an ideal means for women to engage in such suspect political activity.

The food gift most commonly given and received among the aristocracy was venison from their deer parks, which were themselves a very obvious sign of wealth and status. Both women and men participated in the exchange of venison. For the Howards, there are surviving accounts made by Richard Parker, keeper of the deer park at Framlingham, from 1509–13, and 1515–20.[91] These provide a list of the deer given by the Howards to their clients and include deer gifted by Agnes Tylney/ Howard, Duchess of Norfolk. The family used venison as a regular gift for local gentry, family friends, favoured household servants, clergy, and, of course, other nobles. The account records most of these gifts of venison as commanded by Agnes's husband, Thomas, Earl of Surrey and later Second Duke of Norfolk, and only a few were specifically recorded as given by Agnes. However, this does not necessarily mean that Agnes was less active in the gifting of venison than her husband; her commands may simply have been relayed by him, and thus recorded as his desire. Where the account does specify that venison was gifted at Agnes's commandment, it shows she gave it to male and female members of local gentry

[87] Madden (ed.), *The Privy Purse Expenses of the Princess Mary*, 58. See also Herbert, *Female Alliances*, 55–7.

[88] Madden (ed.), *The Privy Purse Expenses of the Princess Mary*, 155; TNA E101/422/15.

[89] TNA SP1/158, fol. 201.   [90] *LP* IV, 6738.

[91] BL Add. MS 27421, fols 11–25; BL Add. Ch. 17745 (unfoliated).

families, such as William Bucknam and Lady Capell, her own servants, such as Robert Hogon, and local clergymen.[92]

The Howard women also received gifts of venison, and even asked for them directly—one of the few instances where *asking* for a gift was socially acceptable.[93] Elizabeth, Duchess of Norfolk, seemed to consider presents of venison as a kind of barometer of social success. Writing to Thomas Cromwell in 1534 after her husband had removed her to Redbourn, she complained that 'there be meny of my ffrendes that sent me venyson the last yere that dare not sende me noon this yere for my lordes displeasure', and claimed that her husband had not sent her any either, which was hardly surprising under the circumstances.[94] To remedy this lack, she asked Cromwell to send her some 'whan you see tyme conuenyent'. Ordinarily, requests for venison were made when a large entertainment was on the horizon, not to try to claw back social prestige or lost connections. It is perhaps significant that Elizabeth phrased her request by asking Cromwell to 'have her in remembrance' for venison, since what she was really seeking was continued social contact and a way out of the isolation in which she now found herself.

As well as food, jewellery was used for gifts designed to be particularly personal, not only because it was valuable but because it was worn close to the body. Among the Howard women and indeed elites in general, rings were used as 'tokens', a word which was used to mean a small, modest gift—'just a token'—or something evidencing a hidden meaning, feeling, or sign, such as the authority or affection of the owner.[95] The 1546 inventory of Howard residences shows that the Duke's mistress Bess Holland participated in the exchange of rings as tokens with her female friends. She possessed one ring which had been sent to her by Mistress Mary Shelton, and another from Mistress Freston, both of whom were local.[96] Elizabeth, Duchess of Norfolk, sent a gold ring to her sister Catherine, Countess of Westmorland, in 1540.[97] The way in which ownership and personal identity remained part of an object even after it had been given away is demonstrated by a Chancery case in which one Lucy Lacy and her new husband sued Ralph Crayford for the return of a number of rings: one was described as having previously belonged to Agnes, Duchess of Norfolk, showing that they thought that this information might lend importance, and thus a fast resolution, to their case.[98] 'Tokens' were also part of marriage negotiation, so much so that when the secret marriage between Lord Thomas Howard and Lady Margaret Douglas was suspected in 1536, one of the questions asked of both parties and of the witnesses was what tokens they had exchanged, presumably to help prove that marriage had been intended. On this occasion, rings again proved key; Lord Thomas had sent Lady Margaret 'oon crampe ring', and had received in return one diamond and her 'phisnamye painted', i.e. her portrait.[99] Material culture could therefore confirm, but also condemn.

---

[92] BL Add. MS 27421, fol. 21, and BL Add. Ch. 17745.   [93] Heal, *The Power of Gifts*, 42.
[94] BL Cotton MS Vespasian F XIII, fol. 151.   [95] Heal, *The Power of Gifts*, 31–4.
[96] TNA LR 2/116.   [97] TNA SP1/158, fol. 201.
[98] TNA C1/147/56.   [99] TNA E36/120/65.

Textiles, too, were personal gifts, particularly embroidery or needlework, since this was usually made by the giver and represented time invested in the relationship.[100] They were also gendered, as men never gave needlework. Some Howard women used embroidery as New Year gifts for the monarch; Agnes, Duchess of Norfolk sent the King 'a table of nedilworke wrought w[i]t[h] golde and silke' in 1534.[101] Elizabeth Howard/Boleyn, Countess of Wiltshire, gave 'a cofer of nedill work' in 1532, and in 1534 'a case of blak velyuet enbrawdered with the kinges armes'.[102] In 1557, Elizabeth, dowager Duchess of Norfolk, sent the queen 'a cusshen cloth frengid & tasselled with golde'.[103] New Year gifts were presented publicly, and were a time-honoured way to gain favour with the monarch as well as to proclaim the loyalty of oneself and one's family.[104] The point, as with all gifts, was to give something that would remind the recipient of the giver. During Henry VIII's reign many noblewomen gave him personal items like shirts or handkerchiefs for this reason, but a glance over the extant lists suggests that the king received so many of these items that he would have been hard put to know whose work—usually black-work embroidery—adorned the handkerchief he picked up on any given day. The Howard women, by giving items like those above, stood out from the crowd, and yet still managed to retain a personal touch by using their own needlework.

Gifts, like everything else, were subject to trend. The most ubiquitous gift that Mary I received from women in 1557 was money in various forms, and both Frances de Vere/Howard, dowager Countess of Surrey, and Margaret Gamage/Howard, Lady Howard of Effingham, gave coins worth £5. Anne Howard/de Vere, dowager Countess of Oxford, however, was older than both of the others and was the only woman to give the Queen a salt.[105] Livestock of various sorts remained popular presents among the nobility, the more exotic the better. Dorothy Howard/Stanley, Countess of Derby, gave Princess Mary a parrot in 1538.[106]

Women also gave expensive decorative items. Some of these, like the carving knives given by Elizabeth, Duchess of Norfolk, to Cromwell in 1535, or the tablet of gold that Mary, Duchess of Richmond, gave to the King in 1534, were relatively common gift items for women of their status.[107] Others, like the needlework gifts above, were more creative, while still being appropriate. Agnes, Duchess of Norfolk, gave the King 'the byrthe of o[u]r lord in a box'—probably a carved nativity scene—in 1532.[108] One Duchess of Norfolk sent Margaret of Austria, Duchess of Savoy, a 'jardin clos'—a three-dimensional artificial garden made of silk flowers, with figures of the holy family in the middle—at some point before 1516.[109]

---

[100] Lisa M. Klein, 'Your Humble Handmaid: Elizabethan Gifts of Needlework', *Renaissance Quarterly* 50 (1997), 459–93.
[101] TNA E101/421/13.   [102] TNA E101/420/15, fol. 5; E101/421/13.
[103] BL Add. MS 62525.
[104] Maria Hayward, 'Gift Giving at the Court of Henry VIII: The 1539 New Year's Gift Roll in Context', *Antiquaries Journal* 85 (2005), 125–75.
[105] BL Add. MS 62525.   [106] BL Royal MS 17 B, xxviii, fol. 41.
[107] TNA SP1/91, fol. 23; TNA E101/421/13.   [108] TNA E101/420/15, fol. 4v.
[109] Dagmar Eichberger, *Leben mit Kunst, Wirken durch Kunst: Sammelwesen und Hofkunst unter Margarete von Österreich, Reentin der Niederlande* (Turnhout, 2002), 398–9. The gift is listed in an inventory taken in 1516, but the exact date of receipt is not given.

Because the gift is listed in an inventory and neither the date of receipt, nor the given name of the Duchess of Norfolk are recorded, it is difficult to be sure who, exactly, the sender was. For any of the possible candidates to send a gift to Margaret of Savoy at all is worthy of comment, since it was not usual for noblewomen of one country to send presents to female rulers elsewhere unless the ruler was English, or unless they were related, and neither of these was true here. Agnes Tylney/Howard, who held the title Duchess of Norfolk from 1514, is the most likely to have met her in person. Agnes and her husband were the escorts for Henry VIII's sister Mary on her marriage to the French King Louis XII in 1514, and it is possible that Margaret also attended, since she had strong links to the French court.[110] We must also note that Anne Boleyn, who was Agnes's step-granddaughter, had been in service with Margaret of Savoy until 1514, at which point she was recalled in order to serve the new French Queen, Princess Mary Tudor.[111] There is a slim possibility that Agnes's gift might have been related to Margaret's care of Anne. Regardless, this demonstrates the vast geographical and political reach afforded to noblewomen through gift-giving.

The household was the site of much of women's material creation and patronage.[112] For women, artistic patronage was an important form of self-expression, and, in many cases, a way to exert direct political, religious, or dynastic influence. Elizabeth Tylney/Bourchier/Howard, Countess of Surrey, is known to have been a patroness of the poet John Skelton during the late fifteenth century. His poem *The Garlande of Laurell* describes a meeting with her at which she calls him 'my clerke' and gives him a garland of laurel leaves woven by her ladies for 'his servyce', in payment for which he then gives each of the ladies a flattering verse.[113] The poem says that this took place at Sherriff Hutton Castle in Yorkshire, which was the then-residence of the Howard family, suggesting some sort of patron–client connection. Walker has argued that Elizabeth's patronage of Skelton at this time—*c*.1494–5—suggests that she was trying to keep up with the movement of fashions at court during her absence.[114] Skelton was a favoured poet of both the King and his mother Margaret, Duchess of Richmond, so by employing him, Elizabeth not only gained whatever court gossip he had to offer her, but demonstrated her continued connection to the centre of politics, as well as perhaps pleasing Skelton's royal patrons. This was important not only for herself but for her family: at this time, her husband was working to gain the favour of Henry VII after his previous support of Richard III. Elizabeth's use of this kind of material culture, then, speaks not only for a potential interest in poetry, but also for the way in which women sought to exercise agency through patronage on behalf of themselves and their families.

---

[110] Leland, *Collectanea*, I, ii, p. 701.

[111] *The Manuscripts of J. Eliot Hodgkin*, HMC Fifteenth Report (London, 1897), 30 (letter from Thomas Boleyn to Margaret of Savoy asking her to release his daughter).

[112] Broomhall, 'Materializing Women'.

[113] John Skelton, 'The Garlande or Chapelet of Laurell' (printed by Richard Faukes 1523). See Greg Walker, *John Skelton and the Politics of the 1520s* (Cambridge, 2002), and M. J. Tucker, 'The Ladies in Skelton's "Garland of Laurel"', *Renaissance Quarterly* 22:4 (1969), 333–45.

[114] Walker, *John Skelton and the Politics of the 1520s*, 22.

Mary Howard/Fitzroy, Duchess of Richmond, used literary patronage for the purpose of religious, rather than political, influence in the 1540s and 1550s. In 1548 she hired John Foxe as tutor to her nieces and nephews, which was surely a conscious attempt to affect the religious inclinations of the next generation, thereby promoting the continuity of the new faith in general and specifically within her own family. It was during this time under her roof that Foxe began work on the earliest form of his infamous *Book of Martyrs*, in which some of Mary's reminiscences of her former mistress and cousin Anne Boleyn are immortalized.[115] Mary also harboured the controversial cleric John Bale on his return from exile in 1547, and he was then her go-between with the translator Nicholas Lesse, who declared in his dedication of St Augustine's *Twelve Steps of Abuse* that she was as desirous as he was that such works should come into the hands of ordinary people.[116] In this way Mary was able to use her status and her connections to promote the evangelical cause.

Art, particularly portraits, also served the purposes of display, of fashion, of commemoration, and of influence through patronage. The same Skelton poem that lauds the Countess of Surrey and her ladies mentions one 'Newton', who was busy drawing the scene before him, suggesting that the family employed a draughtsman of some sort. Princess Mary's privy purse expenses reward 'my lady of Derbys servant for drawing a wourke for my ladys grace', showing that Dorothy Howard/Stanley, Countess of Derby, also had an artist of some sort in her employ, and that apparently this was a way to gain the attention of royalty.[117] The Duke of Norfolk had a collection of twenty-eight portraits of 'dyverse noble persons' at Kenninghall in 1546, as was the fashion; it demonstrated his connectedness to his peers and thus his noble status.[118] Some of the women were also painted by the best artists of their day. Mary Howard/Fitzroy, Duchess of Richmond, was sketched by Holbein, wearing a striking hat adorned with feathers, and Foister suggests that the finished portrait was among her father's collection.[119] There is also a portrait of Mary recorded in the inventory of Henry VIII in 1547, 'with Darbie [probably an animal] sitting upon her knees'. This portrait probably ended up in the King's collection because Mary had married his illegitimate son, and it would therefore have functioned as a remembrance of her connection to the royal family.[120] Frances de Vere/Howard, Countess of Surrey, was sketched by Holbein at a similar time, most likely to mark her marriage to Henry Howard, Earl of Surrey, in 1533.

An extension of the patronage of artists was the commissioning of tomb effigies and brasses, an area in which the Howard women were very active during this period. This, indeed, was a typically female interaction with material culture, because

---

[115] Elizabeth Evenden and Thomas Freeman, *Religion and the Book in Early Modern England: The Making of Foxe's 'Book of Martyrs'* (Cambridge, 2011), 36–52.

[116] Nicholas Lesse (trans.), *The twelfe steppes of abuses write[n] by the famus doctor S. Augustine translated out of laten by Nicolas Lesse*, EEBO [accessed 3 February 1515], dedication (3–4).

[117] BL Royal MS 17 B xxviii, fol. 67, printed as Frederick Madden (ed.), *Privy Purse Expenses of the Princess Mary 1536–1544* (London, 1831), 101.

[118] TNA LR2/116.   [119] Susan Foister, *Holbein in England* (London, 2006), 54.

[120] Ibid.; Starkey, *The Inventory of Henry VIII Vol I. The Transcript*, no. 15406.

widows were generally responsible for carrying out their husbands' requests concerning burial and commemoration.[121] This cast women as custodians of dynastic memory, and meant they were therefore largely responsible for telling or creating the dynastic story remembered by future generations. Naturally, this was a role not only of enormous familial significance, but for families like the Howards, of potentially national political import.[122] Agnes Tylney/Howard, dowager Duchess of Norfolk, appears to have ignored her husband's instructions, which were to carry out the design he had had made for his tomb, including her own effigy as well as his, at Thetford Priory. A contemporary image of his tomb shows only his own effigy, without hers, and without any room to add it later.[123] Instead, she later had a chest tomb with a brass effigy made for herself and placed in the centre of the Howard chapel in St Mary's Church, Lambeth.[124] She was probably behind the creation of this chapel in the first instance. Although most antiquarians state that it was built by her husband, it was she who provided the candles for the consecration of the chapel in July 1522.[125] The churchwardens' accounts consistently describe it as 'my Lady Norfolk's chapel', and she herself called it 'my chappil at Lambhith' in her will.[126] This is the only known instance of a Howard woman undertaking an architectural project during this period.[127] As it turned out, it was lucky that she did. At the dissolution of the family's original burial place, Thetford Priory, in 1540, Agnes was able to move her husband's body to Lambeth, and, as I have argued elsewhere, had a brass set into the floor to commemorate him.[128] She was also most likely responsible for the brass commemorating her daughter-in-law Katherine Broughton/Howard in 1535 in Lambeth, as well as plaques for her daughter Elizabeth Howard/Radcliffe, Lady Fitzwater, in 1534, and her sons who had died in infancy. In fact, Agnes's agency concerning burials in the Lambeth chapel is such that she appears to have been responsible for creating an alternative family mausoleum commemorating her own family line.

Clearly, then, material culture was a key means by which the Howard women could claim and exercise individual agency. Commissioning and purchasing goods and objects gave them economic power. Agnes, Duchess of Norfolk's, commissioning of what would have been expensive tombs and brasses, for instance, supported

[121] Barbara J. Harris, 'The Fabric of Piety: Aristocratic Women and Care of the Dead, 1450–1550', *Journal of British Studies* 48 (2009), 308–35.

[122] For more on women as custodians of familial memory, see James Daybell, 'Gender, Politics and Archives in Early Modern England', in Daybell and Norrhem (eds), *Gender and Political Culture in Early Modern Europe, 1400–1800*, 25–45.

[123] Her will of 1542 shows that she had already built her tomb: TNA PROB 11/30/596. The image of Norfolk's tomb is in BL Add. MS 45131, fol. 85.

[124] This tomb is depicted in Henry Lilly, *The genealogie of the princeley familie of the Howards* (1638), unpublished manuscript, Arundel Castle Archive.

[125] Charles Drew (ed.), *Lambeth Churchwardens' Accounts 1504–1645 and Vestry Book 1610*, Surrey Record Society 18 (1941), 2 vols, I, 41.

[126] Ibid. I, 73–4., 100; II, 195; TNA PROB 11/30/596.

[127] Margaret, Duchess of Norfolk, did supervise building work during her husband's absence, but there is no evidence that she herself commissioned it. Crawford, *The Household Books of John Howard*, I, 184–6.

[128] Clark, 'The Gendering of Dynastic Memory'.

individual craftsmen, the industry as a whole, and thereby the local economy. Materiality could offer religious agency and legacy too, as per Mary, Duchess of Richmond, who offered employment, house-room, and patronage to some of the early Reformation's most influential evangelical writers. Making and distributing objects was an accepted route to political influence, and the Howard women seem to have gifted objects with sensitivity, having a keen grasp of what was both fashionable and appropriate for each recipient.

Materiality also gave these women a means to claim dynastic identity. The objects surrounding them tended to illustrate both natal and marital identities, usually by means of badges or heraldry. However, material culture, most notably the production of objects, allowed them to publicly proclaim their own understanding of their identity at times when that identity was threatened, as Elizabeth Stafford/Howard, Duchess of Norfolk, did by embroidering bed textiles for herself and her husband in the face of their failing relationship. Kinship relations could therefore be played out materially, which affords us another level of insight into the nature of these relationships at different times. Such analysis clearly shows that the Howard women did not use materiality purely in support of their marital families, but were equally concerned to form and maintain personal networks and connections. Aside from the use of dynastic branding on publicly displayed objects, materially speaking, dynasties like the Howards did not operate as collectives. The Howard women did not select their material interests with wider dynastic motives in mind as a deliberate means of advancing the whole family, unlike, for instance, the Orange–Nassau dynasty of early modern Europe as demonstrated by Susan Broomhall and Jacqueline Van Gent.[129] This may be partly because the Howards, unlike many European aristocratic dynasties, were not contending with cultural or dynastic expansion across national borders. However, this chapter has also shown that the uneven nature of material wealth across families was an accepted fact at this time in England: possessing the Howard name did not mean that one could, or was expected to, compete materially with those at the head of the dynasty. In a similar vein, when one individual or family group were materially disadvantaged as the result of political crisis, the rest were not bound to step in and rescue them. On several occasions, this left Howard women materially stranded. For women, then, material culture could function as a way to gain and express agency, but it could also be used against them as a means of control.

---

[129] Broomhall and Van Gent, *Dynastic Colonialism.*

3

'To wise for a woman'
Marital Strife and Dynastic Identity

To marry was, for noblewomen, a non-negotiable duty. While Amy Froide has shown that lower-class women and even a few classed as 'gentry' were able to remain unmarried, this was demonstrably not the case for aristocratic daughters: every girl born into the Howard dynasty across this period married at least once, and part of the Howards' success as a dynasty lay in the fact that they produced plenty of female offspring who could be used to create valuable alliances.[1] However, the way that the family negotiated marriages was no different from other noble dynasties, except perhaps in terms of their success in using marriage to regain status and finances. There is little indication that Howard daughters exercised choice over their first husbands, but they do seem to have had influence over second marriages, either to choose a second husband freely, or to block a distasteful proposal, as Mary Howard/Fitzroy, Duchess of Richmond, appears to have done when faced with marrying Thomas Seymour in 1538.[2] Interestingly, the vast majority of women born into the Howard dynasty across this period married only once, choosing to spend lengthy periods as comparatively independent widows with closer alliances to their natal Howards than to their marital relations.[3] While a number of high-status women chose to marry far beneath them for the second time, no woman born into the Howard dynasty made this choice; only Frances de Vere/Howard, Countess of Surrey, is known to have done so, and it is not difficult to imagine why she may have wanted to retire from public, political life after the execution of her first husband Henry Howard, Earl of Surrey, in 1547.[4] This does suggest that for many Howard women, natal identity was very strong.

While there were clear strategic aims in the way that marriages were made in the Howard dynasty during this period, the family was only unusual in that it operated at the very top of the aristocratic hierarchy and was therefore able to use marital alliances to successfully recover and bolster both status and finances. Where they

---

[1] Amy M. Froide, *Never Married: Singlewomen in Early Modern England* (Oxford, 2005).

[2] TNA SP1/134, fol. 160r–v. For more on choice in marriage, see Harris, *English Aristocratic Women*, 56–8.

[3] Of those born into the Howard dynasty during this period, only Muriel Howard/Grey/Knyvett and Katherine Howard/ap Rhys/Daubeney, Countess of Bridgwater, married more than once. Several more who had married into the Howard dynasty did marry more than once, either before or after their Howard alliance.

[4] See Kimberly Schutte, 'Marrying Out in the Sixteenth Century: Subsequent Marriages of Aristocratic Women in the Tudor Era', *Journal of Family History* 38 (2013), 3–16.

were different, however, was in the experience of some of these women within marriage. By and large, the marriages made by and for members of the family, including women, seem to have been as successful as others of their class, and for several couples there is clear evidence of a happy partnership.[5] However, three women close to the core of the dynasty experienced severe marital problems, even 'failed' marriages, almost simultaneously during the 1520s and 1530s. While marital strife was not unknown among the English aristocracy, it is highly unusual to find so much within one family during such a short space of time.[6] Indeed, the records generated by these episodes tell us more, in some ways, about the way in which the family operated as a whole, and the agency of women in this context, and this chapter therefore reconstructs these disputes for this purpose.

Anne Howard/de Vere, Countess of Oxford, struggled as a young wife to exert any influence over her husband John de Vere, Fourteenth Earl of Oxford, as he frittered away his inheritance, drank and gambled, and allowed his friends to turn him against her in the 1520s. By enlisting the help of her kin and of Cardinal Wolsey, Anne secured an unusual legal intervention to attempt to force her husband to toe the line. Her sister Katherine Howard/ap Rhys/Daubeney, later Countess of Bridgwater, went one step further, formally separating from her second husband Henry Daubeney in 1535 with the help of a church court and Thomas Cromwell. Elizabeth Stafford/Howard, Duchess of Norfolk, in the best-known saga of the three, openly struggled with her husband's adultery until he banished her to a separate house in the mid-1530s. There she remained for much of Henry's reign, writing letters to Cromwell campaigning for alimony and detailing the various abuses she had received at Norfolk's hands. Studies have shown that when early modern aristocratic women ran into marital trouble, they generally turned to their natal families for assistance, as indeed the Howard women did, suggesting that natal identity gained additional importance for women in times of crisis.[7] For those of sufficient rank, the 'state'—usually in the form of the King's chief advisers— might also be called upon, or become involved, in resolving marital issues, as again occurred in these cases.[8] Taken together, however, the three cases discussed here show that the attitudes of the women, their families, and the state towards their marriage problems could often be at odds. It would be easy to assume that when this occurred, the woman would lose out, since by law she was under coverture

---

[5] Thomas Howard, Second Duke of Norfolk, left his second wife Agnes Tylney/Howard all of his movable goods in his will and made her executrix, suggesting a happy marriage. PROB 11/21/249.

[6] The closest comparative I have found is the Brandon family, where Anne Brandon/Grey, Lady Powis, and Mary Brandon/Stanley, Lady Monteagle, daughters of Charles Brandon, Duke of Suffolk, both suffered marital problems across the 1520s, 1530s, and 1540s. See S. J. Gunn, *Charles Brandon, Duke of Suffolk, c.1484–1545* (Oxford, 1988), 94–5 and 174–5.

[7] Tim Stretton, 'Marriage, Separation and the Common Law in England, 1540–1660', in Helen Berry and Elizabeth Foyster (eds), *The Family in Early Modern England* (Cambridge, 2007), 18–39; Susan Dwyer Amussen, ' "Being stirred to much unquietness": Violence and Domestic Violence in Early Modern England', *Journal of Women's History* 6:2 (1994), 70–89; Harris, 'Marriage Sixteenth-Century Style'.

[8] See also S. E. James, 'A Tudor Divorce: The Marital History of William Parr, Marquess of Northampton', *Transactions of the Cumberland and Westmorland Antiquarian and Archaeological Society* 90 (1990), 199–204.

and had no legal recourse. It is argued here, however, that they were often able to exercise agency in 'soft' forms, through letter-writing, seeking appropriate patronage, and—crucially—through enlisting the help of kin.

ANNE: 'FOR THE ST[A]YING OF HIS HONOR AND MYN'

Anne, as the eldest daughter of the Second Duke of Norfolk and his second wife Agnes Tylney, was the first of her full sisters to be married. Her marriage to John de Vere, heir to the earldom of Oxford, was arranged by both their fathers by November 1511, when Anne and John were both about 13, and had taken place by September 1512.[9] The match was marginally more advantageous for the Howards than for the de Veres. In rank and political favour, the two families were equal—both held earldoms, both had equivalent wealth and lands, and both were active at court—but the de Veres held the better, that is the older, noble pedigree, and so this match was part of the Howards' attempt to legitimize their own nobility. Initially, matters unfolded in the best possible way for the Howards. The Earl of Oxford died in 1513, and the Howards were granted the new Earl's wardship.[10] He was brought up in Thomas Howard's household alongside his future wife. On his twenty-first birthday in August 1520 he was granted livery of lands, and it is likely that the couple then moved to Hedingham Castle in Essex, the main seat of the earldom of Oxford, and began married life together as adults.[11] Within three short years, however, the Oxfords' marriage was in serious difficulties.

The major source for this episode is a series of contemporary letters written by Anne to Cardinal Wolsey over the course of a year, beginning in April 1523 and culminating in a Chancery ordinance in February 1524.[12] The root of the problem appears to have been the chasm between ideal noble conduct and Oxford's actual behaviour. The ordinance ordered him to make no grants or annuities without the advice of Cardinal Wolsey, so that 'the great Decaie of his Lands' could be avoided; he was to 'use himself honourably, prudently, and sadly, forbearinge all riotous and wild companies, excessive and superfluous apparel'; 'have a vigilant regard that he use not much to drink hot wines, ne to drink or sitt up late'; 'moderate his hunteing or other Disports'; 'give no Ear to simple or evil tongued Persons'; and 'lovinglie, familiarlie, and kindlie intreate and demeane himself towards the said Countesse his wife', which gives a fairly thorough indication of the issues at hand.[13] Moreover, the letters show that he was failing to retain the officers that were needed to help manage a noble estate and household; he lacked a steward, surveyor, treasurer,

---

[9] As stated in the will of Anne's father-in-law the Thirteenth Earl of Oxford; TNA PROB 11/17/379.

[10] *LP* 1, 2964 (80).   [11] *LP* III, 956.

[12] TNA SP1/27, fols 149–56. Four manuscript copies of the ordinance survive: BL Add. MS 34324, fols 1–2; BL Add. MS 46410, fol. 165; BL Hargrave MS 227, fols 472–76; BL Hargrave MS 249, fol. 226. The latter is printed as Henry Ellis, 'Copy of an Order made by Cardinal Wolsey, as Lord Chancellor, respecting the Management of the Affairs of the young Earl of Oxford', *Archaeologia* 19 (1821), 62–5, and is the one to which this study will refer.

[13] BL Hargrave MS 249, fol. 226.

receiver, and auditor. Evidently the young Earl was not interested in mundane matters like estate management. It seems highly unlikely that he would not have been taught the skills of administration and management that an earl needed during his time as the Duke of Norfolk's ward, which makes this episode look very much as though the freedom of his majority had gone to his head.

It is likely that Anne initially followed the usual strategy of wives experiencing problems with their husbands, and appealed to her natal relatives, the Howards.[14] In one letter, she mentioned 'my cosyn Tylney, my servant' as her go-between with Wolsey.[15] The Tylneys were the natal family of Anne's mother Agnes, Duchess of Norfolk, and it is plausible that Anne's use of a Tylney cousin in this affair reflects her mother's knowledge and involvement—this would argue for the importance not only of natal relatives, but of female kinship networks in such circumstances. The Chancery ordinance enrolled in February 1524 implies her father's involvement as well, stating that the couple were to return to live under his roof.[16] Later in the sequence of letters she also mentioned her half-brother Thomas, later Third Duke of Norfolk.[17] Interestingly, her brother, not her father, was the male relative most active in her cause throughout this year. This may have been because her father was in his eighties and had retired from public, political life by this point, allowing his son to take over many of his former roles; perhaps this applied to familial as well as political concerns.[18] When in need of succour on at least two occasions she was sheltered by her brother and not her parents.[19] After their father's death in May 1524 Anne's brother—now Duke of Norfolk—went to some effort to continue to place the matter before the King despite spending most of 1523 away in his capacity as Lieutenant of the North.[20] Clearly women's marriages continued to be matters of importance to their natal families long after the alliance was concluded, though whether this had more to do with the preservation of a valuable political relationship or with the woman's happiness remains debatable. In Anne's case, this suggests a continued close relationship with the Howards after she had moved into her own household, since they evidently both believed her and were willing to support her against her husband.

It is likely, then, that Anne's letters to Cardinal Wolsey were written with the support, and possibly the help, of her natal family. Her choice of patron was interesting but made sense, and she was not the only woman to petition him regarding marital matters during this period, though most other surviving examples were more directly concerned with finance.[21] Not only did Wolsey have the ear of the King but he was also Lord Chancellor, with the considerable legal jurisdiction that

---

[14] On the role of the family in marital strife, see Sara M. Butler, *Divorce in Medieval England: From One to Two Persons in Law* (London, 2013), 45–7.

[15] TNA SP1/27, fol. 152.

[16] BL Hargrave MS 249, fol. 226: 'The same Earle shall incontinentlie discharge and breake his household, sojourning...with his father-in-law the Duke of Norffolke.'

[17] TNA SP1/27, fols 154v–155.

[18] Head, *The Ebbs and Flows of Fortune*, 68.   [19] UCB, MS UCB 49.

[20] TNA SP1/27, fols 154v–155; Head, *The Ebbs and Flows of Fortune*, 61.

[21] See BL Cotton MS Titus B XI, fol. 362, TNA SP1/26, fol. 183, and SP1/39, fol. 125, for examples of Wolsey dealing with issues of marriage money.

came with this position. The fact that he was Archbishop of York was probably less significant, for although as a clergyman he held authority over spiritual matters—and marriage was a sacrament, governed by canon law—he held none directly over Anne's case, since Essex, her home county, fell into the archdiocese of Canterbury and not of York. At no point is there any suggestion that Anne pursued any kind of separation or restitution through an ecclesiastical court, and so it is fair to assume that she sought Wolsey's secular, rather than spiritual, assistance. Nor should we presume that he was necessarily the only person that she petitioned. It was common for suitors to approach more than one patron, even when they claimed that the recipient was their only 'friend' or 'help' in this matter, and the letters to those whose papers were not subsumed by the state paper office may well have been lost.

The fact that she wrote to Wolsey herself, rather than getting a male relative to approach him for her, shows that noblewomen possessed considerable agency in communication. Anne would undoubtedly have met Wolsey while attending court both before and after her marriage, and so this was not a desperate appeal to a stranger. Nor, however, were they 'private' documents. As scholarship by James Daybell and others has emphasized, the concepts of 'public' and 'private' are largely redundant where early modern correspondence was concerned.[22] More than one person might easily be involved in their composition, and it was (and remains) far safer to assume that more than one person would read them. In fact, as we shall see, Wolsey and Cromwell after him both had something of a side-line of employment as marriage counsellors to the nobility on behalf of the crown, which took its role as marriage mediator seriously.[23] It was therefore highly likely that letters like Anne's were written for several audiences, potentially including the King and his councillors, and this should be borne in mind when reading them.

Anne's letters described both what was happening and what effect it was having on herself and the household. She wrote that 'ther wase never pore woman so trobyll[ed] as I am and all ffor lake off ofycres'.[24] Though she attempted to advise Oxford and to take on some of these duties herself, she complained that he would not let her: 'yf I shuld medyl in anny off these concerns further than I do I surteyne that I shuld never leue in rest ther ffor I meadyll no further than hys household causys'.[25] In the same letter she required Wolsey to intervene in a matter of a debt owed to Oxford, and asked him to ensure that she would not 'bere the reproche to meadyll without offycers'.[26] Anne wrote herself as the quintessentially dutiful wife, assuming the mantel of household control not because she wanted to, but because her husband's hopelessness left her no choice. She asked Wolsey for household officers not because it would make her life easier—though evidently it would—but

---

[22] Daybell, *Women Letter-Writers*; Lynne Magnusson, 'A Rhetoric of Requests: Genre and Linguistic Scripts in Elizabethan Women's Suitors' Letters', and Karen Robertson, 'Negotiating Favour: the Letters of Lady Ralegh', in James Daybell (ed.), *Women and Politics in Early Modern England, 1450–1700* (Aldershot, 2004), 51–66 and 99–113.

[23] Butler, *Divorce in Medieval England*, 97.   [24] TNA SP1/27, fol. 152.

[25] Ibid., fols 154v–155.   [26] Ibid., fol. 154v.

'for the st[a]ying of his honor and myn'.[27] Here, she clearly constructs herself as Oxford's wife, a member of the de Vere family, prioritizing her marital identity in the way that a dutiful wife was supposed to do.

Out of all of Oxford's bad habits, Anne was most disturbed by the company that he kept, notably his cousin and heir, Sir John Vere. Vere was older than Oxford by some years and appears to have had considerable influence over him—Anne wrote that 'my lord wyll do nothing without the counsel off Sir John Vere'.[28] He stood to inherit the earldom unless Oxford and Anne produced an heir and seems to have taken steps to ensure that they did not. Anne wrote to Wolsey that 'they [Oxford's friends] care letyll ffor hys comyng forward so the inherytannce meyt be saved for Sir John Wer hath spoken largely to my fface'.[29] Oxford's friends, led by Vere, were apparently poisoning him against her. Oxford would have known that it was his duty to produce an heir regardless of his feelings towards his wife, or towards his friends: the 1524 ordinance specifies that he should treat Anne kindly 'for bringeing forthe fruit and children between them'.[30] Does this mean he preferred to hand his estates to a paternal cousin rather than trying to create a son and heir with Anne? Or was this a fiction created by Anne to spur Wolsey to action?

In fact, the letters were very carefully constructed, placing herself in the position of dutiful wife and powerless woman dependent on Wolsey's good lordship, scripting the role that she wanted him to play. Her letters followed the tropes of deference used by noblewomen in petitions. All four in this sequence were both written and signed in her own hand, a mark of social courtesy and perhaps of desire for secrecy.[31] They are tidy, with few smudges or crossings out, which could suggest that they were fair copies made from earlier drafts, again a sign of care taken with both presentation and content. Materially, they make obvious use of deferential space.[32] The margins are generally wide, and the signature is consistently at the bottom of the page on the right-hand side, usually leaving a significant gap after the body of the letter, again a sign of respect and deference. The salutations she used, while not untypical, were chosen to set this tone.[33] She began each letter in her 'moste humbylle wise' or 'humbelest wyse', and signed herself as his 'humbyl assured bedwoman'. In the first letter she made reference to his role as her 'good lord' three separate times.[34] She also made her trust in him very clear, explicitly stating not only that he was her sole hope in this matter (which was not entirely true), but even appearing to state that she owed her position to him: 'I troust youe consyder

---

[27] Ibid., fol. 150.　　[28] Ibid., fol. 153.

[29] Ibid., fol. 153.　　[30] BL, Hargrave MS 249, fol. 226.

[31] Both the body of the letter and the signature were written in one hand in this sequence. The signatures on later letters from Anne are also in this hand even where the body of the letter is in another hand, suggesting that she signed all her letters herself, and that she therefore also wrote these four earlier letters herself.

[32] For material analysis of early modern letters, see James Daybell, *The Material Letter in Early Modern England: Manuscript Practices and the Culture and Practices of Letter-Writing, 1512–1635* (Basingstoke, 2012).

[33] See Erin Sadlack, *The French Queen's Letters: Mary Tudor Brandon and the Politics of Marriage in Sixteenth-Century Europe* (Basingstoke, 2011) and Daybell, *Women's Letter-Writing*, for alternative examples of women constructing letters in this way.

[34] TNA SP1/27, fol. 150.

that I haue no nother ffrend nor help but only your grace ffor youe ware the setteyng forward off me ffor I haue notheyng nor wasse nevyr leyke to haue a hade yf yt had natt a byn by your graceshvous goodnes.'[35] We do not know whether this was a reference to a specific event, but if so this was clearly a good time to remind him of it. In the last letter of the sequence she again reiterates the bond of obligation between them and tells him that she is bound 'to do whatever he commands in return for his help. She then gives him a small 'taster' of this by offering to report the gossip she had heard about him in her local area, but without actually doing so, thus providing him with an incentive to write again.[36]

She did not only outline the problems that Oxford's behaviour was causing for her and the household, but especially underlined the ways in which Oxford was neglecting his public duty as an earl, knowing that Wolsey—and through him, the King—would be more concerned with this than with Oxford's treatment of her. The theory here was that an earldom was a public role; if Oxford could not handle that, then he would hardly be fit for any higher office, and that was a problem for a realm reliant on its nobility to fill government positions. To suggest that a man had lost control over his household was deeply insulting, as it implied that he had failed to maintain the natural order by allowing his God-given authority to be usurped.[37] Anne's words plainly demonstrated that this had occurred. She made it clear that she had assumed control of the household finances—concerning the hiring of an officer sent by Wolsey, Oxford wrote rather vaguely that he would be glad to give the man 'suche yerely rewarde and ffee for the same as your grace shall thynk good and resonable', whereas Anne wrote that 'I did offer hym forte pounds a yer hys chamber hys wyffe to be with hym as long as he woll haue hur fower servants and iiij horse'.[38] It is evident that she had taken on more household man-agement than was generally acceptable for women.

Her third letter of the four in the sequence especially revealed her annoyance at her husband's behaviour and her petitionary strategy suffered a little. Complaining that Oxford had acted against her advice in granting an annuity, she snapped that she trusted that the unsuitable recipient 'shall natt in joy yt yf I may haue eny conf-fort of your grace'.[39] This letter failed to provide the same degree of effusive thanks and humble greetings found in her other letters, and was also less respectful on the page, using only half a sheet and cramming the signature into the bottom corner without leaving any deferential space. This is where the role she had created for Wolsey as her sole protector also began to slip. In the last letter of the sequence, she mentioned that her half-brother the Duke of Norfolk had spoken to the King on her behalf and that the latter was anxious to know that things were improving.[40] This made it clear that Anne had felt the need to invoke aid other than Wolsey's, and had gone behind his back to reach the King, a move at odds with her continual assurances that he was her 'sole ffrend'.

[35] Ibid., fol. 152.   [36] Ibid., fols 154v–155.

[37] Elizabeth A. Foyster, *Manhood in Early Modern England: Honour, Sex and Marriage* (London, 1999), 87.

[38] TNA SP1/27, fols 149–50.   [39] Ibid., fol. 153.   [40] Ibid., fols 154v–155.

Measures were certainly taken. Wolsey sent them men from his own retinue to act as the household officers that Anne and Oxford lacked.[41] This was doubtless an attempt to remove a key source of strife by making it unnecessary for Anne to take on so many roles of household management. Not only did this serve to place good, rather than bad, influences around the young Earl, but it also gave Wolsey unbiased eyes and ears within the establishment. Since one of the officers sent by Wolsey was a treasurer, Anthony Hansard, and he also attempted to send them Robert Heneage to be auditor, we might also infer that they were designed to bring Oxford's finances under greater control without recourse to Anne. This, though, proved insufficient, and so a legal ordinance was drawn up by Wolsey in February 1524 and enrolled in Chancery, allegedly under the King's instructions, 'to lymitt John Earle of Oxenford in the orderinge of his Expences of Household and other his Affaires in his yonger yeares, as also for his demeanor towards the Countess his wife'.[42] It ordered Oxford to cease all the behaviours that were considered damaging, placed his estates into Wolsey's nominal keeping, and instructed him to disperse his house-hold and return to his father-in-law the Duke of Norfolk's household until further notice, all under pain of a personal £2,000 bond as well as six sureties bound for 500 marks each.[43] This was draconian. Aside from the financial obligation, the measure most likely to keep Oxford in check was the return to his father-in-law's household. However, Anne's father died in May 1524 and the last letter in the sequence shows that the move had not been effected beforehand.[44] Nevertheless, towards the end of the letter she thanked Wolsey for the 'quyet lyffe that you haue brought me to', so perhaps some change had occurred.[45] Oxford died two years later in 1526. That Anne did not remarry, but remained a widow until her death thirty years later, perhaps shows what a bad experience this had been for her.

What does Anne's experience say about female agency? The episode shows how the domestic and the political could overlap. In attempting to assume some of the duties of estate officers, Anne moved beyond the normal level of estate management undertaken by noblewomen during this period. Though it was done out of neces-sity and she seems to have had an aptitude for the work, all concerned, apparently including Anne herself, were keen to relegate her to a more usual, subordinate, position. But this does not mean that she did not want or was unable to exercise agency within the confines of 'normal' gender relations. Though the resulting ordinance was endorsed by her male relatives and not by herself, it was she who wrote to Wolsey in the first place to get help for her situation. The strategies she used—emphasizing the damaging public aspects of Oxford's behaviour, making it clear that his behaviour was emasculating—were cleverly chosen and effective.

---

[41] Ibid., fols 153 and 156.   [42] BL Hargrave MS 249, fol. 226.   [43] Ibid.

[44] TNA SP1/27, fols 154v–155. Anne wrote that she had lately spoken to her brother the Duke of Norfolk—placing this letter after the death of her father in 1524, and therefore after the ordinance—and had heard from him that the King was very desirous to know 'how that my lord dothe use hym selfe'. The King thought that Oxford should have 'som wysemen a bowt hym', and Norfolk intended to counsel His Majesty to provide such men at their next meeting. This suggests that the couple remained in their own household.

[45] Ibid.

Though arguably she would not have had such success without the support of the Howards, she was also canny enough to capitalize on these connections, taking opportunities to remind Wolsey of her position within the Howard family as well as her marital, de Vere, identity.

KATHERINE: 'MANY KYNE AND FEWE THAT DOTHE FOR ME'

Anne's younger sister Katherine also suffered marital problems, but in her case this was during her second marriage, with Henry, Lord Daubeney (later Earl of Bridgwater). Katherine is the only known Howard woman for whom marriage ended in a legal divorce settlement. This makes her unusual not only within her own dynasty, but within the nobility as a whole during this period. It was possible and, as Butler argues, common for 'ordinary' people to 'self-divorce', meaning to simply separate without any formal legal process and change location in order to avoid detection.[46] This was naturally impossible for the aristocracy, and so while a couple might attempt to live separately for a time, they could not officially end their marriage without due legal process. Helmholz's oft-quoted statement that there was remarkably little divorce litigation therefore still stands where the nobility is concerned, and Katherine's case is significant as part of this minority.[47] It also provides a fascinating juxtaposition to the way that Anne's case above was dealt with. We saw there that initial support in a troubled marriage came from her natal relatives, and they continued to function as a kind of 'pressure group' on the King and on Thomas Wolsey until a satisfactory solution was reached. The title quote for this section, taken from one of Katherine's letters—'I haue many kyne and few that dothe for me'—shows that this was not, apparently, equivalent for her.[48] Her situation therefore provides a different angle on the attitude of the Howard family to these circumstances.

Unfortunately for so unusual a case, the sources for the breaking of this marriage are limited. While we can state categorically that a separation took place, there is little to explain why or how. There are two letters dealing with the topic that have survived among Cromwell's papers, one from Daubeney and one from Katherine, both dated 10 October 1535, a few pieces of contemporary gossip found predominantly in the Lisle letters, and a Chancery petition. These make it clear that a legal divorce was indeed secured. Daubeney's letter concerns negotiations over alimony, clearly showing that the couple were no longer intending to cohabit.[49] A letter from George Rolle to Lady Lisle dated 4 March 1536 stated that 'he [Daubeney] shalbe now dyvorsyd from my lady by there both assentes'.[50] Most significantly, a Chancery petition dating from the chancellorship of Thomas Audley describes the couple as

---

[46] Butler, *Divorce in Medieval England*.
[47] R. H. Helmholz, *Marriage Litigation in Medieval England* (Cambridge, 1974), 74.
[48] TNA SP1/97, fol. 120r–v.
[49] TNA SP1/97, fol. 119 (Daubeney to Cromwell, 10 October 1535).
[50] TNA SP3/9, fol. 36.

'devorcyd and seu[er]yd from bedde and borde by thorder of the spirituell lawe'.[51] It is this which not only makes it clear that a legal separation occurred, but tells us what kind, how it was most likely done, and provides some insight into what the cause(s) may have been.

'Divorce' was a catch-all term used in medieval and early modern England to mean both annulment and judicial separation. An annulment ruled that a marriage had never been valid, and that both parties were now free to proceed as though it had never occurred, whereas a judicial separation allowed separate living without dissolving the marriage. The phrase used in the later Chancery petitions—'devorcyd and seru[er]yd from bedde and borde'—indicates a judicial separation, because the phrase is a literal translation of the legal terminology and was not used when referring to informally negotiated separations.[52] This could only have been granted by an ecclesiastical law court, and is highly unusual among the nobility.[53] For Katherine and Daubeney, there appears to be no written record of the case itself. Helmholz tells us that separations among the nobility rarely came to a court hearing, because they tended to seek sentence privately from a bishop.[54] In this instance they might have gone to John Clerk, Bishop of Bath and Wells (their 'home' diocese), but his registers survive almost unbroken and there is nothing in them to suggest he granted them a separation.[55] Moreover, those who had property in more than one diocese, as this couple did, might well have gone straight to a higher, non-geographical, court, most likely the Court of Arches. Those records no longer survive.[56] Without specific case records, we do not know the details of their divorce.

However, the fact that they obtained a judicial separation at all provides some clues. One could only obtain a separation from bed and board by pleading cruelty, adultery, or heresy.[57] Pleas of heresy were rare, and in any case hardly worth attempting in the troubled atmosphere of the 1530s. Pleas of adultery were almost exclusively made by men against women, and pleas of cruelty by women against men. For both, proof was required, and for cruelty, this had to be proof that at least one party had committed 'repeated, life-threatening acts of physical violence'.[58] Though the legal definition was something of a sliding scale, taken contextually in every individual case, divorces were not granted for casual or occasional blows.

---

[51] TNA C1/777/16.

[52] TNA C1/777/16. See Helmholz, *Marriage Litigation in Medieval England*, 101. My thanks to Professor Tim Stretton for advice on this.

[53] For the technicalities of the divorce procedure, see Helmholz, *Marriage Litigation in Medieval England*, 100–37, and Butler, *Divorce in Medieval England*.

[54] Helmholz, *Marriage Litigation in Medieval England*, 160–1.

[55] Sir Henry Maxwell-Lyte (ed.), *The Registers of Thomas Wolsey, Bishop of Bath and Wells, 1518–1523, John Clerke, Bishop of Bath and Wells, 1523–1541, William Knyght, Bishop of Bath and Wells, 1541–1547, and Gilbert Bourne, Bishop of Bath and Wells, 1554–1559*, Somerset Record Society, 55 (London, 1940). Nor is there any reference to their case in surviving documents from the Baths and Wells consistory court.

[56] M. Ingram, *Church Courts, Sex and Marriage in England, 1570–1640* (Cambridge, 1987), 172.

[57] Helmholz, *Marriage Litigation in Medieval England*, 100.

[58] Joanne Bailey, 'Cruelty and Adultery: Offences against the Institution of Marriage', in Anne-Marie Kilday and David S. Nash (eds), *Histories of Crime: Britian 1600–2000* (Basingstoke, 2010), 39–59 (41); Helmholz, *Marriage Litigation in Medieval England*, 101–5.

Most cases of this kind of separation were brought for cruelty; even where the divorce was a mutual decision (though 'collusion' was in theory not permitted) proof would be required.[59] In theory, then, either Daubeney brought a suit against Katherine for adultery, or she brought one against him for cruelty. What's more, the 'proof' in either case was sufficient for the court to grant them their divorce.

There is no indication in any surviving material that Katherine was an adulteress. Indeed, the very fact that Cromwell was negotiating alimony on her behalf goes some way to suggesting otherwise. There appears to have been a contemporary feeling, echoed in statute law, that a woman's right to jointure or dower depended on her having 'earned' it through good behaviour, namely sexual fidelity and the birth of children. Women who behaved inappropriately during a divorce case might find their alimony either severely reduced or forfeited altogether.[60] Daubeney himself seems to have thought this way; his letter to Cromwell protested at the amount he was expected to give Katherine, arguing, 'I do bey myn hertes ease very dearly consyderyng that I haue had no man of commodyty bey her.'[61] Whether by 'commodyty' he meant children, money, lands, or all three is not further explained, but it does not suggest that her behaviour or fidelity was the problem.

We are left with Daubeney and the issue of 'cruelty', and with speculation. There is no direct contemporary evidence to argue that he was violent either to Katherine or to his previous wife.[62] Yet he was seen as an unpleasant, even violent, figure by some of those around him. The Lisle family had been litigating against him over lands for many years, and their London agent John Husee so disliked Daubeney that he said he wished that he might die childless, 'as I trust he shall do, and that shortly'.[63] Lady Lisle herself spoke wearily of him in 1538: 'I knowe the Erle of bridwatr['s] appetite the mor he ys spokenn unto the warse he wilbe.'[64] When in 1539 it was falsely rumoured that Daubeney was sick and in danger of death, Husee wrote that 'the nyws were to good to be trywe'.[65] During the late 1540s Daubeney's own servant brought a Chancery suit against him for non-payment of debts and unfair dismissal, incidentally complaining that Daubeney had tried to shoot at him with a crossbow.[66] There was also an incident in 1539 where Daubeney, accompanied by eighteen armed servants and a borrowed crossbow, attempted to seize the person of Sir William Baram, who was Sir Thomas Speke's steward. When told that the law would settle whatever the problem was, he replied that 'it wold not be determyned w[i]t[h]out murder'.[67]

Katherine's letter to Thomas Cromwell on 10 October 1535, too, suggests that her husband was not a pleasant man. Written in her own hand, it is long, but tidy, contains little deferential space, but does begin by thanking Cromwell for his 'gret

---

[59] Helmholz, *Marriage Litigation in Medieval England*, 101.

[60] Butler, *Divorce in Medieval England*, 80–1. See also Paul Brand, '"Deserving" and "Undeserving" Wives: Earning and Forfeiting Dower in Medieval England', *Journal of Legal History* 22:1 (2001), 1–11.

[61] TNA SP1/97, fol. 118.

[62] Elizabeth Neville, daughter of George Neville, Third Lord Bergavenny, and his first wife Joan Fitzalan.

[63] TNA SP3/12, fol. 15.   [64] TNA SP3/4 fol. 45; TNA SP3/14, fol. 66v.

[65] TNA SP1/142, fol. 132.   [66] TNA C1/1137/44.   [67] TNA SP1/152, fols 195–7.

goodnes' and contains sundry other messages of thanks for good lordship.[68] She provides no concrete information on why the divorce had been necessary—perhaps everybody already knew—but it transmits a deep feeling of unease that feels less contrived than the sentiments of Anne's letters above. Katherine is also one of the few early modern women who specifically stated that she had used her own hand for the purpose of secrecy:

> that [which] I have wreten herto yow ys my owen hand wyche ys very yll/I have done the best I cane and rather thene I wold trust enny so fare as to knowe my mynd I had lever yt ware undon/and I desyr yow in as myche as none ys prevy of this letter but my selff and yow that yeff yt be yowr plesyr I praye yow that yt be not sene for thowe I befayer spoken unto yet ame I not all wayes in sewrty & I ame very unsewer as yt now chancheyethe.[69]

This desire for secrecy argues that this letter was intended as a 'private', rather than a 'public', document, and that we can bear this in mind when reading it. That the date of composition is the same for her own and her husband's letters seems too odd for coincidence. One must have known that the other was writing, which strongly suggests that in October 1535 they were still living under the same roof, though neither gives a location. This might be why Katherine's contains only vague statements, which show that there had been issues for some time. She spoke of Cromwell's previous promises of help 'at all tymes whene I was asewter to yow an in spechally whene I came to yowr howese by the fryers in London whene I forst sewyd to yow'.[70] She asked him to 'speke yowr good word whane yow thence best to the kynges hyghnes for me' because 'my lord my hosbond hathe payd well fore to make frends a gaynst me . . . my enymyes wull saye the worst'.[71] Though she asks this, the letter otherwise is clearly only intended as a 'reminder' to Cromwell to keep her and her suit in mind. Like Anne, she does use statements which are intended to provoke pity, such as 'I do trust that at lengthe the truthe what I do soffer wylbe knowen', and the complaint that her husband was spreading lies at court. She also mentions those who are on her side, like 'Master Courtenay' and Sir Thomas More, the sheriff of Dorset, but seems actively surprised that the last has apparently been so vocal in her cause, since 'I never ded hyme plesyr nore never desyryd hyme to saye for me more thene I desird all other gentyllmen'. She also stated frankly 'I have not ussyd to talke myche of theme that dothe promyse me to do me enny plesyr or be my frend', suggesting that from experience, she did not trust these promises. In all, the letter is not so carefully constructed as some of Anne's, and the style is franker. This might reflect the fact that she had apparently composed it herself without assistance, but it could also be because Katherine was older when she wrote this letter than Anne was when she wrote hers, and because strictly speaking, there was a lesser difference in rank and status between Katherine and Cromwell than between Anne and Wolsey.

Katherine's letter does not refer directly to finances, but Daubeney's, written on the same day, is chiefly concerned with this. His letter is also written in his own

---

[68] TNA SP1/97, fol. 120r–v.   [69] Ibid.   [70] Ibid.   [71] Ibid.

hand, with clear margins and a fair portion of deferential space.[72] He wrote with a mixture of the authority of rank and the persuasion of a petitioner, beginning, 'Master secretary thys let[er] shall be to deser you to be my good mastr and frynd', and ending 'all youres'. He was using a relative, 'cossen arendel', as his go-between with Cromwell, and began his letter by saying that he 'cad not be in quett' since Arundell had informed him that his offer of £200 yearly in alimony had been refused.[73] He was concerned that Cromwell intended him to give more, and explained that this would be his 'undoyng', and that he and others thought that even his offer of one hundred pounds unfair, since she would also have 'so grett a jointer'. This seems to suggest that he had made two offers, and Cromwell had refused both. This is very interesting. Katherine's jointure from her first marriage was worth £200 per year, and for her receive another £200 on top of this in alimony would have placed her in a better financial position than her own mother, the dowager Duchess of Norfolk, whose jointure was worth £358.[74] For Cromwell to apparently refuse to pass this does appear to suggest that he was 'on her side', particularly since Daubeney's poor financial situation was well known, and alimony payments were usually based on the husband's wealth.[75]

The fact that yearly alimony was under negotiation might also mean that the divorce had been granted by this time, October 1535. However, this makes it difficult to understand George Rolle's letter to Lady Lisle in March 1536, in which he claimed that they 'shalbe now dyvorsyd'; perhaps it was not public knowledge until this time, or perhaps they were only now beginning their officially divorced lives once the alimony was settled. For Rolle also stated that 'my lady to haue nowe lxxx ponndes yerely & hyr hole joyntour aft hys deth as was appoynted the tyme of there furst maryage'.[76] One does not need to be mathematically inclined to note that £80 was considerably less than the £200 that had been rejected in October 1535. It is possible that the original offer had not been predicated on Katherine obtaining jointure from Daubeney after his death, and that once this was included, the yearly payments went down correspondingly. We know that she certainly did keep the lands that she had in jointure from her first marriage. The lawsuit describing herself and Daubeney as divorced was to do with the upkeep of a mill in Carmarthen, south Wales, and it stated that the said mill 'upon the said sep[ara]acion and dyvorce assigned and appoynted by the said Erle unto the sayd lady kat[er]yn yor oratrice during her lyfe'.[77] She also would have received jointure from Daubeney on his death in 1548, had she not previously been attainted for misprision of treason; records show that the lands passed straight to crown control, but were described as belonging to her jointure.[78] Financially, she was not worse-off as a result of the separation. Nor does it seem that custody of her three children caused any issue, even though none had reached their majority and the youngest cannot have been

---

[72] TNA SP1/97, fol. 119.

[73] Probably Thomas Arundell, whose wife was Margaret Howard, sister of the future Queen Catherine, and half-niece of Daubeney's wife.

[74] TNA SC12/25/53 (Katherine's jointure); Arundel Castle Archive, G1/4 (Agnes's jointure).

[75] Butler, *Divorce in Medieval England*, 83.

[76] TNA SP3/9, fol. 36.   [77] TNA C1/777/16.   [78] TNA SC6/EDWVI/420.

older than 10.[79] This was probably because Daubeney was not their father, and therefore had no claim to or responsibility for them in the eyes of the law. By the early 1540s they were living in the household of their grandmother, Katherine's mother Agnes, dowager Duchess of Norfolk.[80] Daubeney, however, did not fare so well. He had warned Cromwell in 1535 that he would be forced to sell lands to make alimony payments, and across the later 1530s and 1540s records show him doing precisely this.[81] He was even forced to sell lands set aside for Katherine's jointure, with the caveat that the heirs and assigns of the new owner (Edward Seymour, Earl of Hertford) would allow her to occupy them for term of her life after his death.[82]

Though the divorce was granted and Katherine does not seem to have suffered financially, her letter nevertheless makes clear that it was a stressful process not to be undertaken lightly. What stands out in this regard is her complaint that she had 'many kyne and fewe that dothe for me', which suggests that she had attempted to follow the usual chain of intervention by asking relatives for aid, but been refused. She caveated; 'I have many kyne and fewe that dothe for me onlese thene the quennes hyghnes wyche I ame very myche bownd unto and yet I do here and perseve as myche as cane be devysyd ys devysyd to compasse yt contenewally to sett her grace to w[i]t[h] drawe here favor frome me.'[83] The evidence does not tell us what help Queen Anne Boleyn, a Howard relative, had given, and it is not clear from this statement whether Katherine thought it was Daubeney poisoning the Queen against her, or her own relatives, the Howards. In their defence, Katherine's urgent secrecy over her letter to Cromwell may suggest that it was difficult for her to send or receive letters, which means her family in London may only have had Daubeney's version of events. This was certainly the case for another abused wife during this period; Lady Hungerford, imprisoned in a turret of her husband's castle during the late 1530s, had had difficulty reaching anybody who might help her.[84] Yet her letter also contains fears of the spread of false rumours at court, and clearly at least one correspondent with the Lisle family in Calais was aware of the situation.[85]

As we have seen, the most important natal relative in circumstances of marital difficulty was a woman's father. Katherine's—Thomas, Second Duke of Norfolk—was dead. But where was his successor, the family patriarch, Katherine's half-brother Thomas, Third Duke of Norfolk, who had been so helpful to their sister Anne in her marital problems ten years previously? Butler emphasizes the rarity of a negative attitude among natal relatives, pointing out that their investment in the making of marriage meant that they were inevitably involved in the breaking of it too, and were generally supportive of wives seeking separation.[86] There is evidence, though, that this was not the case when the woman was perceived to be in the wrong, as

---

[79] Based on birthdates of 1524 and 1526 for the two boys, and possibly 1528 for her daughter Agnes. See Ralph Griffiths, *Sir Rhys ap Thomas and his Family: A Study in the Wars of the Roses and Early Tudor Politics* (Cardiff, 1993), 69.

[80] TNA SP1/168, fol. 124.   [81] TNA E305/7/D61; *LP* XV, 1030 (13); E326/8868.

[82] TNA E328/285.   [83] TNA SP1/97, fol. 120.

[84] BL Cotton MS Titus B I, fol. 388.   [85] TNA SP3/9, fol. 36.

[86] Butler, *Divorce in Medieval England*, 45–7.

indeed we will see in the last case considered in this chapter. Katherine had already made a reputation for herself as a rebellious woman through her activities in south Wales with her first husband Rhys ap Gruffudd, who was executed for treason as a result of this in 1531. It is possible that her brother and other family members had distanced themselves from her at this stage and were not inclined to alter their position. Of course, Katherine had many more Howard relatives than just her brother. When she stated that 'few' of her kin would help her, did she mean that some had, or had tried, but simply did not have the kind of money or influence that her brother did, or that she needed? Was she demonstrating an understanding of 'kin' that essentially meant 'patriarch' in these sorts of scenarios? Alternatively, was she using a broader definition of 'kin'? Daubeney's 'cossen arendel', his go-between with Cromwell, was most probably Thomas Arundell of that great Cornish clan, but as well as being Daubeney's cousin he was also affinally related to Katherine, having married one of her half-nieces, Margaret Howard, in the early 1530s. That he was playing the part of Daubeney's messenger indeed suggests he was not willing to take Katherine's part.

That we do not know how the marriage was made in the first place also makes it difficult to understand her family's alleged attitude. Katherine's first husband, Rhys ap Gruffudd, was executed on a trumped-up charge of high treason in December 1531.[87] She had certainly left Wales by March 1532, but we do not know where she went.[88] The couple had definitely married by the time of Anne Boleyn's coronation in 1533, as Katherine was listed there as 'Lady Daubeney'.[89] They must therefore have married between March 1532 and May 1533, and their marriage had then broken down by 1535. This does raise the question of whether it had ever been a positive or even neutral union. Katherine is one of only a few Howard women to have married more than once during this period, and the reasons behind this second marriage are unclear. It was unusual for a widow to have her second marriage dictated by her natal family in the way that her first marriage probably was, unless she was widowed very young. Katherine was around 30, the mother of three children, and ought in theory to have been able to choose her own second marriage. She may have done so. Daubeney was not the sort of husband usually selected by the Howards, being financially poor, firmly rooted in the west country, not a courtier, and only a baron.[90] Katherine's mother-in-law, another Catherine (St John/ap Rhys/Edgecombe), had married a Cornish knight, Sir Piers Edgecombe, as her second husband, and it is possible that Katherine met Daubeney through this link and chose or was encouraged to accept him. It may simply have been a love match that turned sour very quickly, and her family may have felt that having made her bed, she ought to lie in it.

Though she received no apparent aid from any members of the Howard family per se, there is evidence to show that in 1536 one member of her extended natal

[87] *CSP Spain*, IV, ii, 853.

[88] TNA SP1/53, fol. 129 shows that she had sent her priest back to Wales to collect certain goods, and that she was not there herself.

[89] BL Add. MS 71009, fol. 58v.

[90] Philip Heskith Daubeney et al., *The History of the Daubeney Family* (n.p., 2004), 32–3.

family did come to her assistance. In George Rolle's 1536 letter to Lady Lisle in which he mentions the Daubeneys' imminent divorce, he also states that Daubeney had recently borrowed £400 from the Earl of Wiltshire.[91] This was none other than Thomas Boleyn, father of the Queen, Norfolk's brother-in-law and Katherine's too. In her discussion of this letter, Muriel St Clare Byrne suggested that this loan had something to do with the Daubeneys' divorce and this seems plausible, as court cases were not cheap and Daubeney's finances were not robust.[92] Moreover, Katherine had suggested a year earlier that Queen Anne Boleyn was the only member of her kin who would help her, which suggests that Wiltshire's loan may have been a royal order.[93] This was generous help indeed; without it, the case might have stalled and Katherine might never have escaped from her husband. In the event, she remained separated until Daubeney's death in 1548, notwithstanding a rumour of their reconciliation in February 1540.[94] In her letter of 1535 she also mentioned a 'master Courtenay', who had relayed Cromwell's 'goodness' to her, and this may have been a marital link. Sir William Courtenay of Powderham was married to a member of the Edgecombe family, and so was Katherine's mother-in-law. While 'master Courtenay' was probably not Sir William himself, it may have been one of his sons.

Katherine's divorce case undoubtedly raises more questions than it answers. Nevertheless, it is remarkable that the divorce of a member of the Howard family has remained more or less hidden under the radar, and equally remarkable that two such high-status sisters should both have suffered such severe marital issues. Both followed a similar path to resolution: application to their natal relatives, the Howards, followed by escalation to the King's advisers (Wolsey and Cromwell respectively) and the use of the law. That the outcomes were so different could simply reflect the differences in the issues at hand. Anne's husband the Earl of Oxford was obstreperous and wayward, but not criminal, whereas the problems in the Daubeney case were crimes against canon law. However, it also demonstrates the significant impact of familial assistance at such times. Without the support of her father and brother, Anne would not have been able to secure Wolsey's assistance and bring her husband to heel with the Chancery ordinance. While we cannot be so certain in Katherine's case, it is reasonable to argue that the Queen's assistance and the loan from the Earl of Wiltshire also helped her to reach a satisfactory settlement. Natal intervention could therefore come from extended family members as well as—or instead of—more immediate relations. In Katherine's case it is possible that marital connections could also play an assisting role. These two cases raise the issue of conditional, rather than automatic, familial support. It is impossible to know for sure why Norfolk supported Anne in the 1520s and not Katherine in the 1530s, but it is plausible that prior behaviour, scandal, and social expectations regarding women's roles may all have played a part. It seems evident that aristocratic women did expect their natal relatives to support them in such circumstances, but that this support was not automatically forthcoming.

---

[91] TNA SP3/9, fol. 36.
[92] Muriel St Clare Byrne (ed.), *The Lisle Letters*, IV, 39–40; TNA SP3/9, fol. 36.
[93] TNA SP1/97, fol. 120.   [94] TNA SP3/13 fol. 48r–v.

ELIZABETH: 'BRAKYNG' AND 'FFYTTINGE'

The marriage issues experienced by Elizabeth Stafford/Howard, Duchess of Norfolk, were different again from both Anne's and Katherine's, and this makes it interesting to compare them in terms of individual agency and the Howard family's reaction to their respective situations. While Anne's case is usually only mentioned in passing by historians interested in other people or other themes, and Katherine's barely at all, Elizabeth's is something of a source of fascination. The utter breakdown of a marriage between two such high-status individuals coupled with Elizabeth's emotive, voluble letters, accusations of domestic violence, and the curiosity of a woman who refused to accept the 'double standard' of her day have generated and maintained interest among social and political historians.[95] Elizabeth's own experience, however, is not often placed centre stage, and rarely in the wider context of the Howard dynasty and their activities during the 1530s.

As the daughter of Edward Stafford, Third Duke of Buckingham, Elizabeth had royal blood and was probably one of the most eligible girls on the marriage market in the 1510s. Initially betrothed to her father's ward Ralph Neville, heir to the earldom of Westmorland, this contract was broken when Thomas Howard, then Lord Howard, approached her father for her hand after his first wife's death in 1511.[96] Though Howard would later become Third Duke of Norfolk, at this stage nobody knew this would happen—it was pre-Flodden—and the highest title he could then aspire to was Earl of Surrey. By contrast, Elizabeth's family had a dukedom, more money, and more status. Elizabeth was therefore marrying below her. The marriage took place in 1512 and at first everything seemed to be rosy. The couple had five children together.[97] While away in the north in 1524, Surrey requested that his wife might join him, and she had also accompanied him to Ireland during his spell as lieutenant there in 1520.[98] The first sign that things were not so good between Elizabeth and Norfolk was in 1531, when Spanish ambassador Eustace Chapuys noted that Elizabeth had been sent from court, 'because she spoke too freely, and declared herself more than they liked for the Queen'— Catherine of Aragon.[99] Her husband, of course, was behind Anne Boleyn, as this was the heart of the King's 'great matter', and for his wife to do otherwise did not speak well for their relationship. A few years later in 1533 the crux of the matter became clear: Chapuys wrote that Elizabeth refused to see or speak to her husband because he was having an affair with Bess Holland, who was the daughter of his secretary and also one of Anne Boleyn's ladies in waiting.[100] The comparison with the royal love triangle is difficult to avoid here, and though it must have been

---

[95] Barbara Harris, 'Marriage Sixteenth-Century Style: Elizabeth Stafford and the Third Duke of Norfolk', *Journal of Social History* 15 (1982), 371–82; Jessie Childs, *Henry VIII's Last Victim* (London, 2006), 87–93; W. A. Sessions, *Henry Howard, the Poet Earl of Surrey: A Life* (Oxford, 1999), 41–68; Retha M. Warnicke, 'Family and Kinship Relations at the Henrician Court: The Boleyns and Howards', in Dale Hoak (ed.), *Tudor Political Culture* (Cambridge, 1995), 31–53 (44).

[96] This comes from Elizabeth's description in a letter written later.

[97] Only four are known, but Elizabeth states five, suggesting that one must have died young.

[98] BL Cotton MS Caligula B VI, fol. 429v; SP60/1, fol. 40.

[99] *LP* V, 238.   [100] *LP* VI, 1164.

coincidental, it is nevertheless startling and no doubt helps to explain Elizabeth's support for the Queen. According to Elizabeth's later letters the affair had been going on since 1527, which makes it possible that their relationship had broken down much sooner than the surviving outside evidence shows.[101] It is very clear both from Elizabeth's own letters and other sources that Norfolk's mistress was indeed the major cause of contention here. Although, as Harris has stated, there is hardly sufficient comparable evidence to argue that Elizabeth was unique in expecting fidelity in marriage, nor that she was unusual in disliking her husband's adulteries, it is clear that her *behaviour*, stemming from these views, was considered shocking and wrong.[102]

As in Anne's case, and, indeed, the Queen's, Elizabeth's kin were the first to become involved in seeking resolution. In 1533 Chapuys reported that Lord Bergavenny, Elizabeth's brother-in-law, was called to go and see her in order to mediate between her and Norfolk. Though Bergavenny allegedly promised that Norfolk would henceforth be a good husband, it is difficult to know what was meant by that, since evidently Norfolk was not prepared to give up his mistress.[103] The major difficulty facing Elizabeth here was that her father, the Duke of Buckingham, was no longer alive, having been executed for treason in 1521. As we saw earlier, when Anne ran into difficulties, the fact that her father was the Duke of Norfolk and her brother the Earl of Surrey stood her in good stead, since they outranked her husband. Elizabeth did not have that level of support. It was unlikely that her brother Henry, Lord Stafford, whose major characteristic seems to have been a desire to lie low and stay out of the kind of trouble his father had fallen into, would ever have attempted to chastise the Duke of Norfolk. Though both her brothers-in-law (Lord Bergavenny and her original betrothed, Ralph Neville, Earl of Westmorland) apparently attempted to mediate or to sue to Norfolk on her behalf, neither of them had the clout that her father would have done. Where Katherine had the advantage of kin from a previous marriage, some of whom may have provided minor assistance, Elizabeth did not, and it was unlikely that any other Howards would deliberately intervene in the marriage of the dynasty's patriarch.

In 1534, some kind of 'last straw' event occurred, and Norfolk came 'ryding all night' home to Kenninghall to lock Elizabeth in a room, take possession of her jewels and valuable clothing, and shortly afterwards installed her in her own, much smaller, establishment in Redbourn, Hertfordshire.[104] It was from this time and

---

[101] BL Cotton MS Titus B I, fols 388r–v, in which she states that 'ytt ys xj yere syn my lorde my husband furst fell in love wyth hyr'. This letter was arbitrarily dated to 1537 by the editors of *Letters and Papers,* but the internal context places it in 1538, which means that by Elizabeth's own calculation, Bess Holland came onto the scene in 1527.

[102] Harris, 'Marriage Sixteenth-Century Style'.   [103] *LP* VI, 1164.

[104] This description comes from one of Elizabeth's letters. This event has been variously dated to either 1533 or 1534, often dependent on the way that Elizabeth's own letters have been dated, but can be firmly placed in 1534. She states more than once that it occurred on the Tuesday of the passion week, i.e. Easter week. In 1533, this was 8 April. The Spanish ambassador, Chapuys, stated that the day after this—9 April—the Duke of Norfolk and other noblemen had ridden to the Queen at Ampthill, so it seems highly unlikely that he could have been free to ride to East Anglia to deal with Elizabeth the night before, and still less that he could have returned to court in time to receive this instruction and depart with his colleagues (*CSP Spain*, IV (ii), 1058). In 1534, however, Tuesday of the passion week

place that she began writing to Thomas Cromwell. While Cromwell was the obvious person to petition in these cases, for Elizabeth he was also a somewhat unfortunate choice, for though he and her husband Norfolk are popularly supposed to have been deadly enemies, the evidence in fact shows that they had a cordial, even friendly, relationship. Cromwell owed his 1529 seat in Parliament to Norfolk's patronage; Norfolk entrusted Cromwell with his will when he went north to suppress the Pilgrimage of Grace in 1537.[105] Ironically, in another 1537 letter to Cromwell, Norfolk actually explained that although the house he had found for Cromwell to stay in at York was not 'great', it was the best sort in the city, 'and if ye lust not to daly with his [the host's] wif, he hath a yowng woman with praty proper tetins'.[106] As a widower, Cromwell was, of course, perfectly free to pursue casual liaisons, but that Norfolk saw this as an appropriate recommendation to make, presumably knowing that Cromwell would not be offended, did not bode well for Elizabeth's cause. Though Elizabeth had followed the established process, application to natal relatives followed by petitions to the King's advisers, in light of her husband's relationship to those very advisers it was most unlikely that Cromwell would take her part against him. Elizabeth remained at Redbourn at least until her husband's imprisonment in 1546, and she and her husband were never reconciled.

The episode as a whole is difficult to analyse objectively because Elizabeth's letters are the major source for it, and these were written many years later for a specific purpose. The surviving sequence includes nine letters from Elizabeth to Thomas Cromwell, between 1534 and 1540; one from Elizabeth to her brother Henry, Lord Stafford, and one to her brother-in-law Ralph Neville, Earl of Westmorland; two from her husband, Norfolk, to Cromwell; one from Lord Stafford to Norfolk, and one from Stafford to Cromwell.[107] While this is a reasonable amount of correspondence, it is clearly incomplete. Because it was preserved

---

was 31 March and Norfolk had been in London attending Parliament until its prorogation on 30 March (BL Add. MS 4622, fol. 298). It is entirely possible that he was able to ride to East Anglia that night, and would indeed have been 'rydyng all night' to cover the 100-mile distance.

[105] Michael Everett, *The Rise of Thomas Cromwell* (London, 2015), 59–60; TNA SP1/115, fol. 80.

[106] TNA SP1/121, fol. 55.

[107] BL Cotton Vespasian F XIII, fol. 151 (Elizabeth to Cromwell, 23 August 1534, calendared *LP* VII, 1083); TNA SP1/91, fol. 23 (E to C, 3 March, calendared as 1535 in *LP* VIII, 319, but date unconfirmable); BL Cotton MS Titus B I, fols 392–3 (E to C, 30 December 1536, uncalendared); TNA SP1/115, fol. 80 (Norfolk to Cromwell, 27 January 1537, calendared *LP* XII, I, 252); TNA SP1/106, fol. 219 (E to C, 28 September; calendared as 1536 at *LP* XI, 502, but internal evidence places it in 1537); BL Cotton MS Titus B I, fol. 390r–v (E to C, 24 October 1537, calendared *LP* XII, ii, 976); BL Cotton MS Titus B I, fol. 389 (E to C, 10 November 1537, calendared *LP* XII, ii, 1049); BL Cotton MS Titus B I, fol. 388r–v (E to C, 26 June; calendared as 1537 at *LP* XII, ii, 143, but internal evidence places it in 1538); TNA SP1/144, fol. 16 (E to C, 3 March 1539, calendared *LP* XIV, I, 425); BL Cotton MS Titus B I, fol. 391 (E to C, 29 January, calendared as 1539 in *LP* XIV, I, 160, but internal evidence places it in 1540); TNA SP1/158, fol. 201 (E to Westmorland, 11 April, calendared as 1540 at *LP* XV, 493, but internal evidence places it in 1541). The remainder of the letters are not obviously datable: TNA SP1/76, fol. 38 (Henry, Lord Stafford, to Norfolk, 13 May, calendared as 1533 at *LP* VI, 474); TNA SP1/76, fol. 39 (Stafford to Cromwell, 13 May, calendared as 1533 at *LP* VI, 475); Bl Cotton MS Titus B I, fol. 162 (E to Stafford, calendared as 1537 at *LP* XII, ii, 1332); BL Cotton MS Titus B I, fol. 394r–v (Norfolk to Cromwell, no date).

among Cromwell's papers, which were then amalgamated into the state papers, we do not have Cromwell's replies to Elizabeth, and indeed she herself describes letters and copies of letters that she has sent but that we do not now possess. Many of the surviving letters have been calendared in Henry VIII's *Letters and Papers* but unfortunately this has meant that some have been dated where no date was given by the author, and some have been misdated. While most of the letters include the day and month, they do not give the year, and this means it is simply not possible to date them all. However, Elizabeth's own letters nearly always note how many years she has now been separated from her husband, and using this and other contextual information it becomes clear that some have been placed in the wrong year—usually a year too early—and this affects our understanding of the progression not only of the narrative, but of her petitionary strategy.[108]

There are some stylistic and material constants across almost all of Elizabeth's letters. With one exception, the main body of each letter was written by a secretary, and across the sequence there are at least two different secretaries. She used her own hand for her sign-off and signature, sometimes for a postscript, and on one occasion early in the sequence, wrote a short letter entirely in her own hand. Though ordinarily it was considered polite, respectful, and a sign of deference to write personal letters in one's own hand, as both Anne and Katherine did, it soon becomes very clear why Elizabeth does not: her hand is, to put it plainly, atrocious, even by the standards of the time and of her sex. Her letters are large, ill formed, and inconsistent, and her spelling wild. Writing was evidently a laborious process for her, and she was aware of the poor results, writing anxiously to Cromwell: 'I ffaer me that he kan not rad my hand het hes so hel' (I fear me that ye can not read my hand it is so ill).[109] While it was common for women to apologize for their poor writing, one suspects this is not so much a use of that trope as a reflection of reality. It is surprising that a daughter of the Duke of Buckingham should have such poor penmanship even at the beginning of the sixteenth century, and unfortunate that there is no surviving correspondence from either of her sisters in their own hands. As Daybell has shown, many of her contemporaries wrote perfectly legible, though not professional, hands, though Elizabeth's daughter would in her turn complain about the 'travail' of writing.[110]

Almost all of Elizabeth's letters are written on smaller pieces of paper rather than one large folded sheet, which was most likely due to economy, since paper was expensive and she complained of poverty.[111] This means that she sometimes squeezed several postscripts onto the bottom of the page in a way that makes them almost unintelligible to the reader. The first letter of the sequence, for instance, written on 23 August 1534, uses half a page for the body of the letter written by a secretary, and the second half of the page for a postscript in Elizabeth's own hand. She placed her signature in the bottom right-hand corner directly underneath her postscript, using a sign-off that appears to read 'by yours hass hass [*sic*] lang hass

---

[108] See n. 107 for dating specifics.   [109] TNA SP1/91, fol. 23.
[110] Daybell, *Women Letter-Writers*, 68, 104–5. For Mary's letter see TNA SP10/7/1.
[111] Daybell, *Women Letter-Writers*, 51.

I leffe hass…power ffrend E Norfflkey'. In the bottom left-hand corner, written so that it looks as though it is part of the sign-off, she has added, 'I pra you sand me my boke artycless by thess barer hass my trosst hess in you'.[112] The time, effort, and number of scholars that it has taken to untangle these two sentences suggests that it would not necessarily have made sense to Cromwell, her recipient, either. This is important, because, as we saw with Anne's letters, leaving a degree of blank space was considered polite and deferential. Even where this is not done, as in Katherine's letter, clarity remained a priority. We do have to note that in some cases Elizabeth's original letters have been cut down and bound into manuscripts, making it difficult to tell what the original size of the paper and margins might have been. On many occasions, however, she and/or her scribe have filled every available space on the page, the writing often becoming smaller as the letter goes on in order to cram as many words as possible onto the paper.

It is probable that the letters not in her own hand were written to her dictation, because the style is remarkably similar across the entire sequence.[113] Certain phrases are repeated across letters written by different secretaries; one of her favourites was to tell Cromwell that 'my trust is in you next God'. This means we can be confident that we are reasonably close to Elizabeth's own voice despite the use of an amanuensis. What makes this even clearer is the erratic, 'stream-of-consciousness' style of writing. Though Daybell highlights this as a general trend in noblewomen's letters, the length, degree of repetition, and number of evidently impassioned statements are a hallmark of Elizabeth's letters, particularly by comparison with both Anne and Katherine above, and could not have been invented by a secretary.[114] Again, by comparison with the others, Elizabeth's letters are neither particularly well put together, nor especially well judged as petitions for help. In one she remarked that she had 'not connsayle to put my self in wryttyng of my lettr'—a probable admission of her isolation from family and friends—and it may be that this lack of letter-writing advice was the reason that they read so differently, though Katherine also claimed this and her letter is a far clearer and more sober read.[115]

While Elizabeth's earliest two letters are shorter, more light-hearted, and lean more heavily on the language of friendship than that of lordship, her tone changed with the third letter, which has been dated to 30 December 1536.[116] This letter saluted Cromwell for the first time as her 'very good lord' and contained many more effusive phrases of thanks for his kindness. This tone continued for the remainder of her correspondence with him. This third letter is also the first time that we learn of much of the detail of the episode from her own hand. For the first time she mentioned Bess Holland, stating that her 'ille lyffe' with her husband had begun when he fell in love with Bess, 'which was butt washer of my nurcory' and 'the causer of all my trouble'. In this letter we also learn that her aims had changed since she had been sent to Redbourn. Having sued to her husband three times to take her back, one of these at the King's commandment, his continued

---

[112] BL Cotton MS Vespasian F XIII, fol. 151.
[113] Daybell, *Women Letter-Writers*, 80–2.   [114] Ibid. 44–5.
[115] TNA SP1/144, fol. 16.   [116] BL Cotton MS Titus B I, fols 392–3.

refusal had made her resolve never to sue to him or to anybody else for this again. She wrote impassionedly that 'I woll not do it atte the kynges comanndemet nor at your desire | I woll not doo it for noo frende nor kynnge I haue lyvynge'. Instead, she begged Cromwell to work instead to secure her more alimony, what she termed 'a better lyvyng'. This and other letters suggest that she had been working hard to find a way to force Norfolk to give up Bess and return to her in the two and a half years since their separation. A later letter makes it clear that she had been to petition the King in person when he was at Dunstable nearby, though all that she had gained was a command to sue again to her husband.[117] As was common in petitionary letters from women, she elicited sympathy here by declaring that if she were to return to Norfolk now, it would be even worse, 'bicause I haue lyved quyet this iij yere withoute brakyng or ffyttinge'. Her style is idiosyncratic and creates a jarring dissonance between her defiant stance and refusal to do as Cromwell desires, and the submissive role of petitioner. Seen in this context, the similarity between the Queen's reaction to annulment and Elizabeth's to her husband's behaviour becomes clear. The Queen was implacable, refusing to recognize either the authority of the court that tried their marriage, or the result. In 1528 she informed Cardinal Campeggio that 'neither the whole kingdom on the one hand, nor any great punishment on the other, although she might be torn limb from limb, should compel her to alter this opinion; and that if after death she should return to life, rather than change it, she would prefer to die over again'.[118] Elizabeth, naturally, would have known of the Queen's reactions first hand, and it is impossible not to see that she would undoubtedly have identified with her when faced with her own situation. It is also interesting that she did not cease campaigning for her husband to put aside his mistress and return to her until after the Queen herself had died.

As the years passed, her demand for more money morphed into a plea for her entire yearly jointure payment of 500 marks, as agreed by her father and husband at the time the marriage was made. The request first appeared in a letter in October 1537, and it is perhaps interesting that this letter also saw a slight increase in the level of deference, saluting Cromwell as 'my specyall gud lorde in my most loving wyse that my hertt can thinck I recomend me unto yow'.[119] This letter was the first time (to our knowledge) that she explained at length the circumstances under which her marriage had been made, and it is worth quoting in full:

'[he] had wyth me ij thosannd marks w[i]t[h] ye more by tymes when he had but lytyll to take to when he maryed me furst but hys lands & he wos all ways a grett player: Seyng my lorde my father made me sure off CCCCC marks ayere & seyng yt my lorde my husbande chase me hym sylffe for my lorde my father had borth my lorde off westmereland for me he & I had loved to gether ij yers & my lorde my husband had not sende immedyatly word after my lade an my lords furst wyff wos ded he mad

[117] BL Cotton MS Titus B I, fol. 388r–v. It is not wholly clear when this visit took place; a later letter dated to January 1540 on its own internal context states that it had happened 3.5 years previously, which would place it in the middle of 1536 (see BL Cotton MS Titus B I, fol. 391). I have found no direct evidence for the King being in Dunstable around this time, though he was certainly there in August of the following year, 1537.
[118] *LP* IV, 4875.　　　[119] BL Cotton MS Titus B I, fol. 390r–v.

sute to my lord my father or ells I had be maryed afore crystynmas to my lorde off westmereland & yt was my lord my husbande sute to my lorde my father & neu[er] came off me nor no[ne] off my frynds: & when he came thether at stroft tyde he wold haue no[ne] off my systern but only me.'[120]

She appears to justify her own expectations of fidelity and love from Norfolk by insisting that it had been a love match to begin with. Though we cannot prove or disprove this, it seems highly likely that the childlessness of Howard's previous marriage had much to do with his desire to gain a new wife quickly, and the fact that Elizabeth was, at 15, the eldest sister, was no doubt among the reasons that he was only interested in her and not in the others. She herself gives us another reason for Howard's keenness; she came with a large dowry. Perhaps to her 15-year-old eyes it did seem as though Howard had fallen in love with her, and there is no reason why he might not have had or developed feelings for her in the early days of their courtship and marriage, whatever happened later on. Her motive behind this lengthy description may have been simply to furnish Cromwell with this information, since he had not moved in these circles back in 1512, and to do so in the context of her own suffering. However, we must remember that the case for the Queen's divorce depended on the way the marriage was made, and her virginal state or otherwise at its beginning. Elizabeth's divorce rested on no such pretexts and yet she too made much of these things in her letters to Cromwell. It is as though she was suggesting to Cromwell that the premise on which she thought her married life was based was in fact a lie, and that she was owed something in return; if not a loving husband, then the money that would allow her to live independently as though she had been widowed.

This echoes the understanding given by Daubeney in his letter to Cromwell about maintenance payments that a woman 'earned' her right to jointure by her good behaviour and by bearing children. Elizabeth compares her own situation directly with that of her daughter Mary's quest for her own jointure following the unexpected death of her husband Henry Fitzroy, Duke of Richmond, in 1536.[121] Mary's dowry, she argued, had not been paid, and she had had no children; her own dowry was fully paid, and she had given her husband five children. Thus, 'by the law' she thought she ought to get her jointure before Mary. Had she been genuinely widowed, or undergone a formal divorce procedure, she would have had a point. Without either of these, this was a fruitless quest, since it simply was not how the law worked. This underscores her apparent lack of real legal understanding, and of professional advice. This is unusual for a noblewoman; as Barbara Harris has pointed out, the majority had a keen understanding of the law as it concerned them, as indeed they needed to in order to successfully manage property, estates, and finances on their own or their husband's behalf.[122]

Interestingly, it seems that Elizabeth scuppered her own chances for obtaining her jointure money, whether or not she realized this. In November 1537, she told

---

[120] Ibid.
[121] Mary's father-in-law, the King, was refusing to pay her jointure, claiming that the marriage was not valid because it had not been consummated.
[122] Harris, *English Aristocratic Women*, 66–7.

Cromwell that after she had come to Redbourn, Norfolk had sent his chaplains to tell her that if she would be 'devorsed' he would give her her jewels, apparel, and a lot of plate and household stuff.[123] She 'rebukett' the priests, noting with evident satisfaction that 'he had lever then a thousand li he colde haue brogth me to haue ben devorsed'. It is not difficult to imagine where Norfolk might have got the idea to divorce his wife in light of the 'great matter'. Indeed, his reaction to his own situation was not dissimilar to the King's; Henry had sent Catherine away to a succession of damp castles, and Norfolk sent Elizabeth away to Redbourn. Though 'divorce' was a catch-all term to contemporaries, it also seems more likely that he did intend an annulment like the King, and not a judicial separation like his sister Katherine.[124] For the latter, he would have had to plead that Elizabeth was adulterous, or allow her to plead cruelty; if the former, he would, so far as is known, have had to fabricate his evidence, and given his emphatic denial of the latter in 1536 it is unlikely that he would have allowed her to do this. If successful, the marriage would still not have been officially dissolved. Conversely, an annulment would have allowed him to wash his hands of Elizabeth and even to remarry, though it is not clear what grounds he might have used, since the degree of kinship between them was not sufficiently close to invalidate the marriage.[125]

If Elizabeth had agreed to this, and the suit had been successful, she would have lost her title as Duchess of Norfolk, just as Catherine of Aragon had lost her title as Queen. While in theory she might have regained the dowry that she brought to the marriage, in practice, courts did not always insist on this. That Elizabeth refused so decidedly, despite having 'connsyll inoth yff I wold a followed ytt', seems also to point towards an intended annulment rather than separation. Though she might have gained her 'better living', plus the material goods that she had lost, the loss of her title and rank would have been a disadvantage, and one suspects that she did not want to give Norfolk the liberty to continue his relationship with Bess. It may also have been a deliberate choice taken in light of the Queen's situation, though by 1534, when Norfolk made his request, it must have been clear that the Queen was not going to 'win'. Divorce was also generally considered to carry a label of shame and dishonour, and, like Anne, Elizabeth drew on this in her letters, albeit with less success. In 1536 she wrote that if Norfolk were to take her back, 'it is more for the shame of the world than for eny love he bereth me'.[126] She consistently wrote his affair as a disregard for her status, and thus, implicitly, his own, claiming that 'yt ys spokon off fer & nere to hys grett dyshonnr & schame', and that he was 'so ferre indotyng loffe w[i]t[h] that queyne yt he nother regards god nor hys honor'.[127] The words she employed to describe Bess were all insults relating to rank

---

[123] BL Cotton MS Titus B I, fol. 389.

[124] Although in later years there were a few isolated cases where noblemen divorced their wives by Act of Parliament, these did not occur until the 1550s, and it is doubtful whether any 1530s Parliament would have allowed such a thing, particularly not when reform of the ecclesiastical court system appeared imminent.

[125] Norfolk and Elizabeth would have to have had great-grandparents in common at the very least in order to claim consanguinity, and they did not.

[126] BL Cotton MS Titus B I, fols 392–3.   [127] BL Cotton MS Titus B I, fol. 388r–v.

and status: 'harlot', 'churles dort[er]', 'quene', 'that drabbe'.[128] This implied that Norfolk's choice showed that he was careless of his own nobility. While this tactic had worked for Anne, it did not for Elizabeth; the reason that the affair was widely spoken of was not because of Norfolk's behaviour but because of her own.

Another hallmark of Elizabeth's letters was continued allegations of domestic violence. She made general references to 'brakyng or ffyttyinge' experienced in her former household in a letter to Cromwell in December 1536. In October 1537 she wrote that the women at Kenninghall had 'bounnde me & pynaculled me & satt on my brest tyll I spytt blod' for speaking against Bess Holland.[129] Later in the same letter she complained that 'ever syns ye baude & the drabbys bonnde me I am sycke at the fall of ye leyff & at the spryng of the yere ever syns they bound me pynaculled me & made me speytt blod'. In June 1538 she wrote that 'he sett hys wemen to bynde me tyll blod came out att my fyngars endes & pynnacullyt me & satt on my brest tyll I spett blod and he never ponysched them'; in January 1540, 'he kepeth ye harlot besse holond & all ye resydue off ye harlottes yt bownd me & pynacled me & sat on my brest tyll they made me spytte blode'.[130] The amount of literal repetition here is evident, despite the fact that some of these letters are in different hands, which strongly suggests that this is Elizabeth's own phrase. There is no way to prove or disprove her allegations. That they form part of a petition is significant, since this encouraged exaggeration. As Daybell argues, the truth or otherwise would not have been the point; the point was the emotive language designed to provoke sympathy.[131] She also, according to an undated letter from her husband to Thomas Cromwell, accused Norfolk of abuse dating back to 1519, claiming 'in writing and saying' that 'when she had be in chyld bed [inserted above: "of my doghter of Richmond"] ij nyghts and a day I [Norfolk] shuld draw her out of her bed by the here of the hed aboute the howse and w[i]t[h] my dagar geve her a wonde in the hed'.[132]

Narratives given in such circumstances were designed not only to be emotive but to strike familiar chords with the reader. Women alleging domestic abuse in law courts often claimed to have suffered violence during pregnancy, because it looked worse and created more sympathy; so did Elizabeth.[133] Moreover, there is some evidence that this, at least, may have been a fabrication. Norfolk's letter to Cromwell describing the event was written specifically to deny it: 'my gode lord if I prove not by witnes…that she had the skar in her hed xl monthes before she was delyuerd of my seid doghter and that the sam was cut by a surgeon of London for a swellyng she had in her hed of drawing of ij leth never trust my worde after…ther is no man on lyve that wold handle a woman in child bed or that sort nor for my part wold not so haue done for all that I am worth.'[134] It was highly unusual for men to bother

[128] Ibid.   [129] BL Cotton MS Titus B I, fol. 390r–v.

[130] BL Cotton MS Titus B I, fol. 388r–v.

[131] Daybell, *Women Letter-Writers*, 245–6. For further discussion of this episode in the context of the household, see Chapter 2.

[132] BL Cotton MS Titus B I, fol. 394r–v.

[133] Laura Gowing, *Domestic Dangers: Women, Words, and Sex in Early Modern London* (Oxford, 1996), 42–56 and 189–90.

[134] BL Cotton MS Titus B I, fol. 394r–v.

denying violence against their wives. What they usually did was to contextualize it, explaining that it was done as a form of correction.[135] Elizabeth was certainly deliberately using these descriptions to emphasize her position as the victim. We simply do not know how far she fabricated or exaggerated in order to do so.

Elizabeth's case was therefore somewhat different from both Anne's and Katherine's, and unlike them, she gained no real resolution. Her plea for more money was never granted, and her husband did not give up Bess until his arrest in 1547, after which she seems to have married another man.[136] Though she followed the traditional process of intervention, she was hamstrung by her lack of influential natal kin, and by her husband's powerful position. However, from an early modern perspective one could also argue that she did not help herself. She was undeniably in the wrong here, and it seems likely that even her mistress the Queen would have thought this. Catherine only objected to her husband's affair when it materially threatened her own position, and there is no evidence that Norfolk was seeking to marry Bess. Elizabeth's letters to Cromwell were also not the strongest petitions. Though she drew on some of the same tropes as the other women, she seems to have done so haphazardly, and it was of course difficult to construct an effective petition when half the letter had to be spent apologizing for not following Cromwell's original counsel. Her case, though, was arguably strongly affected by the King's 'great matter'. Elizabeth's own implacable attitude reflected the Queen's; Norfolk's, the King's. This shows that the King's divorce did indeed impact his nobility, since apparently Norfolk felt it appropriate to attempt to divorce his own wife in light of it. The King, however, did not see things in this way. Throughout, he preached reconciliation to Elizabeth, counselling her to return to her husband and accept the situation, and encouraging her to write 'gentle' petitions to Norfolk, clearly intended that Norfolk should accept them. His own divorce was not supposed to be a signal for the nobility to do likewise.

CONCLUSIONS

There is no easy explanation as to why three women at the core of one noble dynasty all experienced serious marital problems within a short space of time. Aside from their kinship to the Howards, there are few common factors. Not all were born into the family, some were first and one a second marriage, there were different reasons for marital breakdown, and not all were encouraged by the family to pursue resolution. To a greater extent, then, these cases occurring so close together was a matter of coincidence. Nevertheless one has to wonder whether the King's annulment created an atmosphere in which 'divorce' of one kind of another was seen as more viable than previously. Surely Norfolk would not have asked

---

[135] Susan Dwyer Amussen, '"Being stirred to much unquietness": Violence and Domestic Violence in Early Modern England', *Journal of Women's History* 6:2 (1994), 70–89 (73).

[136] After Norfolk's arrest, Elizabeth's allowance was paid by the crown, and remained the same amount; *APC* 2, 77.

Elizabeth to divorce had he not had the example of the King in front of him; surely Elizabeth might have been more amenable if she had not seen the Queen's demise; surely Katherine or Daubeney, whichever brought the suit, was encouraged by the recent example of the use of canon law. It is also highly likely that these cases impacted on one another. Elizabeth, for instance, would have known first hand about her half-sister-in-law Anne, Countess of Oxford's, issues; she sheltered Anne at Tendring Hall on a couple of occasions in 1523.[137] She might therefore have thought that she could secure similar help from a royal adviser later on. She would also presumably have known about Katherine's case. Perhaps the court gossip about it helped to firm her own resolution to refuse Norfolk when he asked her for a divorce in 1536.

While the reasons for marital breakdown were different across all three cases, the women reacted in notably similar ways. First they all approached or used natal relatives to try to produce resolution, and from there, whether successful or not, escalated their call for aid to the King's advisers, Wolsey and Cromwell respectively, while continuing to use the assistance of family members where possible. This shows that there must have been a generally understood process of petition for women who found themselves in this situation, but interestingly it shows that lack of familial support did not deter them from seeking higher resolution. Nor did it necessarily stop them gaining it, since Katherine had her divorce regardless. In fact, the support or lack thereof from royal advisers was more crucial for concrete action. The women also behaved similarly in the way that they created their petitions, in terms of the epistolary techniques used and the tropes that they drew on. The necessity for good petitionary strategy and/or good advice is clear, since the two who had resolution (Anne and Katherine) also wrote the better petitions.

These cases therefore allow us to think about female agency. The importance of familial and state support—almost always male—seems to suggest that women in these situations really had very little agency to change their circumstances alone. To a degree, this is true. Anne and Katherine were 'lucky' in that they had husbands who were not especially well regarded by those in positions of power, whereas Elizabeth's was so powerful in his own right that it would have been difficult to find anybody to help her oppose him, whatever the scenario. Broadly speaking, if society, and therefore family, thought that a woman was in the wrong, she was not going to get what she wanted, as Elizabeth's case demonstrates. But Katherine's case shows that things were a little more complicated than that. Her family, allegedly, did not think she warranted their help; but the Church and the state disagreed, and she did gain resolution. Could this be down to Katherine as an individual? Though we do not know whether she or her husband initiated the divorce suit, she clearly took initiative in petitioning Cromwell for help with the financial settlement. Katherine was a similar age to Elizabeth, but arguably had additional 'life experience', having taken part in a rebellion far away in south Wales and seen her first husband executed for treason, before marrying Daubeney. She may simply have had a better idea of how to go about securing what she wanted, or had access

---

[137] UCB, MS UCB 049 (Howard household book, 1523–4).

to better advice. She was also politically savvy, having created some sort of unofficial alliance with Anne Boleyn. Elizabeth, by contrast, was clearly less able to write a good petitionary letter, was self-evidently not a 'politician', and not only misunderstood the law but had no advice.

These cases also show that families did not necessarily behave consistently or collectively when faced with these sorts of crises. For Elizabeth, though her brother was clearly not prepared to support her, there is evidence that one brother-in-law had attempted to act as mediator, and another sued to her husband on her behalf. Though Elizabeth never wavered from her resolution not to return to her husband, it is clear that her brother later 'came around' and the two were reconciled. For Katherine, though her brother Norfolk and other 'kyne' apparently refused to help her, her niece the Queen did, and possibly also the Earl of Wiltshire, alongside a few marital kin. 'Dynasty', then, cast a wide net, and women's agency was not necessarily restricted to or by immediate family.

4

'Yll name or fame'
Courtiers

The Howards are known as one of England's premier 'courtier families' of the sixteenth century, and with good reason. The Second and Third Dukes of Norfolk were Lord Treasurers of England, privy councillors, and Earls Marshal. They, and others, served on numerous occasions as diplomats and military commanders. Many also held humbler court offices that were nevertheless important in an age of personal monarchy; John Howard, First Duke of Norfolk, for instance, began his court career as the King's carver in the 1460s.[1] Howard women, too, held formal offices at court. Two (Anne Boleyn and Catherine Howard) became queen, Agnes Tylney/Howard, Duchess of Norfolk, was godmother to both Princesses Mary and Elizabeth, and many served in various queens' households. Their exact service record, though, is somewhat hazy, and while we tend to assume, for instance, that there were more Howard women in service with Anne Boleyn and Catherine Howard, this deserves proper consideration.

This is closely linked with another common assumption about the point of women's court service: that they were there explicitly to serve their families.[2] It is not that this is untrue. Numerous examples from sources like the Lisle letters, directly contemporary with these women, as well as an increasing body of scholarly research, show that there was indeed an expectation that women would seek to help family members to gain office, grants, information, and favour.[3] Theory, how-ever, sometimes came to blows with practice. This book has already shown that 'family' was not a simple thing for women. Which family, natal or marital, were they supposed to promote first and foremost, and what if they had to choose one above the other, or if interests clashed? The question of loyalties is one that is rarely formally considered, but it was brought sharply into focus for women at court during Henry VIII's reign. Yet again, this rests on the way in which we define 'a Howard woman', and the elasticity of kinship. This chapter explores this from the perspective of the royal court, shedding new light on some well-known episodes

---

[1] Crawford, *Yorkist Lord*, 29.

[2] See, for instance, Harris, *English Aristocratic Women*, chapter 9; Helen Payne, 'Aristocratic Women, Power, Patronage and Family Networks at the Jacobean Court, 1603–1625' in Daybell (ed.), *Women and Politics*, 164–80; Olwen Hufton, 'Reflections on the Role of Women in the Early Modern Court', *Court Historian* 5 (2000), 1–13.

[3] *Lisle Letters*, V, 1513; see also many of the essays in Geevers and Marini (eds), *Dynastic Identity in Early Modern Europe*.

and bringing out some of the difficulties faced by female Howard courtiers across this period.

The context for this is the robust and growing volume of work on women at court during the early modern period. There are now scholarly studies not only of queenship in its many guises, but on the women who served them in courts across Europe.[4] 'Soft power' is now an accepted phenomenon, because, as Olwen Hufton explained, it is evident that women played a role as 'the emollient', the oil on the wheels of the patronage system.[5] Formal office-holding was not the only route to influence. We are now very clear that women did indeed hold political power and operated as political players, and so this chapter does not ask whether or not this was the case, but rather when, how, and why the Howard women were able to play this role.

Before asking when and whom the Howard women served, it is useful to think about what their experience of courtier life might have included. What did it mean to be a female courtier? Contemporaries outside the royal court generally under-appreciated the difficulty of a courtier's job, instead ridiculing them as profligate, vulgarly ostentatious, morally dubious, and sycophantic.[6] Sometimes those things were true. To be a courtier with a long-lasting, successful career, however, required very much more than this. For women, duties varied depending whether or not they were in formal service. The court was not a hermetically sealed entity, and women were able to visit if they were in town, or be brought in by those who held

---

[4] On queenship, see: Theresa Earenfight, *Queenship in Medieval Europe* (Basingstoke, 2013); J. Laynesmith, *The Last Medieval Queens: English Queenship, 1445–1503* (Oxford, 2004); Carole Levin and Christine Stewart-Nuez (eds), *Scholars and Poets Talk about Queens* (Basingstoke, 2015); Alice Hunt and Anna Whitelock (eds), *Tudor Queenship* (Basingstoke, 2010); T. Adams, 'Renaissance Queenship: A Review Article', *Explorations in Renaissance Culture* 42:1 (2016), 87–107. On women at court, see: Nadine Akkerman and Birgit Houben (eds), *The Politics of Female Households: Ladies-n-Waiting across Early Modern Europe* (Leiden, 2013); Hufton, 'Reflections on the Role of Women'; Sharon Kettering, 'The Household Service of Early Modern French Noblewomen', *French Historical Studies* 20:1 (1997), 55–85; Dakota Hamilton, 'The Household of Katherine Parr' (unpublished Ph.D. dissertation, University of Oxford, 1992); Natalie Mears, 'Politics in the Elizabethan Privy Chamber: Lady Mary Sidney and Kat Ashley', in Daybell (ed.), *Women and Politics*, 67–82; Charlotte Merton, 'The Women who Served Queen Mary and Queen Elizabeth' (unpublished Ph.D. dissertation, University of Cambridge, 1990); Rosalind K. Marshall, *Queen Mary's Women: Female Relatives, Servants, Friends and Enemies of Mary, Queen of Scots* (Edinburgh, 2006); Una McIlvenna, *Scandal and Reputation at the Court of Catherine de Medici* (London, 2016); Caroline zum Kolk, 'The Household of the Queen of France in the Sixteenth Century', *The Court Historian* 14 (2009), 3–22; Birgit Houben, 'Intimacy and Politics: Isabel and her Ladies-in-Waiting (1621–33)', in Cordula van Wyhe (ed.), *Isabel Clara Eugenia: Female Sovereignty in the Courts of Madrid and Brussels* (London, 2012), 325–30; Helen Payne, 'Aristocratic Women and the Jacobean Court, 1604–1625' (unpublished Ph.D. dissertation, University of London, 2001); Sara Wolfson, 'Aristocratic Women of the Household and Court of Queen Henrietta Maria, 1625–1659' (unpublished Ph.D. dissertation, University of Durham, 2010); Sharon Kettering, 'Strategies of Power: Favorites and Women Household Clients at Louis XIII's Court', *French Historical Studies* 33:2 (2010), 177–200; Ruth Kleinman, 'Social Dynamics at the French Court: The Household of Anne of Austria', *French Historical Studies* 16:3 (1990), 517–35; Frances Harris, 'The Honourable Sisterhood: Queen Anne's Maids of Honour', *The British Library Journal* 19 (1993), 181–98.

[5] Hufton, 'Reflections on the Role of Women', 11.

[6] See, for instance, John Skelton, 'Bowge of Court' (*c.*1499), or Antonio de Guervara, *A dispraise of the life of a courtier, and a commendacion of the life of the labouring man* (1548).

a position in the queen's household.[7] Those not in formal service would have no official duties except perhaps on ceremonial occasions. Those holding a defined position within the Queen's household, however, were on duty full time, seven days a week, and were not supposed to leave without permission.[8] In essence, they were there to serve the Queen in whatever way she required. Exact duties depended on a woman's specific position within the household, but might include personal service, such as helping the Queen to get dressed and undressed; care of her clothes and jewels; keeping her chambers clean; and attending her wherever she went and whatever she was doing, from banquets with foreign ambassadors to sharing her bed at night. While elsewhere these might be considered menial tasks, at court these were duties of great honour.

Female courtiers, then, needed a large and diverse skillset. They had to be able to converse appropriately with a variety of people of different genders, statuses, and nationalities, meaning that language skills were an advantage. They must be able to dance, and probably to sing and/or play musical instruments; to ride and to hunt; to be able to stay up late and get up early repeatedly without flagging. As Castiglione's *Book of the Courtier*, written in 1528, explains, the female courtier was constantly walking a narrow and difficult tightrope between preserving her virtue without seeming prudish.[9] She was supposed to be entertaining as well as ornamental, but she had to find a way to be witty and vivacious without thereby appearing unchaste, ungentle, or indiscreet. If, for instance, she found herself amidst a group of men indulging in lewd conversation, she should not leave in horror in case it looked as though the lady doth protest too much, but she should certainly not join in, because to do so risked her reputation. Castiglione suggests that she should instead listen silently with a blush of shame, since this was apparently the right balance between her duty to entertain, and her virtue.[10] Indeed, these inherent contradictions were everywhere in Castiglione's ideal woman; she was also supposed to take great care with her appearance, without appearing to have taken any, something that no doubt remains familiar today.[11] Of course, these are ideals, and there are plenty of examples from the English and other courts to show that in reality women at court did not perfectly match this description. But evidence from the Lisle letters in the mid-1530s shows that the concept of the virtuous female courtier was taken seriously. Lady Lisle was advised to make sure that her daughters hoping to enter the Queen's service were 'sober, sad, wise and discreet and lowly above all things, and to be obedient... and to serve God and to be virtuous, for that is much regarded, to serve God well and to be sober of tongue'.[12]

---

[7] See *Lisle Letters*, IV, 868a discussing Katherine Basset's potential placement at court. Though the Countess of Sussex had no space for another gentlewoman in her own retinue, 'Mrs Margery' promised to 'receive her and lay her in her chamber, or else with young Mrs Norris, and bring her with her into the Queen's chamber every day'.

[8] Merton, 'The Women Who Served', 11.

[9] Baldesar Castiglione, *The Book of the Courtier*, trans. George Bull (London, 1976), Book III (207–78).

[10] Ibid. 212.   [11] Ibid. 215.   [12] *Lisle Letters*, IV, 887.

Nevertheless, all the virtue in the world could not make up for good looks, social ease, and general accomplishment, as is made clear by the placement of Lady Lisle's younger daughter over her elder sister.[13] In the same letter as above, the writer went on to describe the court as 'full of pride, envy, indignation and mocking, scorning, and derision'.[14] It must sometimes have seemed so to the women who were on show all day, every day. For those who lodged with their husbands, there was probably a degree of respite at night. For unmarried ladies-in-waiting, and the maids of honour, solitude was in short supply, and their living arrangements were not unlike a girls' boarding school.[15] While no doubt this could have its advantages—many women forged close and lasting friendships through court service—there were, inevitably, cliques, feuds, and favourites. Lady Lisle was forced to pacify the Countess of Sussex with a personal token in 1539 after some incident between the Countess and Lady Lisle's daughter Anne; Husee, her London agent, reported that Lady Sussex remained 'not well plyased' with Anne, and that 'thoughe the mater be forgavin I do p[er]cayve she hathe not fforgotten it'.[16]

Yet the feeling of being part of the most important establishment in the realm, among the biggest movers and shakers, must have been a powerful attraction for many women. Catherine Howard said in 1541 that everybody had known how happy she had been to enter service at court.[17] Undoubtedly there were perks, and the advantages to having a daughter, sister, or other female relative in service to the Queen are usually understood from a dynastic, familial perspective. Though in theory royal servants were not supposed to approach the King or the Queen with personal suits for patronage, in practice their proximity to the monarchs meant that they were considered and used as brokers by their own family and by others, and thus they stood to gain a degree of personal influence.[18] Families wanted eyes and ears near the monarchs. Women in service might well see and hear all sorts of important information that they could then pass on. They also had access to areas of the court which were barred to most or all men: only the Queen's women would enter her bedchamber, for instance. Women therefore functioned as barometers of the Queen's mood, and might be her confidantes, or be used by her to dispense patronage, or even to send out specific political messages.[19] Unmarried women in court service stood in good stead to make a better marriage than they might have managed otherwise, since they came into contact with many more eligible men in this environment, and might even have a marriage arranged for them by the Queen. Competition for places, therefore, was fierce. There were perks for the women as individuals too. Positions in the Queen's household usually, though not always, came with a salary, and though this itself might be meagre, the Queen's women were also entitled to food, fuel, light, and lodging, and a certain amount of

---

[13] See *Lisle Letters*, IV, chapter X for this episode.   [14] *Lisle Letters*, IV, no. 887.
[15] *CSP Dom., 1547–80*, 648.   [16] TNA SP3/11, fol. 121.
[17] Gilbert Burnet, *The History of the Reformation of the Church of England*, 6 vols (London, 1643–1715) VI, 252.
[18] See royal household ordinances in Bodl. Laudian MS Misc. 597, fol. 24v.
[19] See the essays in Akkerman and Houben, *The Politics of Female Households*, for examples of this. See also Natalie Mears, 'Politics in the Elizabethan Privy Chamber: Lady Mary Sidney and Kat Ashley', in Daybell (ed.), *Women and Politics*, 67–82.

clothing provided as livery.[20] Besides this, they often received gifts of clothing or other valuable items from the Queen herself. As with most professions, then, there were pros and cons to court service for women as well as for men. Whatever one's personal attributes, it took time and effort first to gain a place at court, and then to become a good courtier. Serving the Queen was no sinecure.

Although one did not have to hold a salaried position in order to be considered a courtier, official service is nevertheless a helpful place to begin considering the Howard women's court careers. Although we still lack a scholarly study of the women who served Henry VIII's queens, the growing body of work on women at royal courts, including the households of Princesses Mary and Elizabeth and Katherine Parr, means that it is possible to set the Howards' court service into some kind of context.[21] There were many more formal positions available for men than for women throughout the sixteenth century, and consequently more men than women at court. Until *c.*1540, the number of women attending the Queen 'in ordinary', meaning daily service, was not usually more than twenty.[22] During the last years of Henry's reign, under Katherine Parr, the number inflated, and Dakota Hamilton has stated that Parr had around forty-five women in regular attendance by 1547.[23] During Edward's reign, there was of course no household attached to a queen consort, because the King, as a minor, remained unmarried. While most probably the wives of men in royal service continued to lodge at court, they were not in formal service to a female sovereign of any sort. On Mary's accession in 1553, the number of women in her household was around thirty.[24] Of these women, between two and four would be 'great ladies' of high status; seven or more would be classed as 'ladies' or 'ladies and gentlewomen' of the privy chamber; and some-where between two or four would be chamberers, women of lower status whose job it was to look after the queen's rooms and belongings.[25] As the sixteenth century progressed, it became normal for there to be around six 'maids of honour', young, adolescent women in their teens for whom the royal court functioned as a sort of finishing school environment, where they might polish their accomplishments, make useful connections, and serve the Queen.[26] These girls were under the care of the 'mother of the maids'.

---

[20] See, for instance, the 'fees' tabled in BL Add. MS 34320, fols 102v–103. For a clear explanation of 'bouche of court' see Merton, 'The Women Who Served', 12–19.

[21] Merton, 'The Women Who Served'; Dakota Hamilton, 'The Household of Katherine Parr' (unpublished Ph.D. dissertation, University of Oxford, 1992); Akkerman and Houben (eds), *The Politics of Female Households*; Laynesmith, *The Last Medieval Queens*, chapter 5.

[22] Elizabeth Woodville had fourteen female attendants in 1466–7 (A. R. Myers, *Crown Household and Parliament in the Fifteenth Century* (London, 1985), 251–318.); Anne Neville had twelve at her coronation in 1483 (Anne F. Sutton and P. W. Hammond, *Richard III's Coronation: The Extant Documents* (Gloucester, 1983), 84); Elizabeth of York had twenty in 1502–3 (TNA E36/210, privy purse expenses 1502–3); Catherine Howard had twenty four (TNA SP1/157, fols 14–15); Katherine Parr had twenty-seven on a lodgings list from the late 1540s (BL Cotton MS Vitellius C XIV, fols 93–93v).

[23] Forty-five women are listed as 'ordinary' at Henry VIII's funeral in 1547 (TNA LC2/2, fol. 44). Hamilton, 'The Household of Katherine Parr', 13.

[24] For numbers under Mary and Elizabeth, see Merton, 'The Women Who Served'.

[25] See note 19.

[26] It is not clear when this practice emerged. Elizabeth of York's wages list (TNA E210/36, fol. 91) does not appear to show a distinct group of younger women, and the lack of complete wage lists for

As well as the women who served 'in ordinary', there was also a pool of women 'in extraordinary', who effectively functioned as substitutes when those in ordinary had to leave for a period of time, usually because they were pregnant. Peeresses might also be considered as 'extraordinary' ladies in waiting, since they would drop in to attend the Queen when staying in the vicinity. At various points, there were also other royal female households in which women might serve, such as those of Henry VIII's mother Lady Margaret Beaufort, his sisters Margaret and Mary, his daughters Mary and Elizabeth, and, occasionally, former queens, notably Catherine of Aragon and Anne of Cleves, but these households were both smaller and less exalted than that of the Queen herself. No Howard women appear to have served in any royal household except the Queen's own.

The Howard women were no strangers to court life, but their pedigree of court service did not extend as far back as one might assume. No woman born into the Howard family appears to have served Margaret of Anjou, Elizabeth Woodville, Anne Neville, or Elizabeth of York as a daily attendant, though they did attend important ceremonies at court during the latter two reigns. The Howard men's support of Richard III meant that both Margaret Chedworth/Wyfold/Norreys/Howard, Duchess of Norfolk, and Elizabeth Tylney/Bourchier/Howard, Countess of Surrey, received scarlet livery for the coronation of Anne Neville in 1483, but—not surprisingly—no Howard women attended Elizabeth of York's coronation in 1487.[27] The single possible exception to this lack of early service was Anne Plantagenet/Howard, first wife of Thomas Howard, later Third Duke of Norfolk. As the sister of Elizabeth of York, Anne's name does appear on the wages list in the Queen's privy purse expenses of 1502–3. However, Anne was not actually paid any wages in this account. Instead, the entry in the account was a payment to her husband, Lord Howard, for the 'diettes' of his wife for the previous year, as per an agreement made at the time of their marriage.[28] Thus while it is of course plausible that Anne did occasionally attend her sister, the surviving evidence does not show her as an 'ordinary', daily, attendant.[29]

This state of affairs changed from the beginning of Henry VIII's reign. Catherine of Aragon, swiftly made his Queen, had, of course, been in England for some time as Prince Arthur's wife and widow, but her household had been severely reduced after his death and appears only to have included women who had come with her from Spain.[30] On her marriage to Henry VIII, her household more than doubled in size, and for the first time, women related to the Howards held places in it. Though this looks like a sudden change in their fortunes, the reality was probably more measured. The Earl of Surrey's political rehabilitation had been progressing increasingly swiftly post-1500—he was, for instance, chosen to escort Princess

Catherine of Aragon makes it difficult to know when they were introduced, though it was probably during her reign.

[27] Sutton and Hammond, *Richard III's Coronation*, 167–71; BL Cotton MS Julius B XII, fols 43–5.
[28] TNA E36/210, fol. 91; *Rot. Parl.*, 6, 479.
[29] For more on Elizabeth of York's household, see Laynesmith, *The Last Medieval Queens*, chapter 5.
[30] At the funeral of Henry VII, her female retinue comprised only eight women, all Spanish. The largest female household appears to have been that of Princess Mary, who had inherited many of her mother's women. TNA LC2/1, fols 95–6.

Margaret to her marriage with Scottish King James IV in 1502—but because Elizabeth of York died suddenly in 1503, places in her household, the most obvious sign of favour for women, could not be offered to the Howards. The first time that they were able to serve a queen was therefore 1509. It is also fair to note that their rank no doubt increased the demand for their presence; though they had yet to regain the dukedom of Norfolk, even countesses were not in infinite supply, particularly countesses who were geographically close enough to attend, and were not consumed by the need to manage large estates elsewhere.

At the coronation, Agnes Tylney/Howard, Countess of Surrey, and her step-daughters Muriel Howard/Grey, Viscountess Lisle, and Elizabeth Howard/Boleyn, Lady Boleyn, were listed as belonging to the Queen's chamber.[31] Agnes, indeed, was the matriarch of the Howard family by this point, and arguably had the most glittering court career of any Howard woman save, perhaps, those who later became queens. Though she does not seem to have served Elizabeth of York as an ordinary attendant, she did escort Princess Margaret to her wedding in Scotland in 1503, along with her stepdaughter Muriel, showing that even then she was a trusted courtier.[32] As we saw, she belonged to Catherine of Aragon's chamber in 1509, and the records suggest that she continued to serve Catherine at least up until her own widowhood in 1524 and possibly beyond it.[33] During this time, she also took on a number of significant ceremonial roles at court, serving as deputy godmother in the place of Margaret of Savoy at the christening of Prince Henry in January 1511, and as full godmother to Princess Mary in 1516, as well as escorting yet another Princess—Henry VIII's sister Mary, this time—to her wedding with the King of France in 1514.[34] In 1520, Agnes was possibly the only high-ranking peeress not to attend the Field of Cloth of Gold in France; she and her husband were left at home to guard the kingdom against the Scots. During that time some French ambassadors came to see Princess Mary and the court had to scramble in order that the Princess would not look poorly attended. Agnes came to the rescue, bringing herself and her three younger daughters to court.[35] Even after her widow-hood she remained a courtier. The 1526 Eltham Ordinances list her as lodging on the Queen's side, and this was the same in the list of 1529.[36] Though she continued

---

[31] TNA LC9/50, fols 204r–v. While usually lists of female attendants for special events cannot be taken as a list of 'ordinary' because of the many extras brought in for such occasions, this particular account clearly specifies that these women belong to the Queen's chamber, and were not 'extraordinary'.

[32] After Princess Margaret expressed a dislike of her new husband's beard, he enlisted Agnes and Muriel to shave it off as a joke, and paid them in cloth of gold. Sir James Balfour Paul (ed.), *Accounts of the Lord High Treasurer of Scotland A.D. 1500–1504*, 13 vols (Edinburgh, General Register Office, 1900), II, 314.

[33] For the first half of the reign, the King's books of payments list the rewards that he gave to court-iers' servants each New Year. He began rewarding the servants of a few women in 1511, and though the list grew across the 1510s it was never as long as the later gift rolls. This, and the otherwise arbitrary selection of names, suggests these were women who served the Queen, since the King would have known both them and their servants. Agnes's servants are on the list every year between 1513 and 1521. BL Add. MS 21481, fols 111, 141v, 176v, 210, 245, 279; TNA E36/216, fols 59, 146. 235.

[34] BL Add. MS 6113, fol. 79v; BL Harl. MS 3504, fol. 232; Leland, *Collectanea*, I, ii, 701.

[35] BL Cotton MS Caligula D VII, fol. 240v.

[36] Bodl., Rawlinson MS B 47, fol. 34; BL Egerton MS 2623, fol. 7.

to attend special events up until her death in 1545, she did not serve any other of Henry's queens as an ordinary lady-in-waiting.

The nature of recruitment at court—through personal recommendation—meant that particular families did indeed come to dominate particular households, and across Catherine's tenure as Queen consort her ladies-in-waiting took on an increasingly Howard flavour. In 1509 Agnes and her two stepdaughters were listed as members of the Queen's chamber.[37] Margaret Bourchier/Bryan, Lady Bryan, too, was a relative, though not a Howard, being the daughter of Elizabeth Tylney/Bourchier/Howard, the Second Duke of Norfolk's first wife. After serving Catherine of Aragon, she then became 'lady governess' to the royal children.[38] Her sister, Anne Bourchier/Fiennes, Lady Dacre of the South, was also listed in 1509, but does not appear in any court records after that until a list of New Year plate gifts from the Queen in 1522, which may mean that she was not an ordinary attendant.[39] By the New Year list of 1515, Elizabeth Stafford/Howard, the new Countess of Surrey, had joined them, and indeed seems to have been at court before her 1512 marriage.[40] Elizabeth would later say that she had been 'dayly waytar in the courtt' for sixteen years, and her somewhat turbulent court career will be discussed in greater detail below.[41] In 1514, one of the 'demoiselles' sent to France with Princess Mary was a 'Mademoiselle Boleyn', one of the daughters of Elizabeth Howard/Boleyn, Lady Boleyn, and another was Mary Fiennes, daughter of Anne Bourchier/Fiennes, Lady Dacre of the South.[42] Both of these then went on to serve Catherine of Aragon after Princess Mary's second marriage and return to England. Anne Knyvett, daughter of Muriel Howard/Grey/Knyvett, Viscountess Lisle, was also among the Queen's women by 1514, when she received livery.[43] The New Year list for 1519 included Lady Shelton, who belonged to a Howard client family and was also related to them through the Boleyns; she would later, along with her husband, run the princesses' household.[44] By the time of the infamous 'Chateau Vert' masque in 1522, both Anne and Mary Boleyn were among Catherine's maids, along with their future sister-in-law Jane Parker.[45] The rewards to servants at New Year in 1529 show that they were still at court, along with Mary Fiennes, who had since married Henry Norris.[46] Between 1509 and 1529, then, twelve women related to the Howard dynasty definitely held formal positions within the Queen's household, a household that numbered only around twenty at any given time.[47] What we cannot see

[37] TNA LC9/50, fols 204r–v.

[38] Susan Brigden, 'Margaret Bryan, suo jure Baroness Bryan (d. 1552)', *ODNB* [accessed 27 March 2017].

[39] TNA SP1/233, fol. 233.

[40] BL Add. MS 21481, fol. 176v. The Lady Elizabeth Stafford listed at the coronation cannot have been her aunt, because her aunt had married Robert Radcliffe, Viscount Fitzwater, by 1507.

[41] BL Cotton MS Titus B I, fol. 388r–v.

[42] BL Cotton MS Vitellius C XI, fol. 155. It is thought that 'Mademoiselle Boleyn' was probably Anne, since her sister Mary was already on the Continent and joined Princess Mary from there. See Ives, *The Life and Death of Anne Boleyn*, 27–9.

[43] TNA E101/418/6, fol. 30.   [44] TNA E36/216, fol. 59.

[45] Hall, *Chronicle*, 630–2.   [46] TNA E101/420/11, fol. 15.

[47] The lack of clear lists means that there may be more; this figure has been gleaned from a selection of other records.

is whether they saw themselves, or were seen, as 'Howards'. What the identity of these women highlights more strongly is the importance of vertical kinship links in court service. Many of the women who joined as maids of honour during Catherine's reign were the daughters of those who had served earlier on. This predominance of matriarchal, rather than patriarchal, kinship could perhaps indicate that in a court context, it was tangible kinship links, rather than the broader concept of dynastic identity, that was important.

From the late 1520s the situation at court became increasingly complex with the advent of Anne Boleyn. Henry had had mistresses before, including Anne's sister Mary, but his infatuation with Anne coincided with his increasing desperation for a male heir, and this did not bode well for the Queen. It also had an impact on female service at court. Anne is often said to have had the Howard dynasty ranged behind her in support of her alleged bid for the throne.[48] Her personal relationships with Howard individuals will be discussed later on, but looking through the lens of formal service itself provides a new and interesting perspective. Where the women were specifically concerned, the absence of formal records means that we cannot accurately pinpoint any shifts in allegiance from the Queen to Anne. It is also difficult to know when Anne gained her own household, but it is most likely that this occurred in late 1528, when Henry wrote to Anne explaining that he had found a lodging for her.[49] In December, the French ambassador reported that she was better attended than the Queen, but did not name any of her attendants.[50] In fact, the first concrete reference to Anne's own female attendants is not until the New Year gift roll of 1532—after Catherine had departed from court—where five gentlewomen were specifically listed as being 'w[i]t[h] the lady Anne'.[51] These were Anne Savage (later Lady Berkeley), Anne Joscelyn, 'Margaret' (perhaps Margaret Horsman), Jane Asshley, and [blank] Wriothesley; none of them were Howards, Howard relations, or Howard clients. As her reign progressed, Anne was served by her own female relatives in a mirror of the female kinship links seen in her predecessor's household. Her mother, Elizabeth Howard/Boleyn, Countess of Wiltshire, sister, Mary Boleyn/Carey, Lady Carey, sister-in-law Jane Parker/Boleyn, Viscountess Rochford, cousins Mary and Margaret Shelton, and aunt Elizabeth Wood/Boleyn, Lady Boleyn, were all part of her household. The Howards themselves were represented only by Anne's mother, and by Mary Howard, daughter of the Duke of Norfolk.[52] This was not due to a lack of candidates. The dowager Countess of Oxford, the Countess of Derby, Lady Fitzwater, and Lady Daubeney were all born with the Howard name, and there were also a number of wives of Howard men at this point who could have served.

Women born with, or who married, the Howard surname appeared instead at Anne's many formal ceremonies in the early 1530s. At her creation as Marquess of Pembroke in September 1532, her cousin Mary, the Duke of Norfolk's daughter,

[48] Retha M. Warnicke, 'Family and Kinship Relations at the Henrician Court: The Boleyns and Howards', in Dale Hoak (ed.), *Tudor Political Culture* (Cambridge, 1995), 31–53.

[49] Savage (ed.), *Love Letters of Henry VIII*, 37.   [50] *LP* IV, 5016.

[51] TNA E101/420/15, fol. 3v.

[52] One might perhaps count the Duke's mistress Elizabeth Holland, who was among Anne's maids.

bore her mantel, and this is usually taken to be Mary's own debut into court service.[53] A month later, two out of the six women accompanying Anne on the monarchs' trip to Calais were Howards: two of her cousins, Elizabeth Howard/ Radcliffe, Lady Fitzwater, and Dorothy Howard/Stanley, Countess of Derby.[54] Another two were her sister Mary and her sister-in-law Jane, who, as we saw, were in her permanent service. The final two women, Honor Grenville/Basset/ Plantagenet, Lady Lisle, and Elizabeth Harleston/Wallop, Lady Wallop, were clearly deemed necessary or politic choices by dint of their husbands' positions as Deputy of Calais and ambassador to France respectively. It is striking that those deliberately selected for the trip were Howards. Though we do not know whether Elizabeth and Dorothy were officially employed in Anne's service, she could presumably have chosen any of her own women or other peeresses to accompany her, and yet she chose, or was allocated, women who emphasized her own blood relationship to the Howard dynasty, suggesting that this was considered important on public occasions either by herself or by those around her. Senior Howard women continued to attend other high-profile ceremonies during Anne's reign, though apparently not her marriage in January 1533, which was so 'secret' that even several weeks afterwards the Spanish ambassador had not realized that it had occurred.[55] However, Agnes, the dowager Duchess of Norfolk, was certainly present at the feast given in Anne's privy chamber in March 1533, and at her coronation in June, and was then godmother to Princess Elizabeth.[56]

Anne's coronation, indeed, seems to have contained a number of Howard women, if the recollections of gentleman usher John Norreys are accurate.[57] The seven ladies at the top of his list of those who received livery for, and attended, her coronation included Mary Howard (soon to be married to Henry Fitzroy, Duke of Richmond), Dorothy Howard/Stanley, Countess of Derby, and Katherine Broughton/Howard, wife of Lord William. In the first chariot was Agnes, dowager Duchess of Norfolk; those on horseback included Elizabeth Howard/Radcliffe, Lady Fitzwater, and Katherine Howard/ap Rhys/Daubeney, Lady Daubeney. Anne's own relations, her sister-in-law, mother, and aunt, were also present. Interestingly, Elizabeth Stafford/Howard, Duchess of Norfolk, does not appear on Norreys's list, which supports the independent account stating that she had refused to attend.[58]

The point here is that although many Howard women, including the most high-status, turned out in support of Anne on public, ceremonial occasions, these individuals do not seem to have been among her ordinary attendants. There could be a number of interpretations of this. Are we perhaps seeing a division that contemporaries did not? Commentators referred to Anne as Norfolk's niece, which

[53] BL Add. MS 6113, fol. 70.   [54] *LP* V, 1484.

[55] This is usually said to have taken place around 25 January 1533; see Cranmer, *Letters*, 246. There are no contemporary lists of witnesses, but Nicholas Harpsfield later listed only Lady Berkeley in his 'Treatise on the Pretended Divorce between Henry the Eighth and Queen Katherine' (Camden Society, ser. 3, vol. 21, 1838), 234–5.

[56] *LP* VI, 212; Hall, *Chronicle*, 801; BL Harl. MS 543, fol. 128.

[57] BL Add. MS 71009, fols 57v–59.   [58] *LP* VI, 585.

she was, but never explicitly as a member of the Howard dynasty, perhaps because this was considered self-explanatory by that very kinship link. She was clearly considered to be kin by those women who had been born with the Howard surname; her half-aunt Katherine, Countess of Bridgwater, included her under the label of her 'kyne' in a letter written in 1535.[59] But was this the same as being a Howard; did contemporaries think of that as a separate thing? The identities of the women who served her ordinarily versus those attending her at public events seems to suggest that on some level they did. That women who bore or had borne the Howard name were there for the big events suggests that somebody, or several somebodies, were keen to present Anne as a Howard, probably because this bolstered her own individual noble status, and thus her claim to queenship. It made sense to emphasize this link the most wherever Anne's own status was important, and wherever it would be seen by the largest number of observers. That this was not echoed within her privy chamber is interesting. The others of Henry's queens who were English and who had formerly been ladies-in-waiting also prioritized the appointment of their most immediate female relatives to their households, and in Anne's case these were Boleyns, rather than Howards. This was partly to do with prior intimacy. A queen would want those she had known from a young age, or for a long time, or consistently, around her. Anne had been brought up first at Blickling Hall in Norfolk, and then abroad in the household of Margaret of Savoy, and at no point had she been much in the company of her female Howard relations, which might mean that lack of former intimacy was why few were appointed to her household. Did Anne not, therefore, see herself explicitly as a Howard? As time wore on, cracks appeared in the façade of dynastic unity, which might suggest there was a crowbar separation between the two families. Norfolk and Anne quarrelled violently and repeatedly during 1535, and Norfolk complained that he was 'held in no esteem', the inference being that Anne had forgotten who had helped her to her position.[60] Ives has suggested that while Norfolk had been happy for Anne to 'be a Boleyn' while taking risks on the way up, 'he fully expected her to be a Howard when enjoying success'.[61] While there are areas in which this could be disputed, in the area of female service this does indeed appear to be the case, and this potentially demonstrates a striking manipulation of dynastic identity for a public audience.

So far as the records show, no Howard women continued to serve or began to serve Catherine of Aragon in her exile from court.[62] There is little or no additional information regarding changes in Anne's household through the rest of her reign, which itself may suggest that there weren't many. The depositions relating to the discovery of the secret marriage between Lord Thomas Howard and Lady Margaret Douglas, the King's niece, show that both Elizabeth Wood/Boleyn, Lady Boleyn, and Mary Howard, by now Mary Howard/Fitzroy, Duchess of Richmond, were still in her service in 1535/6, and that one of her maids, Mistress Gamage, had

[59] TNA SP1/87, fol. 120r–v.   [60] *LP* VIII, 263 (104).
[61] Ives, *The Life and Death of Anne Boleyn*, 202.
[62] Our knowledge of Catherine's household at this point is somewhat limited, but the list of those who refused to take the oath of supremacy in 1533/4 contains no Howard women (TNA SP1/82, fol. 127).

since become a Howard by dint of her marriage to Lord William Howard.[63] The latter event perhaps shows that Anne had not, in fact, entirely forgotten her Howard relatives, since service in her household could apparently result in marriage into the dynasty. None of the women who accompanied Anne into the Tower in 1536 were Howards, though two were her aunts, Lady Boleyn and Lady Shelton.[64]

Following Anne's fall the Howards were understandably somewhat eclipsed. There is very little evidence for the make-up of Jane Seymour's household, and no handy lists of her women. Though we know who attended her funeral in 1537, the sheer number of women there mean that it is in no way a list of those in ordinary service.[65] Likewise, although there is a list of jewels owned by her with additional marginal notes recording who she gave them to, this does not constitute a reliable household list; it contains thirty-eight separate women, for a start.[66] Nevertheless, many of the names are those of known former or future courtiers, which suggests they either lived at court or visited during Jane's short reign. Though Jane's own relatives are in evidence—her brothers Thomas and Henry received jewels as gifts, as did her sister-in-law Anne Stanhope/Seymour, Lady Beauchamp—there were some missing, including her sister Elizabeth. This suggests her court was not 'packed' with her own relatives, though we must remember that the Seymours were a smaller family than the Howards. Agnes Tylney/Howard, dowager Duchess of Norfolk, Jane Parker/Boleyn, the now widowed Lady Rochford, and Margaret Gamage/Howard, Lady Howard, were all on Jane's jewel list, which suggests at least that they visited court, if they were not in ordinary service. That Mary Howard/Fitzroy, Duchess of Richmond, was not there was probably because she was recently widowed and fighting a jointure case against the King, not necessarily because she had formerly served Anne Boleyn.

The records for female service for the latter three queens are more informative than for the former three, for there are either wage lists or livery lists for Anne of Cleves, Catherine Howard, and Katherine Parr's households. Following Jane's death, her household would have been dispersed and the women returned to their homes, excepting, presumably, those who had husbands at court and might still claim board and lodging on that account. Once it was clear that the marriage to Anne of Cleves was going ahead, recruitment for her household began. A letter sent by a group of ladies who had been to see the King's ships in August 1539 shows that at least some of her future household were already at court, and this included the signature of Margaret Gamage/Howard, Lady Howard, wife to Lord William.[67] Unlike most of the other signatories, however, she did not appear on the list of the Queen's household 'in ordinary' that was made slightly later in 1539, but this could have been a temporary absence due to pregnancy. This list did include Mary Howard/Fitzroy, Duchess of Richmond, and Jane Parker/Boleyn,

[63] TNA E36/120/65.

[64] Letters from William Kingston to Henry VIII, May 1536 (BL Cotton MS Otho C X, fols 222–5).

[65] *LP* XII, ii, 1060.   [66] BL Royal MS 7 C XVI, fols 18–33.

[67] BL Cotton MS Vespasian F XIII, fol. 251r–v.

Viscountess Rochford, the latter of whom had now served each of Henry's queens.[68] More women clearly joined a little later, perhaps after Anne had arrived, as a wages list for the year 1540–1 also includes 'Mistress Howard'—Catherine, the future queen—and Howard relative Catherine Carey, the daughter of Mary Boleyn/ Carey/Stafford.[69]

Once again, things became complicated. Henry was not enamoured of his new wife, but he did very quickly succumb to the apparent charm of Mistress Catherine Howard. Catherine was Anne Boleyn's first cousin, the daughter of Lord Edmund Howard, the most feckless of the Duke of Norfolk's brothers, who had died in 1539. Catherine has not commanded quite the scholarly or popular fascination that her cousin has, due in part to the shortness of her reign and lack of evidence for her life in general, and her rise and fall have been slower to be reconsidered by revisionist historians.[70] Even more than for Anne Boleyn, the classic narrative of Catherine's rise presents her as the pawn of her family. Her uncle the Duke of Norfolk is usually alleged to have engineered her appointment to the Queen's household hoping to push her into the King's bed.[71] This is hindsight at its most breathtaking. Nobody could possibly have known during 1539 that the King would not take to his new queen. What they did know, as indeed did Henry himself, was that even if adoration was not instantly forthcoming, the marriage would have to go ahead for reasons of foreign policy, whatever happened later. Catherine's promiscuous behaviour while in her grandmother's household, known to several of her female relatives if not her uncle the Duke of Norfolk, would also have ruled her out as a choice to seduce the King.[72] Rather, she caught his eye, and the family could only ride the wave and hope that their collective heads would remain above water.[73]

Understandably, given the family link with Catherine, no Howard women remained in Anne of Cleves's household after she ceased to be Queen.[74] The only list of women relating to Catherine Howard's household is headed 'The booke of Certayne of the Quenys Ordynary as yet to no place Appoynted'.[75] It is most likely

---

[68] BL Add MS 45716 A, fols 15v–16.   [69] TNA E101/422/16.

[70] The standard scholarly work remains Lacey Baldwin Smith, but this is now rather out of date (originally published 1961, reprinted 2009). Most 'new' work on Catherine has been done by historians writing for a general audience, e.g. Conor Byrne, *Katherine Howard: A New History* (London, 2014) and Gareth Russell, *Young & Damned & Fair: The Life and Tragedy of Catherine Howard at the Court of Henry VIII* (London, 2017).

[71] Lacey Baldwin Smith, *Catherine Howard* (Stroud, 1961), 62, 95.

[72] The depositions in TNA SP1/167–8 make this clear.

[73] The Duchess of Norfolk was told that the King 'did cast a fantasy' towards Catherine the first time that he saw her. TNA SP1/168, fol. 53.

[74] TNA LC2/2, fol. 267.

[75] TNA SP1/157, fols 12–15. The list clearly refers to the position of a former queen's household at the start of a new reign. For this reason, Pamela Gross wrote that it was Jane Seymour's household recalled for Anne of Cleves, but the reasonable space of time between them makes this seem unlikely (Pamela Gross, *Jane the Quene, Third Consort of Henry VIII* (Lewiston, NY, 1999), appendix 1). Likewise, it cannot relate to Catherine Howard's household moving to Katherine Parr's, again because there was over a year between the execution of the former and the marriage of the latter, and also because several of the women on the list had only recently been pardoned for misprision of treason relating to the late Queen's fall, and one, Jane Parker/Boleyn, Lady Rochford, was dead.

to have been made in the midst of the swift and unexpected changeover between Anne of Cleves and Catherine Howard, meaning that it is a list of Anne's 'ordinary' that had yet to be placed (the inference being that they should be or were going to be) within Catherine's household. To state that it is a list of those in service to Catherine is therefore not strictly accurate, but comparison with other records does suggest that those listed were indeed appointed. The list includes Mary Howard/Fitzroy, Duchess of Richmond, Margaret Gamage/Howard, Lady Howard, Jane Parker/Boleyn, Lady Rochford, and Katherine Tylney, who was one of Agnes, Duchess of Norfolk's, nieces. Later on, the French ambassador reported that Catherine's sister had been dismissed from the privy chamber, and this was probably Margaret Howard/Arundell, wife of Sir Thomas Arundell.[76] One of her half-sisters from her mother's first marriage, Isabel Legh/Baynton, Lady Baynton, wife of Sir Edward Baynton, vice-chamberlain to five of the six queens, was also a fixture in the Queen's privy chamber, and accompanied her to her semi-imprisonment at Syon House.[77]

As with Anne Boleyn, Catherine's immediate female relatives were among her attendants, though there were also other higher-class Howards not quite so closely related to her. Those listed above, however, all appear to have pre-dated her rise to the throne, and there is no real evidence that any other Howard women gained appointments once she became Queen. It is often said that Catherine recklessly welcomed many of her former friends from her grandmother's household into her service, and that her family encouraged her to do this. A recent biography of Catherine written for a general audience even argues that they did so deliberately as a form of 'damage control', an attempt to buy the silence of those who knew about Catherine's chequered past.[78] While it is true that they do appear to have spoken for the appointment of her former lover Francis Dereham, the Queen herself did not have absolute control over her appointments and her family could not have promised positions to all and sundry.[79] Few women were treated to this in any case. Catherine's cousin Katherine Tylney was already in service to Anne of Cleves.[80] Alice Wilkes/Restwold, one of the women who had shared the maidens' chamber at Lambeth, did join Catherine's chamberers, but not until October 1541.[81] Though Joan Bulmer, another chamberer, wrote to her to ask for a position, there is nothing to suggest this was granted.[82] Neither her sister-in-law Anne Howard, nor her aunt Katherine, Countess of Bridgwater, nor, indeed, the latter's daughter, Agnes ap Rhys, joined Catherine's household at court, and they were surely obvious candidates in terms both of their nobility and of their knowledge of Catherine's previous behaviour.

After Catherine's fall the King was again unmarried for a year and a half, and the only women at court were royalty and those whose husbands were in daily service. Henry's last queen, Katherine Parr, was sourced from Princess Mary's household,

[76] *LP* XVI, 1633.   [77] TNA SP1/167, fols 123–4v.
[78] Russell, *Young & Damned & Fair*, 127–9.   [79] TNA SP1/168, fol. 87.
[80] TNA SP1/157, fols 12–15.   [81] TNA SP1/167, fol. 136.
[82] TNA SP1/161, fol. 85.

and the wedding took place on 12 July 1543.[83] Records of Katherine's household are fairly good, and there are several lists of her women.[84] No Howards were among the ordinary at any point during her reign or afterwards in her household as Queen dowager. In a lodgings list from the late 1540s both Mary Howard/Fitzroy, Duchess of Richmond, and Margaret Gamage/Howard, Lady Howard, were listed as 'ladyes of the household extraordynarye attendante at this tyme', but this is all.[85] This provides something of a corrective to accounts that include Mary Howard/Fitzroy, Duchess of Richmond, among this Queen's inner circle of reform-minded women.[86] While we will see that Mary's beliefs did certainly incline this way, she was not in daily service to the Queen, and therefore she was not likely to have been a strong member of this particular clique.

During Edward's reign there was, naturally, no queen in residence at court, and therefore the only royal households in which women could serve were those of the Queen dowager until her death in 1548, and the princesses. No Howard women did so. Lady Jane Grey was famously served by Elizabeth Tylney, niece to the now late dowager Duchess of Norfolk, but no real change in the family's service came until Mary's accession in 1553, and even then it does not seem to have been significant.[87] At her coronation, her train was carried by Elizabeth Stafford/Howard, Duchess of Norfolk, in her first known court appearance since the 1530s.[88] Though Elizabeth does not seem to have served the new Queen in ordinary, the chances are high that she now attended court as an extraordinary 'Great Lady', and other surviving Howard women may well have done so too. Mary's ordinary attendants included Isabel Legh/Baynton, Lady Baynton, half-sister of Queen Catherine Howard, and Mary Howard, probably the daughter of Lord William Howard and Lady Margaret Gamage/Howard, was among the maids of honour in 1556/7.[89] To some degree, the Howards were 'between generations' at this stage. Those like the Duchess of Norfolk who had served during the first half of Henry VIII's reign were no longer young, and perhaps not up to the rigour of daily service. In fact, many of them died during Mary's reign.[90] The newer generation, by now split into more than one family branch, had no experience of court service. The daughters of Henry Howard, Earl of Surrey, and Frances de Vere/Howard, his wife, were about the right age to be in service, as were the rest of the

---

[83] Susan James, *Catherine Parr* (Stroud, 2009), 77.

[84] For the complete list, see Hamilton, 'The Household of Katherine Parr', table 3, 123.

[85] BL Cotton MS Vespasian C XIV, fol. 93.

[86] John N. King, 'Patronage and Piety: The Influence of Catherine Parr,' in Margaret P. Hannay (ed.), *Silent But for the Word: Tudor Women as Patrons, Translators, and Writers of Religious Works* (Kent, Oh., 1985), 43–60; James, *Catherine Parr*, 199; Melissa Franklin-Harkrider, *Women, Reform and Community in Early Modern England* (Woodbridge, 2008), 62.

[87] John Gough Nichols (ed.), *The Chronicle of Queen Jane, and of two years of Queen Mary, and especially of the rebellion of Sir Thomas Wyat* (London, 1850), 25.

[88] J. R. Planché, *Regal Records: or, a Chronicle of the Coronations of the Queens Regnant of England* (London, 1838), 15.

[89] Merton, 'The Women Who Served', appendix 1.

[90] Elizabeth, Duchess of Norfolk, in 1558; Mary Howard/Fitzroy, Duchess of Richmond, *c.*1555; Katherine, Countess of Bridgwater, in 1554; Anne, Countess of Oxford, in 1559. Agnes, Duchess of Norfolk, had already died in 1545.

daughters of Lord William Howard and Margaret Gamage/Howard, and so it is somewhat curious that more of them did not find places in Mary's household, though the fact that the former were the daughters of a traitor may have had an impact here. That they were not old and proven servants of Mary's may also help to explain this, since the majority of household positions went to those who had been with her for some years.[91] It was not until Elizabeth's accession in 1558 that a new generation of Howard women burst onto the court scene.[92]

There is no doubt that if we want to use the term 'courtier family', the Howards fit this description on both sides of the gender divide. However, we need to note that a good deal of this reputation is based more on ceremonial, occasional attendance at special events than it is on 'ordinary', daily, service positions within the queen's household. There was a female Howard court presence of some sort throughout Henry VIII's reign, and again in Mary's reign, but those in attendance were not always the highest-status women of the family, and not always the largest kinship group within the Queen's household. One would expect their pre-eminence to fluctuate depending on the identity of the queen in residence, and it did, but perhaps not as much as historians tend to assume. There were indeed more Howard relations and clients in ordinary service during the reigns of Anne Boleyn and Catherine Howard, but often they were just that, relations and clients, rather than women from the core of the Howard dynasty. This emphasizes the way in which dynastic identity might vary depending on circumstance. At court, kinship links were paramount, but often they were matriarchal. Daughters followed mothers, and queens who had formerly been ladies-in-waiting appointed their closest female relatives, not necessarily those who might bolster their dynastic image. This is particularly clear during the rise of Anne Boleyn, when the highest-status Howard women appear to have remained at a slight distance until it became clear that Anne's bid for the throne was going to be successful, at which point they appeared with her in public ceremonies to mutual advantage. This effectively stymies the traditional narrative whereby both Anne and Catherine Howard were supported, even pushed, onto the throne by the Howards working as a dynastic collective.

Given these close links between women in service, it is clear that being a courtier created potential for conflicts of interest. Women who entered the Queen's household were required to take an oath of service, just as men were, and this was in essence an oath of loyalty to one's new mistress.[93] Of course, women took no comparable oath to the head of their family, but there is considerable evidence to show that their families expected them to fly their flag, promote their interests, and seek patronage for their relatives.[94] The dilemma potentially faced by women when family interests and those of their mistress clashed is one that is rarely considered by historians, but it did sometimes occur and could cause anguish on all sides. The turnover of queens during Henry's reign, and the way in which some of his

---

[91] See Anna Whitelock and Diarmaid MacCulloch, 'Princess Mary's Household and the Succession Crisis, July 1553', *Historical Journal* 50:2 (2007), 265–87.

[92] Merton, 'The Women Who Served', appendix 1.

[93] Anne Basset was described as 'sworn in' as the Queen's woman in 1537. *Lisle Letters*, IV, 895.

[94] See, for instance, *Lisle Letters*, V, 1126, 1513.

marriages ended, created ample opportunity for divided loyalties among the women at court.

It is often difficult to find evidence for the nature of the relationship between a queen and individual female attendants for this period. They cannot all have functioned as her confidantes. It is clear, too, that some of Henry's queens were 'better' at inspiring loyalty in their women than others. One of those who did was Catherine of Aragon, and one of the women most loyal to her was Elizabeth Stafford/Howard, Duchess of Norfolk. As discussed above, Elizabeth herself appears to have joined Catherine of Aragon's household in time for her coronation in 1509, and continued to serve after her marriage to Thomas Howard in 1512. In 1537 she told Thomas Cromwell that she had served at court for sixteen years.[95] These were not consecutive years; in 1520, for instance, Elizabeth accompanied her husband to Ireland, and cannot have been in service at court.[96] The nature of the surviving records makes it impossible to chart her precise periods of service, but she was certainly regularly present at court between 1509 and 1532. Her own household book from 1526/7 shows that by this time she tended to spend periods of a couple of months at a time at court, which might suggest either that at least some of the Queen's women served on a rota system, or that by this time she was in extraordinary rather than ordinary service.[97] Aside from her lengthy presence at court there is little to suggest that she and the Queen had an especially close relationship until the late 1520s and early 1530s.

Their relationship either changed or became obviously closer around the beginning of the royal divorce proceedings. On 27 November 1530, Eustace Chapuys, Imperial ambassador, reported to his master the Emperor that 'a few days since, the duchess of Norfolk sent the Queen a present of "*volaille*" and an orange, enclosing a letter from Gregory Cassal, which I send. The Queen thinks the Duchess did this out of regard for her, but I fear it was done with the knowledge of her husband, as a means of entering into some secret communication with her Majesty more easily.'[98] Gregory Casali was the King's ambassador at the Vatican charged with placing his case before the Pope. For Elizabeth to send the Queen one of his letters reveals that she was taking steps to give the Queen information about progress in Rome that, presumably, the latter might not otherwise have had access to: she was spying for her. Chapuys did not say, and perhaps did not know, whether the letter in question was addressed to the Queen or to somebody else, and so we cannot know whether Elizabeth was merely acting as a go-between for an established chain of illicit communication, or whether she was acting on her own initiative and appropriating a letter that Casali had written to somebody else.

It became abundantly clear that Chapuys was not correct in thinking that Elizabeth was acting with the knowledge of her husband, though it remains interesting that his first response was to assume that she was not acting independently. In January 1531, he reported, 'yesterday the duchess of Norfolk sent to tell the Queen that her opponents were trying to draw her over to their party, but that if

---

[95] BL Cotton MS Titus B I, fol. 388r–v.   [96] SP60/1, fol. 40.
[97] CUL, Pembroke MS 300.   [98] *LP* IV, 6738.

all the world were to try it she would remain faithful to her. She also desired the Queen to be of good courage, for her opponents were at their wits' end, being further off from their object than the day they began.'[99] This sounds very much as though the Duke of Norfolk was leaning on his wife to renounce her support for Catherine, and that she refused to do so. This was a direct clash of loyalties and Elizabeth chose what seems to us to be the less obvious, more difficult path, supporting her mistress above the interests of her husband and family, and, indeed, against the King. In April the same year, 1531, Chapuys wrote:

> 'She [Anne Boleyn] becomes more arrogant every day, using words and authority towards the King, of which he has several times complained to the duke of Norfolk, saying that she was not like the Queen, who had never in her life used ill words to him. The duchess of Norfolk has reported this to the Queen, telling her moreover that her husband [Norfolk] was in marvellous sorrow and tribulation, and that she saw quite well she [Anne] would be considered the ruin of all her family, and that if God wished that she should continue in her fantasy it would be a very good thing for the Queen.'[100]

Yet another reference from Chapuys states that Elizabeth had seen a letter from the Duke of Albany, and reported the contents to the Queen.[101]

Elizabeth was not alone in her support of Catherine of Aragon during this time. Gertrude Blount/Courtenay, Marchioness of Exeter, was described by Chapuys in 1531 as 'the only true comforter and friend the Queen and the Princess have', and she passed on information about Privy Council discussions.[102] Maria de Salinas/Willoughby, Lady Willoughby, rode through the night and then talked her way into Kimbolton Castle in order to be with Catherine as she lay dying in January 1536.[103] Numerous women were among those who had listened to and encouraged the pro-Catherine, anti-Anne prophecies of Elizabeth Barton, the 'nun of Kent', in 1534, including the aforementioned Marchioness of Exeter alongside Margaret Plantagenet/Pole, Countess of Salisbury, Anne Grey/Hussey, Lady Hussey, and Mary Scrope/Jerningham/Kingston, Lady Kingston.[104] All of these women were seasoned courtiers like Elizabeth, and would no doubt have known one another well, though there is nothing to show that they were working as a coordinated group. A significant number of Catherine's daily attendants refused to sign the Oath of Supremacy in 1534, and there is ample evidence of ordinary women slandering Anne in support of Catherine.[105]

The major difference between Elizabeth and these women was that they were not, so far as is known, defying the explicit interests of their families. Most of the women named in the nun of Kent case, or by Chapuys, had husbands who were also either known or suspected as supporters of Catherine. In many cases these men's hands were tied by their service to the King, which is a good example of the political uses for women, because they could risk helping the Queen in ways that

---

[99] *LP* V, 70.   [100] *LP* V, 216.   [101] *LP* V, 238.
[102] *CSP Spain*, IV, ii, 1127 (800).   [103] BL Cotton MS Otho C X, fol. 215.
[104] TNA SP1/80, fols 118–19 (*LP* VI, 1468).
[105] The list of Catherine's household who refused to sign the Oath: TNA SP1/82, fol. 127. The most famous incident of a woman slandering Anne Boleyn took place in 1535, when Margaret Chancellor called her a 'goggle-eyed whore' (*LP* VIII, 196).

their husbands could not. Elizabeth was the only peeress who was obviously, blatantly, going against her husband and family's wishes. As Chapter 3 has argued, she quite clearly identified with the Queen on a personal level, because her husband, too, was in love with another woman. Others recognized this link between the two women as well. One Mistress Amadas was had up in 1533 for saying that 'ther was neuer a good weddid woman in ynglond bot pryns Arthurs dowger The doches of Northfolk and herself'.[106] Probably because of this link, Elizabeth's espionage is often spoken of by historians in a tone of amusement, but it is more significant than has been realized. Elizabeth was not only morally supporting the Queen from a distance, but actively spying for her, reporting what Anne Boleyn and Norfolk had said, passing on letters, and providing comfort. Quite clearly she had access to sensitive information both written and spoken. Whether this was the sort of 'automatic' access occasioned by stumbling across her husband's papers or being in the room when he discussed important matters, or whether Elizabeth made opportunities to rifle his correspondence and to eavesdrop, is not clear. What is plain is that she did not hesitate to use this information in a way that was not supportive of her marital family's broader political goals.

At first glance it seems surprising that she managed to achieve this for so long, and suggests it may have been a reasonably well-kept secret for some time. Chapuys would have known about the Duchess's reports because he was in the Queen's confidence, but it may not have been more generally known. One imagines that if the Duke had been aware of it he would at the very least have rethought the security of his filing system. Could this suggest that not all contemporaries were aware of women's capacity for agency in these sorts of situations? Elizabeth's actions clearly show that women took advantage of the access that they had on both the King's and Queen's sides of the household. For we know that when Elizabeth was at court during this time, she was lodged on the King's side with her husband, and this is undoubtedly how she was able to gain the information that she did.[107] Her access to the Queen's chamber then allowed her to pass it on without suspicion, since there was every reason for her to move between these areas. Elizabeth herself does not seem to have made especial efforts to hide her loyalties. In May 1531 she was sent home, apparently at Anne Boleyn's desire (according to Chapuys), 'because she spoke too freely, and declared herself more than they liked for the Queen'.[108] Who 'they' were is not specified. Evidently, women's roles at court were more than simply backing up the family interests, and loyalties could get complicated when courtiers were forced to 'take sides' in this way. It might be pertinent to note that Elizabeth absented herself from Anne Boleyn's coronation in 1533 on account of her support for Catherine of Aragon.[109]

The issue of loyalty must also have confronted those who were asked to depose as witnesses to Catherine's wedding night with Prince Arthur long ago in 1501. While Elizabeth was too young to have witnessed this, her stepmother-in-law, Agnes Tylney/Howard, dowager Duchess of Norfolk, had been there, and had also

---

[106] BL Cotton MS Cleopatra W IV, fol. 99v.   [107] BL Egerton MS 2623, fol. 7.
[108] *LP* V, 238.   [109] *LP* VI, 585.

served as one of Catherine's women for much of her reign. It is likely that she had no option but to give her statement, since the Council were thorough in their pursuit of those who had witnessed that night. Agnes gave hers on 29 July 1529, in Thetford, Norfolk, and like almost all the others, she said nothing that truly confirmed or denied Catherine's insistence that the marriage was unconsummated, recording only that 'the said prynce Arthur and [K]atheryne nowe beynge queyne wer brought to bedd the next nyght after the said mariage for this deponent dydd se them ... in oone bedd the same nyght in a chamber withyn the said palace being p'pared for them and that this deponent lefte them soo ... [to]gether there the sayd nyght'.[110] When it came to deposing in front of the court set up to rule on the marriage in the summer of 1533, however, she and other ladies seem to have ignored a summons, delaying proceedings and forcing the court to send a commission to examine them in London, rather than with the court at Dunstable.[111] Could this have been a quiet protest? The letters recording their absence say only that 'it was loked for' and 'it had been better that' they were there, not explicitly that they had refused to come, which may mean that their absence was a planning oversight by those in charge and not the fault of the women themselves. Nevertheless, it is not difficult to suppose that they might have felt some reluctance in this matter.

The exploits of Mary Howard/Fitzroy, Duchess of Richmond, also show that for women, being a courtier involved more than simply supporting your family's interests. For Mary, this is partly because—as must have been the case for many individuals—'family interests' could be many, and varied, and were not necessarily collective. What one individual thought was good for the family might not enjoy a general consensus. This was the case in July 1536, when an affair and contract of marriage was discovered to exist between Mary's cousin Lord Thomas Howard and her close friend Lady Margaret Douglas, the King's niece.[112] The inevitable investigation found that the couple had 'loved' for a year, and had been contracted since Easter 1536.[113] Mary had known about their affair and marriage since it began. The deposition of Thomas Smyth, a servant of Lord Thomas Howard's, states that he 'wold watche tyl my lady bulleyn was goon and thenn stele in to her [Lady Margaret's] chambre' while Mary was present.[114] Mary had therefore acted as the couple's accomplice and chaperone. Nor was she the only Howard woman involved. When asked how many people had known, Lord Thomas stated that Lady Margaret had also told 'my lord William's wife that now is'—this was Margaret Gamage/Howard, Lady Howard. That they had to sneak around and wait for Lady Boleyn to leave, however, shows that they clearly understood that what they were doing would be frowned upon not only by the King but by members of the dynasty and its client families. This highlights the difficulty with seeing court families as collectives. The Howards were such a vast family that it would be naive to expect them to hold

---

[110] TNA E30/1456.
[111] BL Cotton MS Otho C X, fol. 164; TNA SP1/76, fol. 34. The other lady mentioned was Lady Guildford.
[112] TNA E36/120/65; *Statutes of the Realm*, III, 680–1.
[113] TNA E36/120/65. [114] Ibid.

unified ambitions at every stated point. Inevitably they sometimes split into smaller groups, and this group were evidently the 'young courtier' set, the Bright Young Things of the 1530s.

The same group of people demonstrates women's participation in the development of court culture during this period. Mary Howard/Fitzroy, Duchess of Richmond, was, along with Margaret Douglas, Mary Shelton, Thomas Howard, Edmund Knyvett, and others, responsible for producing the miscellany of poetry now known as the Devonshire Manuscript.[115] The quarto-sized volume itself was owned originally by Mary, who probably passed it on to Margaret Douglas at some point during the 1530s or 1540s. The manuscript was used as a sort of cultural commonplace book, passed around between friends for them to add poems of their own and others' composition, annotations, pointed comments, riddles, and so forth, and as such it gives enormous insight into the fashions, concerns, and pastimes at court. Poetry was an important form of leisure for courtiers, and the tradition of 'courtly love', in which women were mock-courted by ardent admirers whom they then publicly spurned, was still going strong. As Elizabeth Heale explains, this manuscript shows that women were not only central to this cultural tradition, but 'they actively promote and develop it, copying, answering, appropriating, altering, adapting and composing verses for themselves'.[116] Their literary activities here show clearly that they perceived the difficulty and danger of maintaining Castiglione's 'certain difficult mean' in their behaviour as courtiers. The ubiquity of themes like fickleness, fortune, the anguish of forbidden love, cloaking one's true feelings, all speak volumes about the atmosphere at court during the late 1530s. On the other hand, there is also a lot of light-hearted wordplay and what we might call 'banter' within the pages of the manuscript, between women as well as men and women, and it is clear that poetry was used as an expression of female friendship at court.

This kind of evidence for the breadth and depth of friendships at court does give the impression of a social bubble. Yet the obligations of kinship can never have been far away. It is universally stated that women were placed at court to broker patronage for their families, and there is plenty of evidence to show that they did indeed do this. Although we have seen that the Howard women did not always behave in ways expected by the rest of their family, they were able to act as patronesses in their own right, or as brokers of patronage, for relatives. Most obviously, Anne Boleyn and Catherine Howard were both able to use their position to gain favours for family members. Anne Boleyn allegedly obtained a marriage for the Duke's daughter and her own maid of honour Mary Howard with the King's illegitimate son Henry Fitzroy, and bargained to such a degree that the Duke did

---

[115] The main authority on this manuscript is Elizabeth Heale, the author of the printed edition *The Devonshire Manuscript: A Woman's Book of Courtly Poetry* (Toronto, 2012). See also Helen Baron, 'Mary (Howard) Fitzroy's Hand in the Devonshire Manuscript', *Review of English Studies* 45 (1994), 318–35; E. Heale, 'Women and the Courtly Love Lyric: The Devonshire MS (BL Additional 17492)', *The Modern Language Review* 90 (2005), 296–313; R. Southall, 'The Devonshire Manuscript Collection of Early Tudor Poetry, 1532–41', *Review of English Studies* 15 (1964), 142–50.

[116] Heale, *The Devonshire Manuscript*, 22–3.

not have to pay any dowry.[117] Another of her women, Margaret Gamage, married Lord William Howard, and it seems reasonable to suppose that Anne had something to do with this as well. Two of Catherine Howard's brothers, George and Charles, were showered with grants when she became queen.[118] Women who were not queen also at least attempted to aid the rest of the family, though the records do not generally allow us to draw a clear connection between their suit and eventual action. After the fall of Catherine Howard and the imprisonment of many members of her family in 1541–2, Lady Margaret Howard, following her own release and pardon, was said to have petitioned the King in person on behalf of her husband and her mother-in-law, and Chapuys at least thought it was likely to be successful.[119] There is also evidence that certain Howard women were considered so influential that they were able to exercise patronage outside of their family, and they were asked to do so by men as well as by women. Agnes, dowager Duchess of Norfolk, was petitioned by Thomas Cranmer, Archbishop of Canterbury, in May 1534, to 'cause sume of your speciall frendes nyght aboute the kynges highnes' to promote the suit of one his servants, who was in pursuit of a particular office in the garrison at Calais. Cranmer would, he explained, have promoted the suit himself, but he had used up his patronage 'credit' with the King on his own suits and required the efforts of a broker like Agnes.[120]

They were also able to obtain things for themselves beyond what they were entitled to as part of service in the Queen's household. Clothing, for instance, was sometimes given to women by the Queen as a gift. Agnes, Duchess of Norfolk, received 'a gowne of c[ri]mosyn veluet w[i]t[h] spaynesh slevys lined w[i]t[h] grene clothe of gold of damaske' from Catherine of Aragon in May 1516.[121] This was not only a financially valuable gift, but an important sign of favour from the Queen. It may, given the 'Spanish sleeves', have been a hand-me-down, which gave it additional, symbolic value, because objects were considered to retain something of the spirit of the original owner.[122] Jewels, as well as clothes, might be received by women in service, and these were again valuable gifts both financially and symbolically. A list of gifts given by Catherine of Aragon in 1522, probably at New Year, includes a letter 'A' of pearls set with diamonds, gifted to Agnes, Duchess of Norfolk, from the Queen's own store.[123] This was a particularly personal gift, since most of the others received the standard gift of a piece of plate, the weight representative of the recipient's status. The list of Jane Seymour's jewels made in 1537 shows that Agnes, Duchess of Norfolk, was given 'a pair of beyds of jassinges gauded [gilded] w[i]t[h] golde'; Jane, Lady Rochford, had a tablet of gold at

---

[117] BL Cotton Ms Titus B I, fol. 390r–v.

[118] TNA SP1/163, fol. 61; *LP* XVI, 678 (38), 878 (49), 1056 (16).

[119] *LP* App. B, 11.   [120] BL Harl. MS 6148, fols 44v–45.

[121] TNA E101/418/6.

[122] Arnoud-Jan Bijsterveld, 'The Medieval Gift as Agent of Social Bonding and Political Power: A Comparative Approach', in E. Cohen and M. B. de Jong (eds), *Medieval Transformations: Texts, Power, and Gifts in Context* (Leiden, 2001), 123–56 (125–6).

[123] TNA SP1/233, fol. 233.

New Year 1537, and Margaret, Lady Howard, received 'a great bordello enamelled w[i]t[h] redde and white', and a pair of gold bracelets.[124]

Women in court service, and indeed those who were present but not in service, could expect to receive New Year gifts from both the King and Queen, and as discussed above, these were usually a piece of plate of a certain weight relating to status. Formal New Year gift rolls do not survive for Henry's queens, but we do have some draft lists of plate gifts from Catherine of Aragon, dating to *c*.1520, 1522, and 1528.[125] These include the Howard women who we know were in service with the Queen, and others besides, since as one of the lists makes clear, it was customary for peers and peeresses to come to court for New Year to exchange gifts.[126] There are gift rolls for the King for the years 1528, 1532, 1534, and 1539, besides the lists of rewards to servants found in his payment books. Again, in general, those on the lists are those who were in service at court, and those who were present, probably plus those whose status made it politic for gifts to be exchanged. This makes any omissions interesting. Despite her activity in support of Catherine of Aragon, Elizabeth, the younger Duchess of Norfolk, received a gift from the King in 1532, but though her name is on the list for 1534, the space for what she received has been left blank. This was mutual. In 1532, she gave the King a gold pomander, but the space next to her name on the 1534 list is also blank, which suggests that she and the King did not actually exchange gifts that year.[127] This would not be all that surprising in light of her views on his divorce. By 1539, she was not on the list for giving or receiving at all.[128] New Year gifts as a form of material patronage can therefore be used as a political barometer, and in this case reveal the King showing his displeasure by leaving Elizabeth off the list.

As a group, the Howard women were clearly successful and influential courtiers. Many were employed for very long stretches of time. That several of them gained the Queen's favour is shown by the way in which they were able in time to secure places for their daughters and other female relatives at court. Though there was never truly a Howard 'stranglehold' on female court service, there was, equally, never a time without a Howard woman, relative, or client in service with the Queen, and this is not counting their dominance at many formal court ceremonies and events across the period. Many were able to secure grants and favours for themselves and for family members, and even to act as brokers of patronage for exalted persons outside the family circle.

However, if a female courtier's influence was meant to be used primarily to serve her family, the picture is less clear. Undoubtedly, as I have said, many Howard women did explicitly gain favours for family members by dint of their positions at court. But was Elizabeth Stafford/Howard, Duchess of Norfolk, being a good Howard when she spied for Catherine of Aragon during the 'great matter'? Certainly she was serving the Queen in the most useful way that she could, but by doing so

---

[124] BL Royal MS 7 C XVI.

[125] TNA SP1/73, fol. 70; this was originally dated to 1531, but includes the Duke of Buckingham, so must date before his execution in 1521. TNA SP1/233, fol. 233, and TNA E101/420/4.

[126] TNA E101/420/4 specifies that these were the gifts given 'at Grenewyche'.

[127] TNA E101/420/15; E101/421/13.   [128] Hayward, 'Gift-Giving', 146–7.

she was actively damaging her marital family's prospects. It could work the other way around too. Elizabeth's daughter Mary Howard/Fitzroy, Duchess of Richmond, was arguably being a good Howard by helping to engineer a clandestine marriage between her uncle Lord Thomas Howard and her best friend Margaret Douglas, the King's niece, since this created another marital link between the Howards and the Tudors. The King, however, was far from happy about this aggrandizement, and so Mary did not behave like a wise courtier here. Sometimes it simply wasn't possible for women in service to be both good courtiers and good family members, and the tumultuous marital exploits of Henry VIII serve to highlight this more explicitly than other periods. Families could not work continuously like political collectives or factions. Anne Boleyn, it turns out, was not uniformly surrounded by Howard women helping to push her onto the throne; the female 'core' of the dynasty appear far more visible at the public ceremonies once Anne had gained power, and even after she became Queen, her chamber was staffed by her own Boleyn relatives with far fewer Howards. The Howard women's court service makes it very clear that women as well as men possessed a kaleidoscope of identities: they were courtiers, family members, part of a wider dynastic membership, and circumstances dictated which identity was uppermost for each woman at any given time.

5

'The syknes of mistrust'
Treason and Rebellion

On 15 December 1541, Thomas Howard, Third Duke of Norfolk, penned an extraordinary letter to the King. From his safe refuge at Kenninghall, he wrote:

> Most noble and gracious souerayne lord yesterday came to my knowlege that myn ungracious mother In lawe myn unhappy brother and his wiff w[i]t[h] my lewde suster off brydgewater wer comited to the toure wich by long experience knowyng yo[r] accustomed equetie and justice used to all yo[r] subiectes am sewer is not done but for som their fals and [tr]aytorous procedynges agaynst yo[r] royall maieste/

> wich revoluyng In my mynd w[i]t[h] also the most abhomynable dedes done by ij of my niesys agaynst yo[r] highnes hath broght me in to the grettest p[er]plexite that ever poure wretche was in / ffearyng that [inserted above: yo[r]] maieste havyng so oftone and by so many of my kyn bene thus falsly and traytorously handled myght not only conseyue a displesure in yo[r] hert agaynst me and all other of that kyn but also in maner abhorre to here speke of any off the same.[1]

Written in response to the fall of Queen Catherine Howard, this must be among the best surviving examples of sixteenth-century aristocratic grovelling, and with good reason. As Norfolk explains, a large number of his close relations were arrested alongside the Queen, and he was self-evidently afraid for his own safety. This episode marked the culmination of several cases of high treason directly involving the Howard dynasty during Henry VIII's reign, most of which involved the family's women more they did the men. Here these episodes are examined side by side in a familial context for the first time.

Chapter 4 considered the family's behaviour at court when things were going well for them. This chapter picks up those threads at times of political crisis, which were, it is clear, more frequent for this family than is sometimes recognized. As well as the falls of Anne Boleyn and Catherine Howard in 1536 and 1541–2, Howard women were involved in rebellion in Wales between 1529 and 1531; a poorly timed clandestine marriage in the middle of 1536; and, possibly, the Pilgrimage of Grace towards the end of the same year. Of course, the Howards were not the only aristocratic women involved in rebellion or treason during this period. Many others were caught up in the 'nun of Kent' case in 1534, including Margaret Plantagenet/Pole, Countess of Salisbury, Gertrude Blount/Courtenay, Marchioness of Exeter,

---

[1] TNA SP1/168, fol. 143.

Anne Grey/Hussey, Lady Hussey, and Mary Scrope/Jerningham/Kingston, Lady Kingston.[2] Still others were involved in the Pilgrimage of Grace. Several were even involved in more than one episode; Lady Hussey came within an ace of a treason conviction in 1536 for continuing to refer to Princess Mary as 'Princess' rather than 'Lady'.[3] Most such cases, however, did not involve more than one woman from any given family. Was there something particularly treasonable about the Howards?

Though the cases of treason in which they were involved are well known, they are not usually analysed together, and the role of women is rarely the focus. Sharon Jansen's study of women and popular resistance to Henry VIII's reforms is the only book-length work of this kind.[4] However, she is generally concerned with episodes involving lower-status women. This is not wholly surprising. While Arlette Farge, Rudolf Dekker, and others have shown that some women in early modern Europe did incite, support, and participate in rebellious activity, their work makes clear that it was usually lower-class women who did so during food or taxation riots.[5] There were some exceptions, and the participation of European noblewomen has been considered in reference to some specific wars or rebellions, such as the seventeenth-century English Civil War and the Spanish Revolt of the Comuneros in the 1520s.[6] Nevertheless, though it has been noted that some aristocratic women did participate in sixteenth-century English rebellions such as the Pilgrimage of Grace 1536–7 or the Northern Rising of 1569, there has been no systematic study of their actions.[7]

Yet this period saw the greatest changes to the legal definition and scope of treason for 150 years, and many of these changes came about as direct results of the high-profile cases with which aristocratic women, including the Howard women,

---

[2] *Statutes of the Realm*, III, 446.   [3] BL Cotton MS Otho C X, fol. 254.

[4] Sharon Jansen, *Dangerous Talk and Strange Behavior: Women and Popular Resistance to the Reforms of Henry VIII* (New York, 1996).

[5] On England, see Bernard Capp, 'Separate Domains? Women and Authority in Early Modern England', in Paul Griffiths, Adam Fox, and Steve Hindle (eds), *The Experience of Authority in Early Modern England* (Basingstoke, 1999), 117–45; R. Houlbrooke, 'Women's Social Life and Common Action in England from the Fifteenth Century to the Eve of the Civil War', *Continuity and Change* 1 (1986), 176–86; Muriel C. McClendon, 'Women, Religious Dissent, and Urban Authority in Early Reformation Norwich', in Joseph P. Ward (ed.), *Violence, Politics and Gender in Early Modern England* (Basingstoke, 2008), 125–46. On Ireland, see William Palmer, 'Gender, Violence, and Rebellion in Tudor and Early Stuart Ireland', *Sixteenth Century Journal* 23:4 (1992), 699–712. On France, see Natalie Zemon Davis, 'Women on Top', in *Society and Culture in Early Modern France: Eight Essays* (Stanford, Calif., 1975), 124–51 and Arlette Farge, 'Protesters Plain to See', in David and Farge (eds), *A History of Women in the West, vol. 3: Renaissance and Enlightenment Paradoxes* (Cambridge, Mass., 1993), 489–505. On Holland, see Rudolf Dekker, 'Women in Revolt: Popular Protest and its Social Basis in Holland in the Seventeenth and Eighteenth Centuries', *Theory and Society* 16 (1987), 337–62. On Spain, see Stephanie Fink De Backer, 'Rebel with a Cause: The Marriage of María Pacheco and the Formation of Mendoza Identity', in Helen Nader (ed.), *Power and Gender in Renaissance Spain: Eight Women of the Mendoza Family, 1450–1650* (Chicago, 2004), 71–92.

[6] Katherine A. Walker, 'The Military Activities of Charlotte de la Tremouille, Countess of Derby, during the Civil War and Interregnum', *Northern History* 38:1 (2001), 47–64; David Weigall, 'Women Militants in the English Civil War', *History Today* 22:6 (1972), 434–8; Fink De Backer, 'Rebel with a Cause', 71–92.

[7] Madeleine Hope Dodds and Ruth Dodds, *The Pilgrimage of Grace 1536–1537 and The Exeter Conspiracy 1538*, 2 vols (London, 1971), I, 24–6, 79, 287–8; Jansen, *Dangerous Talk and Strange Behavior*, 24–37.

were involved.[8] It became both easier and more damaging to be convicted for treason as the sixteenth century wore on, and this had a direct impact on courtier families like the Howards. While there were occasions where an individual facing an accusation of high treason might count on familial support, or where a family in collective danger would band together to try to escape it, this chapter shows that kinship was put under severe strain by such crises and that families might temporarily shatter as a result.[9] Norfolk's 1541 letter makes it clear that on many levels the dynasty was seen as a collective entity, and that he feared that disgrace might also be collective. Looking at these cases from a female, familial perspective allows us to test how far this was the case, and whether this was something that developed further during this period.

'[A]T THE COMANNDYME[N]T OF RECE GRIFFITH AND MY LADY HAWARD': WALES, 1529–1531

Though the Howards had been involved in treason before Henry VIII's reign, this was to do with the men, who fought on the 'wrong' side at the Battle of Bosworth in 1485, resulting in an attainder for high treason for the then-Earl of Surrey. After his pardon and release in 1489, all members of the family stayed out of serious trouble for really quite some time. The next involvement of any Howard with treasonous activity began in 1529. This was Katherine Howard/ap Rhys, Lady Rhys, daughter of Thomas Howard, Second Duke of Norfolk, and Agnes Tylney/ Howard, and her behaviour fell into a particular category of treason: rebellion. Her role in this episode was greater than has been recognized, and sheds some interesting light on contemporary understandings of dynastic identity.[10] On 18 June 1529, Walter Devereux, Lord Ferrers of Chartley, Chamberlain and Chief Justice of south Wales, wrote in a panic to Cardinal Wolsey:

> Please it your noble grace to be adu[er]tysede … of the greate rebel[lion] and insurrec-cion of the peple in thys partes at the comanndyme[n]t of Rece griffith and my lady haward as for a troth ther was not such insurrecion in walys at any tyme a man can remebre …[11]

---

[8] John Bellamy, *The Tudor Law of Treason: An Introduction* (London, 1979; repr. 2013). See also K. J. Kesselring, *Mercy and Authority in the Tudor State* (Cambridge, 2003).

[9] For instance, the Pole family in 1538. See Dodds and Dodds, *The Pilgrimage of Grace*, I, 297–328.

[10] See Glanmor Williams, *Recovery, Reorientation and Reformation: Wales c.1415–1642* (Oxford, 1987), 148–57; Glanmor Williams, *Wales and the Reformation* (Cardiff, 1997); Gwynfor Jones, *Early Modern Wales, c.1525–1640* (Basingstoke, 1994); E. Davies, and B. Howells, *Pembrokeshire County History 3: Early Modern Pembrokeshire, 1536–1815* (1987). Lengthier treatment is found in R. A. Griffiths, *Sir Rhys ap Thomas and his Family: A Study in the Wars of the Roses and Early Tudor Politics* (Cardiff, 1993), 66–119, and D. Jones, 'Sir Rhys ap Thomas: A Study in Family History of Tudor Politics', *Archaeologia Cambrensis* 5th ser. 9 (1892), 81–101 and 192–214. The fullest, but now dated, account is W. Llewelyn Williams, 'A Welsh Insurrection', *Y Cymmrodor* 16 (1902), 1–94. Most recently it has been used as the springboard for consideration of Henrician Catholic exile by Peter Marshall, in ' "The Greatest Man in Wales": James Ap Gruffydd Ap Hywel and the International Opposition to Henry VIII', *Sixteenth Century Journal* 39:3 (2008), 681–704.

[11] TNA SP1/54 fol. 93.

A year and four months later, the Imperial ambassador in London, Eustace Chapuys, reported to his master the Emperor Charles V that 'The King has sent to the Tower a Welsh gentleman named Ris because (as report goes) not satisfied with his wife having some months ago besieged the governor of Wales [in his castle] for several days, and had some of his attendants killed, he himself has threatened to finish what his wife had begun.'[12]

The gentleman concerned was Rhys ap Gruffudd, grandson to Henry VII's Welsh crony Sir Rhys ap Thomas (d. 1525), and he was executed for high treason in December 1531. The marriage between him and Katherine had been arranged by Sir Rhys ap Thomas and Katherine's father, the Second Duke of Norfolk, in 1514, and probably took place in 1522.[13] Initially they lived under the guidance of Gruffudd's grandfather, Sir Rhys ap Thomas, and more distantly of Katherine's father Thomas, Second Duke of Norfolk. Within three years, however, both these stalwarts had died, leaving the young couple to carve out their own path in south-west Wales as lord and lady of the wealthy and powerful Dynevor estate. This is where things began to turn sour. Sir Rhys ap Thomas had been Chamberlain and Chief Justice of south Wales, and it was logical to suppose that Gruffudd, his grandson and heir, would inherit these offices. In May 1526, however, Walter Devereux, Lord Ferrers of Chartley, was appointed not only Chamberlain and Chief Justice, but also steward and councillor of Princess Mary's household, recently formed at Ludlow.[14] At one fell swoop Gruffudd was deprived of what he seems—not unreasonably—to have considered his birthright. This was fuel enough for serious rivalry to spring up instantly between the two men.

Throughout the second half of the 1520s, antagonism flared, and in June 1529 matters came to a head at the Carmarthen assize courts. While Katherine's behaviour up to this point remains unknown, she did accompany her husband to Carmarthen and was an eyewitness to some of what occurred there.[15] A quarrel began when both men claimed the same lodgings for their men. On that same evening, Gruffudd allegedly gathered his adherents throughout Carmarthen and Kidwelly, who 'in ruettous maner' assembled 'to a great nombre' intending to murder Ferrers.[16] A day later, Sunday 6 June, he sent out another call of arms across the south-west of the country, allegedly bidding them come to Carmarthen the next day for the same reason.[17] Understandably, such a gathering appears to have taken some time, but roughly a week later—Tuesday 15 June—Gruffudd and more than forty servants broke into Carmarthen Castle and into the privy chamber to attempt

---

[12] *CSP Spain* IV, i, 460.

[13] The marriage contract stipulated that Gruffudd had to reach the age of 14 before the marriage took place. Based on a birthdate of 1508, he would have turned 14 in 1522. NLW MS A59.

[14] Williams, *Recovery, Reorientation and Reformation*, 254; *LP* IV, 2200.

[15] A contemporary letter from Katherine to Wolsey (TNA SP1/54 fol. 87), two letters from Ferrers (TNA SP1/54, fols 85 and 93) and the indictment against Gruffudd, written by Ferrers several months later (TNA STAC 2/18/234, printed in Jones, 'Sir Rhys ap Thomas: A Study in Family History of Tudor Politics', *Archaeologia Cambrensis* 5th ser. 9 (1892), 81–101 and 192–214) all describe the quarrel.

[16] TNA STAC2/18/234.   [17] Ibid.; TNA SP1/54, fol. 85.

to rescue his kinsman Thomas ap Owen, who was imprisoned there.[18] In the heat of the quarrel, somebody drew a dagger; Ferrers claimed that it was Gruffudd after 'many opprobrious words', but Katherine states that it was Ferrers (though she would not have been there to see this), and that Gruffudd only drew his in self-defence and was hurt in the arm for his pains.[19] The end result was that Lord Ferrers immediately imprisoned Gruffudd inside the castle.

The next day, Gruffudd and, apparently, Katherine sent out proclamations across most of south-west Wales summoning Gruffudd's followers to Carmarthen in order to storm the castle and rescue him.[20] According to Ferrers, this rescue attempt took place the next day on Thursday 17th 'at the comanndymet of Rece griffith and my lady haward'. A hundred and twenty ringleaders were later indicted and Ferrers wrote that 'for a troth ther was not such insurrecion in walys at any tyme a man can remebre'.[21] The attempt did not work: the rebels were arrested and indicted, and Gruffudd remained in the castle probably until early July.[22] Nevertheless, something approaching a rebellion clearly took place. Ferrers consistently blamed Katherine for inciting rebellion alongside her husband, and while historians have tended to downplay this, there was no reason for him to say so unless it was in some way true. Moreover, though Ferrers claimed that the second 'call to arms' between 15 and 17 June was sent by Gruffudd and Katherine together, we know that Gruffudd was by then imprisoned 'w[ith]out no plac to wrytt'. The fact that she, not he, wrote to Wolsey suggests that this was true.[23] It also means Gruffudd was probably not the author of this second call to arms, and that it must therefore have been Katherine inciting rebellion on his behalf. Katherine, then, remained in Carmarthen after his imprisonment and tried to raise the country and to rescue him. She was sufficiently involved to make the effort to discover just what had happened between him and Ferrers in Carmarthen Castle before his imprisonment, and she was aware of the conditions under which he was imprisoned. This was not simply passive acquiescence to a rebellion organized in her name. Naturally she did not physically lead the rebels—the indictment would surely have mentioned it—but we should not expect her to have done. Women did not bear arms, and thus their role in violent rebellion was invariably restricted to inciting, raising troops, and organizing.[24] The evidence shows that Katherine did all of these.

The date of Katherine's own petition to Wolsey cements the impression that she was not a passive or unwilling figurehead. Her letter is dated 17 June, a Thursday, the same day as the rescue attempt at the castle and two days after Gruffudd had been imprisoned there by Ferrers.[25] The timing here is significant. The letter

---

[18] TNA STAC2/18/234; TNA SP1/54, fol. 85.

[19] TNA SP1/54, fols 85 and 87. The indictment further claimed that Rhys had drawn his dagger first and that Ferrers was saved from his assault by his own servant Lewis Thomas ap John, who took the dagger from Rhys and was 'sore hurt and wounded w[i]t[h]in his right hand' in the process.

[20] TNA STAC2/18/234.   [21] TNA SP1/54, fol. 93.

[22] TNA STAC2/18/234. By 10 July Rhys was free and busy arresting pirates: TNA SP1/54 fol. 233.

[23] TNA SP1/54, fol. 87.

[24] Jansen, *Dangerous Talk and Strange Behavior*, 29–30; see also Cristian Berco, 'Juana Pimentel, the Mendoza Family, and the Crown', in Nader (ed.), *Power and Gender in Renaissance Spain*, 27–47.

[25] TNA SP1/54, fol. 87.

claimed to be her primary response to her husband's imprisonment and her only attempt to secure his freedom, yet it was written not immediately when Gruffudd was taken into ward nor even the next day, but two days later. It cannot have taken her that long to discover what had happened as she was staying within the city where the fracas took place. Instead, in those intervening days, she sent out proclamations across the country to raise a revolt and rescue him. Clearly the petition to Wolsey was not her first reaction. Yet the fact that she wrote it on the day of the revolt—and presumably before the rescue attempt itself had taken place, since the indictment tells us that it was tried that night—shows that she was not sure that the revolt would succeed. This shows that she fully understood the risk she was taking in reacting in such a violent manner, and that she used her petition as a safeguard against any possible consequences.

Her letter may have had the desired effect, as within two weeks Wolsey had ordered Gruffudd's release from Carmarthen Castle.[26] A year later in October 1530 came Chapuys's report, quoted at the beginning of this section, that Gruffudd had been imprisoned in the Tower because his wife (Katherine) had besieged the governor of Wales (Ferrers) in his castle, and Gruffudd had threatened to finish what she had begun.[27] This extraordinary statement may be something of an exaggeration. Ambassadors would often grasp at gossip simply to have something to report. However, at the same time on 7 October 1530, Gruffudd's cousin James ap Gruffudd ap Howell was arrested for 'fortifying' himself with a force in Emlyn Castle, which belonged to Gruffudd, making it clear that something did occur.[28] Even if Chapuys was exaggerating the extent of Katherine's involvement, it speaks volumes that this rumour was circulating at court, and that it was thought plausible.

Chapuys's reports tell us that Gruffudd was released from the Tower in June 1531 due to ill health, but was taken back into custody in September on charges of conspiracy.[29] He was said to have plotted with Scotland to topple Henry VIII from his throne in favour of James IV, and thus take Wales for himself. He was also accused of using his servant Edward Floyd to carry messages to his cousin James ap Gruffudd ap Howell, urging him to join in this conspiracy. Chapuys believed it to be the other way around, reporting that Gruffudd refused to confess that his own servant had tried to persuade him into such a conspiracy, and though he had not done anything wrong himself, was executed for his refusal to implicate anybody else.[30] Even Chapuys seemed to be aware that this was merely a charge of expediency. No action had been taken to enact any such conspiracy. As Gruffudd's descendant Henry Rice would declare in a detailed written defence of his ancestor in 1625, if Gruffudd really had intended to approach James IV, he would undoubtedly have done some serious damage given his wealth and the size of the army he could command.[31] Nevertheless he was executed on 4 December 1531 on trumped-up

---

[26] TNA SP1/54, fol. 233.   [27] *CSP Spain,* IV, 460.   [28] *LP* IV, 6709 (7).
[29] *CSP Spain,* IV (ii), 796.   [30] *CSP Spain,* IV (ii), 853.
[31] Henry Rice, 'Objections against Rice Griffith in his Indictment, with the Answers thereunto', *Cambrian Register* 2 (1796), 270–7.

charges of high treason in what amounted to a show trial. Katherine, whose whereabouts during her husband's imprisonments in London are unknown, escaped scot-free.

The quarrel at the assizes, the 'insurrection' following that, and Katherine's actions against Ferrers did not form part of the official charge of treason against Gruffudd, but they undoubtedly had an impact on his situation. Gruffudd had not been executed for anything he had actually done, but for what the government was afraid he might do. South-west Wales at this moment was in a state of discontent over religious reform and the abuses of royal officers and was ripe for rebellion.[32] Chapuys offered another reason, reporting that 'there is a rumour about town that had it not been for the Lady [Anne Boleyn], who hated him [Gruffudd] because he and his wife had spoken disparagingly of her, he would have been pardoned and escaped his miserable fate'.[33] Again, Gruffudd was not acting alone: Katherine was also thought to be involved, and once again there seems little reason for Chapuys to have included her name without cause. It is very interesting that a Howard daughter was speaking out against the rise of her own cousin, as it shows that the behaviour of Elizabeth Stafford/Howard, Duchess of Norfolk, was not a dynastic anomaly. Even if this was not the whole truth, it was enough that Gruffudd, a man who had spoken out against the new regime, had control of south-west Wales, a tried and tested invasion route.

It was not the norm for noblewomen like Katherine to incite and organize violent revolt. The few other noblewomen in sixteenth-century England who did so were involved in large-scale rebellion involving those of all classes, such as the Pilgrimage of Grace in 1536–7, or the Northern Rebellion of 1569.[34] It is more difficult to find noblewomen participating in smaller-scale revolts against the crown as most such activities were part of feuds between nobles.[35] Katherine's actions therefore remain unusual even in the context of other disorderly noble-women. There is some evidence that Katherine herself attempted to paint her actions as a feud with Ferrers on behalf of, not against, the King. She referred to one of Ferrers's prisoners as 'servant unto the kings honorable grace', suggesting that Ferrers was himself acting against the crown by imprisoning the King's men.[36] However, all the sources make it clear that Ferrers was in Wales as the King's representative. Katherine would undoubtedly have known that any action taken

---

[32] Williams, *Recovery, Reorientation, and Reformation*, 254–6; Gwynfor Jones, *Early Modern Wales*, xxiii.

[33] *CSP Spain*, IV, (ii), 853.

[34] Jansen, *Dangerous Talk and Strange Behavior*, 24–37. During the Northern Rebellion, Jane Howard/Neville, Countess of Westmorland—another Howard woman—had spurred the men on when they looked to give up the idea, and Anne Somerset/Percy, Countess of Northumberland, allegedly rode up and down the lines of rebel troops to encourage them, despite being heavily pregnant.

[35] Examples include Margaret Beauchamp/Talbot, Countess of Shrewsbury, who imprisoned members of the Berkeley family and participated in the siege of Berkeley castle in the middle of the fifteenth century, and Anne Savage/Berkeley, Lady Berkeley, who ordered her servants to steal fish from a manor she was trying to repossess in 1534. See Harris, *English Aristocratic Women*, 207–8; James Herbert Cooke, 'The Great Berkeley Lawsuit of the 15th and 16th Centuries. A Chapter of Gloucestershire History', *Transactions of the Bristol and Gloucestershire Archaeological Society* 3 (1878–9), 305–24 (305–15).

[36] TNA SP1/54, fol. 87.

against him was equivalent to rebellion against the crown and would have been construed as such. Ferrers certainly understood his own actions in this way, stating that he had taken Gruffudd into ward 'in the kings name'.[37] Kesselring has noted that categorization of an action—i.e. whether it was riot or rebellion, felony, or treason, against the crown or not—lay with the crown's officials and not with participants.[38] Ferrers's indictment does contain the request that Gruffudd be convicted of treason for trying to kill the King's justice, and the fact that Gruffudd was eventually executed on a treason charge does suggest that his actions, and thus Katherine's, were understood as rebellion against the crown.[39] That his charge concerned a conspiracy to place James IV of Scotland on the throne of England, and not his attempts to kill Ferrers, does not detract from this. In 1531, Gruffudd could not legally have been convicted of treason for his attempt on Ferrers's life, and historians agree that the conspiracy charge was a convenient cover for his actual deeds.[40]

The way in which Katherine was represented, and presented herself, in the documents relating to these events is also unusual. Commentators continually referred to her by her maiden name of Howard, not her married name of Rhys, calling her 'Lady Katherine Howard' or sometimes 'Lady Howard'. Ferrers did this in all of his correspondence; the indictment also did so; Henry Rice did it later in his seventeenth-century defence of Gruffudd's actions. This is very unusual. Once married, a woman was known either by her title, her married name, or as 'wife of' her husband.[41] Though the Howards were technically of a higher noble status than the Rhys family, the latter were as powerful in their own domin-ion as the Howards were in England, making it unlikely that remaining 'Lady Katherine Howard', the daughter of a peer, was of more consequence than being the wife of Rhys ap Gruffudd in the geographical context of their marriage. For Ferrers to so consistently use her maiden name therefore seems a deliberate choice. It made it clear that a member of the most powerful dynasty in England, one related to the King's intended queen, was involved in what he obviously perceived to be a disaster in south-west Wales. If he was afraid that the government would not take this seriously, he may have thought the mention of the Howard name would up the ante.

Katherine did not call herself a Howard. Her letter to Wolsey is signed 'Katherine Ryx', a firm identification with her husband and marital identity, and her actions clearly show that she was on his side. She did, however, draw on her Howard links to attempt to achieve an outcome in her own and Gruffudd's favour. Noblewomen generally did call on their natal relatives to help them out of difficult situations

---

[37] TNA SP1/54, fol. 85.

[38] K. J. Kesselring, 'Deference and Dissent in Tudor England: Reflections on Sixteenth-Century Protest', *History Compass* 3 (2005), 1–16 (7).

[39] TNA STAC2/18/234.

[40] Treason law at this time rested on a statute from 1352. Though killing an officer of the King was treasonous, attempting but failing to do so was not. See G. R. Elton, 'The Law of Treason in the Early Reformation', *Historical Journal* 11 (1968), 211–36.

[41] Chapuys refers to Katherine in this way. I have found no other contemporary examples of married noblewomen who continued to be known by their maiden names.

when their marital connections were of no use.[42] Though Katherine did not use her maiden name, her letter made no mention of Gruffudd's family but instead identified herself with her natal family and claimed assistance on those terms, asking Wolsey to be good to Gruffudd and herself 'for the great loue that was betwene yo[r] lordship and my lord my father and that ye will not suffer us to haue no shame nor rebuke'.[43] It is very interesting that she did not mention the current Duke of Norfolk, her half-brother, who was the nominal head of the dynasty in 1529. Instead she rested her plea on the past relationship between Wolsey and her father the Second Duke, a dead man. It is difficult to know whether this says more about the Third Duke's relationship with Wolsey, or with Katherine. While there is no evidence to say that brother and sister did not get on, Norfolk and Wolsey are famously supposed to have been enemies, particularly at this point in time.[44] Arguably, then, reminding Wolsey of her relationship to Norfolk would not have served Katherine particularly well. Her use of the word 'us' ('that ye will not suffer *us* to haue no shame or rebuke') is also interesting. It could be read to mean herself and her husband, but in the context of the full sentence, coming immediately after mention of her father, it sounds more as though she was using it to mean herself and the rest of the Howard dynasty. The idea that the entire Howard dynasty would bear the shame of whatever happened to herself and to Gruffudd clearly shows that some noblewomen continued to identify strongly with their natal families after marriage when it was expedient to do so—and, moreover, felt that others would also continue to identify women with their natal dynasties, as indeed Ferrers was doing. That this did not stop her in the first place, however, suggests that the strength of these ties could be augmented or diminished as the occasion required, and that her identification with the Howards was circumstantially elastic.

Katherine suffered no official consequences for her actions. The fact that he, and not she, was the government's major target, was no doubt the major reason for this. At this point women's lack of individual legal identity in most European countries meant they were not seen as legally responsible for their own actions.[45] Moreover, women were popularly understood as disorderly creatures who simply could not help their rebellious behaviour, and thus their conduct was often ignored.[46] As Katherine's husband, Gruffudd was officially responsible for her actions, and this may have been among the reasons why he was imprisoned and she was left alone.

It is worth noting that from 1530, the government was engaged in drafting new treason legislation. When Henry VII came to the throne, the definition of treason rested on a statute passed in 1352 and was restricted to offences against King's person and his throne, most infamously 'compassing or imagining' the death of the

---

[42] Particularly, but not exclusively, in situations of marital dispute. See Susan Dwyer Amussen, '"Being stirred to much unquietness": Violence and Domestic Violence in Early Modern England', *Journal of Women's History* 6:2 (1994), 70–89.

[43] TNA SP1/54, fol. 87v.

[44] On Norfolk and Wolsey's relationship, see chapter 3 in David M. Head, *The Ebbs and Flows of Fortune: The Life of Thomas Howard, Third Duke of Norfolk* (Athens, Ga, 1995).

[45] Davis, 'Women on Top', 176–7. See also Dekker, 'Women in Revolt', 344–5.

[46] Davis, 'Women on Top', 176–7.

King, his Queen, or the royal heir; violating his female relatives; levying war against him or joining his enemies in doing so; counterfeiting the great seal or coin; and killing the chancellor, treasurer, or a justice of any bench while he was exercising his office. As Bellamy points out, changes to treason legislation were usually made in reaction to specific events, and during the early 1530s there were a number of episodes which made the current provision appear inadequate.[47] The new Act, eventually passed in 1534 as the Treason Act, included a clause making it treasonous to withdraw contemptuously after a summons to appear before the king, to any of his castles and maintain resistance there, which may refer to the behaviour of James ap Gruffudd ap Howell and of Katherine in Wales. It was also made treason for a subject of the English crown to take an oath to a foreign-born prince and agree to pay them money against the King's prerogative, which might reflect Gruffudd's supposed conspiracy with the Scottish King alongside the undoubted fear of the influence of Holy Roman Emperor Charles V and of the papacy at this point. This episode may therefore have contributed to changes to the law.

ANNUS HORRIBILIS: 1536

The 1534 Act was also designed to silence opposition to the Boleyn marriage by making it high treason to slander it in speech or in writing, an attempt at preventing dangerous gossip. The fall of Anne Boleyn was the next case of high treason with which the Howard women were involved, but, frustratingly, there is remarkably little evidence with which to build up a narrative. We saw in the last chapter that Anne's rise was in some ways a dynastic affair, but not to the extent that is often assumed; the Boleyns, rather than the Howards, were the ones immediately surrounding her in her day-to-day activities as Queen. Her fall is also generally thought to have affected the Howards' pre-eminence at court, but can this be quantified?

This analysis is not intended as an exploration of Anne's guilt or innocence, since that has been amply covered elsewhere and to date there is no new material to shed any new light on this.[48] The significance of her fall for the Howards lies both in the fact that Mary Howard/Fitzroy, Duchess of Richmond, and Lady Margaret Howard were in service to Anne at the time, and in its use as a point of a comparison for the more detailed material surrounding the fall of her cousin Catherine Howard five years later. One of the most interesting aspects of Anne's fall is that no women were tried or convicted alongside her, which is more surprising than has been recognized given the nature of her crimes. It would be incredible for her women not to have been questioned. They, more than anybody else, would have been in a position to know the truth or otherwise of the claims against her,

---

[47] Bellamy, *The Tudor Law of Treason*, 23–4.

[48] G. W. Bernard, 'The Fall of Anne Boleyn', *EHR* 106:420 (1991), 584–610; E. W. Ives, 'The Fall of Anne Boleyn Reconsidered', *EHR* 107:424 (1992), 651–64; Bernard, 'The Fall of Anne Boleyn: A Rejoinder', *EHR* 107 (1992), 665–74; Greg Walker, 'Rethinking the Fall of Anne Boleyn', *Historical Journal* 45 (2002), 1–29; Ives, *The Life and Death of Anne Boleyn* (Oxford, 2004–5); Bernard, *Anne Boleyn: Fatal Attractions* (London, 2010).

given the intimate service that they rendered, and we should remember that Catherine Howard's women provided the core of the case against her. It is likely that the depositions given by Anne's women simply have not survived, and the lack of legal records of the trial is also unhelpful.[49]

Yet it is clear that the women around her did play a key role in the investigation. Contemporary accounts furnish us with five names. According to John Husee, court agent of Lord and Lady Lisle, Anne's adulteries came to light through the accusations of Lady Worcester, 'Nan' Cobham, 'and one maid other'.[50] Lancelot de Carles, secretary to the French ambassador Antoine de Castelnau, Bishop of Tarbes, and present in England at the time of Anne's trial, wrote a metrical poem on Anne's death also referencing the role of the Countess of Worcester in accidentally implicating the Queen. During a quarrel with her brother, Sir Anthony Browne, in which he accused her of her loose living evidenced by her pregnancy, Lady Worcester retorted that she was not the only one guilty of such behaviour, and related worse of the Queen.[51] This is supported by a report of Tower constable Sir William Kingston. Whilst awaiting trial, Anne Boleyn apparently lamented the poor mental state of Lady Worcester, whose unborn baby had not stirred since Anne's arrest.[52] Sir John Spelman, a judge present at the trial, wrote that the posthumous words of Lady Wingfield had helped to condemn Anne.[53] Jane, Lady Rochford, wife of George Boleyn, was also rumoured to have provided testimony concerning the incestuous relationship between her husband and the Queen, and of their discussions of the King's impotence.[54] Edward Baynton, the Queen's vice-chamberlain, wrote of Margery Horsman, one of the Queen's maids, that 'no dowte but that she must be of conncell'.[55]

No Howard women, then, were among Anne's most memorable accusers, though they were undoubtedly questioned. Perhaps they were not involved as procuresses, or perhaps, as Ives has argued, the fact that no woman was accused along with Anne suggests that the charge was fabricated.[56] However, we should note that as the law stood in 1536, adultery on the part of a Queen was not actually treasonous, and therefore her women faced no official legal consequences for failing to reveal it.[57] Anne was convicted on a charge of imagining the death of the King by discussing his impotence with her brother, George Boleyn, Viscount Rochford. To be guilty of misprision of treason (knowing of treasonous activity and failing to report it),

---

[49] Bernard also agrees that Anne's women would have been questioned and the depositions must have been lost. 'Fall of Anne Boleyn', 599–600.

[50] The identity of Anne or 'Nan' Cobham has puzzled historians, since the most obvious woman to bear this name was Anne Brooke, Lady Cobham, and it has been thought unlikely that a man of Husee's station would use the diminutive 'Nan' to describe a woman of significantly higher status than himself. However, the New Year gift list of 1534 (TNA E101/421/13) contains a 'Mistress Cobham' among the gentlewomen who received gifts from the King and it seems likely that Nan Cobham was in fact a relatively lowly member of Anne's privy chamber. *Lisle Letters*, III, 703a, 381–2.

[51] Lancelot de Carles, 'Poème sur la mort d'Anne Boleyn', in Georges Ascoli (ed.), *La Grande Bretagne devant l'opinion française* (Paris, 1927).

[52] BL Cotton MS Otho C X, fol. 225.

[53] John Spelman, *The Reports of John Spelman*, ed. J. H. Baker, Selden Society, xciii, xciv (1977), I, 71.

[54] *LP* X, 908.   [55] BL Cotton MS Otho C X, fol. 210.

[56] Ives, 'Reconsidered', 652–3.   [57] Bellamy, *The Tudor Law of Treason*, 41.

Anne's women would have to have known of, and concealed, what was probably a private conversation. Bernard suggests that Anne's women turned 'King's evidence', and it is entirely likely that they did indeed reveal anything that they knew when faced with a frightening examination, but this makes it odd that no commentator on the trial itself made mention of their evidence, and suggests that they were not crucial to the verdict.[58] It would be easy to argue that contemporaries simply attached no value to women's testimony, and it is true that diplomatic or ambassadorial correspondence rarely acknowledges women as a source of information during this period.[59] Yet, the wealth of examples gathered by Sharon Jansen of women's words being construed as treason and taken very seriously indeed by the government strongly suggests that in a case as critical as this one, women's testimony would absolutely have been valued.

Where were the Howards at the time of Anne's fall? We know that Mary Howard/Fitzroy, Duchess of Richmond, who was in service to Anne, was indeed at court, for when her husband died less than two months after the Queen's execution, a letter recorded her departure from London for Kenninghall, implying that she had been at court up until that time.[60] Margaret Gamage, who shortly became the wife of Lord William Howard, was probably also there, since they were married at Westminster less than two months after Anne's execution.[61] The other Howard women were more scattered. It seems likely that Agnes, dowager Duchess of Norfolk, was based in Horsham, Sussex, at this point, since we know that she moved her household from there to Lambeth towards the end of 1536. Anne, dowager Countess of Oxford, was based in Cambridgeshire, and Elizabeth, Duchess of Norfolk, was still under house arrest in Hertfordshire. Katherine, later Countess of Bridgwater, had recently undergone a divorce, and may have been in London, but probably not at court. Lord William Howard was in Scotland.[62] Though his brother Lord Thomas Howard was at court, he seems to have played no role in the trial. The Duke of Norfolk had recently arrived at court, and he and his son are the only Howards known to have taken a prominent place in proceedings.[63] According to the chronicler Wriothesley, Norfolk was among the officials who brought Anne to the Tower on 2 May. He headed the trial of peers and pronounced his own niece guilty and his son and heir, Henry, sat at his feet throughout.[64] Anne's own family likewise rallied to the side of the crown.[65]

The evidence does not show whether the women took part in Norfolk's overt display of loyalty, or whether they simply stayed away from court until the storm had passed. Nothing suggests that there was any kind of collective dynastic action or strategy here, which in itself probably indicates that other members of the family

[58] Bernard, *Fatal Attractions*, 158.
[59] I am grateful to Dr Catherine Fletcher for her advice in this regard.
[60] *LP* XI, 163 (71).   [61] *Lisle Letters*, III, 735.
[62] BL Cotton MS Otho B II, fol. 246.   [63] *LP* X, 759.
[64] Wriothesley, *Chronicle*, I, 36–7.
[65] Anne's father, the Earl of Wiltshire, was among the peers who convicted the men, though he did not sit on the jury to convict the Queen; her aunt, Lady Boleyn, accompanied her to the Tower, undoubtedly chosen as a 'safe' guard.

did not come under suspicion. Either they were not involved, or the case was not designed to bring down the Howards as a whole. Norfolk's swift action in condemning his niece, and Mary's probable testimony, might be considered to be something of a family strategy, if unintended.

Barely a month passed before Mary, Duchess of Richmond, became entangled with the treason laws yet again. In July 1536, an affair and contract of marriage was discovered to exist between Mary's cousin Lord Thomas Howard and her close friend Lady Margaret Douglas, the King's niece.[66] The investigation found that they had 'loved' for a year, and had been contracted since Easter 1536.[67] Following discovery, Lord Thomas and Lady Margaret were imprisoned in the Tower, and Lord Thomas was attainted for high treason and sentenced to death. This was a severe punishment for a crime which was not legally treason.[68] Lady Margaret remained within the Tower until November 1536, when she was moved to Syon Abbey.[69] Lord Thomas was never executed, but died in the Tower in October 1537, two days after Lady Margaret's eventual release.[70]

Mary, Duchess of Richmond, had known about their affair and marriage since it began. When asked whether had had seen Howard 'resort unto hir [Margaret]' when Mary was present, Thomas Smyth, a servant of Howard's, replied, 'diu[er]se tymes'.[71] Mary had therefore acted as the couple's accomplice and chaperone. Several servants on both sides, as well as Lady Margaret Howard, wife of Lord William, and Hastings, servant to Agnes, dowager Duchess of Norfolk, also knew, and Hastings's knowledge might suggest that the Duchess was also involved. That the government chose to view Howard's behaviour as treason should, by rights, have meant that Mary was guilty of misprision of treason, the crime of knowing of treasonous activity and failing to report it that had been introduced with the Act of Succession in 1534. Yet, in a pattern that is becoming familiar, she walked free.

The key to this case lay in the recent execution of Anne Boleyn and its immediate impact in terms of safeguarding the realm. With Anne dead and her marriage annulled, her daughter Princess Elizabeth could hardly remain the King's heir. Thus, the Second Succession Act of 1536 illegitimized Elizabeth and gave the King licence to appoint whomever he liked as his heir.[72] As Head has pointed out, Margaret Douglas's importance within the succession increased immeasurably almost overnight.[73] Clearly she could not now be allowed to make her own marriage, and when it was discovered that she had done, it had to be broken. Unfortunately, by canon law it was both valid and binding, so there was no way to do this save by terming it treason and using an Act of attainder. The attainder construed Lord

---

[66] See David M. Head, ' "Beyng Ledde and Seduced by the Devyll": The Attainder of Lord Thomas Howard and the Tudor Law of Treason', *Sixteenth Century Journal* 13:4 (1982), 3–16, and Kimberly Schutte, ' "Not for Matters of Treason but for Love Matters": Margaret Douglas, Countess of Lennox, and Tudor Marriage Law', in James V. Mehl (ed.), *Laudem Caroli: Renaissance and Reformation Studies for Charles G. Nauert* (Kirksville, Mich., 1998), 171–88.

[67] TNA E36/120/65.   [68] *Statutes of the Realm*, III, 680–1.

[69] TNA SP1/110, fol. 186.   [70] TNA SP1/126, fol. 48.   [71] Ibid.

[72] *Statutes of the Realm*, III, 655–62.   [73] Head, ' "Ledde and Seduced" ', 7–8.

Thomas's action as an attempt to claim the throne of England through Lady Margaret, thus relying on the conventional interpretation of treason as imagining the death of the King.[74] His attainder was one of only three which included clauses extending the treason law so that in future the crime listed, i.e. marrying a relative of the King without permission, would be legally treasonable. Interestingly, it also stated that in future, anybody advising or aiding in the making of a such a match would share the penalties for high treason, a clause which, had it come into immediate effect, would have lost Mary her head.[75]

Happily for Mary, she too had suddenly become important to the succession. Following the Second Succession Act of June 1536 allowing the King to appoint his own heir, it was widely rumoured that this clause was included specifically to allow him to name his illegitimate son Henry Fitzroy, Duke of Richmond, as his heir.[76] Mary was Richmond's wife; if he were the King's heir, she would be queen-in-waiting. It would have been inconvenient, not to say deeply embarrassing, to attaint her for treason, and then to declare her the queen-in-waiting. Indeed, the fact that she walked free gives weight to Chapuys's statement that the King really was intending to name Richmond as his heir.[77] This is bolstered by the inclusion of a clause in the attainder specifically stating that forfeiture of goods applied only to Howard and his direct heirs, which has been construed by Head as 'designed to protect the interests of Howard relatives as well as assuage the anxieties of any others who had some role in Lord Thomas' case'.[78] Margaret Gamage/Howard, wife of Lord William, was also rescued by this. Once again, the family as a whole was evidently not the target of this case, which argues that they were not seen here as a political unit. The point was to discourage others from contracting marriage with royal women without leave, and to dissolve this marriage in order to secure the succession. Lord Thomas Howard was not even executed, dying instead of sickness in the Tower over a year later.[79] Unfortunately for Mary and for the Howards, her husband the Duke of Richmond never was named as Henry's heir. During this investigation, he had fallen ill and declined dramatically. By 22 July Chapuys thought that he did not have long to live, and that this was the reason the King had not named him, and he died a day later on 23 July.[80]

Two major treason cases in one year ought to have been enough for any family. Yet there is evidence to suggest that Katherine Howard/ap Rhys/Daubeney, Lady Daubeney (later Countess of Bridgwater), may have treated them to yet another in the autumn of that year. Following the execution of her first husband, Rhys ap Gruffudd, after their rebellion in 1531, she had married Henry Daubeney, Lord Daubeney. As is discussed in Chapter 3, this marriage ended in divorce in 1535, and it is likely that Katherine now lived in London, though she does not seem to have been involved in either the fall of Anne Boleyn or Lord Thomas Howard's marriage. In the autumn of 1536 she may have become involved in the Pilgrimage of Grace. The evidence for this comes from a spy report made in November 1536 by

---

[74] *Statutes of the Realm*, III, 680–1.   [75] Ibid.   [76] *CSP Spain*, V, ii, 77 (214).
[77] Ibid.   [78] Head, ' "Ledde and Seduced" ', 14.   [79] TNA SP1/126, fol. 48.
[80] *CSP Spain*, V, ii, 77 (214).

a young soldier of the King's host named Harry Osberne.[81] Harry, who according to his report came from Gloucester, went north with his father as part of the host under Sir Charles 'á Trowen' (probably Trahern).[82] He received permission from his father to spend a few days among the rebel enemy in order to 'knowe the facyon off them', returning at the end of the month with information on the size of the rebel force, their morale and state of mind, their equipment, aims, and the rumours flying among them. On 29 November his report was written up probably by John Ingby, to whom Osberne reported verbally, and sent to the Privy Council. In it, Osberne stated that 'my lady Rysse ys come to them w[i]t[h] iij thowsande men and sche browth w[i]t[h] herre halffe a carte loode of plate the whyche plate they doo coine them selffe amonge them ther'. Historians have identified 'lady Rysse' as Katherine.[83]

This is only one report, and there are several difficulties with its veracity. Katherine had indeed once been 'Lady Rhys' by dint of her marriage to Rhys ap Gruffudd, but since then she had remarried and was now known as Lady Daubeney.[84] There is no indication that Katherine ever formally returned to her first married name, and this did not usually happen unless a woman's first marriage was of higher status than her second, which was not true in this case. Yet I have found no other noblewoman to whom the title could apply. The women of the Rhys family, Katherine's first marital family, were all accounted for elsewhere, either dead or under different names. Her grandmother-in-law, Lady Jenet, had died in 1535; her mother-in-law Catherine St John—the widow of Sir Griffith Rhys—had married Sir Piers Edgecombe in 1525, and Katherine's own children were too young either to have wives or to involve themselves in rebellion alone. There appears to be no other noblewoman bearing the name of Lady Rhys at this time who could have offered the rebels troops and plate. The general truth of Osberne's report has also been doubted, largely because he stated that Henry, Lord Stafford, had come in person to the rebels and offered 1,000 troops, when, so far as is known, he did no such thing.[85] However, the involvement of Lord Stafford was widely, if falsely, rumoured among the rebel force throughout the autumn of 1536 so it is not surprising that Osberne reported this.[86] His job was to gather the rumours then current in the enemy camp and pass them to his superiors, not to decide what was true and what was false. Katherine's involvement may well have been rumour or a distortion of some kind. It could equally have been fact.

---

[81] TNA SP1/112, fol. 34. All further quotes from Osberne's report refer to this source.

[82] Trahern and variants thereof was a common surname in Wales and in the south-west, and it has not been possible to link Sir Charles to a particular family.

[83] Dodds and Dodds, *The Pilgrimage of Grace*, 288; Jansen, *Dangerous Talk and Strange Behavior*, 25; J. S. Brewer, the calenderer of the relevant volume of *The Letters and Papers of Henry VIII*, also indexed this letter under Katherine's name.

[84] The report of Jane Seymour's funeral in 1537 calls her 'Lady Dawbeney', and so does John Husee's report of her role as chief mourner at the funeral of Elizabeth Howard/Boleyn, Countess of Wiltshire. There were no other Lady Daubeneys at this time. *LP* XII (ii) 1060; TNA SP3/12, fol. 42.

[85] See C. S. L. Davies, 'Henry Stafford, Tenth Baron Stafford (1501–1563)', *ODNB* [accessed 7 June 2012].

[86] Ibid.; Dodds and Dodds, *The Pilgrimage of Grace*, I, 287.

In which case, how far can we test it? Osberne stated that he came from Gloucester, which is on the border with south Wales, Katherine's home during her first marriage until early 1532, so it is possible that he had heard of her. It is also possible that the people of that region continued to think of Katherine as Lady Rhys, since they had known her under that title and she continued to administer her jointure lands there. The wording of Osberne's report does not suggest that he had met Katherine personally in the north, which means that he must have been given her name by the rebels, perhaps the troops that she was reported to have brought with her. The only place from which Katherine could realistically have gathered troops is from her Welsh jointure lands, because she did not have any authority to call musters on her husband's estates in Somerset and Dorset. These troops would undoubtedly have known her previously as Lady Rhys and not Lady Daubeney. Alternatively, she may deliberately have ensured that her correct name was not known to them, using a false name in order to avoid detection.

Katherine's men, if she sent them, must have joined the revolt at York. Though rebellion had began in Lincolnshire on 1 October, it had petered out there by the middle of the month. Osberne's report was written up on 29 November, suggesting that he had been with the troops perhaps during the middle of that month, most probably somewhere in Yorkshire with the bulk of the rebel force. Osberne's description of the rebels coining Katherine's plate—and the fact that he had come away with one of the groats they had minted—shows that they must have been somewhere with a mint, and York is the only location possible for this. Katherine could easily have mustered troops from Wales and marched northwards in time to join the rebellion at York in mid-November; her brother the Duke of Norfolk mustered troops from Norfolk, almost as far away, and made it to the north within the same timeframe, and Osberne himself had come north with a host from Gloucester.[87] Osberne's wording suggests that Katherine herself had personally escorted the plate and troops to the rebels—'my lady Rysse *ys come to them*'. This too is possible. A woman who had lived in rebellious Wales would not be afraid to venture into unrest, and with a consort of 3,000 troops, she would hardly have been in much personal danger.

She also had connections to the north at this time. Her two sons were being brought up in the household of Cuthbert Tunstall, Bishop of Durham, whose own behaviour during the Pilgrimage has been described as 'suspect'.[88] Alternatively, the Countess of Derby, wife of the equally prevaricating Edward, Third Earl of Derby, was Katherine's younger sister Dorothy.[89] Katherine also had the financial wherewithal to donate plate to the rebels. She had been made rich both from her

---

[87] Head, *The Ebbs and Flows of Fortune*, 136–8.

[88] Though he did not actively join the rebels, he did not oppose them either, fleeing to his strong-hold of Norham-on-Tweed until hostilities had ceased. See D. G. Newcombe, 'Cuthbert Tunstal (1474–1559), Bishop of Durham and Diplomat', *ODNB* [accessed 7 January 2013].

[89] For discussion of the Earl of Derby's behaviour during the rebellion, see B. Coward, *The Stanleys, Lords Stanley and Earls of Derby, 1385–1672* (Manchester, 1983), 164 and Edward M. Zevin, *The Life of Edward Stanley, Third Earl of Derby (1521–1572): Noble Power and the Tudor Monarchy* (New York, 2010), chapter 5.

first marriage and from her recent divorce, and now had an annual income of almost £300.[90] 'Lady Rysse', then, may plausibly have been Katherine.

Motivation for her involvement is not far to seek, since the Henrician government had executed her first husband on a spurious charge of high treason. Despite the usual lack of official punishment for women's actions, Katherine's previous experience shows that it was risky. One of the men responsible for suppressing the rebellion was her half-brother the Duke of Norfolk. Katherine's involvement, if indeed it was her, would hardly reflect credit upon the family, and shows that she was clearly not thinking about this. Family connections were a deciding factor in the treatment of rebellious women, but this could go in either direction: relatives could either save or condemn.[91] Katherine does not seem to have suffered any consequences of her involvement here. This may of course mean that Osberne's report was wrong and she was not there, but it may also mean that her connection to the dynasty had shielded her from repercussions, and that therefore families were understood as collectives from the outside even if they did not behave in this way on the inside.

'A MOST MISERABLE CASE': THE FALL OF CATHERINE HOWARD, 1541–1542

The attainder and execution of Queen Catherine Howard in 1542 demonstrates that involvement in high treason became more dangerous as Henry's reign progressed. This case saw the first convictions of Howard women as part of a treason case: Agnes Tylney/Howard, Duchess of Norfolk, Katherine Howard/ap Rhys/ Daubeney, Countess of Bridgwater, Lady Margaret Howard, and a few others related to the family were attainted and imprisoned for misprision of treason. The story is well known.[92] Catherine Howard, the daughter of Lord Edmund Howard, joined her grandmother Agnes, Duchess of Norfolk's, household probably in 1531, the year in which one of the latter's previous wards (another Catherine) moved out to marry Lord William Howard, and the year in which Catherine's father Edmund secured the controllership of Calais and consequently broke up his English household.[93] At this point the household was based at Chesworth House in Horsham, Sussex, and Catherine was probably aged around 8 or 9.[94] At some point after October 1536, Agnes moved her household to Norfolk House in Lambeth, and

---

[90] Her jointure from her first marriage was worth £200, and her divorce settlement entitled her to £80 per year: TNA SC12/25/53; TNA SP3/9, fol. 36.

[91] Jansen, *Dangerous Talk and Strange Behavior*, chapter 1: 'A Woman's Treason: The Case of Margaret Cheyne', 5–37.

[92] The main scholarly account of Catherine's life remains Lacey Baldwin Smith, *Catherine Howard* (Stroud, 1961; repr. 2009) but this is somewhat outdated. Most newer work on Catherine's life has been undertaken by those writing for a general audience; see Conor Byrne, *Katherine Howard: A New History* (London, 2014) and Gareth Russell, *Young & Damned & Fair* (London, 2017).

[93] *LP* V, 318 (21), 220 (14).

[94] Catherine's exact birthdate is unknown and has been the subject of some debate. Gareth Russell provides a comprehensive and up-to-date review of this in *Young & Damned & Fair*, 16–19, and convincingly argues for a date of 1522 or 1523.

engaged a local music tutor, Henry Mannox, to teach the now-teenage Catherine the accomplishments she needed.[95] The two embarked on an affair that seems to have stopped short of intercourse. By autumn 1538, this had ended and Catherine had moved on, with Francis Dereham, one of her uncle's gentlemen-pensioners. This affair did proceed to intercourse, and continued until Catherine went to court as one of Anne of Cleves's maids of honour in the winter of 1539, where she caught the King's eye and was probably being officially courted by April 1540.[96] After marrying the King in July, Catherine then began an affair of sorts with Thomas Culpeper, a Gentleman of the Privy Chamber. Her world crumbled when Mary Lascelles/Hall, an associate from Norfolk House days, told her brother John Lascelles about Catherine's pre-marital behaviour, and he informed the Privy Council in early November 1541. The resulting investigation discovered the Culpeper affair as well. Depositions were taken from all those involved, and many former employees from Agnes's household. Culpeper and Dereham were executed in early December, thirteen members of the extended Howard family and of Agnes's household were imprisoned on charges of misprision of treason, and Catherine herself, alongside Jane Parker/Boleyn, Viscountess Rochford, was executed in February 1542.[97]

This was a comprehensive take-down of a noble dynasty. Surprisingly, given the family connection and the fact that they were both executed for broadly the same crime, the treason cases of Anne Boleyn and Catherine Howard are rarely directly compared. Catherine's was similar to Anne's in that both women were thought to have been guilty of adulterous liaisons during marriage to Henry VIII, but it was this very similarity that meant that Catherine's case went further in almost every respect. As we saw, only Anne and her alleged lovers had been convicted of any form of treason in 1536, and the case was kept as secret as possible, leading to public doubt as to her guilt. By 1542, lessons had been learned and royal embarrassment was no doubt greater the second time around. This time, the government itself published the detail of Catherine's crimes, and was determined to also secure those who had helped her to commit them, both as an example to everybody else, and perhaps to demonstrate that Henry had not driven his wife into the arms of another man all by himself. In 1536, the judges allowed Anne's alleged adulteries to be counted as treason under the old clause of imagining the death of the King, because they bolstered what was legally the greater crime of discussing the King's impotence and her own future remarriage.[98] In 1542, adultery on the part of a queen was still not legally treasonable, and the judges appear to have objected to using the same legal 'fudge' a second time, not least because Catherine does not seem to have also discussed the King's lack of sexual ability or her own remarriage.[99] She was therefore condemned by parliamentary Act of attainder and not by common law, and her attainder contained a clause to alter the law, ensuring that for the future,

[95] A letter from Lord William Howard to Thomas Cromwell dated October 1536 shows that Agnes was still *in situ* in Horsham at this time. TNA SP1/107, fol. 127.
[96] This is when she received a grant of goods in her own right. *LP* XV, 612 (12).
[97] *Statutes of the Realm*, III, 857–60.
[98] See Bellamy, *The Tudor Law of Treason*, 41, and Ives, *The Life and Death of Anne Boleyn*, 344–5.
[99] Bellamy, *The Tudor Law of Treason*, 41.

adultery on the part of a queen would indeed be considered high treason, as would concealment of unchastity prior to making a royal marriage.[100]

I do not intend to reopen the issue of the extent of Catherine's crimes save to note that she was charged only with intent to commit post-marital adultery, and not with having actually done so, because the former was sufficient to obtain a conviction for high treason and it could not be proven beyond doubt that the act had occurred.[101] About the pre-marital liaisons there was less doubt, since the various testimonies made clear that she and Francis Dereham had certainly behaved improperly. Although this was not itself treasonable, it meant that the government was able to construe her taking Dereham back into her service once she was Queen as intent to commit post-marital adultery. Her relatives and associates were there-fore convicted of misprision of treason not only for concealment of her pre-marital unchastity, but for having helped to bring Dereham back to her service and having therefore connived in their alleged intent to rekindle their relationship.

So what did the family know about Catherine's behaviour in her grandmother's household? For them, the decisive issue was not the Culpeper affair, but the earlier one with Francis Dereham. Once it became clear that Mary Hall was telling the truth, it was assumed that those living in the household must have known about it as an open secret. It is difficult to prove or disprove this entirely. Clearly, most knew something. Mannox deposed that Duchess Agnes had discovered him kissing Catherine, had beaten them both, and forbidden them to be alone together again, and Katherine Tylney said almost the same thing had occurred with Dereham.[102] Agnes herself also made various 'joking' comments, asking 'wher is derhm now, I warrant yow if yow seck him in Catherine howardes chamber ye shall fynd hym ther'.[103] However, she maintained that she had not known that they were having a full-blown sexual affair, and Katherine Tylney also consistently said that 'the sayd duches was neu[er] pryvey or hadd no knowleg of any carnall knowleg between them'.[104] Agnes's daughter Katherine, Countess of Bridgwater (Catherine's aunt), knew about the 'night banquets' that Catherine and the other girls had in their chamber with the boys, remarking that 'if she used that sort it wold hurte her beautye'.[105] Lord William Howard also seems to have had some knowledge, though since he did not live there he may not have known all. On hearing that Mannox had, in a fit of jealousy, left a note for the Duchess telling her to go to the maidens' chamber at night so that she might catch Dereham and Catherine out, Lord William turned up on Mannox's doorstep and bawled him out, after which Mannox appears to have left the Duchess's service.[106] Of the atmosphere of blame in the household afterwards, he supposedly remarked, 'what mad wenches can you not be mery amonge yorselfs but you must thus fall out?'[107] His wife Lady Margaret likewise seems to have had suspicions but may not have known the full extent. The women of the household, some of whom were related to the Howards, knew more, because

---

[100] *Statutes of the Realm*, III, 857–60.   [101] Ibid.
[102] TNA SP1/167, fol. 117v; SP1/168, fols 8r–v.   [103] TNA SP1/168, fol. 8.
[104] Ibid.   [105] TNA SP1/168, fol. 159v.   [106] Ibid., fol. 88.
[107] TNA SP1/168, fol. 157v.

they were the ones who deposed the gory detail, including Mannox's explicit comment that he had 'had here by thow count', and the 'many tymes puffynge & blowyng' between Catherine and Dereham.[108] The Duke of Norfolk himself seems not to have been aware of Catherine's past. He probably hardly knew his niece, and he did not live in the household. His innocence never seems to have been doubted either by the family or by the Council.

The family's behaviour during Catherine's tenure as Queen sheds a little extra light on their knowledge of her past. The Council were concerned with the fact that Catherine's relatives had allegedly sued to her to take Dereham back into her service, and some of them did do this. Agnes, Duchess of Norfolk, stated that her daughter Katherine, Countess of Bridgwater, and daughter-in-law Lady Margaret Howard had sued to her to speak to the Queen on Dereham's behalf.[109] Dereham stated that the Queen had ordered Agnes to come to court and bring him with her, and on hearing that he was there, she allegedly said, 'my Lady of Norff[olk] hathe desired me to be good unto him and soo I woll'.[110] Dereham was in fact brought into the court by Lord William Howard.[111] It is highly unlikely that they wanted to facilitate adultery against the King. Rather, this was staged damage control. Dereham genuinely believed that he and Catherine were married, and since she was happy for people to call them 'husband' and 'wife', one cannot blame him.[112] When she received her place at court and broke it off with him, Dereham was heartbroken, angry, and determined to get her back.[113] Initially he fled to Ireland, but when he returned in the autumn of 1540, he seems to have gone back to the Duchess's house. It is not clear what passed between them at that point, but it seems that he may have threatened to spill the beans, which would have been extremely damaging for Catherine, now Queen, and for her family. To mollify him, it seems to have been agreed that they would find him a place at court in return for his silence. Thus Lord William brought him to court; the Queen, in a fashion that sounds pre-arranged, asked Lady Margaret where Dereham was, whereby she was able to say that he was there; and Catherine, claiming that she did so only because the Duchess had asked her to, gave Dereham a place. Clearly, they knew that they needed his silence, which shows that they knew something untoward had occurred.

It also shows that at this stage, some Howard individuals were working together. Once the stories did come out, though, the family reacted somewhat differently. The Duke of Norfolk was the first to hear of the suspicions against Catherine. Cranmer had informed the King on All Souls' Day, 2 November, 1541, and Norfolk and others of the Council received an urgent summons on the 5th.[114] Agnes, Duchess of Norfolk, had heard about Dereham's arrest by Sunday 6 November, but not the reason behind it. She sent her servant Robert Damport to Norfolk to invite him to sleep at Norfolk House that night, as he generally did when kept late on business.

---

[108] TNA SP1/167, fols 111, 140.   [109] TNA SP1/168, fol. 87.   [110] Ibid., fol. 90.
[111] When Catherine asked where Dereham was, Lady Margaret replied, 'he is here w[i]t[h] my lord'. TNA SP1/168, fol. 90.
[112] Burnet, *History of the Reformation*, IV, 505.   [113] Ibid.
[114] *CSP Spain,* VI (I), 204; *LP* XVI, 1332.

Norfolk refused her offer, saying—legitimately—that he had to remain at court on the King's business regardless of the late hour.[115] He did not pass on any message about the incoming political storm. That it was already too late for him to return home suggests that he had already met with the King and knew about the probable danger the family was in, but did not seek to warn them. Later on he apparently said that he wished Catherine would be burnt alive for her crimes.[116] A number of historians have emphasized Norfolk's self-interest and habit of 'abandoning his relatives at the first hint of trouble', and it is difficult not to feel that he did indeed throw them under a metaphorical bus in order to save himself.[117] Nevertheless, one can appreciate the difficulty of his position. Norfolk's summons to the King was quite clearly his call to prove his loyalty to the crown, and this was not framed as a choice. We might also remember that none of his immediate family, his wife, mistress, or children, were directly involved, and he was responsible for their protection as well as his own.

Whether Agnes really needed concrete information from her stepson is debatable, since she jumped to the correct conclusion instantly, telling Damport that she feared there was 'some ill' and that it was something done when Dereham and Catherine had been in her house.[118] She added, however, that if it was done before her marriage, she would not die for it, but probably be sent back to Lambeth.[119] This demonstrates the Duchess's knowledge of the law. Pre-marital adultery was not treasonable, and Agnes clearly knew that. Once the Culpeper affair was discovered on 13 November Agnes clearly grew more worried and took action to preserve herself, her immediate family, and her household. She took advice, discussing the situation with her female relatives. Her servants stated that her daughter-in-law, Lady Margaret Howard, had 'trobled her moche' by saying that she feared Lord William's knowledge of the adulteries.[120] Agnes's niece-in-law Malyn Chambers/Tylney, who lived in her household, told how Agnes had questioned her closely on what she thought would happen.[121] Agnes also considered sending a warning to her son, Lord William Howard, who was then with an embassy in Calais.[122] However, her steward William Ashby stated that she was 'advised' not to do this—he did not say by whom—perhaps because it would have been more beneficial to preserve his innocence of the affair, or because he had already been officially summonsed.[123]

Once Dereham, Damport, and others had been seized and taken to the Tower, Agnes took more drastic action. The depositions of her steward, William Ashby, her comptroller, and Borough, her chaplain, tell us that on 14 November, in the dead of night, ostensibly searching for material to send to the Council to aid the investigation, but clearly aiming to dispose of any incriminating evidence, Agnes broke open Dereham and Damport's coffers and removed certain of their contents.[124] She took out certain letters and read them, 'sending for her spectacles'.[125] Her comptroller, when questioned, was not certain what she then did with the letters,

---

[115] TNA SP1/168, fol. 48.   [116] *LP* XVI, 1359.
[117] Head, *The Ebbs and Flows of Fortune*, 190.   [118] TNA SP1/168, fol. 14.
[119] Ibid., fol. 48.   [120] TNA SP1/168, fol. 83.   [121] Ibid., fol.145.
[122] Ibid., fol. 83.   [123] TNA SP1/168, fols 90v–91r.
[124] TNA SP1/168, fol. 96.   [125] Ibid.

but thought that she kept them, perhaps burning them.[126] Destroying the evidence was sensible and effective, since, as her comptroller testified, she had done so only three or four days before Norfolk arrived on the same mission, sent by the King.[127] Here, again, Norfolk's instincts for self-preservation become apparent. At first glance it looks as if the Council learned of Agnes' breaking of the coffers through the confessions of her servants, beginning with William Ashby on Sunday 4 December.[128] However, the interrogatories for Agnes included questions concerning the coffers, and these were compiled on 1 December or earlier, showing that they knew about the breaking of the coffers before Ashby confessed it.[129] In his own plea to the King on 15 December, Norfolk reminded him that much had come to light through his report of Agnes's words when he was sent to Lambeth to search Dereham's coffers.[130] He evidently shopped his stepmother to the Council. This was not a family trying to shield its collective self, but one shattering under pressure.

Not only did Agnes destroy what was evidently compromising evidence, but she also used her knowledge of the law and the legal system to try to find a loophole, sending Gruffudd Rhys, her grandson, to her steward to ask for a book of statutes kept within the household. When asked the reason, the boy replied that she wanted to know whether the general pardon was contained within it, so that she could see if it would serve for those who knew of Catherine Howard's 'naughty life' before her marriage.[131] General pardons were issued periodically, and they allowed anybody to go to the court of King's Bench or Chancery, pay a small fee, and obtain a pardon for any treasons, felonies, or other crimes committed, whether one was indicted or not, and were thus a useful way to avoid a conviction.[132] The last general pardon before December 1541 had been issued in July 1540, and might indeed have served to help her were it not for the date: this Act allowed pardons for crimes committed before 1 July 1540, and this would have covered only half of Catherine's 'naughty life'.[133] This is presumably why Agnes gave up the idea. However, it speaks volumes for her caution that she kept a book of statutes within her household. The involvement of her grandson in fetching the book could suggest the knowledge and involvement of his mother, Agnes's daughter Katherine, which might mean that they had discussed the legal nature of the case together and were hoping they would escape any charge through this means.

Under examination, Agnes, Katherine, and William all appear to have remained mute as long as possible. This in itself was some feat; Katherine, for instance, faced ten privy councillors and apparently gave them nothing. Wriothesley declared that 'as for bridgewater she sheweth herself her motheres dowghter, that is oon that will by no menys confesse any thing that may towche her', and Lord William was described as 'as stiff as his mother and made himself most clear from all kind of mystrust or suspition'.[134] Agnes denied everything, even in the face of incontrovertible evidence. Interestingly, they also seem to have refrained from condemning

---

[126] Ibid.   [127] TNA SP1/168, fol. 83.   [128] Ibid., fol. 80.   [129] Ibid., fol. 13.
[130] Ibid., fols 143r–v.   [131] TNA SP1/168, fols 80–83v.
[132] Bellamy, *The Tudor Law of Treason*, 219–24.
[133] *Statutes of the Realm*, III, 809–12.   [134] TNA SP1/168, fols 113 and 122.

Catherine herself any further, whereas many others questioned were eager to do so as a means to prove their loyalty to the crown. Only once it was clear that Agnes and those around her were going to suffer for their knowledge of the Queen's affairs did Agnes fall back on more traditional methods of delaying sentence. By 4 December, she was bed-bound, feigning sickness. The Earl of Southampton, Wriothesley, and Mr Pollard, visiting her in the guise of comforters, wrote that she was not so sick as they had expected to find her, but once they suggested that she visit Mr Chancellor for questioning, she 'began to be very sick, even at the heart'.[135] Agnes's actions show that not only was she trying to protect herself and her children, Katherine and William, but also members of her household who also stood to be indicted for their knowledge.

The Duke of Norfolk's actions show that he feared that the King would treat the Howards as a collective and hold them all equally responsible for his niece's behaviour, but that he himself did not behave in this way. Nor did some others. Katherine's brother George, and her sister Isabel Legh/Baynton, Lady Baynton, may possibly have done more than simply exonerate themselves. Lady Baynton's husband was Catherine's vice-chamberlain and was placed in charge of her much-reduced household at Syon House, while Lady Baynton was one of her attendants.[136] As Anne Boleyn's case shows, those placed around a queen at such times were essentially there to spy on her, and that her own sister was part of this seems to us rather sad. Moreover, the list of grants by letters patent for November 1541 shows that George Howard was granted a licence to alienate an advowson to Isabel in her own right, not for the usual term of her life but with remainder to the heirs of her body.[137] It is odd that the King would grant this while their sister was in this position, and it might mean that it was a reward for their compliance.

Jane Parker/Boleyn, Viscountess Rochford, also played a confusing role. Though not technically a Howard, being the widow of George Boleyn, she is often lumped in with the dynasty by dint of her relationship to the Boleyns. However, no contemporary identified her in this way during this episode. She was not involved in Catherine's pre-marital adulteries, and since those, rather than the Culpeper affair, were the ones that concerned the Howard family the most, she has not so far been considered. But Lady Rochford was allegedly responsible for encouraging and arranging liaisons between the Queen and Culpeper, and 'chaperoning' them during their meetings, and she was executed alongside Catherine for this. Historians have no real answer as to why she, of all people, would encourage another queen of England to actually do what her own sister-in-law had lost her life for allegedly doing. The common speculation that there was no love lost between Jane and the Howards has no factual basis, and in any case it made little sense for Jane to seek to bring them down in this way, since she could not have hoped to keep her own role hidden.[138]

---

[135] Ibid., fols 51r–v.   [136] TNA SP1/167, fols 123–124v.   [137] *LP* XVI, 1391 (59).

[138] For more on Jane see Warnicke, 'Family and Kinship Relations at the Henrician Court: The Boleyns and Howards', in Dale Hoak (ed.), *Tudor Political Culture* (Cambridge, 1995), 31–53; Catharine Davies, 'Jane Boleyn [née Parker], Viscountess Rochford (d. 1542)', *ODNB* [accessed 12 April 2017].

Lady Rochford aside, it is clear that Norfolk was correct in thinking that the Howards were treated and perceived as a disgraced collective. Contemporary commentators described it in dynastic terms. When Chapuys reported the first juicy details to the Queen of Hungary as early as 10 November, he thought it important to note that the Queen's brother had been forbidden the King's chamber, implying that this was a result of the Queen's behaviour, and that the King was wreaking vengeance on her entire family.[139] Actually, this was Charles Howard, and his dismissal was because his ill-timed affair with Lady Margaret Douglas had just been discovered, but Chapuys did not know this and it is significant that he assumed that Charles's treatment was linked to his sister.[140] Marillac, the French ambassador, made exactly the same comment in his own dispatch the next day, which shows how widespread this assumption was.[141] Many comparisons were drawn between Catherine and Anne Boleyn, and not only because both were accused of the same thing. People also pointed out their kinship connection, suggesting it was of some importance. Most strikingly, Marillac wrote that 'Norfolk may well be vexed, seeing that she is his brother's daughter, as Queen Anne was his sister's', implying that these faults would be totted up and counted against the whole family.[142]

The assumption that the Howards had operated as a coherent political unit actually seems to have informed the strategy of the investigation. The Council began by questioning Mary Hall, who had provided the very first information, and moved swiftly onto Catherine's lovers and Catherine herself, all at the beginning of November.[143] Their evidence implicated several members of the Howard family, who were the biggest fish in this case aside from the Queen, and one would think that the next logical step would have been to bring those fish in. But the Council left them alone and continued to interrogate the smaller fish first; former and current servants in Duchess Agnes's household, and maids of honour at court. Only once they had bled these smaller fish dry did they move on to question the Howards, which strongly implies that they deliberately waited until they had enough evidence to convict them regardless.[144] The questions that suspects were asked confirm this. The investigators wanted to know about the Queen's affairs, but they were equally keen to know about the roles played by Duchess Agnes, Lord William and Lady Margaret Howard, and Katherine, Countess of Bridgwater. Katherine Tylney was even examined once for each purpose, since her first deposition concerns her knowledge of the Queen's liking for Culpeper, and the second revolves around whether or not she thought Duchess Agnes knew about the Dereham affair.[145] Lists of interrogatories for most of the 'bigger fish' do survive and these make it clear that although the investigators *were* after confirmation of evidence they had already uncovered, they wanted information on the other Howards even more.[146]

---

[139] *LP* XVI, 1328.   [140] TNA SP1/167, fol. 127r–v.   [141] *LP* XVI, 1332.
[142] Ibid.   [143] TNA SP1/167, fol. 109 onwards.
[144] Agnes, Duchess of Norfolk, was not questioned until 4 December, and her son and daughter not until after this. TNA SP1/168 fol. 51.
[145] TNA SP1/167, fols 131–2; SP1/168, fol. 8.   [146] TNA SP1/168, fols 53–77.

Why were so many Howard women involved in so many cases of treason during this time? It seems fair to say that, by and large, they did not actively intend to commit either treason or misprision of treason, and indeed in most of these cases the crimes committed were not legally treasonous at the time they occurred. Again in many of the cases, the problem for the Howard women was not what they themselves had done, but what they knew other people had done, which was a direct result of their position at court. Statistically, they were more likely than other women to know about potentially treasonous activity, so one could argue that their involvement was often simply bad luck. In this sense the Howard women were not necessarily representative of all noblewomen, only those who were also in close proximity to the centre of power. On the other hand, quite clearly many Howard men had equal opportunity to gain dangerous knowledge at court and yet they appear to have found it easier to stay out of trouble. The women, not the men, were responsible here for leading the family into danger, however accidentally, and this is why the study of women in the context of the whole family is important. The exception to the 'accidental' nature of the women's involvement in treason was Katherine, Lady Rhys (later Lady Daubeney and then Countess of Bridgwater) and her rebellious behaviour first in Wales in the late 1520s and then possibly in the Pilgrimage of Grace in 1536. Her involvement was not an accident on either occasion, and though in both cases she doubtless felt she had legitimate motivation, she cannot have failed to notice that what she was doing verged on treason. That her role has remained somewhat under the radar shows that we really do need a broader study of noblewomen's involvement in treason and rebellion during this period.

It is clear too that perceptions and the reality of dynastic unity could be quite divergent. Unlike some families, but not necessarily surprisingly, the Howards did not generally band together as a whole to find a way out of trouble during times of crisis, but they did sometimes do so in smaller, tighter, kinship groups, as demonstrated by the behaviour of Agnes, Duchess of Norfolk, during the investigation of Catherine Howard in the 1540s. In fact, these cases bring a little-known Howard woman to the forefront in this very area. Lady Margaret Howard, wife of Lord William, is rarely mentioned in Tudor political history, but she played a prominent role in several of these cases, being one of Anne Boleyn's women, concealing Thomas Howard's marriage, and then Catherine Howard's pre-marital love affairs. Though described by Thomas Wriothesley as 'a symple woman', she was sharp enough to have known who might have told what to whom, and to get away with her actions in all but the last case, after which she sued to the King on behalf of her husband and mother-in-law.[147] The Duke of Norfolk, conversely, distanced himself firmly from his relatives in all these cases, even helping, in the latter case, to convict them, which demonstrates clearly that the dynasty as a whole did not act as a collective. Yet clearly other people saw them that way, and they knew it, hence Norfolk's actions in the first place. Here, as elsewhere, how

---

[147] TNA SP1/168, fol. 151; *LP* XVII, 197.

one behaved towards kin and how other people perceived those relationships changed according to circumstance.

One last thing that bears attention is the way that many of these particular treason cases were responsible for changes to the treason law. Over the course of Henry's reign, it became treasonous to slander the King's marriage, the royal succession, and the King's religion in writing or in speech, and the latter was then extended to all existing treasons, making it treasonable to merely discuss harm towards the royal family. It became treasonous to contract marriage with a female member of the royal family without royal permission; to conceal previous sexual liaisons when marrying the King; and to commit adultery when married to him. Concealing knowledge of any of these things ranged from high treason to misprision of treason depending on what had been concealed. John Bellamy has stated that the many changes to the treason law during Henry's reign were a natural result of the royal supremacy and of the King's many marriages, and clearly this is true.[148] But many of the newly treasonous crimes were actions traditionally associated with women: unchastity, adultery, clandestine marriage, gossip, and slander. Never before had these been considered suitable subjects for treason legislation. Were they deemed so now because of the unprecedented involvement of women in cases of treason, or did more women become involved in treason because the scope of the law had increased? To answer this question properly requires a broader analysis than has been possible here, but the implications make it a question worth considering for the future. These legal changes are clear testimony to the importance and influence of women at this time.

---

[148] Bellamy, *The Tudor Law of Treason*, chapter 1.

6

'The healthe of my soule'

Religion

Throughout the sixteenth century and beyond, the Howards are usually described as religiously 'conservative', resisting the reformist impulse of the Reformation while conforming to the royal supremacy over the Church.[1] This is because Thomas Howard, Third Duke of Norfolk, is usually placed squarely at the head of the 'conservative faction' and this has coloured historians' impressions of the rest of the dynasty. Michael Graves in the *Oxford Dictionary of National Biography* has called him 'conservative in religion and consistently hostile to the reformed faith'.[2] For Alec Ryrie, Norfolk was 'England's leading lay conservative'; for Diarmaid MacCulloch, 'the lay embodiment of traditional religion'.[3] The women of the family have played little part in this characterization, yet we know that they were not a small contingent of the dynasty during this time. The women who have formed the focus of this book not only lived through the earliest stages of the Reformation, but cover three different generations, and therefore provide valuable insight into the shifting responses to religious change. This chapter shows that what we see is not a family following the lead of its patriarch in religious matters at this early stage of the Reformation, but that this did not stop them maintaining strong kinship relations across the shifting religious spectrum.

---

[1] A version of this chapter has appeared in print as 'A "Conservative" Family? The Howard Women and Responses to Religious Change *c*.1530–1558', *Historical Research* 90:248 (2017), 318–40. The religious groupings that emerged during the 1530s and 1540s had yet to attain the clarity exhibited during the reigns of Henry's children. The prevailing term 'evangelical' will be used here to describe those who not only supported the break with Rome and the royal supremacy, but pursued a reformist agenda beyond this; while the term is not ideal, since as a category it was itself fluid, it is the one most commonly used to this purpose by both contemporaries and recent historians. 'Conservative' will be used to denote those whom Marshall has termed the 'non-evangelical mainstream of English Christians', who maintained a traditional standpoint on the details of Catholic worship whether or not they conformed to the royal supremacy. See P. Marshall, 'The Naming of Protestant England', *Past & Present* 214 (2012), 87–128, and 'Is the Pope Catholic? Henry VIII and the Semantics of Schism', in Ethan Shagan (ed.), *Catholics and the 'Protestant Nation'* (Manchester, 2005), 22–48. For the characterization of the Howards, see, for instance, D. Starkey, *Six Wives: The Queens of Henry VIII* (London, 2004); Lacey Baldwin Smith, *Catherine Howard* (Stroud, repr. 2010); D. MacCulloch, *Suffolk and the Tudors* (Woodbridge, 1986); K. Stöber, *Late Medieval Monasteries and their Patrons: England and Wales, c.1300–1540* (Woodbridge, 2007).

[2] Michael Graves, 'Thomas Howard, Third Duke of Norfolk (1473–1554)', *ODNB* [accessed 13 April 2017].

[3] Alec Ryrie, *The Gospel and Henry VIII* (Cambridge 2003), 213; Diarmaid MacCulloch, *Thomas Cranmer* (London, 1996), 243. See also Head, *The Ebbs and Flows of Fortune*.

Strangely, there has not been a great deal of scholarship focused on aristocratic religious identities during this period. While it may be wrong to suggest that as a social class they exhibited any religious response or identity distinct from the rest of the population, the reason this remains unclear is because the work has not yet been done. The nobility was intimately involved with the implementation of the Reformation, and the public context in which they lived meant that their religious choices were of unavoidably public significance. Despite this, the aristocracy as a whole tend to be presented as spiritually static and unchanging, and both individuals and whole dynasties are often anachronistically labelled 'conservative' or 'evangelical'.[4] This is in direct contrast with other recent work on religious identities of the lower social orders, which places a strong emphasis on the fluidity of religious beliefs across this period.[5]

Equally, though there has been considerable interest in women's religious roles across the sixteenth century, this has not generally extended to the aristocracy. Where it has, it tends to focus on significant individuals rather than familial groups, and it is generally assumed that women's religion was ruled by the family patriarch despite some evidence to the contrary.[6] Work on women of lower classes, however, has emphasized their centrality to the family's religious identity through means as diverse as control of the family kitchen, which allowed women to dictate the mechanics of religious fasting, and maintenance of religious networks.[7] If the aristocracy and women are important to the study of the Reformation as separate entities, aristocratic women's responses to religious change must surely be worth investigating.

Though this book has raised doubts about the degree to which we ought to count Anne Boleyn in with the Howard dynasty, the fact that some contemporaries appear to have done so means that we must consider her reputation for strong religious opinion in the context of the rest of the family. Most historians support the identification of Anne's beliefs as 'evangelical' or 'reformist', emphasizing her ownership of evangelical books by authors such as William Tyndale, her patronage of continental reformers such as Nicholas Bourbon, and contemporary views of her later immortalized by John Foxe and William Latimer.[8] Freeman has argued

---

[4] Steven Gunn, *Charles Brandon, Duke of Suffolk, c.1484–1545* (Oxford, 1988), Joseph S. Block, *Factional Politics and the English Reformation, 1520–1540* (Oxford, 1993). A noteworthy exception is P. Marshall and G. Scott (eds), *Catholic Gentry in English Society: The Throckmortons of Coughton from Reformation to Emancipation* (Aldershot, 2009).

[5] See, for instance, Ethan Shagan, *Popular Politics and the English Reformation* (Cambridge, 2003).

[6] Such as Melissa Franklin-Harkrider, *Women, Reform and Community in Early Modern England: Katherine Willoughby, Duchess of Suffolk, and Lincolnshire's Godly Aristocracy, 1519–1580* (Woodbridge, 2008); Pauline Croft (ed.), *Patronage, Culture and Power: The Early Cecils 1558–1612* (New Haven, 2002); Retha Warnicke, *Wicked Women of Tudor England* (Basingstoke, 2012). A recent and welcome exception is Gemma Allen, *The Cooke Sisters: Education, Piety and Politics in Early Modern England* (Manchester, 2013).

[7] C. Peters, *Patterns of Piety: Women, Gender and Religion in Late Medieval and Reformation England* (Cambridge, 2003), and P. Crawford, *Women and Religion in Early Modern England 1500–1720* (Oxford, 1999). See also the considerable literature on women and recusant networks, beginning with Marie B. Rowlands, 'Recusant Women 1560–1640', in Mary Prior (ed.), *Women in English Society 1500–1800* (London, 1985), 149–80.

[8] M. Dowling, 'Anne Boleyn and Reform', *Journal of Ecclesiastical History* 35 (1984), 30–46; G. Bernard, 'Anne Boleyn's Religion', *Historical Journal* 36:1 (1993), 1–20; E. Ives, 'Anne Boleyn and the Early Reformation in England: The Contemporary Evidence', *Historical Journal* 37:2 (1994),

that much of Foxe's portrayal comes directly from contemporaries who knew Anne and can be corroborated by other sources, showing that there was a general view of Anne as a 'devout and important promoter of the gospel'.[9] The first version of his martyrology was, indeed, written in a Howard household. This was Mary Howard/ Fitzroy, Duchess of Richmond, a relation formerly among Anne's ladies-in-waiting. Mary gave Foxe anecdotes about Anne's charity in the late 1540s or early 1550s before there can have been a widespread move to rehabilitate her reputation.[10] Foxe's reports of her charity, her promotion of reformist clergy, and how she kept an English bible in her chamber for her household to peruse at leisure all support the interpretation of Anne as a reformer. That those around her believed this strongly suggests that we should also see her in this light.

Our understanding of Anne's religion has affected the way that we see her supporters and her traducers. Anne's own support for the royal supremacy is sometimes seen as purely political, because by that point it had become the only way for her to marry Henry and become Queen.[11] But even if this is true—and it may well be—it does not mean she cannot also have had the genuine religious belief and opinion she regularly expressed, and which contemporaries believed she espoused. Conversely, where Anne is sometimes refused religious sentiment in favour of political ambition, her supporters are given religious motivations that they did not themselves express. It tends to be assumed that Anne's supporters were self-evidently evangelicals, and Catherine of Aragon's, conservatives.[12] Yet Norfolk, for example, consistently supported Anne (though later denied this), but we would struggle to call him an evangelical. Anne's aunt Katherine Howard/ap Rhys, Lady Rhys, and her husband Rhys ap Gruffudd were reported in 1531 as having 'spoken disparagingly' of Anne, and it is historians, not contemporaries, who have inferred a religious element here.[13] Norfolk's wife and Catherine of Aragon's supporter, Elizabeth Stafford/Howard, is assumed to have been a religious conservative, but none of the many contemporary references to Elizabeth's support for Catherine mention religion, and we do not know what Elizabeth's views on the break with Rome were.[14] The motivations behind these kinds of alignments were not straightforward, and need to be approached with the same level of caution whether we are talking about Anne or about those around her.

389–408; T. S. Freeman, 'Research, Rumour and Propaganda: Anne Boleyn in Foxe's "Book of Martyrs"', *Historical Journal* 38 (1995), 797–819. Ives's and Bernard's arguments were revisited in their respective books, *The Life and Death of Anne Boleyn: 'The Most Happy'* (Oxford, 2004) and *Anne Boleyn: Fatal Attractions* (New Haven, 2010).

[9] Freeman, 'Research, Rumour and Propaganda', 801.

[10] *The Unabridged Acts and Monuments Online* [hereafter *TAMO*] (1583 edition) (HRI Online Publications, Sheffield, 2011), Book 8, 1078, available from <http://www.johnfoxe.org> [accessed 12 March 2015].

[11] Bernard, *Fatal Attractions*, 109–11; Ives, *The Life and Death of Anne Boleyn*, 277–9; Warnicke, *Wicked Women of Tudor England*, 31–2.

[12] See, for instance, essays in David Starkey (ed.), *Rivals in Power: The Lives and Letters of the Great Tudor Dynasties* (1990).

[13] *CSP Spain*, IV, ii, 853. Williams, *Recovery, Reorientation and Reformation*, 256; Williams, 'A Welsh Insurrection', 11.

[14] *LP* IV, 6738; *LP* V, 70, 216, 238 *LP* VI, 585.

Queen Catherine Howard's religion is both more and less clear-cut, in part because we know far less about her beliefs. For a long time it was assumed that she was, if not a religious conservative herself, at least a pawn of the 'conservative faction' led by her uncle Norfolk and Stephen Gardiner, Bishop of Winchester, who are supposed to have connived to place her on the throne to achieve conservative ascendancy.[15] We have already considered the problems with this narrative, and Catherine's alleged conservatism is also up for revision. On the one hand, she is known to have actively befriended Thomas Cranmer, and her household contained such evangelicals as Edward Baynton, her vice-chamberlain.[16] On the other, she also pleaded with Henry for the lives of conservatives Sir John Wallop and John Mason.[17] MacCulloch is therefore correct when he states that Catherine appears not to have led or been involved in any religious faction, and that her fall was not an evangelical victory against the conservatives.[18] Away from the Howard queens, the religious activities of Norfolk's daughter Mary Howard/Fitzroy, Duchess of Richmond, provide the strongest evidence for non-conservative responses to the Reformation among the Howards. Mary is known to historians as the patroness of the martyrologist John Foxe and author John Bale, and is remembered as a staunch evangelical.[19] Where the late 1540s and early 1550s are concerned we shall see that this was true. But, like many nobles who emerged as reformers during Edward's reign, Mary did not suddenly materialize fully formed in the late 1540s. She had been a shining light of the royal court since the early 1530s, and is an important example of the way in which new beliefs could develop over time. Mary was born *c.*1519 which meant that she had never participated as an adult in the pre- royal supremacy church.[20] It is logical to assume that she first encountered evangelical beliefs while serving Anne Boleyn, but there is no evidence that the cousins had a particularly close relationship, and no evidence that they formed any kind of coherent evangelical 'party' within the dynasty. In fact, Mary's networks show that the religious parties that are said to have characterized the late 1530s and 1540s were not a strong feature any earlier, since one of her closest friends was Margaret Douglas, who later, as the Countess of Lennox, used her house at Temple Newsom in Yorkshire to host recusant Catholic priests.[21]

Mary was widowed unexpectedly in 1536 without having consummated her marriage to Henry Fitzroy. Though widowhood was often a positive life-change for aristocratic women, Mary was still legally a minor, and returned to a position of

---

[15] Smith, *Catherine Howard*, 109; Starkey (ed.), *Rivals in Power*, 649, 654.

[16] MacCulloch, *Thomas Cranmer*, 272. On Baynton, see Patricia C. Swensen, 'Patronage from the Privy Chamber: Sir Anthony Denny and Religious Reform', *Journal of British Studies* 27 (1988), 25–44.

[17] *LP* XVI, 678 (41).   [18] MacCulloch, *Thomas Cranmer*, 288–9.

[19] Beverley A. Murphy, 'Mary [née Howard] Fitzroy (c.1519–?1555), *ODNB* [accessed 12 March 2015]; John N. King, 'Patronage and Piety: The Influence of Catherine Parr', in Margaret P. Hannay (ed.), *Silent But for the Word: Tudor Women as Patrons, Translators, and Writers of Religious Works* (Kent, Oh., 1985), 43–60; S. James, *Catherine Parr: Henry VIII's Last Love* (Stroud, 2009), 199; S. Brigden, 'Henry Howard, Earl of Surrey, and the "Conjured League"', *Historical Journal* 37 (1994), 507–37; Franklin-Harkrider, *Women, Reform and Community in Early Modern England*, 62, 77–8.

[20] For more on generational responses see Jones, *The English Reformation*, 1–6.

[21] R. K. Marshall, 'Lady Margaret Douglas, Countess of Lennox (1515–1578)', *ODNB* [accessed 16 May 2014].

dependence in her father's household at Kenninghall. This did not appear to halt her spiritual progression. Mary continued to serve at court in ordinary and extra-ordinary, and to visit friends in London, dining often with the Seymours, and a 1545 dispensation for herself and two guests at her table to eat meat during Lent and other prohibited times shows that she entertained company.[22] While her reason for seeking the latter dispensation is not given, both it and her relationship with the Seymours may well be an indication of early evangelical leanings. She has often been identified as one of the tight circle of evangelical noblewomen surrounding Katherine Parr during the 1540s.[23] However, she was not among the Queen's resident ladies-in-waiting, and received no more gifts or attention than other non-resident noblewomen during this period. Neither was she one of the small group of women—all of the Queen's inner circle—to be incriminated in the heresy case of the evangelical Anne Askew in 1546. If Mary was an active evangelical during these years, it is surprising that we do not find her more often among Katherine Parr's women, and this suggests she was not yet at the forefront of these circles. Nevertheless, things were changing. In the deposition she gave for her brother the Earl of Surrey's treason trial in 1546, Mary told her questioners how he had tried to dissuade her from 'going too far' in reading the Scripture.[24] This is probably a reference to Mary reading the Bible for herself in English, something her father had declared he never had and never would do.[25]

The arrest of Norfolk and Surrey for high treason in 1546 was followed swiftly by Surrey's execution. This altered Mary's circumstances yet again, and in this light it is noteworthy that Edward VI's reign saw a sudden increase in Mary's evangelical activity. Once it became clear that Norfolk would remain imprisoned for the fore-seeable future, Mary was given custody of his grandchildren, her brother Surrey's children, for whom she employed John Foxe as tutor in 1548.[26] There can be no doubt that Mary knew exactly what flavour of tutor she was employing. However, it is not clear that Foxe joined Mary's household immediately on a full-time basis as is usually assumed; the description of him in 1550 as 'moram faciens'—staying—within the household of Katherine Willoughby/Brandon, dowager Duchess of Suffolk, complicates this.[27] He was definitely in Mary's full-time employment from 1550 when the household moved out to Reigate, the home of Lord William Howard, where the latter's son and heir Charles joined the schoolroom. During

---

[22] Brigden, 'Henry Howard, Earl of Surrey', 525; D. S. Chambers (ed.), *Faculty Office Register 1534–1549* (Oxford, 1966), 254. Beverley A. Murphy, *Bastard Prince: Henry VIII's Lost Son* (Stroud, 2001), 230. For evidence of Mary's court visits see TNA SP1/155, fol. 21v; BL Cotton MS Vespasian C XIV, fol. 107v.

[23] King, 'Patronage and Piety'; James, *Catherine Parr*, 199; Franklin-Harkrider, *Women, Reform and Community in Early Modern England*, 62.

[24] E. Herbert, Lord Herbert of Cherbury, *The Life and Reign of Henry the Eighth* (1672), 627.

[25] TNA SP1/163, fol. 38.

[26] *Calendar of Patent Rolls, Edward VI*, IV, 237; Thomas Freeman, 'John Foxe: A Biography', *TAMO* [accessed 3 February 2015]; Elizabeth Evenden and Thomas Freeman, *Religion and the Book in Early Modern England: The Making of Foxe's 'Book of Martyrs'* (Cambridge, 2011), 36–52.

[27] Ordination book of Nicholas Ridley, printed verbatim in W. H. Frere, *The Marian Reaction in its Relation to the English Clergy* (1896), 181–210. See also Brett Usher, 'Foxe in London, 1550–87', *TAMO* [accessed 13 March 2015].

this time Foxe openly began to write the first version of what would later be known as his Book of Martyrs.[28] As well as Foxe, Mary also harboured John Bale on his return from exile in 1547 and thus facilitated their meeting.[29] Bale acted as go-between for her and the Protestant translator Nicholas Lesse, who described Bale as Mary's 'faithful and loving servant'.[30] Lesse's dedication of his translation of *St. Augustine's Twelve Steppes of Abuse* to Mary in 1550 states that Mary undertook such patronage because she was desirous for such works to 'come in to [the] handes of [the] people', and had 'ofte[n] times...com[mun]ed' with the radical printer John Day in order to achieve this. Day is actually described here as 'hers'.[31] The evangelical writer Thomas Becon also dedicated a collection of prayers, 'The Castell of Comforte', likewise printed by Day, to Mary around the same time.[32]

Nor did Mary confine her patronage to writers. In 1549 she wrote to Secretary of State Sir Thomas Smith to ask him to speak to Protector Somerset for royal licences to allow Dr King of Norwich, Thomas Some (or Solme), and John Huntingdon to preach.[33] The latter two had reputations as radical evangelicals and all three had already been given what were presumably licences of less authority by Thomas Cranmer, Archbishop of Canterbury.[34] Smith evidently responded negatively towards Huntingdon, as Mary then wrote in no uncertain terms demanding that he withdraw his 'evell opynion', stating that 'I am assured he is not only off a godly commorsarye but allso w[i]t[h] lerneynge & eloquens abell to edyfye his audytory'.[35] To write such a letter was a clear and public statement of Mary's own faith and an example of her determination to have her own way regarding it. Mary's religious agency during this period is underappreciated. She was not simply passively receiving dedications from Protestant writers, but had John Foxe writing what would arguably become the most influential Protestant text of the early modern period in her household. She was actively working with printers to secure the publishing of reformist literature, while educating the next generation of Howards in the most reformist atmosphere it was possible to contrive. She did all this against the probable wishes of her father, whose first action on release from the Tower in 1553 was to sack Foxe.[36]

Her activity during Edward's reign is all the more remarkable because she blossomed so quickly. Within a year, Mary hired Bale and Foxe, demanded patronage

---

[28] His *Commentarii rerum in ecclesia gestarum*, published in Strasbourg in 1554. See Evenden and Freeman, *Religion and the Book in Early Modern England*, 52.

[29] J. N. King, 'John Bale (1495–1563)', *ODNB* [accessed 16 May 2014].

[30] Nicholas Lesse (trans.), *The twelfe steppes of abuses write[n] by the famus doctor S. Augustine translated out of laten by Nicolas Lesse*, *EEBO* [accessed 3 February 2015], dedication (3–4).

[31] See 'Fitzroy (Howard), Mary', in F. B. Williams, Jr, *Index of Dedications and Commendatory Verses in English Books before 1641* (London, 1962); Lesse (trans.), *The twelfe steppes of abuses*, 3–4; E. Elizabeth Evenden, *Patents, Pictures and Patronage: John Day and the Tudor Book Trade* (Aldershot, 2008), 24.

[32] Williams, *Index of Dedications*.   [33] TNA SP10/7, no. 1.

[34] See W. R. D. Jones, 'Thomas Solme [Some]', *ODNB* [accessed 16 May 2014], and 'John Huntingdon', *TAMO* [accessed 16 May 2014].

[35] TNA SP10/7, no. 3. Ian Archer states that Smith had a reputation for being religiously lukewarm, blunt, and not very personable (Archer, 'Sir Thomas Smith (1513–1577)', *ODNB* [accessed 16 May 2014]). Mary's tone is probably also a reflection of the difference in their statuses.

[36] Freeman, 'John Foxe', *TAMO* [accessed 13 March 2015].

for preachers, made acquaintance with printers like Day, and put them to good use. Is this because her beliefs had suddenly radicalized, or because she was suddenly free to exercise them in more practical ways? The latter seems more likely. Mary had ceased to live under her father's rule, and religious policy altered enormously in her favour under Edward. But with the coming of the Marian regime Norfolk was released from prison. Mary lost her independence and correspondingly disappears from the historical record, suggesting she ceased all her former activities as swiftly as she had begun them. Norfolk immediately sacked Foxe, placing his eldest charge, Thomas Howard, under the tutelage of Stephen Gardiner, and the younger son Henry within the household of staunch Catholic John White, Bishop of Lincoln.[37] Foxe fled into exile shortly after this, as did many of Mary's other evangelical protégés and a significant number of aristocratic female contemporaries.[38] Mary did not, remaining once again under her father's roof and rule. This is surprising, but was probably because she had neither the support of a husband nor the financial capital to attempt such a move.[39] Mary did not attend the coronation and nothing more is heard of her until her death in 1555. Despite the fact that Norfolk's presence seems to have been a major factor in Mary's inability to express her evangelical beliefs, there was no apparent animosity between them. Though she spent Edward's reign educating his grandchildren in a way he would not have approved, she also spent it visiting Norfolk in the Tower and badgering the Council for his release.[40] He in turn left her five hundred pounds in his will for the pains she had taken.[41] This does not suggest a family riven by religious differences. Rather, it supports recent research showing that families divided by ideology could still enjoy functional relationships across these divides.

Evidence for the beliefs of the rest of the Howard women is thinner on the ground, but nonetheless illuminating. Katherine Howard/ap Rhys/Daubeney, then Lady Daubeney, spoke up in support of Richard Whiting, Abbot of Glastonbury, in a letter to Cromwell in 1535, describing him as 'a good relligous mane'.[42] Throughout the 1530s the elderly Whiting earned the especial enmity of Thomas Cromwell, and was executed in 1539 on a trumped-up charge of treason. Although he and the rest of his house had taken the Oath of Supremacy in 1534, nevertheless the management of the abbey continued to be overseen by Cromwell, and when Katherine wrote in October 1535 injunctions had recently been passed restricting Whiting's personal movements.[43] Katherine's plea was made in a postscript to a letter concerning her own suit for help to dissolve her unhappy marriage to Henry Daubeney, Lord Daubeney. In this light it was arguably unwise to weigh in on behalf of a man who had incurred her patron's displeasure. That she did so, and moreover that she went to the length of describing him as 'a good religious man', makes it likely that her sympathy was not only for the man but also for his beliefs.

[37] Ibid.; Graves, 'Thomas Howard, 4th Duke of Norfolk', *ODNB* [accessed 16 May 2014].

[38] John Foxe, John Bale, Thomas Becon, John Huntingdon, and possibly Thomas Some all fled into exile on the Continent after 1553.

[39] TNA SP10/14, nos 45 and 53.   [40] *APC* II, 400.

[41] See Marshall and Scott, *Catholic Gentry*.   [42] TNA SP1/97, fol. 120r–v.

[43] *LP* IX, 685.

Anne Howard/de Vere, dowager Countess of Oxford, born *c.*1497, was in her thirties when the Reformation began and had been a widow since 1526, living primarily at Castle Camps in Cambridgeshire. As we have seen, her marriage, to John de Vere, Fourteenth Earl of Oxford, had not been a happy one and Anne had had particular support from her half-brother Thomas, Third Duke of Norfolk, during the 1520s.[44] Their closeness extended into their religious activities post-Reformation. In 1538, Anne became involved alongside Norfolk in the eradication of evangelical preaching in East Anglia. According to a letter written by Thomas Dorset, vicar of St Margaret's Lothbury, London, to the Mayor of Plymouth in 1536, 'one Lambert'—John Lambert, formerly Nicholson—'was detect of heresy' for declaring that it was a sin to pray to saints.[45] The detection, according to Dorset, had come from the Duke of Norfolk, the Earl of Essex, and Anne, the dowager Countess of Oxford, who had collectively written to three different bishops about Lambert. Dorset stated that 'men suppose they handelid hym so to please theym [Norfolk, Essex, and Anne] to grate favor'.[46] These three were certainly three of the biggest fish among the East Anglian elite and the two men were perhaps also the most conservative. That Anne joined them, thus actively maintaining the tradition of praying to saints in 1538, suggests she may have been religiously conservative too.

Another key form of patronage providing an insight into these women's responses to religious change across the early Reformation period is their appointments of clergy to benefices. The influence of a parish priest within the local community could be considerable, and it has been posited that in some areas the priest's own response to religious change could affect the direction of the entire region.[47] Patrons were well aware of this. The lengthy widowhoods of many of the Howard women during these years ought in theory to make it easier to trace their patronage in this regard, because during widowhood women not only held advowsons in their own right, but made appointments under their own names rather than being subsumed within a husband's patronage. However, tracing the ownership of advowsons can be a tricky business, since they did not always descend in linear fashion along with a manor or estate.[48] Even more pertinently, the survival rate for bishops' registers, which document institutions to benefices, is low across a number of dioceses for this period. This has meant that systematic analysis of appointments to benefices is only truly possible for Anne Howard/de Vere, Countess of Oxford.

Anne's jointure from the de Veres was large; twenty-two manors, the residue of two more, and reversion of another three.[49] Of the twenty-two, five definitely included the rights to the advowson, while six definitely did not, and the remaining

[44] See Chapter 3.   [45] BL Cotton MS Cleopatra E IV, fol. 110.   [46] Ibid.

[47] David Crankshaw, 'Chaplains to the Elizabethan Nobility: Activities, Categories and Patterns', in Hugh Adlington, Tom Lockwood, and Gillian Wrights (eds), *Chaplains in Early Modern England: Patronage, Literature and Religion* (Manchester, 2013), 36–63 (37).

[48] On the legal mechanics of advowsons, see Peter M. Smith, 'The Advowson: The History and Development of a Most Peculiar Property', *Ecclesiastical Law Journal* 5:26 (2000), 320–39.

[49] See *Statutes of the Realm*, III, 413–14; TNA E41/220.

eleven are doubtful or unknown.[50] Numerically this was a reasonable number of advowsons for a widowed noblewoman to possess.[51] Anne's were spread across Buckinghamshire, Cambridgeshire, Norfolk, and into Kent. She appointed to all of them several times across the 1530s, 1540s, and 1550s, making it possible to spot patterns where they occur.

A note of caution must be sounded. Nominally, Anne was in control. There is only one noted instance of her allowing someone else to present to one of her benefices, and this was for one turn only in 1558, right at the end of her life.[52] Nevertheless, we know that clergy appointments were very often made through personal recommendation, and the number of well-known, senior individuals who made it into Anne's benefices might well indicate this. Kinship connections, indeed, undoubtedly played a role; William Hatch, appointed by Anne to Knapton in 1548, was later appointed to Gaywode in 1556 by Frances de Vere/Howard/ Staynings, Countess of Surrey.[53] However, there is no conclusive evidence to show that any of Anne's appointments were specifically affected by recommendation, and in any case Anne's visible networks do not appear to have been of one religious dimension across this period.

For those of Anne's priests who are traceable, a linear pattern of some kind does emerge. Those appointed in the 1530s and 1540s give the least indication of religious direction. Richard Marvyn, appointed by Anne to her local parish church in Castle Camps, Cambridgeshire, in 1540, left sixteen dairy cows to his home parish of St Peter Mancroft in Norwich in 1543 'for a certen memorie to be wreten in the bed-roll booke, wherby the curate every Sunday shall reherse and pray for the sowles of the sayd Richard Marvyn and Jone his wyff, his father and mother, and John Tevell and all frends'.[54] William Cutler, however, Rector of Knapton from 1529, wrote 'a book for ye Instruction of ignorant people' against the Bishop of Rome in 1536 and was sent by Anne to show it to Thomas Cromwell.[55] Though at first glance these might appear to suggest different religious objectives, the two are not necessarily contradictory. There is no reason why a priest who supported the royal supremacy

[50] Anne's definite advowsons: Knapton in Norfolk, Castle Camps in Cambridgeshire, Calverton and Aston Sandford in Buckinghamshire, and Baddlesmere in Kent. See the relevant volumes of the *Victoria County History* [hereafter *VCH*] at <http://www.british-history.ac.uk>, Francis Blomefield, *An Essay towards a Topographical History of the County of Norfolk*, 11 vols (1810) at <http://www.british-history. ac.uk>, The Clergy of Church of England Database at <http://www.theclergydatabase.org.uk> [hereafter CCED], and relevant episcopal registers for Norwich, Ely, London, and Canterbury dioceses.

[51] For instance, Franklin-Harkrider has worked out that in Lincolnshire sixteen women presented to benefices during this period but only six presented to multiple livings, and Allen states that Lady Bacon held the rights to only two benefices during her widowhood. Franklin-Harkrider, *Women, Reform and Community in Early Modern England*, 89; Allen, *The Cooke Sisters*, 177.

[52] 'Calverton [Location ID 7102], CCED [accessed 13 March 2015].

[53] Blomefield, *An Essay towards a Topographical History of the County of Norfolk*, 8 [accessed 31 March 2015].

[54] Castle Camps [Location ID 883], CCED [accessed 13 March 2015]; Blomefield, *An Essay towards a Topographical History of the County of Norfolk*, 4 [accessed 31 March 2015].

[55] TNA SP1/113, fol. 151. Cutler was Rector of Knapton in Norfolk between 1529 and 1542 (Blomefield, *An Essay towards a Topographical History of the County of Norfolk*, 8 [accessed 13 March 2015]). Cutler's letter states that he left the book with Dr Bellose. Neither the book nor Cutler's description of it survives.

during this period might not also continue to believe in the efficacy of prayers for the dead, or vice versa. A more reformist appointment was John Whitwell, who— if the same person, and we cannot be sure—was chaplain to Thomas Cranmer, Archbishop of Canterbury, at the same time. Records show that he was among the stipendiary curates at Stony Stratford, sister parish to Calverton and probably under Anne's patronage, in 1540.[56] Anne's personal chaplain Richard Pranke was also a feature of this period of her widowhood, holding four out of five of her benefices at various points across the 1540s. His will preamble of 1547 is brief and neutral, bequeathing his soul to Almighty God only.[57] Anne's choices during her early widowhood were generally neither overtly reformist, nor rigidly traditional, but that nebulous thing, 'Henrician Catholic'.

During Edward's reign, Anne's choices again appear to conform to religious policy, though perhaps with varying degrees of alacrity. William Roberts, appointed Rector of Badlesmere, Kent, in 1552, renounced papal supremacy by proxy at the time of his appointment.[58] She also appointed John Redman, the well-known theologian, to Calverton in 1548.[59] He had been prominent during Henry VIII's reign, accepting the royal supremacy and serving on committees charged with drawing up articles for the King's Book of 1543, preparing a new translation of the Bible, and convincing Nicholas Shaxton to accept the Six Articles. However, during Edward's reign he also defended clerical marriage, preached at the funeral of Martin Bucer, and on his death-bed, criticized several key aspects of the old faith. Amanda Null has described him as 'theologically compatible with the king [Henry VIII]' but served the Edwardian regime 'as best he could'.[60] Alec Ryrie has nuanced this further, arguing that Redman's career demonstrates the difficulties faced by open-minded conservatives in the 'rapidly shifting intellectual climate' of Edward's reign.[61] Redman took the benefice of Calverton in 1548 after resigning his more exalted and presumably more financially rewarding position as Archdeacon of Stafford in 1547.[62] Could it be that Calverton, and Anne's patronage, provided a more congenial haven for such open-minded but generally conservative souls in the Edwardian religious climate?

The appointments that Anne made under Mary undoubtedly included her most conservative: Stephen Bayly, an ex-Benedictine of the monastery at St Albans, appointed to Knapton, Norfolk, in 1553. He resigned the benefice in 1556 in

---

[56] Stony Stratford [Location ID 7251] CCED [accessed 13 March 2015]; MacCulloch, *Thomas Cranmer*, p. 15, 284. Stony Stratford had formerly been part of the manor and parish of Calverton, to which Anne held the advowson. The close association between the two places, and the fact that Anne held both manors, makes it likely that she also held the advowson to Stony Stratford alongside Calverton. See *VCH Buckingham*, 4, 476–82.

[57] TNA PROB 11/31/403. Digitized by The Oxford Authorship Site at <http://www.oxford-shakespeare.com/Probate/PROB_11-31_f_403.pdf> [accessed 20 February 2015].

[58] 'Robartus, William' [Person ID 38160], CCED [accessed 13 March 2015].

[59] Calverton [Location ID 7102], CCED [accessed 13 March 2015].

[60] Ashley Null, 'John Redman (1499–1551)', *ODNB* [accessed 2 February 2015].

[61] Alec Ryrie, 'Paths not Taken in the British Reformations', *Historical Journal* 52:1 (2009), 1–22 (12–17).

[62] Ibid.

order to return to religious life in the newly restored monastery of St Albans.[63] Conversely, though, they also included Edward Keble, former chaplain of the alleged evangelical Edward Seymour, Duke of Somerset, a married priest who was deprived of his previous benefice of Upminster in 1554 and who held on to Badlesmere successfully until his death in 1560.[64] John May or Man, instituted to Aston Sandford on the death of James Charnock in 1557, would later marry, became a court preacher under Elizabeth I, and made his will in 1597 before a trip to the wilds of Cumbria to capture a seminary priest.[65]

Mary's reign also saw the deprivation of three of Anne's priests, and the most common cause of deprivation in 1554–5 was marriage. At that point the heresy laws had not yet been revived, and one could not therefore be deprived for 'being a Protestant' this early in the reign.[66] This suggests that Lucas Taylor and William Bull, deprived in 1554, were or had been married, and are therefore unlikely to have been strict religious conservatives. Those clergymen whose wives were dead, or had been put away, were to be dealt with more leniently, and permitted to return to the priesthood, albeit in a different place; a concession to the severe deficit of suitably Roman Catholic candidates in the Marian church at this time.[67] We see this among Anne's priests. Edward Keble, instituted to Badlesmere, Kent, in 1557, had previously been married, but his wife had died in 1551 and he had been deprived of Upminster in 1554.[68] Geoffrey Astley, instituted to Castle Camps in 1557, had previously been deprived of his benefices at Snave and Shadoxhurst, Kent, in 1554.[69] For those who would not put away their wives, no leniency was offered. Since there is no evidence of further employment for William Bull, it is possible that he fell into this category. Lucas Taylor, indeed, probably fell into Mary I's most hated clerical group: a former monk (from the Grey Friars at Cambridge) who had married.[70] For men like him there could be no re-employment. They were forced to divorce from their wives and to undergo 'due punishment'.[71] This shows that Anne, as a patroness, did not object to clerical marriage.

The last of Anne's priests to be deprived was Richard Wadnowe of Castle Camps in 1557.[72] He had been the replacement at Castle Camps for Lucas Taylor, deprived in 1554. He was probably also the Richard/Nicholas Wadnowe employed as Rector of Bradfield St George (also known as Bradfield Monachorum) and Bradfield St Clare in Suffolk in the 1550s, and as stipendiary curate of Bradfield in the mid-1570s.[73]

---

[63] Thomas F. Mayer and Courteney B. Walters (eds), *The Correspondence of Reginald Pole, Volume 4: A Biographical Companion: The British Isles* (Ashgate, 2008), 236 n. 112.

[64] Ibid. IV, 313–14; Badlesmere [Location ID 19], CCED [accessed 13 March 2015].

[65] Ibid. 360; Aston Sandford [Location ID 7076], CCED [accessed 13 March 2015].

[66] Richard M. Spielmann, 'The Beginning of Clerical Marriage in the English Reformation: The Reigns of Edward and Mary', *Anglican and Episcopal History* 56:3 (1987), 251–63 (259).

[67] Ibid. 251–63.

[68] 'Keble, Edward' [Person ID 36629], CCED [accessed 31 March 2015].

[69] *Correspondence of Reginald Pole* IV, 28–9.

[70] John R. H. Moorman, *The Grey Friars in Cambridge* (Cambridge, 1952), 132.

[71] Spielmann, 'The Beginning of Clerical Marriage in the English Reformation', 256.

[72] 'Castle Camps' [Location ID 883], CCED [accessed 13 March 2015].

[73] Bradfield [Location ID 19463], Bradfield St George [20818] and Bradfield St Clare [20817], CCED [accessed 31 March 2015].

The reason for his deprivation at Castle Camps is unclear. If he were married, surely this would have blocked his original appointment in 1554. By 1557 one could be deprived for 'heretical' Protestant views, but in Wadnowe's case this is necessarily speculative. The surviving records suggest that he remained in post at Bradfield St George until the next candidate was instituted in 1575, and we do not know what happened at Bradfield St Clare.

Anne seems not to have followed one clear religious viewpoint when she chose priests to appoint to her benefices. Three of her appointees were ex-monks: Stephen Bayly, Lucas Taylor, and Richard Pranke, who became one of Anne's chaplains, but this does not necessarily mean that she, or indeed they, were religiously conservative.[74] For a start, only Bayly appears to have retained definably 'Catholic' beliefs after the dissolution while Taylor and Pranke conformed to the new changes. Taylor, indeed, was deprived by Mary I in 1554. Even confirmed evangelicals like Katherine Willoughby/Brandon, Duchess of Suffolk, appointed ex-monks to their livings, usually from houses under her own or her husband's patronage.[75] This was not the case for Anne, as neither St Albans, the Cambridge Grey Friars, nor West Acre Priory, the houses of Bayly, Taylor, and Pranke respectively, were patronized by either the Howards or the de Veres at the dissolution. It would also be difficult to claim that these particular candidates reflected her own views, since they appear to have held quite different religious positions. In terms of overall analysis, then, a few things can be said with fair certainty. Anne was not an opponent of clerical marriage. What is more, she was not opposed to ex-monks taking wives post-dissolution, and was indeed happy to employ ex-religious. These things suggest that she was not of a very strongly conservative bent. Beyond this, her appointments generally conformed to the religious standards of each given regime. I would argue that this was a choice in itself.

Another kind of clerical appointment which might in fact say more about the women's individual religious positions is their choice of personal chaplains, a theme which has received more scholarly consideration than appointments to advowsons.[76] Members of the aristocracy generally employed at least two household chaplains if not more. Chaplains resided within their patron's house and were chosen specifically for their abilities as preachers, confessors, and spiritual guides, but might also work in a medical capacity, or function as legal witnesses to indentures, and were often used as trusted messengers.[77] Dorothy Howard/Stanley, Countess of Derby's, chaplain in the mid-1530s, Thomas Bradshaw, held a Bachelor of Arts and Bachelor of Canon Law degree.[78] John Bale, chaplain to Mary, Duchess of Richmond, in the 1540s and 1550s, was a Doctor of Theology.[79] This emphasis on learning suggests

---

[74] *LP* XV, 1032, 547; Moorman, *The Grey Friars in Cambridge*, 132; A. Jessopp (ed.), *Visitations of the Diocese of Norwich 1492–1532* (1888), 310; *LP* XXI ii, 146 (3).

[75] Franklin-Harkrider, *Women, Reform and Community in Early Modern England*, 86.

[76] Adlington, Lockwood, and Wright (eds), *Chaplains in Early Modern England*.

[77] Crankshaw, 'Chaplains to the Elizabethan Nobility'.

[78] Joseph Foster (ed.), *Alumni Oxonienses 1500–1714*, at <http://www.british-history.ac.uk> [accessed 13 March 2015].

[79] *Alumni Cantabrigienses*, at <venn.lib.cam.ac.uk> [accessed 13 March 2015].

that for the Howard women, priests probably were the 'educational elite' of the household and as such were held in some importance, but on its own it does not give much insight into the religious tone of these establishments. It is interesting that for the majority of these chaplains there is little or no further information regarding religious position, and this may suggest that the women were concerned to appoint those who were not likely to prove controversial.[80] Indeed, the only known chaplain of these women who did not hold a degree was Richard Pranke, chaplain to Anne, Countess of Oxford, and we have already seen that his will of 1547 was non-committal. Pranke made Anne the sole beneficiary and executrix, and expressed the hope that she would be good to his brother and his brother's children, which suggests a close relationship between chaplain and patroness.[81]

There is also evidence for the beliefs of 'Sir William', chaplain to Elizabeth, Duchess of Norfolk, in the late 1530s. These gave her considerable cause for alarm in 1539 as a letter from her to Thomas Cromwell reveals.[82] Elizabeth had asked him whether he intended to fast during the coming Lent, to which he responded that he had fasted since childhood, but that he 'wold nat ffast thys lent tyll he dyde se a new world'. Elizabeth rebuked him and asked him what he meant by this new world, and he replied 'a nother way'. Taking alarm, she sent for the Archdeacon of St Albans and a local JP and had the priest put into the bailey for questioning. A search of his belongings turned up a 'booke of juyggelyng' which he had kept for the past three years. Coningsby, the JP, advised her to send the man to Cromwell, which, to judge by her letter, she did, but the case is untraceable beyond this point.

The priest's replies to her questions about fasting suggest an evangelical viewpoint, since this and the concept of a 'new world' are associated more closely with evangelicals than with any other religious persuasion. The 'book of juyggelyng' is a little trickier. The most common use of 'juggling' around this time was in reformist polemic referring to popery or practices of Roman Catholicism, particularly transubstantiation.[83] Yet few individuals were openly questioning transubstantiation in England at this point and there is no indication that Elizabeth was among them. Her description of the text as 'uncomely ffor ony p[re]st to haue' is perhaps more revealing. This suggests it was something heretical or unorthodox, rather than a mass-book or similar which one might expect a priest to own. Sir William's reported comment that 'he wold nat for nothyng it shuld be knowen ffrom thens the boke dyd come', and his claim that he had had it for three years since 1536 also supports this interpretation. If it had been a classic mass-book or similar papalist text, its origin would not have been questioned, since there were still many such texts floating

[80] John Bale excepted.   [81] TNA PROB 11/31, fol. 403.

[82] TNA SP1/144, fol. 16. All further references to this source.

[83] Oxford English Dictionary at <http://www.oed.com> [accessed 15 March 2015]; Nicoletta Caputo, 'Entertainers "on the Vagabond Fringe": Jugglers in Tudor and Stuart England', in Paola Pugliatti and Alessandro Serpieri (eds), *English Renaissance Scenes: From Canon to Margins* (Bern, 2008), 311–48, especially 338–48; Stuart Clark, *Vanities of the Eye: Vision in Early Modern European Culture* (Oxford, 2007), 186. The *OED* records the first usage in this sense in 1531. It is possible that the book could have had something to do with magic or prophecy since books of prophecies were popular at this time. However, prophecy was not yet a treasonable offence in 1539, and I have found no references to the word 'juggling' being used directly to mean 'prophecy' or indeed 'magic' during this specific period.

about in England in 1539. He would also most likely have had it for longer than three years—or rather, it would have been more expedient for him to claim this. Quite clearly there was something recent and illicit in this text and he saw no way to disguise these facts.

Consequently, Elizabeth was concerned to make it clear that the book was not her own, stating that her priest had kept it 'by hys owne conffessyon as my servant p[ar]ker can shewe yowr lordeshipe howe I came by hyt'. She was keen to assure Cromwell that she had told him 'eu[ery] thyng of thys mattr'. Elizabeth's evident desire to dissociate herself from the episode underlines the level of religious uncertainty prevalent in England at this time. She reported Sir William's actions and speech with an apparent concern for accuracy, and though she stated that she had rebuked him at the time, she did not take the time to censure him or make a religious standpoint herself in her letter to Cromwell. Indeed, her letter seems to indicate that she was genuinely not sure whether she had done the right thing by sending this man on to Cromwell. That a member of the nobility would be so unsure of the correct protocol for this kind of situation could show that Sir William and his book were themselves outside the common way. It could also show that Elizabeth herself had no strong partisan views in either direction, and was merely doing her best to navigate through religious ambiguity.

Alongside evidence of clerical appointments, several of these women left wills which provide a snapshot of their religious concerns towards the ends of their lives. Wills are controversial sources. It has been said that they are not reliable indicators of religious preference, because the preamble, the part most likely to contain a statement of faith, tends towards the formulaic and may have been chosen by the scribe rather than the testator.[84] However, others have continued to assert the value of wills in this regard, with the caveat that one must look at the entire will, not just the preamble, and do so alongside other surviving evidence for the individual's beliefs where possible.[85] For literate aristocratic women like the Howards it seems unlikely that the preamble would have been chosen by the scribe without any input from the testatrix. Even if this were the case, the scribe himself would be chosen by the testator.[86]

Wills have survived for Agnes Tylney/Howard, dowager Duchess of Norfolk, written in 1542, her daughter Katherine Howard/ap Rhys/Daubeney, Countess of Bridgwater, in 1554, and Elizabeth Stafford/Howard, Duchess of Norfolk, in 1558.[87] Each written under different regimes, the differences between them are not as overt as might be expected. Considering the preambles first, that of Agnes's,

---

[84] J. D. Alsop, 'Religious Preambles in Early Modern English Wills as Formulae', *Journal of Ecclesiastical History* 40:1 (1989), 19–27, and Eamon Duffy, *The Stripping of the Altars: Traditional Religion in England 1400–1580*, 2nd edn (London, 2005), 504–23.

[85] Lorraine C. Attreed, 'Preparation for Death in Sixteenth Century Northern England', *Sixteenth Century Journal* 13:3 (1982), 37–66; Caroline Litzenberger, 'Local Responses to Changes in Religious Policy Based on Evidence from Gloucestershire Wills, 1540–1580', *Continuity and Change* 8:3 (1993), 417–39.

[86] Attreed, 'Preparation for Death in Sixteenth Century Northern England', 39.

[87] TNA PROB 11/30/596 (Agnes); PROB 10/27 (Katherine); PROB 11/42A/285 (Elizabeth).

written in 1542, is 'neutral'.[88] She commended her soul to 'almightie god my Creator and Redemer' without any mention of the Virgin Mary or the saints, and without referring on the other hand to assurance of salvation. Officially this is unproblematic. We should note, however, that Agnes was a little ahead of her time here, as in 1542 there had not yet been any legislation outlawing traditional forms in wills, and local studies show that the majority of testators still continued to use them.[89] Her daughter Katherine in 1554 also placed her soul neutrally 'in to thandes of Almightye God my Savyour & Redemo[r] & c'. The inclusion of '& c' at the end may give us pause for thought; it could sometimes be used as a 'cover up' of traditional beliefs to stand for 'and the Virgin Mary and all the company of Heaven' or some such traditional variant. However, it could also be a literal attempt to save time and ink.[90] Elizabeth Stafford/Howard, dowager Duchess of Norfolk, did include a much more 'traditional' preamble in 1558, bequeathing her soul 'to almighte god to oure lady seynt marye and to all the blessed companye of heaven'. The specific date of Elizabeth's will makes this very interesting as it was written on 30 November 1558, barely a fortnight after Elizabeth I's accession. This could mean that Elizabeth was simply conforming to what was still, legally and in most people's eyes, 'the norm' of Mary's Catholic revival. On the other hand, neutral preambles were still very much in vogue and acceptable to all, so there was no need for Elizabeth to include such an overtly Catholic preamble at this time except by specific choice.

It is easy to see that the preambles alone are not enough to tell the whole story here. The body of the will, the identity of the witnesses, and, where known, the circumstances under which the will was made are equally as important. Agnes, dowager Duchess of Norfolk's will of 1542 with the neutral preamble was written while she was still imprisoned in the Tower of London on a charge of misprision of treason for her part in the fiasco of Queen Catherine Howard's adulteries. To write her will at this time, after 'rype and good deliberacion', suggests she did not expect to survive this experience. In fact she was released a few months later and lived until 1545, but did not alter this will in the meantime.[91] Did the hope of reprieve, and the fact that at least one of her two witnesses was an ecclesiastical commissioner for the crown, lead her to dampen expressions of religious belief?[92] It is often assumed in the absence of concrete evidence that women of Agnes's generation were strongly conservative.[93] In fact Agnes's will is tempered. She did leave bequests to religious personnel and institutions—two silver spoons to John Rabon, 'channtery priste of Lambithe', and her best chalice to 'my chapple at Lambith'.[94]

---

[88] For categorization of will preambles, see Attreed, 'Preparation for Death in Sixteenth Century Northern England', 40, and Litzenberger, 'Local Responses to Changes in Religious Policy', 422–5.

[89] This was not the case until 1544 with Cranmer's litany.

[90] Litzenberger, 'Local Responses to Changes in Religious Policy', 425.

[91] *LP* XVII, 362 (25).

[92] The witnesses were John Lynsey and Henry Whitereason Esq., the latter being originally from Hackney (BL Add. Ch. 45875) but later one of the chantry commissioners for Northumberland (Richard Welford, *History of Newcastle and Gateshead*, vol. 2 (1885), 25).

[93] Smith, *Catherine Howard*, 47.

[94] The Howard chapel in St Mary's Lambeth across the street from Norfolk House.

The Howard chapel was not an officially endowed chantry and Rabon was not employed by the Howards, since he received his salary from the Southwark deanery.[95] The bequests themselves were not religious items, and she did not specifically ask for prayers for her own or anybody else's soul, which was a cautious move given that they were not yet legally outlawed. Nevertheless, Attreed has argued that at this time bequests like this 'did not exclude a religious motivation' and that there remained an unwritten expectation of prayers in exchange for such gifts.[96] Taken as a whole, the will is undoubtedly religiously cautious, with indications of attachment to traditional religion but nothing definite to go on. The circumstances under which it was written seem especially important here. In fear for her life and under the eye of the crown, Agnes may well have felt that discretion was the better part of valour.

Her daughter Katherine, Countess of Bridgwater's will of March 1554 is remarkably similar. By this date Mary I was on the throne. The Edwardian reforms had been repealed, Mass had been restored, and injunctions for the deprivation of married clergy had just been passed. Officially, therefore, the Church was at the point it had been in 1546, but was in transit and it is easy to see why people might have been cautious about expressions of belief. Katherine was living on the estate of the Archbishop of Canterbury in Lambeth and described herself as 'sycke of bodye'. Like her mother, her preamble was neutral. She too left bequests to religious personnel: 20s. to Thomas Bentley, the curate of St Mary's Lambeth where all three women were buried, and 10s. to the parson John Whitwell, who was also Thomas Cranmer's chaplain and who we know was an evangelical.[97] Like her mother, Katherine included no open exhortations for prayers, but again it is possible that these were supposed to be inferred. Where once such bequests would have been placed at the beginning of the will immediately after the preamble, signifying their importance, Katherine placed them towards the end of the will, after bequests to kin, friends, and servants.

Only one recipient is of obvious religious note aside from the clergymen. Emery Tilney, described as 'kinesmane'—a relation of her mother Agnes, née Tylney—had been the pupil of reformer George Wishart at Cambridge in the 1540s, and gave a memorial of Wishart to John Foxe for his martyrology.[98] He was also probably the author of a metrical poem, *Song of the Lord's Supper*, in 1550, which upheld Edwardian policy in its description of the Eucharist as a symbolic representation of Christ's sacrifice.[99] Whether Katherine included him in her will because of his beliefs, because he was her kin, or because he turned up on her doorstep at the time of writing (invited or uninvited, he signed as a witness to the will) we do not know.

---

[95] *LP* IV, 5125. Rabon's traditional will dated 1559 makes no mention of any relationship with the Howards (TNA PROB 11/42A/483).

[96] Attreed, 'Preparation for Death in Sixteenth Century Northern England', 48.

[97] MacCulloch, *Thomas Cranmer*, 15.

[98] He later wrote a memorial of Wishart for Foxe's *Acts and Monuments*. See *TAMO* (1583 edition), Book 8, p. 1291 [accessed 31 March 2015].

[99] Emery Tilney, *Here beginneth a song of the Lordes Supper* (imprinted at London by William Copland, 1550), *EEBO* [accessed 31 March 2015].

That she did include him might at least suggest that kinship 'trumped' religious beliefs. Alongside Tilney, the witnesses included Whitwell and Bentley, parson and curate respectively of St Mary's Lambeth; Arthur Assheby, one of Katherine's servants of a line who had served the Howards for more than one generation; and four more men, two unidentifiable (John Bever and Thomas Bystare) and two illegible. Those we can identify makes this appear a remarkably reformist line-up. At the end of her will, however, Katherine took the trouble to write that she had set her seal and signed her will 'the daie & yere of lorde abouesayed and in the ffirst yere of the reigne of most drede sou[er]ayne Ladie Quene marye by the grace of God Quene of Englond ffrance & Irelond defender of the ffayeth & of the churche of Englond & Irelond'. This seems unnecessarily lengthy, and signs of support for the Marian regime could more easily have been inferred through a Catholic preamble and religious bequests. In the context of the rest of the will, this reads as a deliberate statement of conformity with the Marian regime from an individual who was nevertheless not prepared to fully re-embrace traditional Catholicism.

The will of Elizabeth, Duchess of Norfolk, in November 1558 had a traditional preamble, but this is less clearly reflected elsewhere in the will. Like Agnes and Katherine, Elizabeth's bequests show a preoccupation with helping family and friends first and foremost. Like them, she did not ask for any prayers, but unlike them she left no bequests to religious personnel or institutions. She did leave her 'greater tablettes' to her grandson Thomas, Fourth Duke of Norfolk. These were probably religious images or icons, in which case it may have been significant that she chose to leave them to the family's undeniably Protestant heir. She alone of the three left money for her funeral, £25 to be bestowed 'by the discretion of myn execut[or]', and in like vein she charged her executor (her brother Henry, Lord Stafford) to perform her will 'for the healthe of my sowle'. Both of these are deliberately neutral and have been described by Duffy as examples of testators' caution.[100] Of her three witnesses, two, John Knight the clerk and Robert Sutton the notary public, are unremarkable.[101] The third signed himself 'Anthony ffortescue'. If this was the Roman Catholic Sir Anthony Fortescue who had been released from custody only five days earlier, having attempted to cast the horoscope of the new Queen Elizabeth, his presence is revealing. It suggests that her house was his first port of call, a safe place after his release. Since he came from Punsbourne in Hertfordshire, only fifteen or so miles away from Elizabeth's home at Redbourn, it is not implausible that the two knew each other. If this Anthony was her witness it would indeed suggest that she identified as a Catholic by this point in her life. Taken as a whole, Elizabeth's will is cautiously Catholic, and seems to indicate some desire to remain under the religious radar.

The women of the Howard dynasty were involved in religious and political culture at an extremely elite level. They employed chaplains and priests already renowned,

---

[100] Duffy, *The Stripping of the Altars*, 513.
[101] This may be the John Knight who was recorder of Hythe, Kent, during this time. See <http://www.historyofparliamentonline.org/volume/1509-1558/member/knight-john-ii-1520-66> [accessed 31 March 2015].

and several who would go on to carve out prestigious careers. They were in regular contact with both secular and spiritual architects of the Reformation, such as Thomases Cromwell and Cranmer. They actively patronized religious writers and Mary, Duchess of Richmond's patronage in particular reads like a roll-call of influential evangelical polemicists. Mary was, perhaps, on another level in this regard, but these women as a group are not especially unusual. Other noblewomen also had contact with a variety of elite figures and were making many of the same choices about spiritual employees and patronage. The Howard women did not, however, share the same religious beliefs, but occupied different positions on the early Reformation religious spectrum, and in some cases these changed with time. Aside from Mary, who develops unequivocally evangelical beliefs, it is impossible to pin down the rest of these women to a defined religious position. This is important as it shows there was no collective dynastic religious identity among the Howards during this period, and argues strongly for the inclusion of women in our assessment of elites for this purpose.

The fact that we cannot identify these women's specific beliefs tells us a lot in itself about their response to religious change across this period. What the evidence appears to show above all else is an active desire to conform. Take, for instance, Elizabeth, Duchess of Norfolk's, clear concern to remove herself from the situation of her priest with his controversial 'book of juggelyng', the way that Mary, Duchess of Richmond, kept a lid on her religious activity until Edward's reign, and the demonstrable caution of bequests and sentiments in their wills. But to what were they conforming? Conformity is a problematic concept and has had a complicated historiography. It used to be seen by historians (and some contemporaries) as an easy, lazy option for those who went along unthinkingly with religious change or who perhaps did not care much either way. Alexandra Walsham did much to challenge this perception with her study of 'church papists'—it is now generally accepted that conformity was as much a choice as any other religious position—but as with so much of the work on this topic it is focused on the Elizabethan era.[102] Conformity might, also, mean more than simply an attempt to stay out of trouble; in an era when kings were believed to be divinely appointed, conformity might well be founded in ideological commitment. Generally speaking, conformity during Henry's reign is used to mean agreement with, or lack of opposition to, the Act of Supremacy (1534), but appears to mean more than this during Edward and Mary's reigns, where acceptance and repudiation respectively of royal supremacy became insufficient as their policies became more 'extreme'.[103] Partly this was because religious positions themselves evolved over these years, making the 'dos and do-nots' less ambiguous for both sides and by extension defining conformity more clearly. Nevertheless its definition remains problematic as it depends on the viewpoint taken. When the King, the Church, the state, the law, and the people were not speaking with one voice about religious policy, whose conformity should historians use? The evidence for the Howard women makes it clear that for them, at least, it was the state—in

---

[102] Walsham, *Church Papists*; see also Lake and Questier, *Conformity and Orthodoxy*.
[103] Shagan, *Popular Politics*, and O'Grady, *Henry VIII and the Conforming Catholics*.

the form of the King, his officials, and the law—who decided what was conformist and what not, what was acceptable behaviour and what would lead you into trouble, since it is in their correspondence with state officials that we see the clearest desire to conform. Their attitudes also strongly suggest that conformity during the latter half of Henry's reign was about more than acceptance of the royal supremacy, as their concerns and caution appear to have more to do with the letter of the law in addition to this.

Epilogue
'Sore perplexed': Twilight Years

The Howard dynasty tumbled dramatically from its position of power and favour at the very end of Henry VIII's reign in 1546 with the arrest and imprisonment (until 1553) of the family patriarch Thomas Howard, Third Duke of Norfolk, and the arrest and subsequent execution (in January 1547) of his son and heir Henry, Earl of Surrey. The 'fall of the Howards' is often considered to have set the tone for the Howard family's fortunes until Mary I's accession in 1553, and is thus of considerable importance to the dynasty's post-Henrician narrative. Beginning with an analysis of this episode, this epilogue explores the activities and experiences of the Howard women from the end of Henry VIII's reign onwards, until the accession of Elizabeth in 1558, at which point a new generation of Howard women flooded into the new Queen's household.

Most existing examinations of this episode have focused on the male narrative, with little consideration of the role of the women involved.[1] Yet Mary Howard/ Fitzroy, dowager Duchess of Richmond, is often said to have given damning testimony against her father and brother, aided by her mother, Elizabeth Stafford/ Howard, Duchess of Norfolk, and this is probably the major reason why the dynasty as a whole is sometimes described as disunited. The basic narrative is well known. Thomas Howard, Third Duke of Norfolk, and his eldest son Henry, Earl of Surrey, were accused of high treason, imprisoned in the Tower, and convicted in December 1546. Surrey was executed on 19 January 1547 and Norfolk's death warrant was signed by the King on 27 January.[2] He was saved by the death of the King only one day later, and remained imprisoned and under attainder until dramatically released by Mary I on her entry into London in August 1553.

The case against Norfolk and Surrey is considered one of the best examples of the elasticity of the treason law during this period and of the tyranny of a paranoid

---

[1] Diarmuid MacCulloch, ' "Vain, proud, foolish boy": The Earl of Surrey and the Fall of the Howards', in David Starkey (ed.), *Rivals in Power: Lives and Letters of the Great Tudor Dynasties* (Basingstoke, 1990), 86–113; Brigden, 'Henry Howard, Earl of Surrey, and the "Conjured League" ', 507–37; Peter R. Moore, 'The Heraldic Charge against the Earl of Surrey, 1546–7', *EHR* 116 (2001), 557–83. Norfolk and Surrey's biographers have also discussed this: see Head, *The Ebbs and Flows of Fortune*, 221–8; Casady, *Henry Howard, Earl of Surrey*, 184–221; Sessions, *Henry Howard, the Poet Earl of Surrey*, 352–87; Childs, *Henry VIII's Last Victim*, 269–313; Cherbury, *The Life and Reign of Henry the Eighth*, 623–32; J. J. Scarisbrick, *Henry VIII* (London, 1968), 482–4; Murphy, *Bastard Prince*, 231–6; Loades, *Intrigue and Treason*, 493–6.

[2] Childs, *Henry VIII's Last Victim*, 311; *LP* XXI (II), 761.

King. Their conviction rested on their alleged misappropriation of the royal arms, and this was used alongside poorly considered remarks made by Surrey about the likelihood of his father's potential future position as royal regent, in order to claim that the two of them were plotting to take control of the throne. It is a charge almost beyond credulity until understood in the specific context of 1546. Henry VIII's health was failing. In September, he had a serious lapse and it was thought that he was probably dying. Access to him was correspondingly restricted to his doctors and an inner circle of Privy Chamber men, none of them Howards; Norfolk complained that he had been excluded from the King's 'most secret (or, as it is there term'd, the Privie privie) Councel'.[3] Those around the King began to prepare for the accession of his son, Prince Edward, and the inevitable regency government that would need to govern during his minority, and tensions, therefore, were running high. Many of the men then closest to Henry were of a Reformist bent, and it has been argued that Norfolk, specifically, was targeted because he was not, and that this 'faction' wanted him out of the way before the regency was decided.[4] Norfolk himself, if the depositions recorded by Lord Herbert of Cherbury in the late seventeenth century are accurate, thought that this was among the reasons for his arrest.[5] The King himself grew increasingly paranoid as his health declined, until he was ready to see conspiracy everywhere it was proposed. This may help to explain why the Earl of Surrey was targeted. He was accused of bearing an illegal coat of arms, including those of Edward the Confessor. To use royal arms at this moment, even if one was in theory entitled to them, displayed a stunning lack of common sense. Surrey's exhibition of military incompetence in France and brash boasting earlier in the 1540s cannot have helped his cause.[6]

Historians now largely accept that the heraldic charge itself was spurious. Surrey had formulated his new coat of arms with the agreement of both the King's Council and the College of Arms, and had a valid claim to them; his ancestor Thomas Mowbray, First Duke of Norfolk, had been granted the right to use them by Richard II in 1397.[7] This line of enquiry seems to have been created in order to secure his destruction, since, as Moore's detailed study points out, it had not formed part of the initial investigation but was added later as a means to an end.[8] Surrey was arrested first. That his misplaced dynastic pride was part of the case against him was made clear when his courtesy title, Earl of Surrey, was ignored, and he was treated to the ignominy of being marched through the streets of London to imprisonment at the Tower like a commoner.[9] On the same day, Norfolk was arrested and also taken to the Tower. Two days later, on 14 December, John Gates, Sir Richard Southwell, and Wymond Carew arrived at Kenninghall early in the morning. They found Mary and the Duke's mistress, Elizabeth Holland, 'newlie risen and not redie'.[10] The councillors had been sent by the King to bring news of

---

[3] Herbert, *The Life and Reign of Henry the Eighth*, 563.

[4] MacCulloch, ' "Vain, proud, foolish boy" ', 109; Head, *The Ebbs and Flows of Fortune*, 223–8.

[5] Herbert, *The Life and Reign of Henry the Eighth*, 563.

[6] Childs, *Henry VIII's Last Victim*, 264–5, 286.   [7] *Cal. Pat. Richard II*, V, 1391–6, 350.

[8] Moore, 'The Heraldic Charge against the Earl of Surrey, 1546–7', 559–60.

[9] *Chronicle of the Grey Friars of London*, 52.   [10] TNA SP1/227, fol. 82.

the arrests, to search the property, and question those inside.[11] Mary's reaction to the news shows that she knew immediately how serious things were; in their report, they described her as 'sore perplexed fumbleng and lik to fall downe'.[12] The women were told that they would be questioned and advised to cooperate. Mary stated that she would not hide anything from them, 'specellie if it be of weight'; she would set everything down 'as it shall fall in her remebrance which she hathe promised for the better declaracon of her integrity to exhibite in writeng unto your highnes'.[13]

Unfortunately, her deposition, and several other important ones, have not survived. That we know broadly what they are supposed to have contained is thanks to Henry VIII's seventeenth-century biographer, Lord Herbert of Cherbury, who saw them before they were lost, but he did not publish a direct transcription, which means that we are reliant on his own construction of their words.[14] According to Cherbury, a key point of Mary's deposition was her relation of her father's second attempt to marry her to Sir Thomas Seymour in 1546, and her brother's reaction to this. Mary had declined the match. According to courtier Gawain Carew in his deposition, she did so because 'her ffanterey [fantasy] would not serve to marry w[i[th him'.[15] Surrey, hearing of this, allegedly told Mary that instead of refusing outright, she ought instead to have prevaricated, using the time to inveigle her way into the King's affections so that she might become his mistress, and 'beare as great a stroke about hiim as Madame destamps doth abowte the ffrenche king'.[16]

Surrey's apologists have argued that this was a sarcastic suggestion and that Mary should not have taken him seriously, thereby attaching blame for the consequences to her instead of to him.[17] Surrey's hatred of the Seymours is often cited, but as Brigden notes, during the late 1530s Surrey had been a frequent guest at their home of Beauchamp Place.[18] In fact, Mary deposed that Surrey actually wanted her to marry Seymour, in order that she might get closer to the King.[19] She was an intelligent woman, and there is no reason to assume that she must have misunderstood him. Horrified by his suggestion that she should seduce her father-in-law, Mary expressed her disgust in no uncertain terms, allegedly saying that 'they should perushe & she would cutt her own troate rather then she would consent to such a villany'.[20] She further deposed that she had recently quarrelled with her brother on religious grounds too, because he had discouraged her from 'going too far' in reading the Scriptures. Two quarrels between evidently passionate characters, however, do not bosom enemies make, and allegations that they had grown to 'hate' each other seem overblown.[21] She remained close enough to her brother to make him steward of some of her lands.[22]

---

[11] Ibid., fols 82–3.   [12] TNA SP1/227, fol. 82.   [13] TNA SP1/227, fol. 88.
[14] Cherbury, *The Life and Reign of Henry the Eighth*, 626–7.   [15] TNA SP1/227, fol. 105.
[16] Ibid., fols 104r–v.
[17] Casady, *Henry Howard, Earl of Surrey*, 179–80, 197–9. See also Murphy, Bastard Prince, 231–2.
[18] Brigden, 'Henry Howard and the "Conjured League"', 525.
[19] Cherbury, *The Life and Reign of Henry the Eighth*, 627.
[20] TNA SP1/227, fols 104–106v.
[21] Brigden, 'Henry Howard and the "Conjured League"', 522.
[22] Murphy, *Bastard Prince*, 235.

On 14 December she told the three councillors that nature constrained her to love her father, 'whom she hathe ever thought to bie a trew and faithfull subject'.[23] Cherbury was of the opinion that the evidence Mary gave was designed to exonerate her father of any treasonable word or act that they might bring against him: he stated that she reported many 'passionate words' of her brother's, which were not to his advantage, but 'did much to clear the father'.[24] She said that her father was not worried about any ill will from the Seymours or other new nobility, saying that 'His truth should bear him out', and that he had never said that the King hated him.[25] Murphy argues that Mary knew that the execution of her father, not her brother, was the Council's real aim, and that she was trying to protect him.[26] She had every reason for doing so. A cynic might note that her refusal to marry Sir Thomas Seymour meant that she was still a single widow, and her continual sales of land during the 1540s imply that she was not very well off.[27] If her father was executed, Mary would lose her source of financial support and accommodation. She might even have to marry Sir Thomas Seymour after all.

None of the evidence provided by Mary was directly used to convict either her father or her brother, but some of it cannot have helped their cause. When questioned about his heraldry, she responded that she thought he had more than seven rolls of arms, that he had resumed the Stafford arms of their grandfather, and that the crown above them, in her judgement, looked like a close crown.[28] These confidences have been taken as evidence of her complicity with the government in attempting to destroy her father and brother, yet it is clear that she temporized and caveated her responses, saying that a thing looked so in her judgement, rather than that it *was* so. Nevertheless there was enough there to provoke further investigation. Her description of the crown that he had put in place of the duke's coronet to which he was entitled added that 'underneath the Arms was a cipher, which she took to be the King's cipher, *HR*'.[29] This, surely more than anything else, argued that Surrey was setting himself up as royalty and would undoubtedly have been used in the trial. Likewise, Mary's descriptions of her brother's 'passionate speeches', while not used to convict him, would not have helped his case. Surrey evidently thought her evidence had an impact on the verdict: he allegedly exclaimed, 'must I, then, be condemned on the word of a wretched woman?'[30] It would be unfair to state that Mary single-handedly caused her brother's execution, or that she desired to accomplish this, because there were plenty of other depositions which condemned him. Nevertheless, whether accidentally or on purpose, Mary did play a role in her brother's conviction. Mary was in an immensely difficult position. She could not refuse to answer an examination, for this was itself treason. Likewise, if she said nothing, or appeared to know nothing of events described by others, they would know she was lying. Mary had to tread a very careful line between saying too

---

[23] TNA SP1/227, fol. 82.   [24] Cherbury, *The Life and Reign of Henry the Eighth*, 627.
[25] Ibid. 628.   [26] Murphy, *Bastard Prince*, 235.
[27] *LP* XIX (ii), 690; *LP* XX (i), 624 (15); *LP* XXI (i), 1383 (110).
[28] Cherbury, *The Life and Reign of Henry the Eighth*, 627–8. The following refers to this account.
[29] Ibid. 628.   [30] *CSP Spain*, IX, p. 4.

much or too little, and given her fright, it is hardly surprising that she was not wholly successful.

Her mother Elizabeth, Duchess of Norfolk, was also said by Cherbury to have given evidence against her husband, and most commentators have taken this at face value. After all, if the Council really were seeking any possible avenue against Norfolk, it would make sense to question his estranged wife. Yet what Cherbury says of Elizabeth's evidence does not sound like a deposition. Apparently, '...divers occasions of scandal were given: Insomuch, that not being content with having surmised a long while since two Articles against him, she again in sundry Letters to the Lord Privie-Seal, both averr'd the Articles, and manifestly accused some of his Minions, repeated divers hard usages she pretended to receive from them, and briefly discovered all the ordinary passions of her offended sex. This...was not unwillingly heard.'[31] This sounds like a description of the letters that Elizabeth had written to Cromwell during the late 1530s and 1540s, not evidence given specifically for this trial. Cherbury notes that she had been 'now for above four yeers been separated from him', which, while true, was a little out of date, since by this point she had in fact been sequestered for twelve years. There is nothing in Cherbury's account of Elizabeth's evidence that relates directly to anything that the Council were asking about. Norfolk himself commented in a letter after his arrest that even if questioned, Elizabeth knew nothing against him since they did not live together.[32] It seems, therefore, that Cherbury had somehow stumbled across Elizabeth's earlier letters and assumed that they related to this trial. If Elizabeth was questioned specifically on this occasion, none of her evidence was used in the trial.

Mary's actions after her brother's execution and her father's imprisonment further underline the fact that she did not deliberately seek to condemn either of them. She was granted custody of her brother's four children in 1547, and spent the reign of Edward VI raising them at her half-uncle Lord William Howard's manor of Reigate.[33] Throughout this period she also sued to the King to try to improve her father's situation in the Tower.[34] Norfolk recognized her actions on behalf of himself and the family in his 1554 will, granting Mary £500 because she had made 'great shift' to get him out of prison.[35] Mary, then, was responsible for raising the next generation of the Howard dynasty and for maintaining its existence until they were able to rise to prominence once more with the accession of Mary I in 1553. Far from revealing internal fractures in the Howard family, this demonstrates the importance of the Howard women as the glue holding the dynasty together.

By 1547 several Howard women had already died. Of the Second Duke's daughters by his first wife, Elizabeth Howard/Boleyn, Countess of Wiltshire, was the longest lived, dying in 1538, where Muriel had died in 1513 and Katherine, Lady Berners, allegedly in 1535. His second wife, Agnes Tylney/Howard, passed away in 1545, not long after the fall of Catherine Howard had reduced her circumstances. She was predeceased by two out of her four surviving daughters; Elizabeth, Lady

---

[31] Cherbury, *The Life and Reign of Henry the Eighth*, 626.   [32] TNA SP1/227, fol. 101.
[33] TNA SP10/14/45; TNA SP10/14/53.   [34] TNA SP10/13, fol. 22.
[35] TNA PROB 11/37/345.

Fitzwater, died in 1534, and Dorothy, Countess of Derby, at around the same time. Several others, however, survived well beyond Henry VIII's reign, into the 1550s. The effect of the Duke of Norfolk's disgrace during Edward's reign and his release and restoration under Mary I on the rest of the Howard dynasty, however, has never been properly examined. This is partly because the kind of gossipy, correspondence-led evidence does not survive for Edward VI's reign in the same way that it has for Henry VIII's, largely because the papers of chief ministers were not seized like those of Thomas Cromwell had been. However, it is also because the women genuinely seem to have 'gone to ground' to a certain extent.

Uniquely among the women, the dynasty's fall proved somewhat advantageous to the remaining Duchess of Norfolk, Elizabeth. Though the execution of her son Henry, Earl of Surrey, was undoubtedly very painful for her, her estranged husband's indefinite imprisonment was fortuitous as it allowed her to escape his control. Financially, she was no worse off. She continued to receive her annuity of £200 out of Norfolk's estate, but this was now paid by the crown, which had confiscated Norfolk's lands.[36] She also seems to have taken over control of at least some of her jointure properties. A letter from her brother Henry, Lord Stafford, in 1547, asked her to permit him to rent a house in London which formed part of her jointure.[37] This, and the fact that she continued to foster Stafford's daughter Dorothy, shows that she maintained good relations with her Stafford relatives.[38]

In 1550 the Privy Council permitted her to visit her husband in the Tower.[39] There is no evidence to show whether or not she did so, and the fact that they were never reconciled strongly suggests that neither desired to see the other. The visitation rights may have been granted primarily to allow the couple's daughter Mary, dowager Duchess of Richmond, to visit her father, as she had been busy suing for his freedom. Elizabeth appears to have spent most of Edward VI's reign firmly in the background, which is not necessarily surprising for an older noblewoman without a queen to serve. Queen Mary's accession in 1553, however, seems to have changed things for her. She may have been staying in London at the time, as Wriothesley's *Chronicle* tells us that she was present when Mary entered the city and proceeded to free political prisoners—including Norfolk—from the Tower.[40] Elizabeth then carried Mary's train at her coronation, a position undoubtedly denoting her past friendship with Mary's mother.[41] She never reconciled with her husband, who died in 1554, and was not mentioned in his will.[42] Her annuity from the crown had been renewed on the accession of Mary I, and after 1554 she gained access to her jointure estates.[43] After widowhood she continued to play a more important role than she had done during Edward's reign, and was at the forefront of the funeral procession for Anne of Cleves in 1557.[44] Elizabeth died within weeks of Elizabeth I's accession in November 1558 at Lambeth. She was buried in the Howard chapel of St Mary's Church, Lambeth, as directed in her will.[45]

---

[36] *APC*, II, 77. [37] SRO, D(W) 1721/1/10/1–432, fol. 331. [38] Ibid., fol. 248.
[39] *APC*, II, 400. [40] Wriothesley, *Chronicle*, 94–5. [41] Planché, *Regal Records*, 15.
[42] TNA PROB 11/37. [43] *APC* IV, 273.
[44] S. Bentley, *Excerpta Historica* (London, 1831), 303–13. [45] TNA PROB 11/42A/285.

Other Howard women also appear to have remained in the background during Edward and Mary's reigns. Even Elizabeth's daughter Mary, Duchess of Richmond, who spent Edward's reign bringing up her nieces and nephews and petitioning the crown for their maintenance, and for the freedom and comfort of her father, was not involved in politics in the same way that she had been during the 1530s and 1540s.[46] Though surviving letters show that she was active in promoting evangelical preachers at the beginning of Edward's reign, evidence for this tails off after 1550.[47] She does not appear again in the record until 1553, when her father removed her nieces and nephews from her custody. We do not know what happened to Mary after this and she had died by January 1556.[48]

Anne, dowager Countess of Oxford, also faded from the record. There is no evidence that she came to court at any point after Henry's reign, and she was certainly not involved in any tumultuous political events. By the end of her life in the late 1550s she had become querulous and unpopular with her servants. A number of Chancery suits were initiated against her for non-payment of wages and unfair dismissal both from her service and from her lands.[49] An entry in Henry Machyn's diary shows that she died in February 1559 and was buried at Lambeth.[50] Her sister Katherine, Countess of Bridgwater, lay low too. She remained in Lambeth after her pardon for misprision of treason in 1543 and was granted an annuity of £120 by the crown. This continued to be paid until 1550, when she was granted access to the revenue from her jointure estates in Wales from her first marriage to Rhys ap Gruffudd, though she never gained those from her second marriage to Henry Daubeney (d. 1548).[51] In 1552, a summary of poor relief given by the inhabitants of Lambeth parish shows that she was living on the estate of Thomas Cranmer, Archbishop of Canterbury, and was able to contribute a yearly sum of 6*s*. 8*d*.[52] There is no other record of Katherine during these years and her will shows that she died in 1554, and was likewise buried at Lambeth.[53] It is possible that some or all of them were struck down by the epidemic of pneumonia that is estimated to have carried away a considerable proportion of the country's noblewomen during the late 1550s. Margaret Gamage/Howard, second wife of Lord William, however, escaped it, and lived on until 1581, outliving her husband by nine years.[54] She took up court service again during Mary's reign, and remained an important courtier until her death, introducing many of her daughters into service as well. Frances de Vere/Howard, widow of Henry, Earl of Surrey, took a different path, fading, like some of the others, into relative obscurity. In her case this was because she chose to remarry, and to do so to Thomas Staynings, a man considerably below her own status. Frances spent the rest of her life living in Earl Soham in Suffolk, though she did come to court for occasional ceremonial events, and was eventually buried at Framlingham when she died in 1577.

[46] TNA SP10/13, fol. 22; TNA SP10/14, fols 45, 53.   [47] TNA SP10/7, fols 1, 3.
[48] *Cal. Pat. Philip and Mary*, III, 46.   [49] TNA C1/1486/63–5, 89–92.
[50] *Diary of Henry Machyn*, 889–90.   [51] *APC*, II, 232, 271, 275, 297, 328, 411.
[52] T. Allen, *The history and antiquities of the parish of Lambeth* (London, 1826), 439.
[53] TNA PROB 10/27.
[54] Unusually for an aristocratic widow, she left no will.

The burial places of the Howard women, as I have argued elsewhere, are an intriguing testament to their dynastic identities, and the way in which they wanted these to be remembered.[55] The vast majority of the Howard women from this period were buried and commemorated in the Howard chapel of St Mary's, Lambeth, which had been commissioned and built by Agnes, Duchess of Norfolk, in the early 1520s. While it was probably not originally intended as a site specifically for female memory, it developed in this way largely as a result of the Dissolution of the Monasteries, which rendered the family's original mausoleum at Thetford Priory in Norfolk unusable. Thomas Howard, Third Duke of Norfolk, seized on the church of St Michael's in Framlingham, the site of the family seat, as his favoured alternative, and moved several ancestral tombs there.[56] Agnes, conversely, chose Lambeth as her own burial space, and moved her husband's body there during the later 1530s, an act which suggests that her rights as his widow 'trumped' those of his son and heir in terms of choosing his final resting place. Across the 1530s she was also most likely responsible for the burial of several female family members in this place, notably her daughter Elizabeth, Lady Fitzwater, in 1534, and daughter-in-law Katherine Broughton/Howard a year later.[57] Elizabeth Howard/Boleyn, Countess of Wiltshire, also chose burial at Lambeth. Given the Boleyn family's reduced political position at the time of her death in 1538, this may have been an attempt not only to redeem her own perpetual memory, but to remind those left behind that her remaining children were Howards as well as Boleyns.

By Agnes's own death in 1545, the Lambeth chapel had become a memorial of her own specific branch of the Howard dynasty, with her husband and all bar two of the children who had predeceased her buried there.[58] Interestingly, it seems that she had already had her own tomb designed and made by the time that she moved her husband there, which meant while she was laid to rest in a chest tomb in the very centre of the chapel, he had had to make do with a brass set into the floor.[59] This does not follow the usual patriarchal commemorative pattern, for it elevates Agnes above her husband, where, according to bloodline and status, she had no right to be. This is clearly an accidental consequence of the upheaval caused by the dissolution and had not originally been planned in this way. Yet the fact that Agnes left it that way places her among those women who worked commemoration to their own dynastic advantage, as the effect created is of a dynastic matriarch at the head and heart of her family.

[55] Nicola Clark, 'The Gendering of Dynastic Memory: Burial Choices of the Howards, 1485–1559', *Journal of Ecclesiastical History* 68:4 (2017), 747–65.

[56] See Phillip Lindley, 'Materiality, Movement and the Historical Moment', in Lindley (ed.), *The Howards and the Tudors: Studies in Science and Heritage* (Donington, 2015), 43–75.

[57] See Clark, 'The Gendering of Dynastic Memory'. Their brasses are depicted in Henry Lilly, *The genealogie of the princeley familie of the Howards* (1638), unpublished manuscript, Arundel Castle Archive. See also D. Lysons, *Environs of London* (London 1792), 5 vols, vol. 1, 286.

[58] Her son Thomas was buried in Thetford Priory and probably moved to Framlingham; *Register of Thetford Priory*, II, 695. We do not know the exact death date or burial place of Dorothy, Countess of Derby.

[59] Agnes's will of 1542 makes reference to 'suche place whereas I haue prepared my Tombe' (TNA PROB 11//30/596). Norfolk's brass is depicted in the Lilly *Genealogie*.

Following Agnes's death, other women of the family perpetuated Lambeth's position as a place for female memory. In 1554, Agnes's daughter Katherine, Countess of Bridgwater, asked in her will to be buried 'in my Ladie my mother tombe in the chapell w[ith]in the p[ar]ryshe churche in Lambeth'.[60] It was unusual for women to choose to be commemorated according to their natal identity when they could have been buried with a husband, but Katherine's first husband, Rhys ap Gruffudd, had been laid to rest in the Crutched Friars in London, now dissolved, and her second marriage to Henry Daubeney, Earl of Bridgwater, had not been a success. Her sister Anne, dowager Countess of Oxford, also chose burial at Lambeth in 1559, which might again have been because her husband had been buried in a priory where she could not join him.[61] Elizabeth Stafford/Howard, Duchess of Norfolk, was something of an 'odd one out' in the dynastic scheme when she, too, specified burial at Lambeth in her will of November 1558, since by rights she ought to have been placed alongside her husband and children in Framlingham.[62] However, again, her acrimonious relationship with her husband was probably why she chose not to lie beside him in perpetuity, and since her natal family, the Staffords, had no fixed mausoleum at this time, she may have felt she had no other choice.

When taken together, the Howard women's burials at Lambeth look as though they might be a typical dynastic fiction, set up at one time by one individual to commemorate the family's women.[63] In fact, only the memorials to the sole Howard man and the children fall into this category, which in many ways makes the female burials all the more interesting. They seem to imply that the Howard identity was particularly important to all of these women, regardless of whether it was their natal or marital identity. Since most other female memorialization is based on patriarchal dynastic inheritance, these commemorations document an unusually strong case of dynastic loyalty.

[60] TNA PROB 10/27.

[61] 'Houses of Benedictine monks: Priory of Earl's Colne', in William Page and J. Horace Round (eds), *A History of the County of Essex: Volume 2* (London 1907), 102–5. Anne's burial, like the others, is listed in St Mary's Lambeth burial register: London Metropolitan Archives, P85/MRY1/342, fols 143, 151v, 155, 155v.

[62] TNA PROB 11/42A/285.

[63] For more on aristocratic burial traditions, see Peter Sherlock, *Monuments and Memory in Early Modern England* (Aldershot, 2008).

Conclusion
'A man can not haue his cake and eate his cake'

In 1639, Frances Howard/Pranell/Seymour/Stewart, the infamous 'double Duchess' of Richmond and Lennox, made her will. In it she left her niece Elizabeth, Lady Maltravers, 'the H with seven diamondes and three pendant pearles which was Queen Katherine howardes which my godson Thomas [Howard] must have alsoe and not altered as an heire loome to remaine to him and to the heires of the howse of Arundell foreu[er]'.[1] Whether the pendant had really belonged to Catherine Howard is unclear. It is not among those listed in the inventory of her jewels taken shortly before her execution in 1541.[2] How Frances had got hold of it is also a matter for conjecture. What this shows, however, is that 100 years later, the Howard generation of this book remained a source of dynastic pride and fascination. Frances Howard had never known Catherine, but she clearly felt that she was important to her own and her relatives' dynastic identity. By this time it apparently no longer mattered that Catherine Howard had been executed as a traitor to the realm: what was important to her family was that she had been, however briefly, Queen of England. This demonstrates the way in which families and individuals were themselves responsible for writing and rewriting their own dynastic history, and, therefore, their dynastic identity. Women could be the source of its creation, its subject, and the means by which it was passed on. It also shows that throughout the early modern period, a Howard woman remained a Howard woman, even after three marriages.

This has been the central issue of this book. It has demonstrated conclusively that one cannot simply explain a woman's actions in terms of a single family identity. 'Oh well, she was a Howard' is not sufficient; early modern elite women's identities were much more complex. She might have been a Howard by marriage, for example, but who were her natal family, what did they think about any given situation, who else were they allied with politically or through marriage, and which individuals was this woman particularly close to? Come to that, what did she herself feel? All of these need due consideration, and we need to understand that women's identities, just like men's, were a kaleidoscope, each valid under different circumstances. This is not to say that family identities were not important. This book has shown that they clearly were, to the point where outside commentators also explained women's

---

[1] TNA PROB 11/181/222. [2] BL Stowe MS 559, fols 55–68.

behaviour in this way. It has also shown, though, that women's dynastic identities were open to interpretation by themselves and by those around them.

Do the Howard women exhibit an unusual attachment to their Howard identity? This is a difficult question to answer contextually without similar studies of other families, something this book has clearly shown is needed. However, the answer appears to be 'yes', to some degree, in certain circumstances, both to themselves and to outsiders. The number of women related to the Howard dynasty who actively chose to commemorate themselves not only as Howards, but specifically in a place redolent with the memory of Howard *women*, is something I have not found replicated elsewhere during this period, and is a strong indication of their dynastic feelings at the time of death. The way that the justiciar of south Wales deliberately described Katherine, then Lady Rhys, as 'Lady Howard' during her involvement with rebellion demonstrates not only that women did not leave their natal identities entirely behind when they married, but that that identity might be resurrected if others thought it useful.[3]

There is no single explanation as to why the Howard women in particular behaved in this way. To some degree, it may simply have been a reflection of their very high status throughout this period. There were few other families into which Howard daughters could marry that might be considered to have 'trumped' the Howards, and one could not marry royalty all of the time. It was therefore to their advantage to maintain strong relationships with their natal family, and to continue to identify with them. A number of the women considered here experienced poor relations with their other families, and, as was usually the case for women experiencing marital difficulties, this probably made them cling all the more tenaciously to their natal identity. The strong relationships between many of the Howard women may also have led them to give this identity undue weighting. This elasticity of kinship relations and family identities was therefore a core element of early modern politics and society where women were concerned.

The Howard men, however, particularly the family patriarchs, may well have rued the strength of the Howard women's agency in this regard, since many of these women were undeniably, and unusually, drawn to political and personal trouble throughout this period. While many chapters of this book have shown that the Howard women were invaluable to the dynasty as a whole, managing its resources competently, forming and maintaining useful contacts, and raising the profile of the family at court, it is impossible to escape the realization that inasmuch as they helped, so too did they hinder. The title quote of this chapter is taken from a letter written by Thomas, Third Duke of Norfolk, to Thomas Cromwell in the 1530s, and though when he said that 'a man can not haue his cake and eate his cake' he was referring to his finances, he might just as well have been referring to his female relations.[4] Involvement in rebellion was not something likely to advance one's family. Involvement in treason, even less so. As Chapter 1 explained, it was generally accepted to be the job of the family patriarch, or paterfamilias, to keep control of

---

[3] TNA SP1/54 fol. 93.   [4] TNA SP1/130, fol. 43.

his family and prevent them from behaving in damaging ways, and to mitigate the consequences when they did so.[5] In this, Thomas Howard, Third Duke of Norfolk, faced considerable difficulties. This book has uniquely showcased his troubles with his female relatives, but has argued that he should not necessarily be blamed entirely for this. It would be unrealistic to fault him alone for failing to prevent them leading the dynasty into trouble. Indeed, we might even feel a little sorry for him. Few men were faced with such difficult female relations during this period and it seems that he, like several others they encountered, was often baffled as to how to deal with them. That his response when faced with a recalcitrant female was usually to distance himself and the rest of the family, doing whatever possible to cut her off from familial support and to deny her identity as a member of the dynasty, should be seen as protection of the inheriting line, the most important duty of a paterfamilias.

While comparative analysis has shown that subversion, wilfulness, and outright rebellion in the face of male authority were not unique to the Howard women, to find so many such episodes within one generation of one dynasty is not common. This study approaches these women with the understanding that they necessarily operated within the confines of patriarchy; to suggest otherwise would be an anachronistic form of wishful thinking. However, it is important to remember that 'patriarchy' was and is not only about personal relations between women and men, but was also about women's interactions with the man-made and primarily male-dominated systems that made up aristocratic society in general, such as the law, the monarchy, and the royal court. Clearly it is not realistic to lean on an old-fashioned model of purely oppositional gender relations, because this would mean that women were permanently working against all of the structures of early modern society. This book itself has offered plenty of evidence that men and women were often united in pursuit of shared goals, and that women were able to use those social structures to their benefit. Yet much of the evidence for the Howard women suggests that as a group and as individuals they were not always in tune with those goals, and many successfully followed an alternative path to that laid out for them. The book therefore offers a flexible definition of patriarchy heavily dependent on the state of individual relationships. These women were not changing the system; rather, they were changing their immediate experience of the system.

This raises the question of the existence of any form of 'family strategy' among dynasties like the Howards. The actions of these women suggest that there were sometimes coherent group strategies, most discernibly in efforts to evade life-threatening legal convictions, or, more usually but less obviously, in attempts to augment the family's fortunes by promoting family and clients. Among the Howards, however, collective strategy was rare. Where there is evidence for such a thing, as in the wake of Catherine Howard's arrest in 1541, it becomes apparent that the

---

[5] Broomhall and Van Gent, 'In the Name of the Father: Conceptualizing Pater Familias in the Letters of William the Silent's Children', *Renaissance Quarterly* 62:4 (2009), 1130–66.

efforts to protect relatives and friends involved only a small portion of the family. Anne Boleyn's rise, too, demonstrates the difficulties faced by families like the Howards at court: to support a client family in a risky venture, or not? That the Howard women themselves were largely absent until Anne had clearly made a success of things is significant, and is an example of the way in which this book has nuanced, and even dispelled, many traditional narratives about the Howard dynasty as a whole.

Bibliography

MANUSCRIPT SOURCES

Arundel Castle Archive, Arundel
A Accounts
AP Acts of Parliament, bills and associated documents
G Documents relating principally to the Howard family
M Manorial Documents
MD Miscellaneous Documents
T Testamentary Records
Henry Lilly, *The genealogie of the princeley familie of the Howards* (1638)

Bancroft Library, University of California, Berkeley (UCB)
Bancroft MSS

Bodleian Library, Oxford (Bodl.)
Laudian MSS
Rawlinson MSS

British Library, London (BL)
Additional MSS
Additional Charters
Arundel MSS
Cotton MSS
Egerton MSS
Harley MSS
Hargrave MSS
Lansdowne MSS
Royal MSS
Stowe MSS

Cambridge University Library (CUL)
Baker MSS
Cambridge University Library MSS
Pembroke MSS

London Metropolitan Archives
P85/MRY1 Parish records, St Mary's Lambeth

The National Archives, Kew (TNA)
C Court of Chancery
CP Court of Common Pleas
E Exchequer
LC Lord Chamberlain's Accounts
LR Land Revenue

REQ Court of Requests
SC Special Collections
SP State Papers
STAC Court of Star Chamber
PROB Probate
WARD Court of Wards

The National Library of Wales (NLW)
Dynevor Estate Records
Dynevor Parcels

Norfolk Record Office, Norwich (NRO)
Bishops' registers
BL Bradfer-Lawrence Collection
JER Jerningham Collection
PD Parish Registers
Phi Manuscripts of Sir Thomas Phillips
LEST Le Strange of Hunstanton Collection
NNAS Norfolk and Norwich Archaeological Society Collection
NRS Norfolk Record Society Collection
RYE Rye Collection
WLS Walsingham (Merton) Collection

Somerset Heritage Centre, Taunton
D\D/cd Diocese of Bath and Wells, court deposition books

Staffordshire Record Office, Stafford (SRO)
D(W) 1721 Stafford family

Surrey History Centre, Woking
LM Loseley collection

PRINTED PRIMARY SOURCES

Accounts of the Lord High Treasurer of Scotland A.D. 1500–1504, ed. Sir James Balfour Paul, 13 vols (Edinburgh, General Register Office, 1900), II
Acts of the Privy Council, ed. John Roche Dasent, new series, 32 vols (London, 1890–1964) (*APC*)
Alumni Cantabrigienses, at <venn.lib.cam.ac.uk>
Alumni Oxonienses 1500–1714, ed. Joseph Foster, at <http://www.british-history.ac.uk>
The Antient Kalendars and Inventories of the Treasury of His Majesty's Excheqer, ed. F. Palgrave, 3 vols (London, 1836)
The Antiquarian Repertory, ed. F. Grose et al., 4 vols (London, 1809)
Bentley, S., *Excerpta Historica* (London, 1831)
Burnet, Gilbert, *The History of the Reformation of the Church of England*, 6 vols (London, 1643–1715)
Calendar of Inquisitions Post Mortem, Henry VII, 3 vols (London, 1898–1955) (*Cal. IPM*)
Calendar of Institutions by the Chapter of Canterbury Sede Vacante, ed. C. E. Woodruff and I. A. Churchill, Kent Archaeological Society Records Branch 8 (Canterbury, 1924)

Calendar of Entries in the Papal Registers relating to Great Britain and Ireland, ed. W. H. Bliss et al., 19 vols (London and Dublin, 1893–)

Calendar of State Papers Relating To English Affairs in the Archives of Venice, ed. Rawdon Brown, 38 vols (London, 1867)

Calendar of State Papers, Domestic: Edward, Mary and Elizabeth, 1547–1580, ed. R. Lemon, 8 vols (London, 1856) (*CSP Dom.*)

Calendar of State Papers, Spain, ed. G. A. Bergenroth et al., 19 vols (London, 1866–1954) (*CSP Spain*)

Calendar of State Papers, Milan, ed. A. B. Hinds (London, 1912)

Calendar of the Patent Rolls: Richard II, 1391–1996, vol. 5, ed. G. J. Morris and H. M. Maxwell-Lyte (London, 1905)

Calendar of the Patent Rolls: Edward VI–Philip and Mary, 9 vols (London, 1924–9)

Castiglione, Balthasar, *The Book of the Courtier*, trans. George Bull (London, 1976)

Cavendish, George, *Thomas Wolsey, Late Cardinal, his Life and Death*, ed. Roger Lockyer (London, 1973)

Chronicle of the Grey Friars of London, ed. J. G. Nichols, Camden Society Old Series 53 (London, 1852)

Chronicle of King Henry VIII of England, trans. Martin A. S. Hume (London, 1889)

The Chronicle of Queen Jane, and of two years of Queen Mary, and especially of the rebellion of Sir Thomas Wyat, ed. John Gough Nichols (London, 1850)

Cockayne, G. E., *Complete Peerage of England, Scotland, Ireland and Great Britain*, 12 vols (London, 1910–59)

Collection of Ordinances and Regulations for the Government of the Royal Household, printed by J. Nichols (London, 1790)

Cranmer, Thomas, *Miscellaneous Writings and Letters of Thomas Cranmer*, ed. John Edmund Cox (Cambridge, 1846)

Crawford, A. (ed.), *The Household Books of John Howard, Duke of Norfolk, 1462–1471, 1481–1483* (Stroud, 1992)

de Carles, Lancelot, 'Poème sur la mort d'Anne Boleyn', in *La Grande Bretagne devant l'opinion française*, ed. Georges Ascoli (Paris, 1927)

The Devonshire Manuscript: A Woman's Book of Courtly Poetry, ed. Elizabeth Heale (Toronto, 2012)

The Diary of Henry Machyn, Citizen and Merchant-Taylor of London, from A.D. 1550 to A. D. 1563, ed. John Gough Nichols (London, 1848)

Ellis, H. (ed.), *Original Letters illustrative of English History*, 3 series, 11 vols (London, 1824–46)

Ellis, H., 'Copy of an Order made by Cardinal Wolsey, as Lord Chancellor, respecting the Management of the Affairs of the young Earl of Oxford', *Archaeologia* 19 (1821), 62–5

Faculty Office Register 1534–1549, ed D. S. Chambers (Oxford, 1966)

Foxe, John, and Tom Freeman, *The Acts and Monuments Online*, <http://www.johnfoxe.org> (*TAMO*)

The Great Wardrobe Accounts of Henry VII and Henry VIII, ed. M. Hayward (Woodbridge, 2012)

Griffiths, R. A., *The Household Book of Sir Edward Don: An Anglo-Welsh Knight and his Circle, Buckinghamshire Record Society* 33 (Aylesbury, 2004)

Gunn, S. J., 'A Letter of Jane, Duchess of Northumberland, 1553', *EHR* 114 (1999), 1267–71

Hall, Edward, *Hall's Chronicle*, ed. H. Ellies (London, 1809)

The Herald's Memoir 1486–1490: Court Ceremony, Royal Progress and Rebellion, ed. E. Cavell (Donington, 2009)

Herbert, Edward, Lord Herbert of Cherbury, *The Life and Reign of Henry the Eighth* (London, 1672)

Howard, C., *Historical Anecdotes of Some of the Howard Family* (London, 1769)

Howard, H., *Indication of Memorials of the Howard Family* (Corby, 1834–6)

Howard, L., *A Collection of Letters, from the Original Manuscripts of Many Princes, Great Personages, and Statesmen* (London, 1753)

Howlett, R., 'The Household Accounts of Kenninghall Palace in the Year 1525', *Norfolk Archaeology* 15 (1904), 51–60

Illingworth, W., 'Copy of an original Minute of Council for the Preparations for the Ceremonial of the Funeral of Queen Catherine, the divorced Wife of King Henry the Eighth', *Archaeologia* 16 (1812), 22–8

The Inventory of Henry VIII, vol. I: The Transcript, ed. D. Starkey (London, 1998)

Jerdan, W. (ed.), *The Rutland Papers*, Camden Society, old series, 21 (London, 1842)

Lambeth Churchwardens' Accounts 1504–1645 and Vestry Book 1610, ed. Charles Drew, 2 vols, *Surrey Record Society* 18 (London, 1941)

Leland, J., *De Rebus Britannicis Collectanea*, ed. T. Hearne, 6 vols (London, 1774)

Lesse, Nicholas (trans.), *The twelfe steppes of abuses write[n] by the famus doctor S. Augustine translated out of laten by Nicolas Lesse*, EEBO (1549)

Letters and Papers, Foreign and Domestic, of the Reign of Henry VIII, ed. J. S. Brewer, J. Gairdner, and R. H. Brodie, 22 vols (London, 1862–1932)

Letters and Papers Illustrative of the Reigns of Richard III and Henry VII, ed. J. Gairdner, 2 vols, Rolls Series 24 (London, 1861–3)

Lewer, H. W., 'The Testament and Last Will of Elizabeth, Widow of John de Veer, Thirteenth Earl of Oxford', *Transactions of the Essex Archaeological Society* 20 (1933), 7–16

The Lisle Letters, ed. M. St Clare Byrne, 6 vols (Chicago, 1981)

Lloyd, Charles (ed.), *Formularies of Faith Put Forth by Authority During the Reign of Henry VIII* (Oxford, 1825)

London and Middlesex Chantry Certificate 1548, ed. C. J. Kitching, London Record Society 16 (London, 1980)

The Manuscripts of His Grace the Duke of Rutland, G. C. B., preserved at Belvoir Castle, HMC Twelfth Report, Appendix, Part IV (London, 1888)

Nicolas, N. H. (ed.), *Proceedings and Ordinances of the Privy Council of England*, 7 vols (London, 1834–7) (*PCP*)

Nicolas, N. H. (ed.), *Testamenta Vetusta*, 2 vols (London, 1826)

Nott, George Frederick (ed.), *The Works of Henry Howard, Earl of Surrey, and of Sir Thomas Wyatt The Elder*, 2 vols (London, 1815)

Original Letters illustrative of English History, 3rd ser., ed. H. Ellis, 4 vols (London, 1846)

Partridge, Charles, 'Will of Sir Philip Tylney of Shelley Hall, Suffolk, 1532', *Notes and Queries* 192 (1947), 297–300

The Paston Letters, 1422–1509, ed. J. Gairdner, 3 vols (London, 1872–5)

Pizan, Christine de, *The Treasure of the City of Ladies; or the Book of the Three Virtues*, trans. Sarah Lawson (New York, 1985)

The Privy Purse Expences of King Henry the Eighth, ed. N. H. Nicolas (London, 1827)

The Privy Purse Expenses of Princess Mary, ed. F. Madden (London, 1831)

The Receyt of the Ladie Kateryne, ed. G. Kipling, EETS 296 (Oxford, 1990)

The Register or Chronicle of Butley Priory, Suffolk, 1510–1535, ed. A. G. Dickens (Winchester, 1951)

The Register of Thetford Priory, ed. D. Dymond, 2 vols, Norfolk Record Society 59–60 (Oxford, 1995–6)

Registers of Stephen Gardiner and John Poynet, Bishops of Winchester, ed. Herbert Chitty, Canterbury and York Society 37 (Oxford, 1930)

The Registers of Thomas Wolsey, Bishop of Bath and Wells, 1518–1523, John Clerke, Bishop of Bath and Wells, 1523–1541, William Knyght, Bishop of Bath and Wells, 1541–1547, and Gilbert Bourne, Bishop of Bath and Wells, 1554–1559, ed. Sir Henry Maxwell-Lyte, *Somerset Record Society* 55 (Taunton, 1940)

The Reports of Sir John Spelman, ed. J. H. Baker, 2 vols (London, 1976–7)

Rice, Henry, 'Objections against Rice Griffith in his Indictment, with the Answers thereunto', *Cambrian Register* 2 (1796), 270–7

Ridgard, John, *Medieval Framlingham: Select Documents 1270–1524*, Suffolk Record Society 27 (Woodbridge, 1985)

Rotuli Parliamentarium, ed. J. Strachey et al., 6 vols (London, 1767–77) (*Rot. Parl.*)

Smyth, J., *The Berkeley Manuscripts: The Lives of the Berkeleys*, ed. J. Maclean, 3 vols (Gloucester, 1883)

The Statutes of the Realm, ed. T. E. Tomlins and W. E. Taunton, 9 vols (London, 1810–25), III

Stow, John, *A Survey of London*, ed. C. L. Kingsford, 2 vols (Oxford, 1971)

Strype, J., *Ecclesiastical Memorials*, 3 vols (Oxford, 1822)

Testamenta Eboracensia, A Selection of Wills from the Registry at York, III, ed. J. Raine and J. W. Clay, *Surtees Society* 45 (York, 1864)

Testamenta Vetusta, ed. N. H. Nicholas, 2 vols (London, 1842)

The Survey of London, ed. C. R. Ashbee et al., 47 vols (London, 1854–)

Valor Ecclesiasticus, ed. H. Caley, 6 vols (London, 1810–33)

The Visitacion of Norffolk, made and taken by William hervey, Clarencieux King of Arms, anno 1563, enlarged with another Visitacion made by Clarenceux Cooke, with many other Descents; and also the Vissitation made by John Raven, Richmond, anno 1613, ed. W. Rye (London, 1891)

The Visitation of Norfolk in the Year 1563, ed. G. H. Dashwood and E. Bulwer Lytton, 2 vols (Norwich, 1878–95)

Weever, J., *Ancient Funerall Monuments* (London, 1631)

Williams, Franklin B., *Index of Dedications and Commendatory Verses in English Books before 1641* (London, 1962)

Wood, M. A. E. (ed.), *Letters of Royal and Illustrious Ladies of Great Britain*, 3 vols (London, 1846)

Wriothesley, Charles, *A Chronicle of England During the Reigns of the Tudors, from A. D. 1485 to 1559*, ed. William Douglas Hamilton (London, 1875–7)

York Civic Records, ed. A. Raine, 8 vols (Wakefield, 1939–53)

SECONDARY SOURCES

Adams, T., 'Renaissance Queenship: A Review Article', *Explorations in Renaissance Culture* 42:1 (2016), 87–107

Agren, Maria, and Amy Ericksen (eds), *The Marital Economy in Scandinavia and Britain, 1400–1900* (Aldershot, 2005)

Akkerman, Nadine, and Birgit Houben (eds), *The Politics of Female Households: Ladies in Waiting Across Early Modern Europe* (Leiden, 2013)

Algazi, Gadi, Valentin Groebner, and Bernhard Jussen (eds), *Negotiating the Gift: Pre-Modern Configurations of Exchange* (Göttingen, 2003)

Allen, Gemma, *The Cooke Sisters: Education, Piety and Politics in Early Modern England* (Manchester, 2013)

Allen, Thomas, *The History and Antiquities of the Parish of Lambeth* (London, 1826)

Alsop, J. D., 'Religious Preambles in Early Modern English Wills as Formulae', *Journal of Ecclesiastical History* 40:1 (1989), 19–27

Amussen, S. D., '"Being stirred to much unquietness": Violence and Domestic Violence in Early Modern England', *Journal of Women's History* 6:2 (1994), 70–89

Archer, Rowena. E., 'Rich old ladies: The Problem of Late Medieval Dowagers', in A. J. Pollard (ed.), *Property and Politics: Essays in Later Medieval English History* (Gloucester, 1984), 15–35

Archer, Rowena E., '"How ladies…who live on their manors ought to manage their households and estates": Women as Landholders and Administrators in the Later Middle Ages', in P. J. P. Goldberg (ed.), *Woman Is a Worthy Wight: Women in English Society c.1200–1500* (Wolfeboro, NH, 1992), 149–81

Archer, Rowena E., and B. E. Ferme, 'Testamentary Procedure with Special Reference to the Executrix', in Keith Bate (ed.), *Medieval Women in Southern England* (Reading, 1989), 3–34

Ashdown-Hill, John, 'Lady Eleanor Talbot: New Evidence; New Answers; New Questions', *The Ricardian* 16 (2006), 1–20

Attreed, Lorraine C., 'Preparation for Death in Sixteenth Century Northern England', *Sixteenth Century Journal* 13:3 (1982), 37–66

Aubrey, John, *The Natural History and Antiquities of the County of Surrey*, 5 vols (London, 1719), V

Backscheider, Paula R., and Timothy Dykstal, *The Intersections of the Public and Private Spheres in Early Modern England* (London, 1996)

Bagley, J. J., *The Earls of Derby 1485–1985* (London, 1985)

Bailey, Joanne, 'Cruelty and Adultery: Offences against the Institution of Marriage', in Anne-Marie Kilday and David S. Nash (ed.), *Histories of Crime: Britian 1600–2000* (Basingstoke, 2010), 39–59

Baron, Helen, 'Mary (Howard) Fitzroy's Hand in the Devonshire Manuscript', *The Review of English Studies* 45 (1994), 313–35

Barrow, Lorna G., '"The Kynge sent to the Qwene, by a Gentylman, a grett tame Hart." Marriage, Gift Exchange and Politics: Margaret Tudor and James IV, 1502–1513', *Parergon* 21 (2004), 65–84

Beattie, Cordelia, '"Living as a Single Person": Marital Status, Performance and the Law in Late Medieval England', *Women's History Review* 17:3 (2008), 327–40

Bellamy, John, *The Tudor Law of Treason: An Introduction* (London, 1979)

Ben-Amos, Ilana Krausman, *The Culture of Giving: Informal Support and Gift-Exchange in Early Modern England* (Cambridge, 2008)

Bennett, Judith M., *History Matters: Patriarchy and the Challenge of Feminism* (Manchester, 2006)

Bernard, G. W., 'The Fall of Anne Boleyn', *EHR* 106 (1991), 584–610

Bernard, G. W., *Anne Boleyn: Fatal Attractions* (London, 2010)

Bernard, G. W., 'The Fall of Anne Boleyn: A Rejoinder', *EHR* 107 (1992), 665–74

Bernard, G. W., *The King's Reformation: Henry VIII and the Remaking of the English Church* (London, 2007)

Bernard, G. W., *The Power of the Early Tudor Nobility: A Study of the Fourth and Fifth Earls of Shrewsbury* (Brighton, 1985)

Bernard, G. W. (ed.), *The Tudor Nobility* (Manchester, 1992)

Berry, Helen, and Elizabeth A., Foyster (eds), *The Family in Early Modern England* (Cambridge, 2007)

Bevington, David, and Milla Riggio, ' "What revels are in hand?" Marriage Celebrations and Patronage of the Arts in Renaissance England', in Paul Whitfield White and Suzanne Westfall (eds), *Shakespeare and Theatrical Patronage in Early Modern England* (Cambridge, 2002)

Biksterveld, Arnoud-Jan A., 'The Medieval Gift as Agent of Social Bonding and Political Power: A Comparative Approach', in Esther Cohen and Mayke B. De Jong (eds), *Medieval Transformations: Texts, Power, and Gifts in Context* (Leiden, 2001), 123–56

Blakeway, Amy, 'The Attempted Divorce of James Hamilton, Earl of Arran, Governor of Scotland', *Innes Review* 61:1 (2010), 1–23

Blomefield, Francis, A*n Essay Towards a Topographical History of Norfolk*, 11 vols (London, 1811)

Bonfield, Lloyd, 'Seeking Connections between Kinship and the Law in Early Modern England', *Continuity and Change* 25:1 (2010), 49–82

Bossy, J., 'Blood and Baptism: Kinship, Community and Christianity in Western Europe from the Fourteenth to the Seventeenth Centuries', in D. Baker (ed.), *Sanctity and Society: The Church and the World* (Oxford, 1973), 129–44

Braddick, Michael J., and John Walter, *Negotiating Power in Early Modern Society: Order, Hierarchy and Subordination in Britain and Ireland* (Cambridge, 2001)

Brady, Ciaran, 'Comparable Histories?: Tudor Reform in Wales and Ireland', in Steven G. Ellis and Sarah Barber (eds), *Conquest and Union: Fashioning a British State, 1485–1725* (London, 1995), 64–86

Brand, Paul, ' "Deserving" and "Undeserving" Wives: Earning and Forfeiting Dower in Medieval England', *Journal of Legal History* 22:1 (2001), 1–11

Breen, Dan, 'Power and Authority in Tudor England (Review Article)', *Reformation* 10 (2005), 129–34

Brenan, Gerald, and Edward Phillips Statham, *The House of Howard*, 2 vols (London, 1907)

Brigden, Susan, 'Youth and the English Reformation', *Past and Present* 95:1 (1982), 37–67

Brigden, Susan, 'Henry Howard, Earl of Surrey, and the "Conjured League"', *Historical Journal* 37 (1994), 507–37

Brigden, Susan, 'Religion and Social Obligation in Early Sixteenth-Century London', *Past and Present* 103 (1984), 67–112

Bristow, Cyril, *Tilney Families* (Tonbridge, 1988)

Broomhall, Susan (ed.), *Emotions in the Household, 1200–1900* (Basingstoke, 2008)

Broomhall, Susan (ed.), *Authority, Gender and Emotions in Late Medieval and Early Modern England* (Basingstoke, 2016)

Broomhall, Susan, 'Materializing Women: Dynamic Interactions of Gender and Materiality in Early Modern Europe', in Amanda L. Capern (ed.), *The Routledge History of Women in Early Modern Europe* (London, 2017)

Broomhall, Susan, and Jacqueline Van Gent, 'In the Name of the Father: Conceptualizing Pater Familias in the Letters of William the Silent's Children', *Renaissance Quarterly* 62:4 (2009), 1130–66

Broomhall, Susan, and Jacqueline Van Gent, 'Corresponding Affections: Emotional Exchange Among Siblings in the Nassau Family', *Journal of Family History* 23 (2009)

Broomhall, Susan, and Jacqueline Van Gent (eds), *Governing Masculinities in the Early Modern Period: Regulating Selves and Others* (Aldershot, 2011)

Broomhall, Susan, and Jacqueline Van Gent, *Dynastic Colonialism: Gender, Materiality and the Early Modern House of Orange–Nassau* (London, 2016)

Broomhall, Susan, and Stephanie Tarbin (eds), *Women, Identities and Communities in Early Modern Europe* (Aldershot, 2008)

Brundage, James A., *Medieval Canon Law* (London, 1995)

Burghartz, D., 'Tales of Seduction, Tales of Violence: Argumentative Strategies before the Basel Marriage Court', *German History* 17 (1999), 41–56

Bush, Michael, *The Pilgrimage of Grace: A Study of the Rebel Armies of October 1536* (Manchester, 1996)

Bush, Michael, *The Pilgrims' Complaint: A Study of Popular Thought in the Early Tudor North* (Aldershot, 2009)

Butler, Sara M., *The Language of Abuse: Marital Violence in Later Medieval England* (Leiden, 2007)

Butler, Sara M., *Divorce in Medieval England* (London, 2013)

Byrne, Conor, *Katherine Howard: A New History* (London, 2014)

Calvi, Giulia, and Isabelle Chabot (eds), *Moving Elites: Women and Cultural Transfers in the European Court System*, EUI Working Papers HEC, 2 (Florence, 2010)

Capern, Amanda, 'The Landed Woman in Early Modern England', *Parergon* 19:1 (2002), 185–214

Capp, Bernard, *When Gossips Meet: Women, Family, and Neighbourhood in Early Modern England* (Oxford, 2003)

Caputo, Nicoletta, 'Entertainers "on the Vagabond Fringe": Jugglers in Tudor and Stuart England', in Paola Pugliatti and Alessandro Serpieri (eds), *English Renaissance Scenes: From Canon to Margins* (Bern, 2008), 311–48

Carley, James Patrick, *The Books of Henry VIII and his Wives* (London, 2004)

Carlson, E. J., *Marriage and the English Reformation* (Oxford, 1994)

Casady, Edwin, *Henry Howard, Earl of Surrey* (New York, 1938)

Chalus, E., ' "To Serve my friends": Women and Political Patronage in Eighteenth-Century England', in Amanda Vickery (ed.), *Women, Privilege and Power: British Politics, 1750 to the Present* (Stanford, Calif., 2001), 57–88

Chapman, Sara, 'The Role of Women in the Patron–Client Network of the Phelypeaux de Pontchartrain', *French Historical Studies* 24 (2001), 11–35

Chedgzoy, Kate, 'The Civility of Early Modern Welsh Women', in Jennifer Richards (ed.), *Early Modern Civil Discourses* (Basingstoke, 2003), 162–82

Chew, Elizabeth V., 'The Countess of Arundel and Tart Hall', in Edward Chaney (ed.), *The Evolution of English Collecting: Receptions of Italian Art in the Tudor and Stuart Periods* (New Haven and London, 2003), 285–314

Childs, Jessie, *Henry VIII's Last Victim: The Life and Times of Henry Howard, Earl of Surrey* (London, 2006)

Clark, Nicola, 'A "Conservative" Family? The Howard Women and Responses to Religious Change c.1530–1558', *Historical Research* 90:248 (2017), 318–40

Clark, Nicola, 'The Gendering of Dynastic Memory: Burial Choices of the Howards, 1485–1559', *Journal of Ecclesiastical History* 68:4 (2017), 747–65

Clark, Stuart, *Vanities of the Eye: Vision in Early Modern European Culture* (Oxford, 2007)

Collinson, Patrick, 'The Role of Women in the English Reformation Illustrated by the Life and Friendships of Anne Locke', *Studies in Church History* 2 (1965), 258–72

Cooke, James Herbert, 'The Great Berkeley Lawsuit of the 15th and 16th Centuries: A Chapter of Gloucestershire History', *Transactions of the Bristol and Gloucestershire Archaeological Society* 3 (1878–9), 305–24

Coster, W., 'Purity, Profanity, and Puritanism: The Churching of Women, 1500–1700', in William J. Shiels and Diana Wood (eds), *Women in the Church* (Oxford, 1990), 377–88

Coster, W., 'From Fire and Water: The Responsibilities of Godparents', *Studies in Church History* 31 (1994), 301–12

Coster, W., *Baptism and Spiritual Kinship in Early Modern England* (Aldershot, 2002)

Coster, W., *Family and Kinship in England, 1450–1800* (London, 2015)

Couchman, Jane, and Anne Crabb (eds), *Women's Letters Across Europe, 1400–1700: Form and Persuasion* (Aldershot, 2005)

Coward, B., *The Stanleys, Lords Stanley and Earls of Derby, 1385–1672* (Manchester, 1983)

Craig. J., and C. Litzenberger, 'Wills as Religious Propaganda: The Testament of William Tracy', *Journal of Ecclesiastical History* 44 (1993), 415–31

Crankshaw, David, 'Chaplains to the Elizabethan Nobility: Activities, Categories and Patterns', in Hugh Adlington, Tom Lockwood, and Gillian Wrights (eds), *Chaplains in Early Modern England: Patronage, Literature and Religion* (Manchester, 2013) 36–63

Crawford, Anne, 'Victims of Attainder: The Howard and De Vere Women in the Late Fifteenth Century', in Keith Bate (ed.), *Medieval Women in Southern England* (Reading, 1989), 59–74

Crawford, Anne, *Yorkist Lord: John Howard, Duke of Norfolk, c.1425–1485* (London, 2010)

Crawford, Julia, *Mediatrix: Women, Politics and Literary Production in Early Modern England* (Oxford, 2014)

Crawford, K., 'Catherine de Medici and the Performance of Political Motherhood', *The Sixteenth-Century Journal* 31 (2000), 643–73

Crawford, Patricia, *Bodies, Blood and Families in Early Modern England* (Harlow, 2004)

Cressy, D., 'Kinship and Kin Interaction in Early Modern England', *Past and Present* 113 (1986), 38–69

Cressy, D., *Birth, Marriage and Death: Ritual, Religion, and the Life-Cycle in Tudor and Stuart England* (Oxford, 1997)

Cressy, D., *Dangerous Talk: Scandalous, Seditious, and Treasonable Speech in Pre-Modern England* (Oxford, 2010)

Croft, Pauline (ed.), *Patronage, Culture and Power: The Early Cecils* (London, 2002)

Cross, Claire (ed.), *Patronage and Recruitment in the Tudor and Early Stuart Church* (York, 1996)

Cross, Claire, 'Noble Patronage in the Elizabethan Church', *Historical Journal* 3 (1960), 1–16

Cunningham, Karen, *Imaginary Betrayals: Subjectivity and the Discourses of Treason in Early Modern England* (Philadelphia, 2002)

Daubeney, Philip Heskith, et al., *The History of the Daubeney Family* ([n.p.], 2004)

Davidson, Peter, and Jane Stevenson, 'Elizabeth I's Reception at Bisham (1592): Elite Women as Writers and Devisers', in Jayne Elisabeth Archer, Elizabeth Goldring and Sarah Knight (eds), *The Progresses, Pageants, and Entertainments of Queen Elizabeth I* (Oxford, 2007), 207–20

Davis, Natalie Zemon, 'Women on Top', in *Society and Culture in Early Modern France: Eight Essays* (Stanford, Calif., 1975), 124–51

Davis, Natalie Zemon, 'Beyond the Market: Books as Gifts in Sixteenth-Century France', *Transactions of the Royal Historical Society* fifth series 33 (1983), 69–88

Davis, Natalie Zemon, *The Gift in Sixteenth Century France* (Oxford, 2000)

Daybell, James (ed.), *Women and Politics in Early Modern England, 1450–1700* (Aldershot, 2004)

Daybell, James (ed.), *Early Modern Women's Letter Writing, 1450–1700* (Basingstoke, 2001)

Daybell, James, ' "I wold wyshe my doings myght be…secret": Privacy and the Social Practices of Reading Women's Letters in Sixteenth-Century England', in Jane Couchman and Ann Crabb (eds), *Women's Letters Across Europe, 1400–1700: Form and Persuasion* (Aldershot, 2005), 143–61

Daybell, James, 'Scripting a Female Voice: Women's Epistolary Rhetoric in Sixteenth-Century Letters of Petition', *Women's Writing* 13 (2006), 3–20

Daybell, James, 'Gender, Obedience, and Authority in Sixteenth-Century Women's Letters', *Sixteenth Century Journal* 41 (2010), 49–67

Daybell, James, 'Gender, Obedience and Authority in Sixteenth-Century Women's Letters', *Sixteenth Century Journal* 11:1 (2010), 67–86

Daybell, James, 'Social Negotiations in Correspondence between Mothers and Daughters in Tudor and Early Stuart England', *Women's History Review* 24:4 (2015), 502–27

Daybell, James, *Women Letter-Writers in Tudor England* (Oxford, 2006)

Daybell, James, *The Material Letter in Early Modern England: Manuscript Practices and the Culture and Practices of Letter-Writing, 1512–1635* (Basingstoke, 2012)

Daybell, James, and Svante Norrhem (eds), *Gender and Political Culture in Early Modern Europe, 1400–1800* (London, 2016)

De Trafford, Clare, 'Share and Share Alike? The Marriage Portion, Inheritance, and Family Politics', in Christine E. Meek and Catherine Lawless (eds), *Studies on Medieval and Early Modern Women: Pawns or Players?* (Dublin, 2003), 36–48

Dekker, Rudolf, "Women in Revolt: Popular Protest and its Social Basis in Holland in the Seventeenth and Eighteenth Centuries', *Theory and Society* 16 (1987), 337–62

Dodds, Madeleine Hope, and Ruth Dodds, *The Pilgrimage of Grace 1536–1537 and the Exeter Conspiracy 1538*, 2 vols (London, 1971)

Donawerth, Jane, 'Women's Poetry and the Tudor–Stuart System of Gift Exchange', in Mary Elizabeth Burke, Jane Donawerth, Linda L. Dove, and Karen L. Nelson (eds), *Women, Writing, and the Reproduction of Culture in Tudor and Stuart Britain* (New York, 2000), 3–18

Doolittle, M., 'Close Relations? Bringing Together Gender and Family in English History', *Gender and History* 11:3 (1999), 542–54

Dowling, M., 'Anne Boleyn and Reform', *Journal of Ecclesiastical History* 35 (1984), 30–46

Duffy, Eamon, *The Stripping of the Altars: Traditional Religion in England 1400–1580*, 2nd edn (London, 2005)

Duffy, Eamon, 'The Reformation After Revisionism', *Renaissance Quarterly* 59:3 (2006), 720–31

Duindam, Jeroen, *Dynasties: A Global History of Power, 1300–1800* (Cambridge, 2015)

Earenfight, Theresa (ed.), *Women and Wealth in Late Medieval Europe* (Basingstoke, 2010).

Earenfight, Theresa, *Queenship in Medieval Europe* (Basingstoke, 2013)

Eichberger, Dagmar, 'The Culture of Gifts: A Courtly Phenomenon from a Female Perspective', in Dagmar Eichberger (ed.), *Women of Distinction: Margaret of York; Margaret of Austria* (Leuven, 2005), 287–96

Eichberger, Dagmar, *Leben mit Kunst, Wirken durch Kunst: Sammelwesen und Hofkunst unter Margarete von Österreich, Reentin der Niederlande* (Turnhout, 2002)

Eisenstadt, S. N., and R. Lemarchand, *Political Clientelism, Patronage and Development* (London, 1981)

Ellis, S. G., 'Henry VIII, Rebellion, and the Rule of Law', *Historical Journal* 24 (1981), 513–31

Elston, Timothy G., 'Widow Princess or Neglected Queen? Catherine of Aragon, Henry VIII and English Public Opinion 1533–1536', in Carole Levin and Robert O. Bucholz (eds), *Queens and Power in Medieval and Early Modern England* (Lincoln, 2009), 16–30

Elton, G. R., *England Under the Tudors*, 2nd edn (London, 1974)

Erickson, Amy L., *Women and Property in Early Modern England* (London, 1993)

Erickson, Amy L., 'Possession—and the Other One-Tenth of the Law: Assessing Women's Ownership and Economic Roles in Early Modern England', *Women's History Review* 16:3 (2007), 369–85

Erler, Mary C., and Maryanne Kowaleski (eds), *Gendering the Master Narrative: Women and Power in the Middle Ages* (Ithaca, NY, and London, 2003)

Evenden, Elizabeth, *Patents, Pictures and Patronage: John Day and the Tudor Book Trade* (Aldershot, 2008)

Evenden, Elizabeth, and Thomas Freeman, *Religion and the Book in Early Modern England: The Making of Foxe's 'Book of Martyrs'* (Cambridge, 2011)

Everett, Michael, *The Rise of Thomas Cromwell* (London, 2015)

Farge, Arlette, 'Protesters Plain to See', in Natalie Zemon Davis and Arlette Farge (eds), *A History of Women in the West, vol. 3: Renaissance and Enlightenment Paradoxes* (Cambridge, Mass., 1993) 489–505

Federico, Sylvia, 'The Imaginary Society: Women in 1381', *Journal of British Studies* 40:2 (2001), 159–83

Ferraro, Joanne M., 'The Power to Decide: Battered Wives in Early Modern Venice', *Renaissance Quarterly* 48:3 (1995), 492–512

Finch, Andrew, 'Repulsa uxore sua: Marital Difficulties and Separation in the Later Middle Ages', *Continuity and Change* 8:1 (1993), 11–38

Flather, Amanda, *Gender and Space in Early Modern England* (Woodbridge, 2007)

Fleming, P. W., 'Household Servants of the Yorkist and Early Tudor Gentry', in D. Williams (ed.), *Early Tudor England: Proceedings of the 1987 Harlaxton Symposium* (Woodbridge, 1989)

Fletcher, Anthony, *Gender, Sex and Subordination in England, 1500–1800* (London, 1995)

Fletcher, A. J., and J. Stevenson (eds), *Order and Disorder in Early Modern England* (Cambridge, 1985)

Fogle, F., and L. Knafla (eds), *Patronage in Late Renaissance England* (Los Angeles, 1983)

Fox, Julia, *Jane Boleyn: The Infamous Lady Rochford* (London, 2007)

Foyster, Elizabeth A., *Manhood in Early Modern England: Honour, Sex and Marriage* (London, 1999)

Freeman, T. S., 'Research, Rumour and Propaganda: Anne Boleyn in Foxe's "Book of Martyrs"', *Historical Journal* 38 (1995), 797–819

Friedman, Alice T., '"Portrait of a Marriage": The Willoughby Letters of 1585–1586', *Signs* 11:3 (1986), 542–55

Froide, Amy M., 'Female Relationships in Early Modern England', *Journal of British Studies* 40 (2001), 279–89

Frye, Susan, and Karen Robertson (eds), *Maids and Mistresses, Cousins and Queens: Women's Alliances in Early Modern England* (Oxford, 1998)

Gage, J., 'The Household Books of Edward Stafford, Duke of Buckingham', *Archaeologia* 25 (1834), 311–41

Geevers, Liesbeth, 'The Miracles of Spain: Dynastic Attitudes to the Habsburg Succession and the Spanish Succession Crisis (1580–1700)', *Sixteenth Century Journal* 46 (2015) 99–119

Geevers, Liesbeth, 'Dynasty and State Building in the Spanish Habsburg Monarchy: The Career of Emanuele Filiberto of Savoy (1588–1624)', *Journal of Early Modern History* 20 (2016) 267–92

Geevers, Liesbeth, and Mirella Marini (eds), *Dynastic Identity in Early Modern Europe: Rulers, Aristocrats and the Formation of Identities* (Aldershot, 2015)

Gilchrist, Roberta, *Gender and Archaeology: Contesting the Past* (London, 1999)

Goldberg, Jeremy, 'Gender and Space in the Later Medieval English House', *Viator* 42:2 (2011)

Gonzalez Cuerva, Ruben, and Alexander Koller (eds), *A Europe of Courts, A Europe of Factions: Political Groups at Early Modern Centres of Power (1550–1700)* (Leiden, 2017)

Gowing, Laura, 'The Politics of Women's Friendship in Early Modern England', in Laura Gowing, Michael Hunter, and Miri Rubin (eds), *Love, Friendship and Faith in Europe, 1300–1800* (Basingstoke, 2005), 131–49

Gowing, Laura, *Domestic Dangers: Women, Words, and Sex in Early Modern London* (Oxford, 1996)

Griffiths, Paul, Adam Fox, and Steve Hindle (eds), *The Experience of Authority in Early Modern England* (Basingstoke, 1999)

Griffiths, R. A., 'The Trial of Eleanor Cobham: An Episode in the Fall of Duke Humphrey of Gloucester', *Bulletin of the John Rylands Library, Manchester* 51 (1968–9), 381–99

Griffiths, R. A., *Sir Rhys ap Thomas and his Family: A Study in the Wars of the Roses and Early Tudor Politics* (Cardiff, 1993)

Groebner, Valentine, *Liquid Assets, Dangerous Gifts: Presents and Politics at the End of the Middle Ages* (Philadelphia, 2000)

Gross, Pamela, *Jane the Quene, Third Consort of Henry VIII* (Lewiston, NY, 1999)

Gunn, S. J., *Charles Brandon, Duke of Suffolk c.1484–1545* (Oxford, 1988)

Gunn, S. J., 'Peers, Commons and Gentry in the Lincolnshire Revolt of 1536', *Past and Present* 123 (1989), 52–79

Gunn, S. J., 'Chivalry and the Politics of the Early Tudor Court', in Sydney Anglo (ed.), *Chivalry in the Renaissance* (Woodbridge, 1990), 107–28

Gunn, S. J., *Early Tudor Government, 1485–1558* (Basingstoke, 1995)

Gunn, S. J., 'The Structures of Politics in Early Tudor England'. *Royal Historical Society Transactions* 6:5 (1995), 59–90

Hacke, Daniela, *Women, Sex and Marriage in Early Modern Venice* (Aldershot, 2004)

Haigh, C., *Reformation and Resistance in Tudor Lancashire* (Cambridge, 1975)

Hammons, Pamela S., 'Rethinking Women and Property in Sixteenth- and Seventeenth-Century England', *Literature Compass* 3:6 (2006),1386–407

Hanawalt, Barbara A., 'Lady Honor Lisle's Networks of Influence', in Mary Erler and Maryanne Kowaleski (eds), *Women and Power in the Middle Ages* (Athens, Ga, 1988), 181–212

Hanawalt, Barbara A., 'The Dilemma of the Widow of Property for Late Medieval London', in Sherry Roush and Cristelle L. Baskins (eds), *The Medieval Marriage Scene: Prudence, Passion, Policy* (Tempe, Ariz., 2005), 165–80

Hanley, Sarah, 'Engendering the State: Family Formation and State Building in Early Modern France', *French Historical Studies* 16:1 (1989), 4–27

Hannay, Margaret Patterson (ed.), *Silent But for the Word: Tudor Women as Patrons, Translators, and Writers of Religious Works* (Kent, Oh., 1985)

Hardwick, Julia, 'Widowhood and Patriarchy in Seventeenth-Century France', *Journal of Social History* 26 (1992), 133–48

Hardwick, Julie, *Family Business: Litigation and the Political Economies of Daily Life in Early Modern France* (Oxford, 2009)

Harpsfield, Nicholas, 'Treatise on the Pretended Divorce between Henry the Eighth and Queen Katherine' (London, 1838)

Harris, Barbara J., 'The Fabric of Piety: Aristocratic Women and Care of the Dead, 1450–1550', *Journal of British Studies* 48 (2009), 308–35

Harris, Barbara J., 'The Trial of the Third Duke of Buckingham: A Revisionist View', *American Journal of Legal History* 20 (1976), 15–26

Harris, Barbara J., 'Marriage Sixteenth-Century Style: Elizabeth Stafford and the Third Duke of Norfolk', *Journal of Social History* 15 (1982), 371–82

Harris, Barbara J., 'Power, Profit, and Passion: Mary Tudor, Charles Brandon, and the Arranged Marriage in Early Tudor England', *Feminist Studies* 15 (1989), 59–88

Harris, Barbara J., 'Property, Power, and Personal Relations: Elite Mothers and Sons in Yorkist and Early Tudor England, *Signs* 15:3 (1990), 606–32

Harris, Barbara J., 'Aristocratic Women and the State in Early Tudor England', in Charles Carlton with Robert L. Woods, Mary L. Robertson, and Joseph S. Block (eds), *State, Sovereigns and Society in Early Modern England; Essays in Honour of A. J. Slavin* (Stroud, 1998), 3–24

Harris, Barbara J., 'The View from my Lady's Chamber: New Perspectives on the Early Tudor Monarchy', *Huntingdon Library Quarterly* 60 (1998), 215–47

Harris, Barbara J., 'Space, Time, and the Power of Aristocratic Wives in Yorkist and Early Tudor England, 1450–1550', in Anne Jacobson Schutte, Thomas Kuehn, and Silvana Seidel Menchi (eds), *Time, Space, and Women's Lives in Early Modern Europe* (Kirksville, Mo., 2001), 245–64

Harris, Barbara J., *English Aristocratic Women 1540–1550* (Oxford, 2002)

Harris, E. Kay., 'Censoring Disobedient Subjects: Narratives of Treason and Royal Authority in Fifteenth-Century England', in Douglas L. Biggs, Sharon D. Michalove, and A. Compton Reeves (eds), *Reputation and Representation in Fifteenth-Century Europe* (Leiden, 2004), 211–34

Harris, Frances, 'The Honourable Sisterhood: Queen Anne's Maids of Honour', *The British Library Journal* 19 (1993), 181–98

Hayward, Maria, 'Gift Giving at the Court of Henry VIII: The 1539 New Year's Gift Roll in Context', *Antiquaries Journal* 85 (2005), 125–75

Hayward, Maria, *Dress at the Court of Henry VIII* (Leeds, 2007)

Hayward, Maria, *Rich Apparel: Clothing and the Law in Henry VIII's England* (Aldershot, 2009)

Head, David M., ' "Being ledde and seduced by the Devyll": The Attainder of Lord Thomas Howard and the Tudor Law of Treason', *Sixteenth Century Journal* 13 (1982), 3–16

Head, David M., *The Ebbs and Flows of Fortune: The Life of Thomas Howard, Third Duke of Norfolk* (Athens, Ga, and London, 1995)

Heal, Felicity, *Hospitality in Early Modern England* (Oxford, 1990)

Heal, Felicity, 'Food Gifts, the Household, and the Politics of Exchange in Early Modern England', *Past and Present* 199 (2008), 41–70

Heal, Felicity, *The Power of Gifts* (Oxford, 2013)

Heal, Felicity, and Clive Holmes, ' "Prudentia ultra Sexum": Lady Jane Bacon and the Management of her Families', in Muriel C. McClendon, Joseph P. Ward, and Michael Macdonald (eds), *Protestant Identities: Religion, Society and Self-Fashioning in Post-Reformation England* (Stanford, Calif., 1999), 100–24

Heale, Elizabeth, 'Women and the Courtly Love Lyric: The Devonshire MS (Bl Additional 17492)', *The Modern Language Review* 90 (1995), 296–313

Heale, Elizabeth, *The Devonshire Manuscript: A Woman's Book* (Chicago, 2012)

Helmholz, R. H., *Marriage Litigation in Medieval England* (Cambridge, 1974)

Henstra, Froukje, 'Social Network Analysis and the Eighteenth-Century Family Network: A C ase Study of the Walpole Family', *Transactions of the Philological Society* 106 (2008), 29–70

Herbert, Amanda E., *Female Alliances: Gender, Identity and Friendship in Early Modern Britain* (New Haven , 2014)

Hicks, Michael A., 'Cement or Solvent? Kinship and Politics in Late Medieval England: The Case of the Nevilles', *History* 83 (1998), 31–46

Hodgkin, Katharine, 'Women, Memory and Family History in Seventeenth-Century England', in Erika Kuijpers, Judith Pollmann, Johannes Muller, and Jasper van der Steen (eds), *Memory before Modernity: Practices of Memory in Early Modern Europe* (Leiden, 2013)

Hohkamp, Michaela, 'Do Sisters Have Brothers? The Search for the "rechte Schwester": Brothers and Sisters in Aristocratic Society at the Turn of the Sixteenth Century', in Christopher H. Johnson and David Warren Sabean (eds), *Sibling Relations and the Transformations of European Kinship, 1300–1900* (New York, 2011), 65–84

Houben, Birgit, 'Intimacy and Politics: Isabel and her Ladies-in-Waiting (1621–33)', in Cordula van Wyhe (ed.), *Isabel Clara Eugenia: Female Sovereignty in the Courts of Madrid and Brussels* (London, 2012), 325–30

Houlbrooke, R. A., *Church Courts and the People During the English Reformation, 1520–1570* (Oxford, 1979)

Houlbrooke, R. A., 'Women's Social Life and Common Action in England from the Fifteenth Century to the Eve of the Civil War', *Continuity and Change* 1 (1986), 176–86

Hoyle, R., *The Pilgrimage of Grace and the Politics of the 1530s* (Oxford, 2003)

Hufton, Olwen, 'Reflections on the Role of Women in the Early Modern Court', *Court Historian* 5 (2000), 1–13

Hufton, Olwen, *The Prospect Before Her: A History of Women in Western Europe* (London, 1995)

Hutchinson, Robert, *House of Treason: The Rise and Fall of a Tudor Dynasty* (London, 2009)

Ingram, M., *Church Courts, Sex and Marriage in England, 1570–1640* (Cambridge, 1987)

Ioppolo, Grace, ' "I desire to be helde in your memory": Reading Penelope Rich through her Letters', in Dympna Callaghan (ed.), *The Impact of Feminism on English Renaissance Studies* (Basingstoke, 2007), 299–325

Irish, Bradley J., ' "The Secret Chamber and Other Suspect Places": Materiality, Space, and the Fall of Catherine Howard', *Early Modern Women* 4 (2009), 169–73

Irish, Bradley J., 'Gender and Politics in the Henrician Court: The Douglas–Howard Lyrics in the Devonshire Manuscript (BL Add 17492)', *Renaissance Quarterly* 64:1 (2011), 79–114

Ives, E. W., 'The Fall of Anne Boleyn Reconsidered', *EHR* 107 (1992), 651–64

Ives, E. W., *Faction in Tudor England*, Issue 6 of *Appreciations in History* (London, 1979)

Ives, E. W., *The Life and Death of Anne Boleyn: 'The Most Happy'* (Oxford, 2004)

James, S. E., 'A Tudor Divorce: The Marital History of William Parr, Marquess of Northampton', *Transactions of the Cumberland and Westmorland Antiquarian and Archaeological Society* 90 (1990), 199–204

James, S. E., *Catherine Parr: Henry VIII's Last Love* (Stroud, 2009)

James, S. E., *The Feminine Dynamic in English Art, 1485–1603 : Women as Consumers, Patrons and Painters* (Aldershot, 2009)

James, S. E., *Women's Voices in Tudor Wills: Authority, Influence, and Material Culture* (London, 2015)

Jansen, Sharon L., *Dangerous Talk and Strange Behavior: Women and Popular Resistance to the Reforms of Henry VIII* (Basingstoke, 1996)

Jones, Gwynfor, *Early Modern Wales, c.1525–1640* (Basingstoke, 1994)

Jones, Michael K., and Malcolm G. Underwood, *The King's Mother: Lady Margaret Beaufort, Countess of Richmond and Derby* (Cambridge, 1992)

Kalas, Robert J., 'The Noble Widow's Place in the Patriarchal Household: The Life and Career of Jeanne de Gontault', *Sixteenth Century Journal* 24 (1993), 519–39

Kent, Ernest A., 'The Houses of the Dukes of Norfolk in Norwich', *Norfolk Archaeology* 24 (1932), 73–87

Kesselring, K. J., *Mercy and Authority in the Tudor State* (Cambridge, 2003)

Kesselring, K. J., 'Deference and Dissent in Tudor England: Reflections on Sixteenth-Century Protest', *History Compass* 3:1 (2005), 1–16

Kesselring, K. J., *The Northern Rebellion of 1569: Faith, Politics and Protest in Elizabethan England* (Basingstoke, 2007)

Kesselring, K. J., 'Felony Forfeiture and the Profits of Crime in Early Modern England', *Historical Journal* 53 (2010), 271–88

Kettering, Sharon, *Patrons, Brokers, and Clients in Seventeenth Century France* (Oxford, 1986)

Kettering, Sharon, 'Gift-Giving and Patronage in Early Modern France', *French History* 2 (1988), 131–51

Kettering, Sharon, *Patronage in Sixteenth and Seventeenth Century France* (Aldershot, 2002)

Kettering, Sharon, 'Strategies of Power: Favorites and Women Household Clients at Louis XIII's Court', *French Historical Studies* 33:2 (2010), 177–200

King, Catherine, *Renaissance Women Patrons: Wives and Widows in Italy c.1300–1550* (Manchester, 1998)

King, D. J. C., and J. C. Perks, 'Carew Castle, Pembrokeshire', *Archaeological Journal* 119 (1962), 270–307

Kisby, F., '"When the King Goeth a Procession": Chapel Ceremonies and Services, the Ritual Year, and Religious Reforms at the Tudor Court, 1485–1547', *Journal of British Studies* 40:1 (2001), 44–75

Klein, Lisa M., 'Your Humble Handmaid: Elizabethan Gifts of Needlework', *Renaissance Quarterly* 50 (1997), 459–93

Klein, Lisa M., 'Lady Anne Clifford as Mother and Matriarch: Domestic and Dynastic Issues in her Life and Writings', *Journal of Family History* 26 (2001), 18–38

Kleineke, Hannes, 'Lady Joan Dinham: A Fifteenth-Century West Country Matriarch', in Tim Thornton (ed.), *Social Attitudes and Political Structures in the Fifteenth Century* (Stroud, 2000), 69–87

Kleinman, Ruth, 'Social Dynamics at the French Court: The Household of Anne of Austria', *French Historical Studies* 16:3 (1990), 517–35

Kolkovich, Elizabeth Zeman, 'Lady Russell, Elizabeth I, and Female Political Alliances through Performance', *English Literary Renaissance* 39 (2009), 290–314

Lamb, Mary Ellen, 'The Countess of Pembroke's Patronage', *English Literary Renaissance* 12 (1982), 162–79

Lander, J. R., 'Attainder and Forfeiture, 1453–1509', *Historical Journal* 4 (1961), 127–58

Laynesmith, J., *The Last Medieval Queens: English Queenship, 1445–1503* (Oxford, 2004)

Lehmberg, S. E., 'Parliamentary Attainder in the Reign of Henry VIII, 1536–1547', *Historical Journal* 18 (1975), 675–702

Leigh-Hunt, A., *The Capital of the Ancient Kingdom of East Anglia* (London, 1870)

Leivers, Clive, 'Family and Community in Early Modern England : A Study of Selston, Nottinghamshire 1550–1699', *Family and Community History* 14:1 (2011), 41–56

Levin, Carole, and Christine Stewart-Nuez (eds), *Scholars and Poets Talk about Queens* (Basingstoke, 2015)

Lewis, E. A., 'Materials Illustrating the History of Dynevor and Newton', *West Wales Historical Records* 1 (1910–11) and 2 (1911–12)

Liddington, Jill, 'Beating the Inheritance Bounds: Anne Lister (1791–1840) and her Dynastic Identity', *Gender and History* 7:2 (1995), 260–74

Litzenberger, Caroline, 'Local Responses to Changes in Religious Policy Based on Evidence from Gloucestershire Wills, 1540–1580', *Continuity and Change* 8:3 (1993), 417–39

Loach, J., 'The Function of Ceremonial in the Reign of Henry VIII', *Past and Present* 142 (1994), 43–68

Loades, David, *Intrigue and Treason: The Tudor Court, 1547–1558* (Harlow, 2004)

Loades, David, *Henry VIII: Court, Church and Conflict* (Kew, 2007)

Loades, David, *The Six Wives of Henry VIII* (Stroud, 2009)

Luxford, Julian M., *The Art and Architecture of English Benedictine Monasteries, 1300–1540: A Patronage History* (Woodbridge, 2005)

Lysons, Daniel, *Environs of London*, 5 vols (London, 1792), I

Lytle, Guy, and Stephen Orgel (eds), *Patronage in the Renaissance* (Princeton, 1981)

MacCaffrey, W., 'Place and Patronage in Elizabethan Politics', in S. T. Bindoff, J. Hurstfield, and C. Williams (eds), *Elizabethan Government and Society* (Oxford, 1961), 95–126

McClendon, Muriel C., 'Women, Religious Dissent, and Urban Authority in Early Reformation Norwich', in Joseph P. Ward (ed.), *Violence, Politics and Gender in Early Modern England* (Basingstoke, 2008), 125–46

McCracken, G., 'The Exchange of Children in Tudor England: An Anthropological Phenomenon in Historical Context', *Journal of Family History* (1983), 303–13

MacCulloch, Diarmaid, *Suffolk and the Tudors: Politics and Religion in an English County 1500–1600* (Oxford, 1986)

MacCulloch, Diarmaid, *Thomas Cranmer* (London, 1996)

MacCulloch, Diarmaid, *The Boy King: Edward VI and the Protestant Reformation* (New York, 1999)

MacCulloch, Diarmaid, *Reformation: Europe's House Divided, 1490–1700* (London, 2003)

MacFarlane, Alan, *The Family Life of Ralph Josselin, a Seventeenth-Century Clergyman* (Cambridge, 1977)

McIntosh, J. L., *From Heads of Household to Heads of State: The Preaccession Households of Mary and Elizabeth Tudor, 1516–1558* (Columbia, NY, 2008)

Majendie, Revd Severne A. Ashhurst, *Some Account of the Family of De Vere, the Earls of Oxford, and of Hedingham Castle in Essex* (London, 1904)

Mann, Catherine, 'Clothing Bodies, Dressing Rooms: Fashioning Recundity in the Lisle Letters', *Parergon* 22 (2005), 137–57

Manning, Roger B., 'Violence and Social Conflict in Mid-Tudor Rebellions', *Journal of British Studies* 16 (1977), 18–40

Marks, Richard, 'The Howard Tombs at Thetford and Framlingham: New Discoveries', *Archaeological Journal* 141 (1985), 252–68

Marshall, Peter, 'Is the Pope Catholic? Henry VIII and the Semantics of Schism', in E. Shagan (ed .), *Catholics and the 'Protestant Nation'* (Manchester, 2005), 22–48

Marshall, Peter, *Religious Identities in Henry VIII's England* (Aldershot, 2006)

Marshall, Peter, '"The Greatest Man in Wales": James Ap Gruffydd Ap Hywel and the International Opposition to Henry VIII', *Sixteenth Century Journal* 39:3 (2008), 681–704

Marshall, Peter, 'The Naming of Protestant England', *Past & Present* 214 (2012), 87–128

Marshall, Peter, and A. Ryrie (eds), *The Beginnings of English Protestantism* (Cambridge, 2002)

Marshall, Peter, and G. Scott (eds), *Catholic Gentry in English Society: The Throckmortons of Coughton from Reformation to Emancipation* (Aldershot, 2009)

Marshall, Rosalind K., *Queen Mary's Women: Female Relatives, Servants, Friends and Enemies of Mary, Queen of Scots* (Edinburgh, 2006)

Mauss, Marcel, *The Gift: The Form and Reason for Exchange in Archaic Societies*, trans. W. D. Halls (New York and London, 1990)

Mayer, Thomas F., and Courteney B. Walters (eds), *The Correspondence of Reginald Pole, Volume 4: A Biographical Companion: The British Isles* (Aldershot, 2008)

Mears, Natalie, 'Historiographical Review: Courts, Courtiers and Culture in Tudor England', *The Historical Journal* 46 (2003), 703–22

Mendelson, Sara, and Patricia Crawford, *Women in Early Modern England, 1550–1720* (Oxford, 1998)

Mertes, Kate, *The English Noble Household, 1200–1600* (Oxford, 1988)

Merton, Charlotte, 'Women, Friendship, and Memory at the Late Tudor Court', in Alice Hunt and Anna Whitelock (eds), *Tudor Queenship: The Reigns of Mary and Elizabeth* (Basingstoke, 2010), 239–50

Miller, H., 'Subsidy Assessments of the Peerage in the Sixteenth Century', *Bulletin of the Institute of Historical Research* 35 (1962), 15–34

Miller, Naomi J., and Naomi Yavneh (eds), *Sibling Relations and Gender in the Early Modern World: Sisters, Brothers and Others* (Aldershot, 2006)

Mills, Rebecca M., '"To be both Patroness and Friend": Patronage Friendship, and Protofeminism in the Life of Elizabeth Thomas (1675–1731)', *Studies in Eighteenth Century Culture* 38 (2009), 68–89

Moore, Peter R., 'The Heraldic Charge against the Earl of Surrey, 1546–7', *English Historical Review* 116 (2001), 557–83

Moorman, John R. H., *The Grey Friars in Cambridge* (Cambridge, 1952)

Moring, Beatrice, 'Widows and Economy', *History of the Family* 15:3 (2010), 215–21

Muldrew, Craig, *The Economy of Obligation: The Culture of Credit and Social Relations in Early Modern England* (Basingstoke, 1998)

Murphy, Beverley A., *Bastard Prince: Henry VIII's Lost Son* (Stroud, 2001)

Myers, A. R., *Crown Household and Parliament in the Fifteenth Century* (London, 1985)

Nader, Helen (ed.), *Power and Gender in Renaissance Spain: Eight Women of the Mendoza Family, 1450–1650* (Urbana, Ill., and Chicago, 2004)

Neuschel, Kristen B., 'Noble Households in the Sixteenth Century: Material Settings and Human Communities', *French Historical Studies* 15 (1988), 595–622

Niles, Philip, 'Baptism and the Naming of Children in Late Medieval England', in Dave Postles and Joel T. Rosenthal (eds), *Studies on the Personal Name in Later Medieval England and Wales* (Kalamazoo, Mich., 2006), 147–58

Nugent, Janay, '"None Must Meddle Betueene Man and Wife": Assessing Family and the Fluidity of Public and Private in Early Modern Scotland', *Journal of Family History* 35:3 (2010), 219–31

O'Day, Rosemary, *Women's Agency in Early Modern Britain and the American Colonies: Patriarchy, Partnership, and Patronage* (Harlow, 2007)

Offer, Avner, 'Between the Gift and the Market: The Economy of Regard', *Economic History Review* 50 (1997), 450–76

O'Grady, Paul, *Henry VIII and the Conforming Catholics* (Collegeville, Minn.,, 1990)

O'Hara, Diana, *Courtship and Constraint: Rethinking the Making of Marriage in Tudor England* (Manchester, 2006)

Orlin, Lena Cowen, 'Spaces of Treason in Tudor England', in Orlin (ed.), *Center of Margin: Revisions of the English Renaissance in Honor of Leeds Barroll* (Selinsgrove, Pa, 2006), 158–95

Outhwaite, R. B.,'Marriage as Business: Opinions on the Rise in Aristocratic Bridal Portions in Early Modern England', in Neil McKendrick and R. B. Outhwaite (eds), *Business Life and Public Policy* (Cambridge, 1986), 21–37

Outhwaite, R. B., *The Rise and Fall of the English Ecclesiastical Courts, 1500–1860* (Cambridge, 2006)

Palmer, William, 'Gender, Violence and Rebellion in Tudor and Early Stuart Ireland', *Sixteenth Century Journal* 23:4 (1992), 699–712

Panek, Jennifer, 'Why did Widows Remarry? Remarriage, Male Authority, and Feminist Criticism', in Dympna Callaghan (ed.), *The Impact of Feminism in English Renaissance Studies* (Basingstoke, 2007), 281–98

Paul, John E., *Catherine of Aragon and her Friends* (London, 1966)

Peck, Linda Levy, *Court Patronage and Corruption in Early Stuart England* (London, 1993)

Peters, Christine, *Patterns of Piety: Women, Gender and Religion in Late Medieval and Reformation England* (Cambridge, 2003)

Phillips, R., *Putting Asunder: A History of Divorce in Western Society* (Cambridge, 1988)

Pierce, Hazel, *Margaret Pole, Countess of Salisbury, 1473–1541: Loyalty, Lineage and Leadership* (Cardiff, 2003)

Pointon, Marcia, 'Women and their Jewels', in Jennie Batchelor and Cora Kaplan (eds), *Women and Material Culture, 1660–1830* (Basingstoke, 2007), 11–20

Pointon, Marcia, 'Material Manoeuvres: Sarah Churchill, Duchess of Marlborough and the Power of Artefacts', *Art History* 32 (2009), 485–515

Polito, Mary, *Governmental Arts in Early Tudor England* (Aldershot, 2005)

Pollock, L. A., '"Teach her to live under obedience": The Making of Women in the Upper Ranks of Early Modern England', *Continuity and Change* 4 (1989), 231–58

Pollock, L. A., 'Embarking on a Rough Passage: The Experience of Pregnancy in Early Modern Society', in V. Fildes (ed.), *Women as Mothers in Pre-Industrial England* (London, 1990), 39–67

Pollock, L. A., 'Anger and Negotiation of Relationships in Early Modern England', *Historical Journal* 47 (2004)

Poos, L. R., 'Sex, Lies, and the Church Courts of Pre-Reformation England', *Journal of Interdisciplinary History* 25:4 (1995), 585–607

Questier, Michael C., *Catholicism and Community in Early Modern England: Politics, Aristoctratic Patronage and Religion, c.1550–1640* (Cambridge, 2002)

Richardson, Catherine, '"A very fit hat": Personal Objects and Early Modern Affection', in Tara Hamling and Catherine Richardson (eds), *Everyday Objects: Medieval and Early Modern Material Culture and its Meaning* (Aldershot, 2010), 289–98

Richardson, Catherine, Tara Hamling, and David Gaimster (eds), *The Handbook of Material Culture in Early Modern Europe* (London, 2016)

Richardson, Malcolm, '"A Masterful Woman": Elizabeth Stonor and English Women's Letters, 1399–c.1530', in Jane Crouchman and Ann Crabb (eds), *Women's Letters Across Europe, 1400–1700: Form and Persuasion* (Oxford, 2005), 43–62

Richardson, R. C., *Household Servants in Early Modern England* (Manchester, 2010)

Roberts, Michael, and Simone Clarke, *Women and Gender in Early Modern Wales* (Cardiff, 2000)

Robinson, J. M., *The Staffords* (Chichester, 2002)

Robinson, John M., *The Dukes of Norfolk: A Quincentennial History* (Oxford, 1982)

Rosenthal, Joel, *The Purchase of Paradise: Gift Giving and the Aristocracy, 1307–1485* (London, 1972)

Ross, James, *John de Vere, Thirteenth Earl of Oxford (1442–1513)* (Woodbridge, 2011)

Rowlands, Marie B., 'Recusant Women 1560–1640', in Mary Prior (ed.), *Women in English Society 1500–1800* (London, 1985), 149–80

Rowse, Alfred Leslie, 'Honor Grenville, Lady Lisle and her Circle', in Rowse (ed.), *Court and Country: Studies in Tudor Social History* (Athens, Ga, and Brighton, 1987), 1–60

Russell, Gareth, *Young & Damned & Fair: The Life and Tragedy of Catherine Howard at the Court of Henry VIII* (London, 2017)

Ryrie, Alec, *The Gospel and Henry VIII* (Cambridge, 2003)

Ryrie, Alec, *Being Protestant in Reformation England* (Oxford, 2013)

Sadlack, Erin, *The French Queen's Letters: Mary Tudor Brandon and the Politics of Marriage in Sixteenth-Century Europe* (Basingstoke, 2011)

Scarisbrick, J. J., *Henry VIII* (London, 1968)

Schutte, Kimberly, *A Biography of Margaret Douglas, Countess of Lennox, 1515–1578: A Niece of Henry VIII and Mother-in-Law of Mary, Queen of Scots* (Lewiston, NY, 2002)

Schutte, Kimberly, 'Marrying out in the Sixteenth Century: Subsequent Marriage of Aristocratic Women in the Tudor Era', *Journal of Family History* 38:1 (2013), 3–16

Schutte, Kimberly, ' "Not for Matters of Treason but for Love Matters": Margaret Douglas, Countess of Lennox, and Tudor Marriage Law', in James V. Mehl (ed.), *Laudem Caroli: Renaissance and Reformation Studies for Charles G. Nauert* (Kirksville, Mich., 1998)

Schwyzer, Philip, 'The Bride on the Border: Women and the Reproduction of Ethnicity in the Early Modern British Isles', *European Journal of Cultural Studies* 5 (2002), 293–306

Sessions, W. A., *Henry Howard, the Poet Earl of Surrey: A Life* (Oxford, 1999)

Shagan, Ethan, *Popular Politics and the English Reformation* (Cambridge, 2003)

Shagan, Ethan (ed.), *Catholics and the 'Protestant Nation': Religious Politics and Identity in Early Modern England* (Manchester, 2005)

Shepard, A., *Meanings of Manhood in Early Modern England* (Oxford, 2003)

Shepard, A., 'From Anxious Patriarchs to Refined Gentlemen? Manhood in Britain *c.*1500–1700', *Journal of British Studies* 44:2 (2004), 281–95

Shepard, A., 'Manhood, Patriarchy and Gender in Early Modern History', in Amy E. Leanard and Karen L. Nelson (eds), *Masculinities, Childhood, Violence: Attending to Early Modern Women and Men* (Newark, Del., 2011), 77–95

Sherlock, Peter, *Monuments and Memory in Early Modern England* (Aldershot, 2008)

Smith, Helen, *'Grossly Material Things': Women and Book Production in Early Modern England* (Oxford, 2012)

Smith, Lacey Baldwin, 'English Treason Trials and Confessions in the Sixteenth-Century', *Journal of the History of Ideas* 15 (1954), 471–98

Smith, Lacey Baldwin, *Catherine Howard* (Stroud, 1961)

Smith, Peter M., 'The Advowson: The History and Development of a Most Peculiar Property', *Ecclesiastical Law Journal* 5:26 (2000), 320–39

Somervell, Donald, 'Acts of Attainder', *Law Quarterly Review* 66:267 (1951), 306–13

Southall, R., 'Mary Fitzroy and O Happy Dames in the Devonshire MS', *Review of English Studies* 45 (1994), 316–18

Southall, R., 'The Devonshire Manuscript Collection of Early Tudor Poetry, 1532–41', *Review of English Studies* 15 (1964), 142–7

Spangler, Jonathan, *The Society of Princes: The Lorraine–Guise and the Conservation of Power and Wealth in Seventeenth-Century France* (Aldershot, 2009)

Spielmann, Richard M., 'The Beginning of Clerical Marriage in the English Reformation: The Reigns of Edward and Mary', *Anglican and Episcopal History* 56:3 (1987), 251–63

Stacy, William, 'Richard Roose and the Use of Parliamentary Attainder in the Reign of Henry VIII', *Historical Journal* 29 (1986), 1–15

Starkey, David, 'The Age of the Household: Politics, Society and the Arts *c.*1350–*c.* 1550', in Stephen Metcalf (ed.), *The Later Middle Ages* (London, 1981), 225–90

Starkey, David, 'Intimacy and Innovation: The Rise of the Privy Chamber, 1485–1547', in David Starkey, D. A. L. Morgan, John Murphy, Pam Wright, Neil Cuddy, and Kevin M. Sharpe (eds), *The English Court: from the Wars of the Roses to the Civil War* (London, 1987), 71–118

Starkey, David (ed.), *Rivals in Power: Lives and Letters of the Great Tudor Dynasties* (Basingstoke, 1990)

Starkey, David (ed.), *Henry VIII: A European Court in England* (London, 1991)

Starkey, David, *Six Wives: The Queens of Henry VIII* (London, 2004)

Stober, Karen, *Late Medieval Monasteries and their Patrons: England and Wales, c.1300–1540* (Woodbridge, 2007)

Stone, Lawrence, *The Family, Sex and Marriage, 1500–1800* (New York, 1977)

Stone, Lawrence, and Howard Colvin, 'The Howard Tombs at Framlingham, Suffolk', *Archaeological Journal* 122 (1965), 159–71

Streitberger, W. R., *Court Revels, 1485–1559* (Toronto, 1994)

Stretton, Timothy, *Women Waging Law in Elizabethan England* (Cambridge, 1998)

Stretton, Timothy, *Marital Litigation in the Court of Requests: 1542–1642* (Cambridge, 2008)

Stretton, Timothy, and Krista J. Kesselring (eds), *Married Women and the Law: Coverture in England and the Common Law World* (Montreal, 2013)

Sutton, Anne F., and P. W. Hammond, *Richard III's Coronation: The Extant Documents* (Gloucester, 1983)

Swensen, Patricia C., 'Patronage from the Privy Chamber: Sir Anthony Denny and Religious Reform', *Journal of British Studies* 27 (1988), 25–44

Tadmor, Naomi, *Family and Friends in Eighteenth Century England: Household, Kinship and Patronage* (Cambridge, 2001)

Tadmor, Naomi, 'Early Modern Kinship in the Long Run', *Continuity and Change* 25:1 (2010), 15–48

Tanswell, John, *The History and Antiquities of Lambeth* (London, 1858)

Terrasa-Lozano, Antonio, 'Legal Enemies, Beloved Brothers: High Nobility, Family Conflict and the Aristocrats' Two Bodies in Early-Modern Castile', *European Review of History* 17:5 (2010), 719–34

Thorne, Alison, 'Women's Petitionary Letters and Seventeenth-Century Treason Trials', *Women's Writing* 13 (2006), 21–37

Tilly, L. A., 'Women's History and Family History: Fruitful Collaboration or Missed Connection?', *Journal of Family History* 12 (1987), 303–15

Tomas, Natalie R., *The Medici Women: Gender and Power in Renaissance Florence* (Aldershot, 2003)

Torlesse, C. M., *Some Account of Stoke by Nayland, Suffolk* (London, 1877)

Tremlett, Giles, *Catherine of Aragon: Henry's Spanish Queen* (London, 2010)

Trull, Mary E., *Performing Privacy and Gender in Early Modern Literature* (Basingstoke, 2013)

Tucker, Melvin, 'The Ladies in Skelton's "Garland of Laurel"', *Renaissance Quarterly* 22 (1969), 333–45

Tucker, Melvin, *The Life of Thomas Howard, Earl of Surrey and Duke of Norfolk, 1443–1524* (London, 1964)

Verschuur, Mary, *A Noble and Potent Lady: Katherine Campbell, Countess of Crawford* (Dundee, 2006)

Vickery, Amanda, 'Golden Age to Separate Spheres? A Review of the Categories and Chronology of English Women's History', *Historical Journal* 36 (1993), 383–414

Virgoe, R., 'The Recovery of the Howards in East Anglia, 1485–1529', in E. W. Ives, R. Knecht, and J. J. Scarisbrick (eds), *Wealth and Power in Tudor England* (London, 1978), 1–20

von Bülow, Gottfried, and Wilfred Powell, 'Diary of the Journey of Philip Julius, Duke of Stettin-Pomerania, through England in the Year 1602', *Transactions of the Royal Historical Society* 6 (1892), 1–67

Walker, Garthine, 'Expanding the Boundaries of Female Honour in Early Modern England', *Transactions of the Royal Historical Society* 6th ser. 6 (1996), 235–45

Walker, Greg, *Persuasive Fictions: Faction, Faith and Political Culture in the Reign of Henry VIII* (Aldershot, 1996)

Walker, Greg, *John Skelton and the Politics of the 1520s* (Cambridge, 2002)

Walker, Greg, 'Rethinking the Fall of Anne Boleyn', *Historical Journal* 45 (2002), 1–29

Walker, Katherine A., 'The Military Activities of Charlotte de la Tremouille, Countess of Derby, during the Civil War and Interregnum', *Northern History* 38:1 (2001), 47–64

Walsham, Alexandra, *Church Papists* (Woodbridge, 1993)

Walsham, Alexandra, *Charitable Hatred: Tolerance and Intolerance in England, 1500–1700* (Manchester, 2006)

Walsham, Alexandra, 'The Reformation of the Generations: Youth, Age and Religious Change in England, *c.*1500–1700', *Transactions of the Royal Historical Society* 21 (2011), 92–121

Ward, Jennifer C., *English Noblewomen in the Later Middle Ages* (London, 1992)

Ward, Joseph P. (ed.), *Violence, Politics and Gender in Early Modern England* (Basingstoke, 2008)

Warnicke, Retha M., 'Family and Kinship Relations at the Henrician Court: The Boleyns and Howards', in Dale Hoak (ed.), *Tudor Political Culture* (Cambridge, 1995), 31–53

Warnicke, Retha M., *The Rise and Fall of Anne Boleyn: Family Politics at the Court of Henry VIII* (Cambridge, 1989)

Warnicke, Retha M., *Wicked Women of Tudor England* (Basingstoke, 2012)

Weigall, David, 'Women Militants in the English Civil War', *History Today* 22:6 (1972), 434–8

Weiner, Annette, *Inalienable Possessions: The Paradox of Keeping While Giving* (Berkeley, 1992)

Westcott, Margaret, 'Katherine Courtenay, Countess of Devon, 1479–1527', in Todd Gray, Margaret M. Rowe, and Audrey Erskine (eds), *Tudor and Stuart Devon: The Common Estate and Government* (Exeter, 1992), 13–38

Whitelock, Anna, and Diarmaid MacCulloch, 'Princess Mary's Household and the Succession Crisis, July 1553', *Historical Journal* 50:2 (2007), 265–87

Whittle, Jane, 'Inheritance, Marriage, Widowhood and Remarriage: A Comparative Perspective on Landholding in North-East Norfolk, 1440–1580', *Continuity and Change* 13:1 (1998), 33–72

Williams, Franklin B., 'The Literary Patronesses of Renaissance England', *Notes and Queries* 207 (1962), 364–6

Williams, G., *Recovery, Reorientation and Reformation: Wales, c.1415–1642* (Oxford, 1987)

Williams, Neville, *Thomas Howard, Fourth Duke of Norfolk* (London, 1964)

Williams, William Llewelyn, 'A Welsh Insurrection', *Y Cymmrodor* 16 (1902), 1–94

Wilson, Adrian, 'The Ceremony of Childbirth and its Interpretation', in V. Fildes (ed.), *Women as Mothers in Pre-Industrial England* (London, 1990), 68–107

Wilson, Derek, *In the Lion's Court: Power, Ambition and Sudden Death in the Reign of Henry VIII* (London, 2001)

Wood, Andy, *Riot, Rebellion and Popular Politics in Early Modern England* (Basingstoke, 2002)

Wooding, L., *Rethinking Catholicism in Reformation England* (Oxford, 2000)

Woolgar, C., *The Great Household in Late Medieval England* (London, 1999)

Wrightson, Keith, 'Household and Kinship in Sixteenth-Century England', *History Workshop Journal* 12 (1981), 151–8

Wunderli, Richard M., *London Church Courts and Society on the Eve of the Reformation* (Cambridge, Mass., 1981)

Zevin, Edward M., 'A New Wife for Edward, 3rd Earl of Derby', *Transactions of the Historic Society of Lancashire and Cheshire* 134 (1985 for 1984), 1–16

Zevin, Edward M., *The Life of Edward Stanley, Third Earl of Derby (1521–1572): Noble Power and the Tudor Monarchy* (New York, 2010)

zum Kolk, Caroline, 'The Household of the Queen of France in the Sixteenth Century', *The Court Historian* 14 (2009), 3–22

UNPUBLISHED THESES

Bundesen, Kristen, ' "No Other Faction But my Own": Dynastic Politics and Elizabeth I's Carey Cousins' (unpublished doctoral thesis, University of Nottingham, 2008)

Clarke, Catherine, 'Patronage and Literature: The Women of the Russell Family, 1520–1617 (unpublished doctoral thesis, University of Reading, 1992)

Hamilton, Dakota, 'The Household of Katherine Parr' (unpublished D.Phil. thesis, University of Oxford, 1992)

Merton, Charlotte, 'The Women Who Served Queen Mary and Queen Elizabeth: Ladies, Gentlewomen and Maids of the Privy Chamber, 1553–1603' (unpublished doctoral thesis, University of Cambridge, 1990)

Payne, Helen, 'Aristocratic Women and the Jacobean Court, 1603–1625' (unpublished doctoral thesis, Royal Holloway, University of London, 2001)

Vokes, S. E., 'The Early Career of Thomas, Lord Howard, Earl of Surrey and Third Duke of Norfolk, 1474–c.1525' (unpublished doctoral thesis, University of Hull, 1988)

Wolfson, Sara, 'Aristocratic Women of the Household and Court of Queen Henrietta Maria, 1625–1659' (unpublished doctoral thesis, University of Durham, 2010)

ONLINE DATABASES

The Clergy of the Church of England Database 1540–1835 <http://www.theclergydatabase. org.uk> (CCED)

Early English Books Online <eebo.chadwyck.com/home> (EEBO)

History of Parliament Online <www.historyofparliamentonline.org>

Oxford Dictionary of National Biography <www.oxforddnb.com> (ODNB)

The Unabridged Acts and Monuments Online or *TAMO* (HRI Online Publications, Sheffield, 2011). Available from: <http//www.johnfoxe.org> (TAMO)

Index

.